A Decade of Negative Thinking

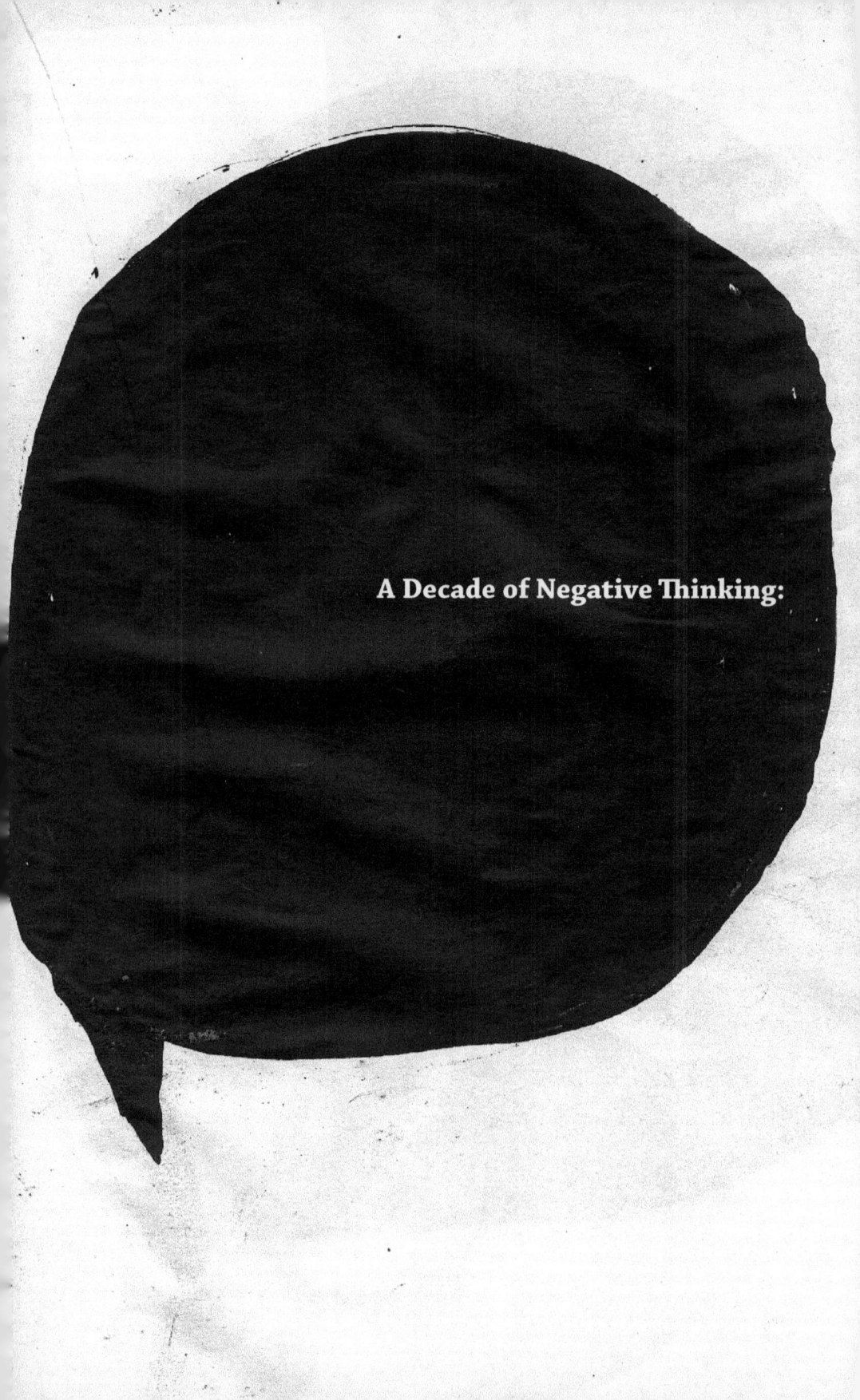

A Decade of Negative Thinking:

Mira Schor

Essays on Art, Politics, and Daily Life

Duke University Press

Durham and London

2009

© 2009 DUKE UNIVERSITY PRESS
All rights reserved
Designed by Amy Ruth Buchanan
Typeset in Chaparral Pro by Tseng
Information Systems, Inc. Library
of Congress Cataloging-in-
Publication Data appear on the last
printed page of this book.

CONTENTS

In the middle of my writing this book, barely three months after September 11, 2001, my sister, Naomi Schor, died suddenly. I write about the relationship between the two events in "Weather Conditions in Lower Manhattan: September 11, 2001, to October 2, 2001." My sister was a theoretician of the "detail,"[1] and the purposefully detailed texture of the everyday found in this essay marks the importance of a few unusual days in the life of New York and is pivotal to the transformation of meaning they engendered.

It is interesting that some of my friends seemed to feel that the loss of a sister entailed an appropriate but also measurable, that is to say *finite*, period of mourning. The idea that there is some sort of definitive closure on mourning was a theme of much journalistic writing after September 11: people were seeking closure; this or that event or memorial or building would give them closure. But if I know anything from having lost my father when I was eleven and hearing my mother retell her experiences of the Second World War all the rest of her life, it is that there is no such thing as closure in the life of a person and perhaps also in the life of a country. My writing's meditations on the past as it affects the present are meant as positive interpretations of that observation, as a useful corrective to the dominance of the relentless marketing of the new.

When, very early on a morning in May 1972, I returned to Kennedy Airport on a red-eye flight at the end of my first year in graduate school at the California Institute of the Arts, I was surprised and thrilled to find my sister and a friend of hers waiting to pick me up. They were young professors in the French department at Columbia University, incredibly excited about the structuralist theory then espoused by the chair of their department. They had been at a party the night before and decided on the spur of the moment to keep talking, stay up all night, and drive out to the airport to meet me. I had just spent a year deeply involved in the personal and political dynamics of the Feminist Art Program at CalArts and in the loopy, Fluxus-influenced atmosphere of the school, an atmosphere certainly filled with ideas and ideologies but taken in mostly through embodied experience rather than ingested through text: on the way to my studio, I looked down a hallway and saw the experimental dancer Simone Forti blindfolded, being guided by a squat, powerfully muscular, black karate teacher so that she could experience sightlessness; it was early evening on a weekend and John Baldessari sat impassively in the cafeteria, implicitly encouraging a group of us who were protesting the awful food supplied to those living in the dorms by cramming some of it into manila envelopes to be sent to the management; it was lunchtime and the gamelan orchestra played for everyone in the school, cardamom-scented Indonesian cigarettes filling the air. Now as I sat in the backseat as we drove through Queens and I listened to my sister and her friend talking passionately about literature and theory, I sank back with a sense of luxurious refreshment as one luminous word crossed my mind: *ideas*. For me that moment crystallizes the productive duality of my visual and critical practice and also of the complex symbiotic but foundational relationship between my sister and me as representatives of theory and practice (theory *as* practice and practice *as* theory), a contested but generative ecology that shaped my work and my identity but that has now been radically disrupted. The effects on my work of this rupture are only beginning to make themselves clear. Maybe they will emerge in another book.

In the summer of 2005 my then ninety-four-year-old, Polish-born mother, Resia Schor, stayed up one night bravely plowing through the heavy printout of an early draft of this book. The next morning she said, "Before, you were *against*. Now this is more personal." She always liked that I find it hard to flatter even when it might serve me best to do so, so the maverick tendencies of my critical practice owe much to her. I was very close to my mother and I admired her. She had personal courage, rigorous self-discipline, fierce independence; she loved deeply but without false sentiment. She was a talented professional artist who taught me the importance of daily practice and formal ambition whatever one's current relation to the art market. She was passionately interested in politics throughout a long life that had been dramatically affected by the Second World War and the Holocaust, and, gifted to her last day with an incredible memory, she was deeply interested both in the latest news and in history. She too died "suddenly" one day in 2006, in her ninety-sixth year. I have completed the preparation of this manuscript in the grip of a deep existential loneliness. But the historical dimension of this loneliness, of being the last person left of my beloved and interesting family—Ilya, Resia, and Naomi Schor—imposes a responsibility of preserving their complex, unique artistic and intellectual historical legacy. That too may be the subject of another book, but all my work carries my family's trace and is dedicated to them.

Acknowledgments

It is customary to thank one's friends for their patience and help. When viii | ix a book takes ten years to write, there are a great many friends to thank and their patience must be enormous. My friends Tom Knechtel, Susan Bee, Maureen Connor, Susanna Heller, Lenore Malen, Nancy Bowen, Faith Wilding, Jennifer Liese, Robin Mitchell, Michael Mazur, Gail Mazur, Elizabeth King, Amelia Jones, Ida Applebroog, Joanna Frueh, Mary Garrard, Johanna Burton, and Sheila Levrant de Bretteville, among others, have all had large packets of text mailed and emailed to them, have listened to me read long portions over the phone or talk at length about essays they couldn't see the full shape of, and have always responded with generous, supportive, and scrupulous attention. I thank my students, who over the years have unwittingly been the lab rats for my thinking and my imagined audience. A half-year sabbatical from the Parsons School of Design in 1999 gave me some time for preliminary research. I thank the family of Alice Neel for their generosity and for allowing me the deep privilege of visiting her studio.

I cannot thank the Rockefeller Foundation enough for the unique privilege of being able to spend a month in their exquisitely appointed and beautifully organized study and conference center in Bellagio, Italy, where I worked on the early drafts of a number of essays in this book.

And I thank my editor, Ken Wissoker, for his continued support and his astute criticism. I thank the Duke University Press staff for their unfailing courtesy and professionalism.

A few years ago, during a break from teaching, I was enjoying my favorite snack: a madeleine dipped in espresso. One of my students asked me what I was eating. A madeleine, I said. I explained that it was an important part of the history of literature, that in Marcel Proust's *Remembrance of Things Past*, the act of dipping a madeleine into lime-tree tea, or *tilleul*, released the totality of the author's memories of his childhood and the meaning of the work he was undertaking. "Oh," my student said as he walked away, "I learned something new today." "About Proust?" I said hopefully, ever the pedagogue. "About a new cookie," he said.

This book is not exactly about new cookies.

It is perhaps a liability to advertise that to my prospective readers! People are interested in books that will give them a heads-up on the next cookie—I look for such volumes myself. But, in fact, most books are about the past: only the journalistic publishing cycle and Internet manifestations occur in the present, everything else is by necessity retrospective or predictive. In a culture focused on the celebrity of the new, there may be some material of interest nestled elsewhere.

The first several pages of Proust's *Du côté de chez Swann* are devoted to an extended, detailed to the point of being soporific, description of the mechanics of falling asleep. I considered reading it aloud to my class that year but thought that the slow pace would seem like abuse to them. Yet we all need sleep, we yearn for deep and restful sleep; desperate, we skip the stages of experience described by Proust and just reach for the Ambien.

In this space bracketed by artificial stimulation and sedation, I want to address artists who are encouraged on many fronts to operate in a limited field of new cookies by exploring instead the potential of a critical but productive temporal counterpoint, a constant movement between the undertow of the past beneath the wave of the present, and the powerful counterflow of the present over reiterations of the past in contemporary artworks and ideologies. Contested histories, networks of influence, and feedback loops of recurrent tropes emerge as major themes.

As my writing of this book was slowed by rapidly shifting ideological conditions, the effects of epochal disasters, religious and market fundamentalisms, personal grief, and minute pleasures on art and on the daily life of individuals deepened my initial general interest in writing about "the past" as a space with material of value for contemporary artists.

In 1997 I published *Wet: On Painting, Feminism, and Art Culture*, a collection of essays written during the previous decade, from the mid-1980s to the mid-1990s. My overarching premise in those diverse writings was that feminist politics, engagement with the many critical discourses then telegraphically described as "theory," and a commitment to the discipline of painting were not mutually exclusive concerns. The essays in *Wet* traced my intervention as an artist and writer into a particular set of polemic conditions, beginning in the early 1980s, at the same time that, in the spirit of that contentious but intellectually charged moment, I also co-founded the journal *M/E/A/N/I/N/G* with Susan Bee. I wrote about gender representation in the work of female and male artists, I wrote about painting in relation to the critique of painting that was a dominant feature of art discourse at the time, and I wrote about teaching art. In all cases I wrote with a feminist analysis of power relations and from my own experience as a studio-based visual artist.

The essays in this book build on what I wrote before: here, as in *Wet*, there are essays on feminism and feminist art history, essays on painting, and essays that emerge from my experience as a teacher of art at the graduate level. There is a mix of theory and practice and of the personal and the political. But within these realms, my focus has shifted. Iterations and manipulations of art history are more central than issues of gender representation. While some texts do have feminist histories and debates as their subject, in others feminist or political themes are not always evident. This change is consistent with the development of many women artists who consider themselves feminists but who now apply feminism's critical point of view or basic tendency to think in political terms to subjects and forms other than the sexualized or gendered body, and who may even create works that offer no representational clues as to a political intent.

The underlying theme is of how the past is perceived or misused: in the persistence of past styles, tropes, and histories—sometimes self-consciously, sometimes unconsciously—in contemporary art modes; and in the disavowal of the (feminist) past by young women artists and the distortion of the (art historical) past by artists arrogating value, in both cases for advantage in the art market.

Wet has a provocatively lubricious title and its cover image neatly tele-graphs the book's major theme: a semi-colon is nestled in a vaginal slit created by thickly applied oil paint, which emerges from a smooth, flesh-colored field. The picture is a detail of a painting that imagines a gyneco-logical examination during which it is discovered that, just where Western philosophy has located the darkness of unreason—in woman and paint- 2 | 3 ing—there is language. To explain how I got from there to *A Decade of Negative Thinking*, with its title like a minus sign splitting the silence of a black thought-balloon, I need to take a moment to unfold some stories of sensory events, embedded in private and public consciousness and im-bued with cultural and personal meaning, which reveal my initial goals for this book and what happened to these in the process of writing and of living.

This narration is in keeping with my dual practice as a visual artist and writer, a painter and "a sort of art historian,"[1] writing across disciplines and committed to the fluid interrelationship between a formalist aes-thetic, a literary sensibility, and a strongly political viewpoint. I also write as a figure in the portal between the darker but rich transitory space of the near-past and the bright anticipation of the "nextmodern,"[2] imbued with values and histories of the past but tuned to challenges of the present. The emphasis is not on nostalgia but on what, from an awareness of history, can enrich a young artist today.

When I began to make notes for a new book shortly after *Wet* came out, I was clear about two things: I wanted to write a book about painting, and I wanted to write a book in which the word *feminism* did not appear. This last wish reflects how sick I was of the way in which the anti-essentialism of poststructuralist art and feminist theory had inaccurately and, to my mind, unjustly marginalized so much art practice by women, as well as painting as a discipline. I was frustrated by my sense that my essays on painting were, at least for some readers, equally marginalized by my per-ceived identification as a feminist. That I would be brought to such a desire places me squarely in the same political dilemma as the younger women artists I criticize in "The *ism* that dare not speak its name," who under-stand that they must sacrifice an overt identification with feminism in order to be allowed into the art industry, and as many women artists of my own and earlier generations who at times have themselves struggled against the limitations of a political identity.

A year later, a taxi ride through Times Square near midnight on May 29, 1998, revealed that temporally stratified, brilliantly lit yet dark urban space as a suitable initiatory metaphor for the trajectory of my thought for this book.

Times Square may symbolize relentless pressure for the new embodied in its identity as the site where the new year is celebrated for the United States and then viewed around the world, but its structure is intrinsically atavistic, created by the awkward intersection of the modern urban grid of streets and avenues — Forty-second to Forty-seventh Streets, geometrically crossed by Sixth, Seventh, and Eighth Avenues — with the old cow path that Broadway once was, a pounding of the earth along the length of the island of Manhattan. Broadway drives in a relentlessly irregular pattern against the grain of the grid, jagging its way eastward and southward, backwards through history to the origin of European settlement on the southern tip of the island.[3]

Crossing it are side streets, whose plainness in the day and relative darkness at night are necessary to create the bright effect of the glowing core. Along these streets are theaters, churches, older hotels, garages, and all kinds of small businesses, somewhat like those observed by Walter Benjamin in the Paris arcades of the 1930s: "Often these inner spaces harbor antiquated trades, and even those that are thoroughly up to date will acquire in them something obsolete. They are the site of information bureaus and detective agencies, which there, in the gloomy light of the upper galleries, follow the trail of the past."[4] If my emphasis on these side streets as an organizing metaphor pays homage to the auratic influence of Benjamin's Paris arcades project on art and cultural analysis within the academy, common sense would dictate that in the real estate environment of New York City, any businesses that remain in such a high rent neighborhood must be profitable, although they may give the faint appearance of obsolescence. They merely represent a peculiarly American kind of darkness, that of the place where work actually gets done. We are famously obsessed with celebrity rather than accomplishment, and value instant product over long germination and revelations arrived at through constant failure, a focus that filters down into the formation of American art students.

Times Square may seem an unlikely starting point for essays that propose alternative artistic processes and histories, yet it provides me with a useful organizational frame for these writings on contemporary art and daily life's effect on one's expectations of art.

This topographical metaphor may mark my thinking as New York–centered. I do write as a New Yorker. But I do so with a bittersweet awareness that from a globalist perspective, New York may now be a cultural backwater, the creative capital of a dying empire—even the glitter of Times Square may be quaint in relation to gaudier displays in other cities around the world. Yet there is a variety of human experience and of lived art history under the surface of what is still one of the thriving centers of the world art market that makes New York an inspiring place from which to observe contemporary art and culture.

In keeping with the topography of Times Square, each major grouping of essays begins in or close to the bright lights of the center of media focus, is filled with distracting asides and images, and, like Broadway, moves backward in time, swerving into personal recollection, drifting toward the marginal and then back to the center. The tension between the brightness of the unstable center and the darkness of its most immediate frame mirrors the tension in my critical writing between attention to the present—the latest art star, the most current stylistic recipe, the most recent yet eternally similar debates about feminism or painting—and attention to subjects from the near and the more distant past that affect these present manifestations. In each section of the book and even within each essay I often work my way backward from the latest to the latent.

In the darkest side street of the book are the endnotes: there, I have stashed the pleasure I take in research, but to these nether regions of the book I have relegated not only the requisites of academic information, but also personal, embarrassing, and risky backstories, along with archeological traces of some essays' previous versions.

On the night of my taxi ride in May 1998, vehicular and pedestrian motion had come to a complete standstill in Times Square while everyone watched Michael Jordan and the Chicago Bulls play a semifinal basketball game on the giant NBC TV screen on the façade of 1 Times Square, so I had plenty of time to gaze out the window of the taxi. As if I had just landed on earth, instead of having been born and lived in New York most of my life, I experienced with a pure intensity the brightness, color, and movement "in the theater of the world,"[5] a great black box, an enormous public exhibition space in which the most effective wall is the darkness of night, where pictorialism has been emblematically displaced, for the urban flâneur, from painting to architecturally scaled electronic signage entirely devoted to money. While the Bulls game played on center stage before me, the Morgan Stanley Dean Witter ticker ran stock prices and international financial information and news in bright yellow lights on a dark ground against the darker ground of night at the northern boundary of the square. Several stories high and moving at great speed, it embodied the dominance of the market itself as the ultimate product. At that moment I fully perceived something I already knew but had never felt so intensely: *this* is really the world, and, if this is really the world, then painting really *is* dead.

I returned one night two weeks later to take some pictures. I clutched in my hand two lists of categories. The first I had transcribed from Baudelaire's essay "The Painter of Modern Life": Beauty, Fashion and Happiness; The Sketch of Manners; The Artist, Man of the World, Man of the Crowd, and Child; Modernity; Mnemonic Art; The Annals of War; Pomps and Circumstances; The Military Man; The Dandy; Woman; In Praise of Cosmetics; Women and Prostitutes; Carriages.[6] The second list was of categories Susan Buck-Morss based on Benjamin's arcades project: Arcades; World Expositions; Phantasmagoria of Politics; National Progress on Display; Urbanism; Progress Deified; Bigger is Better; Dust; Fragility; Fashion; Sterility; Death; Chthonic Paris; Recurrence; Sin; Boredom.[7] I planned to apply these to contemporary painting, looking for the painter of postmodern life, but first I would look for them in Times Square.

By a convenient coincidence, conditions were almost identical to the night of my taxi ride: traffic was again stopped and people stood facing the giant screen to watch a Bulls' game, now in the finals. However this time I was on foot and at ground level, where, even in the glowing brightness of night, when the electronic signage is most brilliant, my experience was less rapturous, more complex. I passed many a darkened doorway, shabby storefronts—perhaps no longer the sexual tawdriness of the years before the corporate clean-up of the 1980s, just insidious and endemic urban grubbiness and a complete lack of interest in elegance at street level, with only the top of the skyscrapers around the square attempting some kind of modern design ambition.

That evening, adding to the paradoxically contingent atmosphere, there was an array of cheap lawn chairs along the curb, set up by Chinese portrait painters; their seated subjects seemed alone, dejected, and vulnerable amidst crowd and traffic. And, in the central traffic island

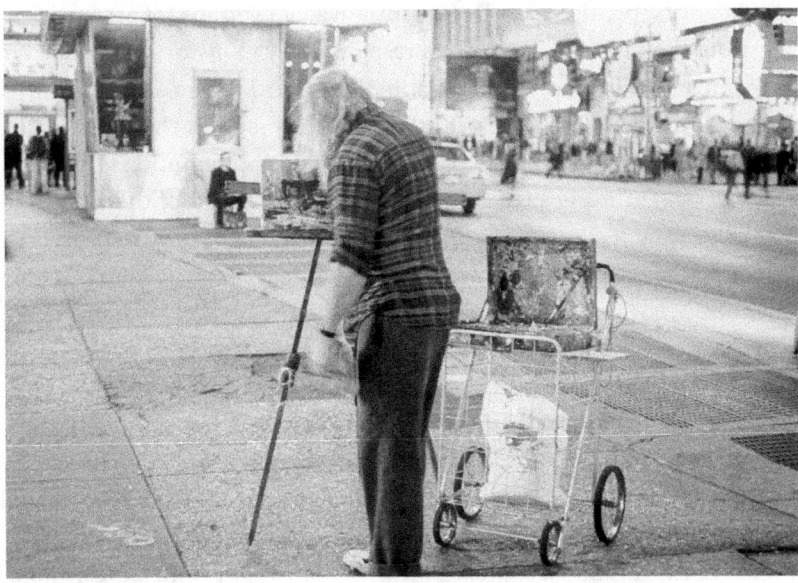

Mira Schor, *Street Painter*, Times Square, New York, June 1998.
Photograph © by Mira Schor.

where Broadway and Seventh Avenue cross paths, just north of the army
recruiting stand, at the empty eye of this quintessentially urban space,
positioned so as to be part of the spectacle but overshadowed by the giant
live television broadcast of the basketball game, a scruffy street person
with a palette stuck on a shopping cart worked on a *landscape* painting on
a rickety portable easel. Either this was a sign of the persistence of painting in the face of electronic imaging technologies or proof that painting
is a delusional space, unable to accept what is right in front of it, be it the
dirty pavement below or the electric whiteness of the illumination above
or the moving ticker of money.

The street painter tuned into some reality other than the one swirling
around him may stand as an uneasy indicator of my critical focus. Like
the lonely landscape painter, I have written about what I thought was
relevant, rather than serving the dictates of the art market. I've tried to
slow down the forward motion of the art-critical apparatus so that I could
stop to think about questions raised by art works and events after their
moment in the spectacle's bright light, or by those in its shadow.

Nevertheless the questions I examine are ones frequently raised in conversations with other artists and with art students. These concern his-

tory, identity, politics, and the currently available means for aesthetic expression. First, what is the artist's responsibility to history and identity? Is feminism still a necessary political discourse? Is there such a thing as "feminist art"? Can political art be good art? Second, is there now an irreconcilable separation between expression and appropriation? How does this work out at the level of art making, even at the level of the individual stroke of paint? Why are certain styles of "personal expression" in contemporary art so generic in appearance and methodology? Finally, how does one negotiate the increased influence of the market even within art education without either essentializing private studio practice or over-accepting market values to the point that one essentializes the market?

My writings on such questions often begin with a supposition, an intuition, the crystallization of something that emerges from what I have seen or read. An essay can also serve as a magnet for stray flickers of matter; a memory, an image, a word held in my mind for years finally finds a place for me to expel it into a context in which it can at last contribute. Among such suppositions, images, and words that led to essays was the frequent assertion, "I am not a feminist artist," pronounced by young women artists but also by women artists whose work was included in major survey exhibitions of feminist art.

Despite my initial desire to keep feminism out of the picture, that proved to be impossible. The market viability of certain types of representation of female sexuality still intrudes at every moment into contemporary painting and its marketing, yet there is a lack of sustained feminist analysis of such imagery just as there is little feminist analysis applied to many relevant events in the news. When they do appear, such feminist interventions are either ignored or preemptively condemned: it is still common in art reviews to encounter the kind of "some feminists may say but" phraseology that I first noted when I researched the collaborationist critical support of David Salle's depiction of women for my essay "Appropriated Sexuality" from 1986. The clear inference is that what "some feminists say" is old-hat, marginal, and irrelevant. That this sentiment is felt and expressed even by women has been the impetus for some of the writing here. As I wrote in 2006 in a polemic piece provocatively titled "She Demon Spawn from Hell," "At times the debates over feminism and feminist art take on the characteristics of daytime soap opera, complete with contested inheritances, angry aging divas, and beautiful young women suffering from the convenient onset of amnesia."[8]

In the same piece I noted the irony that I too was affected by the same impulse in wanting to eradicate feminism from my writings, which proved impossible, practically speaking, because I often respond to requests to write about feminist-related issues thereby creating a body of text on the subject. And anyway, like Michael Corleone in *The Godfather, Part III* trying to escape his identity as a Mafia don but being "pulled back in," the word *feminism* cannot be erased in my work because of my history with it and my commitment to the recognition of female subjectivity and agency.

The first section of the book, "She Said, She Said: Feminist Debates, 1971–2009," tracks recent internecine debates over feminism and feminist art evident in numerous panel discussions, symposia, and art magazine forums on feminist art over the past ten years. "The *ism* that dare not speak its name" was inspired by telling comments on feminism made by Vanessa Beecroft on one such panel and by events at the "F-Word" confer-ence held at the California Institute of the Arts (CalArts) in 1998; I analyze the phenomenon of "F-word" denial by women artists who have come of age since the 1980s in relation to continued patterns of discrimination against women in the art world and society at large. My investigation of denial continues in "Generation 2.5," whose subject is the omission of a generation of women from the most recent major cycle of historicizing the feminist art movement. By recalling important but forgotten works of feminist art in "The *ism* that dare not speak its name" and, in "Generation 2.5," calling attention to a community of women artists who have carried the ideals of the feminist art movement through hostile times, I stress, as I do throughout the book, the importance of challenging the very notion of canonicity in art historical production and the cult of celebrity in con-temporary culture. I also look at new sites of cultural commentary in "Ano-nymity as a Political Tactic: Art Blogs, Feminism, Writing, and Politics." Also in part 1, I revisit some of these themes in "Email to a Young Woman Artist," where I try to re-create some of the excitement of the women's liberation movement in the early 1970s. Finally the retrospective aspects of all the writings in part 1 are capped by two texts about my experiences working on the *Womanhouse* project when I was in the feminist program at CalArts from 1971 to 1972. In "The *Womanhouse* Films" I compare the two documentaries made at the time of this historical project, calling atten-tion to the less well-known KCET television documentary *Womanhouse is Not a Home*, which featured extended interviews with some of the student participants. In "Miss Elizabeth Bennett Goes to Feminist Boot Camp," the letters and diaries I wrote in the moment of my first encounter with feminism also document the point of the view of the student rather than the teacher. These letters may also serve as a reminder that I once was on the other side of the generational divide that I now invoke with some frustration in "The *ism* that dare not speak its name," "Anonymity as a Political Tactic," and "Generation 2.5."

Part 2 of the book is about painting. Again I apply a feminist-inflected analysis to the production of art history. In many cases I contrast artists' efforts to shape their place in that narrative with information contained in the works themselves. I write against the grain of standard narratives and the self-historicizations of my subjects, and in detail, stroke by stroke, close to the surface of the paintings. In "Some Notes on Women and Abstraction and a Curious Case History: Alice Neel as a Great Abstract Painter," I look at the way in which biographical information, when used as a keystone of interpretation (a process often initiated by the artist herself), may distract from the formal strengths of the work even as it enriches the viewer's understanding. The nature of Neel's painterly skills allows for an examination of the problematic of abstraction within feminist art discourse, and it suggests an antithesis of the simulationist "painterly value" in the work of Lisa Yuskavage and John Currin that is the subject of "Like a Veneer."

In that chapter, I analyze Yuskavage's successful promotional meme — that she paints "like Vermeer" — and expand my analysis of this intriguing proposition by searching for other artists who might also have a claim to that legacy. "Like a Veneer" could potentially be misinterpreted by some (and by the same token dismissed) as an example of seventies feminist political correctness and essentialist desire for more positive images of woman, or as having an unexamined reliance on the artist's intention. In fact, it is about the usage of art history to generate market value and determine what constitutes aesthetic capital, and also about how immersion in simulacra has impaired our ability to differentiate between apparently related painting signifiers (or, to put it more simply, people are indiscriminating suckers when it comes to stand oil and sable brushes).

In "Modest Painting" I argue for an alternative to the respect that massive size and scale impose on art audiences. I examine the works of artists, including Myron Stout and Jack Tworkov, which I consider as possible exemplars of the ambition for painting that "modest" paintings may contain and look at some contemporary manifestations of what might appear to be "modest" paintings. I also suggest the importance for art histories to more expansively consider networks of practice by a mixed field of "minor" and "major" artists.

During the years I was working on these writings, I also was engaged in another major book project, compiling and editing *The Extreme of the Middle: Writings of Jack Tworkov*. My work on the Tworkov book began when I sought out some excerpts of Tworkov's writings while I was working on the essay "Modest Painting." A noted abstract expressionist painter, Tworkov was a close family friend, so editing his writings was a task with great personal meaning but also an influential and affirming experience of communion with another painter who was deeply committed to writing. Even so, I would have found the work difficult had I not found many commonalities between Tworkov's critical views and my own. His writings from the late 1940s and early 1950s, when he was a founding member of the Eighth Street Club, addressed major issues of his time, yet he also often went against the grain of the New York school canon. He wrote, "I ask myself questions and I try to come up with answers that are as close to me as possible. They represent not what I ought to believe but what I know I believe."[9] He was not interested in writing manifestos. Rather he was profoundly averse to ideologies that set out to dominate and exclude: "Finally I am against any ideology which takes any significant part of humanity as its 'enemy' whose extermination it seeks in order to insure its own survival"; "All programs represent future sorrows."[10] He valued the specificity of art works over celebrity-driven art criticism and felt that art critical fashions left out much that was valuable in the creative practice taking place within a wider field: "A dozen or so artists in fashion have put some truly fine artists in undeserved shadow and prevent the rising of numerous others all over the country, because the critics and the museums are busy with names rather than art, and they are searching for the birth of stars."[11]

My work on Tworkov's writings emphasizes a paradoxical duality in my interests: a friend once chided me for appearing nostalgic for a time when, it would seem, men were men and everyone knew what to do, yet I am the first to note the deep strangeness of my serving as the mediating voice for a patriarchal figure who was critical of the content and medium of my early artwork. As a feminist I am deeply invested in a critique of the kind of power structures that Tworkov represented to me in my youth. However, as an artist I was instructed deeply in the beliefs of the system that wished to exclude me: in "Modest Painting," I honor Tworkov's work while recontextualizing it into a feminist-inspired analysis of painting, and showing that his fate was to be in some way feminized within the masculinist history of the New York school.

The initial question that led to the final essay in this section, "Blurring Richter," was "Why does the past always have to be grey and out of focus?" This question arose when I considered the stream of generic images of the blur that I regularly saw in exhibitions and received in the mail on exhibition-show cards with respect to a line in Benjamin Buchloh's essay "Divided Memory and Post-Traditional Identity: Gerhard Richter's Work of Mourning" (1996) that caught my attention like a garment of fine mohair caught on a thorn: "A full-size portrait of the artist's uncle in the uniform of the German Wehrmacht, the painting retains the naive central composition typical of a family photograph (which was its source), thereby generating a first conflict within the reading of the painting."[12] With my murdered Uncle Moishe in mind, my first conflict "within the reading of the painting" was that to me it represented a Nazi.

The conceptual clarity and formal acuity of Richter's use of the blur in his painting *Uncle Rudi* created for me a point of entry for tracking the influence of Richter's blurring of the photographic source on contemporary painting and photography back to its roots in the Holocaust. This essay is the final result of the longest research project that I engaged in for this book and for me the riskiest: I am used to writing as a feminist; it was more terrifying to write as a Jew and to discuss publicly the effects that my family's experiences of the Holocaust have had on my artistic and critical practice as an American-born artist working since the early 1970s.

The blur was only one of many recurrent tropes that I noticed in artworks of the past decade. In fact, "trawling for tropes" became my survival modus operandi during visits to art fairs and biennials — creating categories among the seemingly infinite variety of art material rather like children called out state license plates during long family car trips in the days before cars were turned into multiplex entertainment systems on wheels. The related essays "Trite Tropes, Clichés, or the Persistence of Styles" and "Recipe Art" address the ubiquity of such tropes at different levels of the art world, from the college art students unwittingly working in established but unnamed substyles specific to American regional art education to the most sophisticated practitioners of a kind of international avant-garde academy.

"Weather Conditions in Lower Manhattan—September 11, 2001, to October 2, 2001" represents the rupture that made such clichés, trite tropes, and recipe art so intolerable. As a native New Yorker who witnessed some of the events of September 11 with my own eyes and who lived in the city in its aftermath, it would be impossible for me to leave my experiences of this event out of a book of writings from the past decade, whose organizing metaphor is Times Square. Keeping in mind the image of the street painter at the center of Times Square, oblivious to the surrounding barrage of lights, images, and traffic, the moment near high noon on September 13, 2001, when I realized that, had I wanted to, I could have lain down to sleep in the middle of the deserted intersection of Broadway and Grand Street without any risk of being run over was as searing as the more obviously shocking events that I had witnessed two days before. This essay is an exception to the tone and otherwise fairly straightforward sequence of sections in the book—it is off the grid of feminist politics and critical analysis of visual art. Yet these events affected my perceptions of the art that I saw thereafter.

These perceptions are developed in the section of the book titled "Trite Tropes," which groups four distinct yet interrelated essays. The second, third, and fourth follow from the first, but each has a different focus, tone, and timeframe. "Trite Tropes, Clichés, or the Persistence of Styles" calls attention to the continued currency, in American art and art education, of a multitude of obsolete styles, often transmitted to and practiced by art students with an eroded consciousness of these styles' original histories. In "Recipe Art" I examine the flip side of this phenomenon: the success in recent years of a style that is constituted by the ability to successfully configure a set of diverse but predictable tropes in terms of subject and types of appropriated material—one from column A, one from column B—into an art work that can be quickly described. In "Work and Play" I look at political video cartoons from the 2004 election cycle, and in "New Tales of Scheherazade" I examine recent art videos with political content, all works which offered me as a viewer an escape from the predictability of much recipe art.

In keeping with my invocation of the topography of Times Square, the appendix, "Work document: *Grey*," is an off-shoot of "Blurring Richter" and an eccentric text about the conventional uses of black and white to denote the past, which nevertheless adds some inflections to my interest in how the past colors the present. After the failure of collective imagination discussed in "Trite Tropes, Clichés, or the Persistence of Styles," it returns the reader, in a somewhat belle-lettrist though I hope also a playful and suggestive manner, to the beauty of painting.

The appearance of the words *negative thinking* in my title may indicate more of a programmatic belief in modernist ideas of resistance via the methodology of negative dialectics than is actually in play. I can't deny a generationally based frame of mind in which activism, formalism, and even some ideas about resistance do have a place, but my approach to art and culture is more informal and contingent. My title for a lecture from 2006 on my art writing was "The Art of Nonconformist Criticality; Or, On Not Drinking the Kool-Aid."[13] I began work on this lecture with a few words scribbled on a page: *criticality* and *time*, then *time vs. schedule* and *speculativity* (I'm not sure this last one is even a word, but I was thinking about the process of speculative thought as opposed to commodifying text). I also sketched two circles representing the two main forces between which I feel I must navigate when I write. I named these forces for the fabled nautical perils Scylla and Karybdis, located where the Ionian and the Mediterranean seas meet between Sicily and the Italian mainland. According to Greek mythology, both were once beautiful nymphs transformed by a god or goddess. Karybdis had stolen the oxen of Hercules and was turned by Zeus into a whirlpool whose vortex swallows the waves of the sea and anything upon them three times a day. Scylla was a nymph turned into a monster because of the jealousy of the gods: either Poseidon's wife or, in other versions of the tale, Circe was jealous of her and she was turned into a creature with six vicious dog-heads springing from her neck. At first she was horrified at her transformation, but then she began to enjoy her anger, and relished devouring passing sailors.

Two themes emerged from these stories: first the theme of jealousy—and we can trace onto this theme the zero-sum game of power and exclusion created by the art industry's obsession with celebrity and art history's work of canon formation. Secondly, the stories share a theme of cooperation between forces that appear to oppose each other. Only together do they threaten the passage of sailors through the sea between them, because as you move to avoid one you risk getting too close to the other.

In terms of my own navigational chart as a writer, I place academic journals such as *October* on the side of Scylla, an impressive ideological structure, impermeable to influence and interested in absolute aesthetic power in the real world of art institutions. Karybdis, the whirlpool sucking into the deep all who pass, is the mainstream art press, whose requirements for content is never satisfied and whose obsession with discovering and marking celebrity for the market entails the disappearance of the recently new in a constant swirl that eventually tosses up its wrecked victims to float off into the vast ocean and be replaced by the newer new.

Contrary to what some of my writings might indicate, I generally am more interested by what Scylla has to offer as a spur to my thinking, because Karybdis's supportive and dependent relation to the market is enacted in work rules and schedules that enforce conformism.

Let's take the question of time, for instance. If you examine *Artforum*, the actual magazine, not the trope, you see that it's as predictably scheduled as a minuet. If it's September it must "season preview" month, if it is December it must be "best of the year," if it's January it must be "first takes" and "winter preview," then there's the Venice Biennale and the Whitney Biennial to cover. Major retrospectives are planned years in advance as are the articles to be published just before the show. Anything that is not specifically about something that is occurring in the market bracketed by the present tense of "first takes" and the immediate past tense of "best of" cannot appear, though it may nevertheless have import for art practice.

Neither Karybdis nor Scylla is likely to publish much in the way of negative criticism. In the case of Karybdis, the editorial space is essentially bought back from the advertising space, and the advertisers including most of the art world obviously don't want truly negative criticism of their product. Despite hollow reiterations of avant-garde principles of Oedipal rebellion, the market frowns on writing *against* anything. The question of negative criticism comes up a lot when art criticism is discussed: in 2004 at a panel on art criticism entitled, "The Crisis in Criticism," a number of the panelists, who included Saul Ostrow, Nancy Princenthal, Raphael Rubinstein, Jerry Saltz, and Katy Siegel, made a point of saying that they mostly wrote positive articles and reviews about artists they could praise, rather than wasting the precious space they have been allotted in the public arena on a negative review.[14] The press release, always a basic building block for critical exegesis, takes ever greater precedence over more resistant responses. The pressure comes from all sides. The imperative from the market is to write positively for an artist or a movement in order to stake your own claim on the new and correctly bet on futures. And, quite distressing to me, I have at times been chastised from the other side by some older feminist art icons for giving unnecessary attention to bad seeds instead of helping in the career formation of artists I might feel more inclined to champion.

Am I a negative thinker? My title plays with that image, and now that I'm finished with this decade of negative thinking, I can see more clearly the outlines of the "positive" criticism I could have written during the same time period. But no one else was writing what certain art works suggested to me, just as when I began to write in the early 1980s, I wrote in a certain way that sometimes appeared negative because I perceived a political valence in some critically and economically acclaimed works that no one else was writing about from the same point of view. And as always, I want to stress that the artists I seem to write negatively about are all very interesting to me. Their artworks have stayed in my mind as important markers of contemporary thought although I may not write about them according the terms prescribed by their press releases.

Art works and discursive or market patterns must be discussed and analyzed even if that analysis may be negative from the point of view of the market. I want to encourage curiosity and skepticism. I do not want to foster cynicism, which would mean just staying at the level of "that sucks" or "it's all bullshit" that is notable in many of the comments sections on blogs, including art blogs, as I discuss in "Anonymity as a Political Tactic." This is just a micro version of the condition of political discourse in America during the Bush administration: appearance trumped substance, branding as corporate methodology was absorbed into art career management, history was fiction, and longer format, thoughtful criticism of the regime disappeared from mainstream media while the rhetoric of the regime was that criticism equals treason.

It may seem that when I refer to a decade of negative thinking I am referring to my own life, but really the first decade of the twenty-first century has been a terrible decade for democracy in the United States, for the environment, and for the world in terms of war and political extremism. At times it has seemed as if we all were caught in a hall of mirrors, between the violent tactics of previously obscure geopolitical forces and the dark world of Dick Cheney's negative thinking. Things may get better: the election of Barack Obama to the presidency of the United States in November 2008 enabled the hope that political life will make a shift toward less disastrous engagements. In this hoped-for new atmosphere, where a measure of intelligence and reason has begun to replace much criminality and stupidity, it is all the more important to present alternative critical views about the recent past—here of recent cultural utterances—to help develop critical approaches in the coming years.

If I refer to the political situation during the past decade, it is because the ideas and values of the art world do not exist in a vacuum, and there are similarities between the pervasive attitude toward the past, which are outlined in my writings about feminism and art, and the attitude toward realities of geopolitical history expressed by the powers that be.

Notions of "resistance" have been declared passé during a time when academia is under enormous pressure to succeed in the market. (I was even chided by a colleague for using the word *criticality* in the title of my lecture from 2006—she said that was, "SO twenty years ago.") However, the work of scholarship continues: in the past few years, a number of books, including Hal Foster's *Design and Crime (and Other Diatribes)* and Susan Buck-Morss's *Thinking Past Terror*, exemplified a shift to more accessible language and less dogmatic or exclusionary views, including suggestions of theoretical positions, such as a strategic essentialism, that would have been previously unthinkable. These books and also the less scurrilous blog writing by some art writers and poets encouraged my desire for a book more diverse in terms of voice, levels of scholarship, and means of address.

I hope that the time I have taken to play out the meanings of some of the sentences and images that inspired my writing can generate for my readers a different view of the art industry's critical mechanisms, offer less conforming interpretations of some contemporary art, and suggest other possibilities and sources for making art. I am particularly interested in the artists who form part of the MFA generation. My students have inspired much of my writing, as I see my own points of view in the mirror of their generation's needs and preferences. One thing is certain: the present conditions and belief structures that this or any generation takes for granted will influence their views for the rest of their life, as my varied beginnings influenced mine, but also these conditions will change and their beliefs will be tested in ways that cannot be anticipated.

There are times that I have wished that I could declare a moratorium, not just on the art with squiggles, images of childhood, cute animals, and hair that I have tracked, but also on spending six years in art school and on cradle-robbing by dealers and collectors. Young artists should have breathing space to grow up, test their desire to make art, and figure out what subjects they really want to explore, instead of just ordering from column A or column B of the menu of recipe art. I've wished that I could give my students and myself the gift of time, time to work or *not* work in the studio, and, more importantly, to forget about ART; time to just take a walk, not to go somewhere but to experience the city or land in which one lives.

What I can do is to slow the critical traffic down a bit and tease out the meaning of art works and debates that caught my interest.

I began this introduction with the updated anecdote of the madeleine, admitting that, desperate for deep and restful sleep in a daily life crowded by information and signs, I too often skip the stages of experiences described by Proust and just reach for the Ambien. But the sleep that I long for is not the anesthesia and hypnosis of the alienated participant of the spectacle, nor is it the phantasmatically nostalgic return to a series of pasts that never were exactly as one may imagine them. It is the regenerative sleep of open search and fertile dreams that may lead to an art of nonconformist criticality.

I have suggested that ideas and images from the deeper past may provide fuel to go a distance in one's life as an artist. Throughout this book, I apply feminism's willingness to identify and critique power structures to wider fields of inquiry in the hope that, at the very least, I can bring to my examination of contemporary culture the ability to disbelieve. I can assert the value of a grain of salt—and a healthy dash of negativity about present appearances can't hurt.

Part One

SHE SAID, SHE SAID: FEMINIST DEBATES, 1971–2009

"My mother was communist, feminist, vegetarian, and everything," said Vanessa Beecroft, speaking at the conference "The Body Politic: Whatever Happened to the Women Artist's Movement?" held at the New Museum in December 1998. In a sense, she provided at least one answer to the question posed in the title of the panel: *she* had happened to it. It is, of course, the third term in her description that is key, epitomizing one way in which feminism is perceived by a new generation of women artists, in this case quite literally the daughters' generation. In the mysterious way in which a good joke works, it is the word *vegetarian* that reduces the two other terms, which represent major political and social movements of the nineteenth and twentieth centuries, to the kind of self-indulgent, crackpot movements which now reductively sum up the sixties and seventies. Although it may be a healthful practice, here vegetarian is the coded caricature that trivializes communism and feminism.

Speaking last, Beecroft, the youngest member of the panel—which also included Nancy Spero, Mary Kelly, and Renée Cox—opined that she was against work that "screamed." Beecroft herself disconcertingly matched the affectless pose of the women in her videos, which ran continuously during her talk as well as during the discussion period that followed. According to her, such "screaming" work may have been necessary to make polemic points and get attention early on in the feminist art movement, but she herself had encountered no problems in her four-year career. In response to comments about statistics showing the still deplorably low numbers of women exhibiting their work—Spero mentioned that the initial gains achieved in the mid-seventies through demands and protest, from about 4 percent to 25 percent of women in group exhibitions,[1] had never been exceeded to this day—Beecroft stated that she never counted. However, she admitted in a quick aside, her work was often shown with other women's; she did not elaborate further on why this might be the case. She also traced her interest in the female nude to her grounding, as an Italian, in Italian Renaissance art, with no acknowledgment of feminist art historians' extensive iconographic analysis of this history of representation. As disaffected, Barbie doll–figured, half-naked women milled around the atrium of the Guggenheim Museum in the video of her performance there the previous year, she said she was "always impressed by beauty in women, the ability to be objectified, and to objectify themselves." As for the question of power, she expressed some nostalgia for art done under repressive totalitarian regimes when subversion had to be done through covert, non-screaming codes: "I don't mind even the condition of non-power. I think it's more stimulating. Let's say, in old dictatorships, all the intellectuals, they were in this condition. If it's this level, I like, I don't like when it's against, so obvious."[2]

The other panelists and the audience, largely composed of women in their forties and fifties (and about ten hardy men) did not seriously question Beecroft on the political content of her work and her statements. No one noted that if we've learned anything from thirty years of feminist and postmodern critiques of representation, it is indeed that every representation serves an ideology, not just those that "scream." Unfortunately, but as so often happens, the "bad girl" got most of the attention of the audience, although negatively, despite the depth of experience of the other panelists—Nancy Spero in particular was luminously brilliant that evening. None of the other artists on the panel addressed Beecroft with any direct remarks on the dangers of flirting so closely with traditionally exploitative figurations. Perhaps they felt that it would have been like shooting fish in a barrel. Nevertheless, I suspect that many in the room that evening were appalled by Beecroft's complacency, her sense of entitlement, and her apparent contempt for the work that had enabled her sense of privilege.

And yet, isn't that what the early feminist artists' movement had worked for, the day when young women artists would feel only entitlement and possibility? After all, in the Bible, God made the Jews wander in the desert until all those who remembered slavery had died out so that only a fresh, amnesiac but free generation would enter the promised land of milk and honey. The difference here is that only thirty years have passed since the beginning of the women artists' movement, and many of those who first worked in feminism are still alive and not even that old, and are only now doing mature work that synthesizes a broad experience encompassing feminism as well as later discourses. But they haven't forgotten how it was. More importantly, they still see and experience the underlying discriminatory practices of patriarchal systems because they were trained to look for them in the world *and in themselves.*

The ideological schism made evident at this event has been revisited and reenacted at several panels organized on feminism "then and now," including a panel moderated by Faith Wilding held in conjunction with "Between the Acts," an exhibition of works by young women artists at Art in General, curated by Juana Valdes (September 11, 1997 to October 25, 1997); a series of panels held at the A.I.R. Gallery from 1997 to 1998 to celebrate its twenty-fifth anniversary;[3] and "The F-Word: Contemporary Feminisms and the Legacy of the Los Angeles Feminist Art Movement," a symposium organized in October 1998 by the Feminist Art Workshop (FAWS), a group of California Institute of the Arts (CalArts) students, alumni, and faculty, at which I was a participant. Toward the end of "The F-Word" symposium, the question was asked, "Where is feminism going?" While predictive comments are probably futile, one can attempt to pinpoint where feminism has come to. Tracing the progression of events at "The F-Word" provides a few impressions of what is admittedly a complex subject of inquiry.

"The F-Word" included an evening of "Videos from the Woman's Building," presented by Annette Hunt and Nancy Buchanan, who had both been involved in the Woman's Building in Los Angeles in the mid-1970s.[4] The fervor and sincerity of a new political movement was expressed in works by Suzanne Lacy and Leslie Labowitz, Nancy Buchanan, and Nancy Angelo, interviews with Arlene Raven and Sheila de Bretteville, and in archival footage of the construction of the Woman's Building.

In *Memory and Rage*, a 1978 video documentation of Lacy's and Labowitz's performance piece in front of the LA city hall to protest a series of killings of women, women clad in dowdy dresses and sensible shoes and masked by long black veils recite statistics of violence toward women, backed by a chorus of participants yelling out, "We fight back!" The video records every detail in real time, no matter how silly or boring, so that a local black male councilman is seen to be both supportive and opportunistic, and local female TV reporters earning their stripes on the street (and reporting back to the invariably male anchors) seem to understand their own stake in the issues raised by the event. At the end a young Holly Near sings her song "Something About the Women." One young woman in the symposium's audience said, "This [violence against women] is all still happening but there seems to be more silence." The power of group action, the power of anger informed by facts, and the total sincerity of the participants burned through any cynicism that the contemporary media-savvy audience might have brought to a retrospective viewing of its traces.

THE *ISM* THAT DARE NOT SPEAK ITS NAME

Another powerful work was a fictional video from 1977: *On Joining the Order* by Nancy Angelo. In it a woman's voice tells a story of a young girl who can't understand why puberty has caused a loss of intimacy with her father. One night, when her mother is away, she gets into her parents' bed, waits for her father to stumble home in a drunken haze, and lets him have sex with her, as he mistakes her for his wife, her mother. When he awakens and realizes what he has done, he turns his face away and weeps. The mother returns, they all have breakfast, and nothing is said. The narrative is told so that it seems like a true story yet with the strange pace and eerie plotting of a folktale. Although the topic of incest is incendiary, the story here is morally ambiguous and not didactic; it isn't clear who is more culpable, the girl who slipped into her father's bed, or the father who had distanced himself from her precisely because of his fear of incestuous intimacies.

While the quality of the black and white video now seems primitive, the aural narrative is juxtaposed with astonishingly effective metaphoric rather than illustrative imagery. No people are pictured; during much of the tale, fingers of what look like a woman's hand stroke a rose suspended in clear gel. The slow manipulation of the rose in this primal goo as a visual accompaniment to a narrative of incest seems like a perfect example of what early feminist art in the United States sought: visual art that would depict and embody sexuality as experienced by the woman as subject. In this case one intuited, correctly, a lesbian erotics.

At the end of this evening the pervasive feeling was that the seventies ROCKED! Yet two facts shadowed the presentation. First both Hunt and Buchanan expressed their gratitude that anyone was interested in what they had been involved with so many years ago. More tragically from a historical point of view, the material we were watching had almost been lost: Hunt, after safeguarding these hours of tape for nearly twenty years, recently had put them on the curb for garbage collection. Only a providential call inviting her to place the tapes in the Long Beach Museum of Art's archives saved this historically valuable material. The fragility of feminism's legacy was baldly evident.

Two overarching themes were established at "The F-Word" symposium's official opening reception: gratitude for the pioneering work of feminist artists of the 1970s generation, who were invited to participate and be honored at the "F-Word" symposium, and loss, both of the focus and energy of that moment and of documentation of the work made by

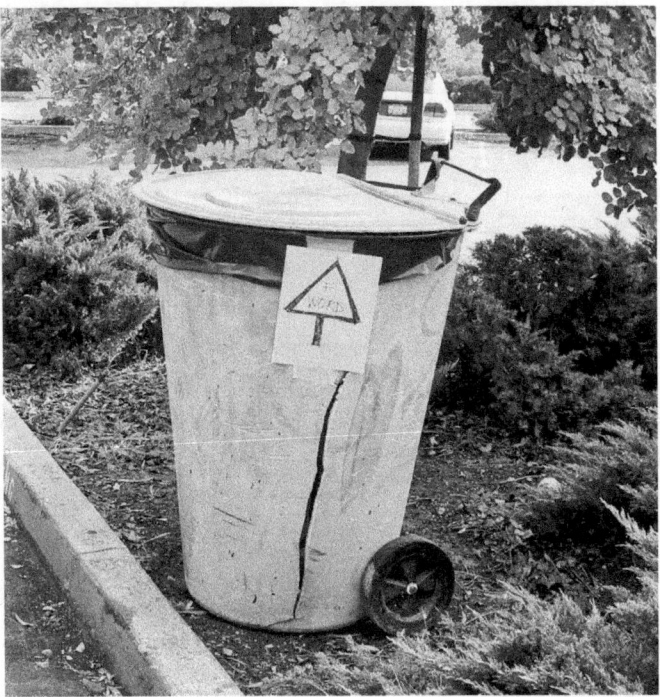

Directions to the "F-Word" symposium at CalArts, 1998.
Photo © by Mira Schor.

these women. The FAWS collective and the symposium grew from the FAWS member Karina Combs's discovery, in the CalArts archives, of evidence of a feminist art program at CalArts, which she had never heard of! Documents, in some cases already in the dumpster, led to the rediscovery of material and events jettisoned from institutional memory, even though it might be argued that the existence of the Feminist Art Program at CalArts from 1971 to 1975 was one of its principle and most innovative contributions to contemporary art history. Those of us involved in the program and the Woman's Building in LA certainly had not forgotten, and now we were told that we were honored guests. Liz Barrett, a current faculty member and part of FAWS, said, "What was really important to us was to meet you all, to meet the people who had been part of the Feminist Art Program. We wanted to create an occasion for you to come and reflect with us on your experiences with those programs and your stories—your personal stories—and your art practices."

So we did tell our stories. That night there were vivid and funny testimonies from the women who had been in Judy Chicago's original Feminist Art Program at the California State University, Fresno, as well as participants in the *Womanhouse* project and the Woman's Building. The next day the symposium began with a panel which included Faith Wilding, Cheri Gaulke, Sue Maberry, and me. Each of us spoke about our early experiences but also about our current work—in our art, jobs, and teaching— where feminism operates in a complex field of interests. Wilding spoke of her involvement with cyberfeminism, for example. Gaulke spoke of collaborative projects in the public-art field and in teaching, and Sue Maberry about a recent grant from the Getty that allowed her to transfer slides of early feminist artworks to digital form (but she had to choose only 1,500 out of 10,000 images). I spoke about the dilemma I experience between feeling the responsibility to continue to represent feminism in my work, for pedagogic purposes, and moving toward other intellectual and formal concerns, for my own growth. As a group, we seemed to have an engaged but also a balanced and reflective view of the past and, at the same time, we existed very much in a developing present of contemporary artistic and pedagogic practice.

In the informally circulated "Journal Notes from F-Word Symposium Week at CalArts," FAWS notes that the final discussion "got bogged down in some of the usual dichotomies between 1970s and 1990s feminisms which once again enforced a simplistic and somewhat false division between essentialist and constructivist views of the body." This was surely not the intention of FAWS, whose "Working Papers for Themes and Topics," prepared just before the symposium, put forth well-informed and wide ranging questions and strategies.[5] But indeed, by the end of the symposium, the still considerable living power of "seventies feminism's legacy" had been overshadowed by a curious reenactment of the way in which it was condemned to the essentialist scrap heap of history by certain aspects of postmodernist discourse predominant in the 1980s.

This was largely effectuated through interwoven presentations by Simon Leung and Juli Carson, who both paid particular homage to the work of Mary Kelly. While the intellectual rigor of Kelly's critique of traditional representation of woman becomes ever more significant in the face of a less theoretically inclined moment, it is important to remember the extent to which, in the 1980s, the discourses of which Mary Kelly is considered the exemplar represented not only a necessary corrective to some work from the 1970s, but also a new prescriptive and divisive hierarchy within feminist art. Those involved in a critique of totalizing systems and essences seemed to display totalizing impulses of their own: to replace Woman with the concept of Human Vehicle for constructed gender signifiers, a shift that continues to leave out the more complex lived experience of interwoven biological and social construction. As I have discussed in other contexts,[6] the critique of essence also favors certain visual strategies, doubling the prescriptive effect of the new hierarchy. Thus, the evocation of Mary Kelly by Carson and Leung—in the context of a symposium dedicated to the reconsideration of the feminist legacy of the 1970s (implicitly, the American version of that legacy, given the location and circumstances)—felt like a reenactment of the repressive aspects of the postmodernist discourse and set into motion the familiar miasmic atmosphere described in the FAWS report.[7]

Certainly more fluid movement along the previously frozen vectors of masculine/feminine and male/female has opened up a wider range of identities. But when Leung said, "I don't know what a body is," he did not allow for the very real social, legal, and economical consequences that still devolve from living in a biologically sexed body. The pitfalls of the rhetoric about a post-sexed body were illustrated by the question one student posed: "I think it's still problematic; as a visual artist, as a woman, as a black woman, where do I put my body? . . . I just want to hear the body talked about. . . . Do we address the body and therefore play into notions of [the] essential, of fetish, or do we not address the body and try to make a theoretical model of the body? But where's the body? . . . In my studio this is kind of daunting." Indeed, how do you deal with conflicting theoretical positions when in the studio? "The language" doesn't help beyond a certain point in the struggle to visually represent experience of the lived body, especially if the concept "woman" has been so successfully problematized that a woman doesn't trust her own experience.[8] If Woman with a capital "W" is an essentializing concept that silenced differences among women, nevertheless the confusion and doubt evident in some of the students' questions and faces made it clear that if you can't say that actual women, embodied and enculturated, exist, then women are silenced yet again.

It is just at this point that my mapping of "The F-word" leads back to what seemed so infuriating about Beecroft at "The Body Politic" panel. For, just beyond the ivory walls of sophisticated gender theory, the post-feminist sense of complacency about the success of feminism is challenged by a proliferation of facts available daily in the mass media that point to how much women in our culture are still enslaved to, and sometimes endangered by, the demands of an ideological and commercial system committed to their objectification.

In the art world, the situation is certainly complex—women have created and inspired some of the most significant work of the past two decades, in large part under the influence of ground-breaking investigations of gender and sexuality by early feminist artists, who often used non-traditional media (including video, performance, installation, and text as image). Women also exhibit more now and are reviewed more frequently. Young women artists enter the art world with a sense of opportunity and at least an illusion of equality with their male cohorts. Despite the fact that, under the glass ceiling of major institutions, museums, galleries, and academic journals and centers, women usually are still only accorded token representation, one can assert that things are certainly measurably better than they were thirty years ago. But what about life outside the art world? Of the many articles on issues relevant to women that I habitually clip from the *New York Times*, *Harper's Bazaar*, *Time*, and *Newsweek*, among other publications, here are some headlines and quotes, from 1998 alone:

> "An Old Scourge of War Becomes Its Latest Crime": "More to the point, it is becoming increasingly apparent that the new style of warfare is often aimed specifically at women and is defined by a view of premeditated, organized sexual assault as a tactic in terrorizing and humiliating a civilian population. . . . achieving forced pregnancy and thus poisoning the womb of the enemy. . . . Largely because of the systematic use of sexual assault in ethnic wars in the Balkans and Rwanda, the [international criminal] court is expected to rank rape as an internationally recognized war crime for the first time in history.[9]

> Impeaching a President on charges of lying about sex with an office underling? Surely it's time to listen to female voices. But when Republican congresswomen held a press conference after the House's historic impeachment vote, the Capitol Hill newspaper *Roll Call*'s only coverage was a photo documenting the legislators' almost identical footwear.[10]

The way Dr. David L. Matlock sees it, he's the Picasso of vaginas. But this gynecologist is just one of many doctors practicing the latest cosmetic-surgery technique: female genital reconstruction. From remodeling the appearance of the labia minora and labia majora (the inner and outer vaginal lips, respectively) to reducing the diameter of the vaginal canal ... gynecologists and plastic surgeons are altering private parts at the request of women willing to shell out thousands of dollars for these procedures. . . . Matlock is so busy he hasn't even had time to finish putting together the photo album of before and after pictures.[11]

If you can't bring a feminist analysis to these and many other examples of women's current place in society, you are dangerously disabled and this disabling is all the more pernicious because it is occurring *after* the women's liberation movement, consciousness-raising, and feminist theory seem to have preempted the need for continued critical vigilance, when people think these discussions have been resolved. Vaginal cosmetic surgery is taking place years after the rarely seen *Near the Big Chakra*, a 1972 film by Ann Severson entirely composed of close-ups of an astonishing variety of palpitating and bubbling labia, like mollusks from the deep: small ones, big loose ones, ones masked by black pubic hair, and ones sparsely haloed by gray hairs, all making the case for the female sexual organ as a varied and fascinating species of living organism. While early feminist movements and practices dreamed of new generations of empowered women, those involved could not have imagined women losing the ability, will, and courage to look at societal structures critically, or women losing solidarity with other women. Terms such as "male-identified" float back into one's mind, but no consciousness-raising sessions now exist to examine what that might mean. Women accept advances owed to an activism whose premise and engagement they now mock—*and often know very little about*, because this history is not widely taught. They take as a birthright rights and opportunities that are not foundational but that were granted due to the courageous efforts of "screamers."

By foundational, I don't mean to speak of hard-wired, biologically based essence, but, rather, of hierarchies that may be soft-wired yet are deeply entrenched throughout recorded history. Perhaps here one can usefully look to the example of the African American experience: slavery was ended by the Emancipation Proclamation and blacks have benefited from laws rectifying previous injustices, but in America, while equality may be legislated, racism is foundational. In the 1990s and the first decade of the twenty-first century, legally mandated roll-backs of affirmative action—before equal opportunity has been achieved—indicate the fragility of what is not foundational. Similarly, while women have undoubtedly achieved substantial legal, economic, and political rights in the twentieth century, agency and subjectivity are not considered women's birthright in the way that they are, albeit in a very relative fashion, for men: rights granted by law are contingent, sexism is foundational. After all, to name just one example, the right to abortion granted in *Roe v. Wade* has already been seriously constrained and several times in the past fifteen years has been just a couple of Supreme Court votes away from being revoked completely. Complacency, combined with contempt for the people who fought for such rights, makes it even easier for the forces some assumed were defeated to take these rights away again.[12]

At the beginning of the feminist movement, women also often denied that there was a problem. It was painful and risky to take off those rose-colored glasses, to criticize Daddy and rethink Mommy. But it was also a time when one generally tended to think politically and to believe that activism could bring change; it is well known that the feminist art movement emerged from the civil rights, anti-war, and women's liberation movements. Although the CalArts Feminist Art Program and other early separatist feminist programs could be as psychologically wrenching for many of the participants as they were challenging and empowering, they did provide basic and enduring models of women supporting women.

Perhaps the most important political act I perform is to identify myself publicly as a feminist. I use the word, the F-word. But, nearly thirty years after the beginnings of the most recent major feminist movement, like the love that dare not speak its name, feminism is the ism that dare not speak its name. Students in the early feminist programs, such as the CalArts Feminist Art Program, were taught to say the word *cunt* until it lost its derogatory nature and female sexuality was revalued, and yet just a few years ago at "The F-Word" symposium, an event organized to honor their legacy, its organizers were so tentative that they were unable to even spell out the word that defined the movement. It was an apt title and also quite cute and funny, but if women can't spell out *feminism*, then feminism is in big trouble—or is it women who are in big trouble? At the very end of the symposium, Faith Wilding got up and did the Fresno "cunt cheer." *Give*

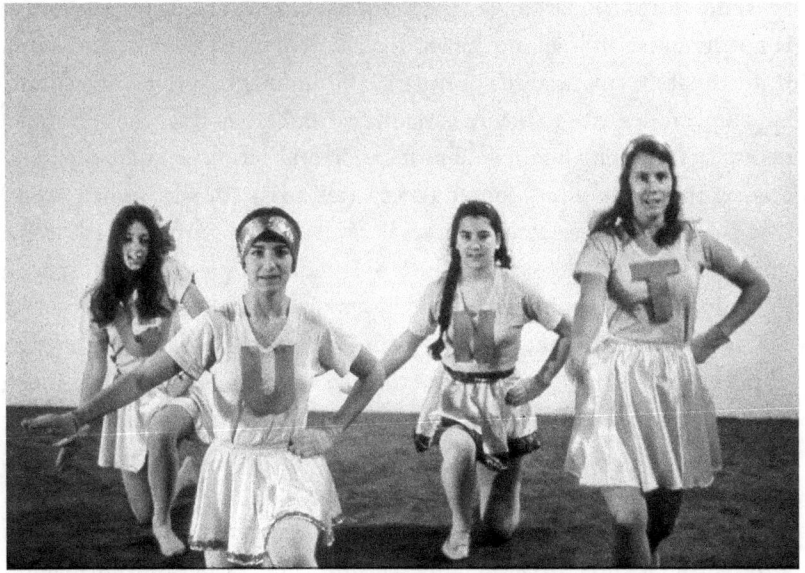

Judy Chicago and the Feminist Art Program, "Cunt Cheerleaders,"
1970–1971. Photograph courtesy of Through the Flower.

me a C. . . . The audience's embarrassment, discomfort, but perhaps also
awe could scarcely have been more palpable if she'd peed on the floor![13]

My own basic view on *feminism* is perhaps a nineteenth-century one:
that women are still, despite major changes, not seen as intrinsically
having equality or parity of agency and subjectivity, but rather are most
valued for their sexuality as a commodity. Culture, both in the capitalist first world and in the recesses of dusty villages of the third world, is
still intent on the objectification of women. Paradoxically, the story of
women's experiences of their own lives and bodies is a rich one, but it
remains largely untapped in the larger scope of the history of civilization.[14] "The Body Politic" and "The F-Word" symposia revealed disturbing
examples of how easily and quickly even recent, self-consciously historical
contributions of women may be lost.

There is no doubt that public identification as a feminist does carry risk.
Young women are often afraid of the word, even when they are drawn to
the concepts. They want to be at the center. Who wouldn't? And, largely because of feminist activism and feminism's analysis of societal hierarchies,
this has become an achievable goal. But feminism is seen as by definition

speaking from the margin, for the margin. Thus, by extension, the center is not feminist and will not reward overt demonstrations of feminism. Unfortunately, this analysis of the risk of feminism is probably accurate, but surely it describes a devil's bargain that only reinforces the continued necessity for strong feminist identification and action. And, further, embracing the nonfeminist center also carries a risk for the woman artist: that the new postgendered universal of the center turns out to be the (male) universal of the past in which only feminist specificity can spare a woman artist from being subsumed by a male-oriented art history.

One could argue that on these panels about the feminist legacy, the young women artists who distance themselves from feminism have been set up to play the role of the bad seed. It could further be argued that their attitude toward feminism is certainly not their fault since feminist accomplishments are often not preserved and not taught. Rather, women who came of age in the 1980s and 1990s have been bathed in and have internalized a three decades–long, culture-wide backlash against feminism. This backlash increasingly operates in a covert manner that is hard to guard against because it seems to take feminism into account, yet in it feminism is manifested either as a culture of victimization, as seen in repressed-memory narratives or other afternoon talk show excesses, or in the simulation of feminism enacted by the "bad girl."

One must also question why it is that young women who are not feminists are so often selected over their feminist contemporaries to publicly represent their generation in these contexts. Perhaps this is because the feminists are less successful or "hot," in art market terms. But, again, it is likely that one condition for art market viability is precisely to abjure feminism.[15] That also may not be "their (the nonfeminists) fault." But the tools are there for any young woman to deconstruct the hierarchies that seek to determine her moral and political choices, and those choices are hers to make.

My comments in this essay may at times appear to speak with a tinge of bitterness toward discord between generations of women artists, but in fact the generational schism is a red herring in the backlash. I've referred to my time in the Feminist Art Program at CalArts as "boot camp for feminists," and no one in their right mind longs to go back to boot camp. Change should be something positive and progressive, which I believe feminism is for society as a whole. Certainly education would help such development. If artists, in the course of a standard art education, were as well-versed in the rich legacy of feminist art as in Italian Renaissance art and other major movements in art history, they could not fail to be inspired.

In the late nineties, I showed a senior class of mostly women art students the *Womanhouse* film by Johanna Demetrakas (1974), which documents the CalArts Feminist Art Program's site-specific installation art project of the same name from 1972, and the performances presented during that exhibition,[16] and *Reclaiming the Body: Feminist Art in America*, a video documentary by Michael Blackwood, which presents the curators of and some of the artists included in the "Bad Girl" exhibition at the New Museum in 1994. During even the most primitive agit-prop performances of *Womanhouse*, such as the Punch and Judy–like "Cock and Cunt Play," their faces were agape, riveted to the screen. A few said that those two hours provided the most concentrated information about women artists they'd ever been exposed to. And at least one immediately put the inspiration to good use, sitting in the front row of a critique with a fake penis conspicuously strapped under a very short skirt and shocking her good-natured but slightly antediluvian male sculpture teacher!

My students' interest is heartening, as is the fact that at every panel discussion I've been to where the generations seem pitted against each other and a Vanessa Beecroft is in evidence, there is always another young woman who speaks up for feminism.

There have been many feminist art panels and symposia since "The F-Word." Among these is "Exquisite Acts and Everyday Rebellions: 2007 CalArts Feminist Art Project." Like "The F-Word," this was a student-organized event held at CalArts, but this time the organizers took a very different overall attitude to the legacy of their school's feminist art program and feminism in general, with the organizers expressing "solidarity" with the frustration and disappointment expressed to varying degrees by women of my generation, including Faith Wilding and myself.[17]

At every panel, there is always a young woman who speaks up for feminism. Nevertheless familiar patterns of behavior and strategic positioning emerge, one of which is the considerable reluctance to downright hostility on the part of young women toward any association with the word *feminism*, the F-word. Various protestations, from "Yes, I'm a feminist *but* . . . ," to "I'm a woman, so of course I am working from that experience, but I'm not a feminist," or "above all, I'm an artist," are again expressed. And, when the panels in question feature (or pit against each other) "generations" of women artists, a new Vanessa Beecroft may appear. One such recurrence was acted out at the panel "'Feminisms' in Four Generations," moderated by the *New York Times* art critic Roberta Smith in January 2006. The Israeli performance artist Tamy Ben-Tor seemed to unknowingly re-perform Beecroft's 1998 performance, with a vengeance. Taking the position that she found it problematic to associate herself with any ideology, she said that feminism is "fine if it serves the 'weak.'"[18] These comments incurred the hostility of the audience and appeared to blindside some of the other panelists, who included Collier Schorr, Barbara Kruger, and Joan Snyder.

While Ben-Tor's aversion to ideology is brilliantly expressed in her unique characterizations of often composite-gendered figures from every side of the charged political and historical narratives of racism and anti-Semitism, her attitude toward feminism as expressed on the panel was not one that seemed to necessarily flow from her work. Indeed, an American viewer could easily see her work, including her hilarious video *Women Talking about Adolf Hitler* (2005) and her searing performance piece, *Judensau* (2007), as existing in a continuum with the early, equally radical, and sometimes terrifyingly embodied performances of someone like Karen Finley. While no one suggested to Ben-Tor that her vehement anti-feminist position was itself *ideological*, her fellow panelist Schorr did ask if such a position might not strategically ensure a certain access to (male) power. (Ben-Tor had previously noted that she had mostly affiliated herself with her male faculty during her theater arts education in Israel, even though there were women teaching there.) Additionally, on the subject of the Holocaust, Ben-Tor said, "The Holocaust is an issue for humanity, not just for Jews." She continued, "If you do work as a woman, it hides the truth."

The writer Lynne Tillman responded from the audience. She said that feminism is not just about specific bodies; feminism is a critique of power. She said that Ben-Tor spoke of "humanity" but feminism is part of the discursive process that questions what is "humanity" and who is allowed to be called "human."

I was grateful to Tillman for the content and the clarity of her statement because of the particular association that the word *humanity* has for me in relation to the word *feminism*. Once upon a time, when I was twenty years old, a little man who taught art told me that I would never be an artist. A few years after that, when I was still in my twenties but had in fact become an artist in the world, I confronted him about this as something outrageous to say to a young person. He thought about it and a few weeks later said that he had never said that I would never be an *artist*, he'd said that I would never be a *painter*! Many more years passed and I ran into him again. "How are you?" he asked. "Still fighting the good fight?" I puzzled over that cryptic question. Later that same summer, I found myself near this man again at a beachside memorial party for a re- cently deceased, much loved artist. "Still fighting the good fight?" he asked again. "The feminist fight?" Ah, the truth was revealed. A short man with a Hercule Poirot mustache, he waved at the ocean and announced, "*I'm interested in humanity.*" "I am too," I began to say, after having stared out at the water for a minute as if to see all the humanity floating about in it, "but I feel I have to start with a group that I am part of most closely. . . ." I stopped trying to engage him in a real conversation when I realized that he wasn't listening to me.[19]

Singular or plural, feminism nonetheless, the word spelled out in full. New nomenclatures and particular causes specific to the historical moment must necessarily apply. But the legacy must be preserved and political analyses of women's societal positions continued, which may take some additional "screaming." Or perhaps less unpleasantly charged strategies and attitudes can contribute to a different method of communication. But, finally, feminism is not a matter of one generation's bitterness, but of everybody's business.

ANONYMITY AS A POLITICAL TACTIC: ART BLOGS, FEMINISM, WRITING, AND POLITICS

I would venture to guess that Anon, who wrote so many poems without signing them, was often a woman.—Virginia Woolf, *A Room of One's Own*

In the historical situation described by Virginia Woolf, writing in 1929 at the end of the first great wave of the suffrage movement, anonymity was the tragic fate of the brilliant woman whose existence one can only deduce based on the laws of chance and general experience of human talents, just as one deduces the existence of dark stars by the gravity that veils their presence from our traditional measuring devices. If ever, or whenever genius existed in a woman and made its way into cultural form, it was reattributed to a named man or relegated to "Anon.," her name erased by propriety, misogyny, and neglect.

In recent years, anonymity has been used as a protective political tactic: for instance in the 1980s and 1990s, the Guerrilla Girls chose anonymity in order to foreclose on career retribution and the danger of being individually dismissed as untalented artists operating out of a sense of sour grapes in their critiques of the inequitable representation of women and artists of color in the art world.[1]

The question of anonymity as a political tactic is of particular interest when discourse occurs in a space without physical presence. Debate and discourse on art now frequently take place on blogs, which often rely on anonymity to enable uncensored speech. These new blogs and websites, with varying degrees of intellectual ambition, political focus, and textual informality, suggest a reconsideration of the role of anonymity as a political tactic for any political cause, but here specifically as it relates to feminist activism at a time when there seem to be fewer public voices for feminism, in a media atmosphere that is generally repressive of alternate points of view, and where collaborationist dissimulation of a clear feminist position may be seen by younger women as necessary for career survival.

My interest in these sites, particularly those run by artists, develops from my own experience as an artist and writer and as the co-editor, with the painter Susan Bee, of *M/E/A/N/I/N/G*, an art journal that was published between 1986 and 1996 and which itself now has a presence on the web.[2] Bee and I began from a position of relative anonymity: that is, our identities were public but relatively unmarked in the art world. However, by creating a space for cultural discourse, we staked out a certain visibility and associated ourselves with and also against various figures and institutions in the art world, with corresponding rewards and risks.

In January 2006, we put back online two issues of $M/E/A/N/I/N/G$ that we had originally created in 2002 and 2003 for the Artkrush website.[3] A few days later I updated our site with "She Demon Spawn from Hell," a brief essay I wrote about the artist Tamy Ben-Tor's anti-feminist statements on the New York Times–sponsored panel, "'Feminisms' in Four Generations," held in New York City on January 7, 2006. This in turn sparked a lively debate on a new blog, Anonymous Female Artist (A.K.A. Militant Feminist Bitch), run by an anonymous woman artist, self-styled as "Miss Edna V. Harris." Through this blog I was made aware of a network of art blogs, including the "artsoldier" blog, PainterNYC, and Brainstormers, among others, and I followed them in the months that followed. Among the twenty or thirty blogs that constitute this nodule of the web, "Anonymous Female Artist" was the only one that focused on feminism and art. I was interested in what these blogs might reveal about the strengths and the pitfalls of blogs as a medium for discourse, and in what they suggested about anonymity as a political strategy.

Further, art writing on blogs presented the possibility of an alternative to the mainstream art media, which is reluctant to publish much in the way of negative criticism, given that the editorial space in many major art publications is essentially bought back from the advertising space, and the advertisers, including most of the art industry, obviously would prefer positive views of their product. Thus the non-commercial aspect of blogs and the anonymity of many of the participants held the possibility of a freer environment for criticism, but, as further experience proved, the sucks/bullshit mode that is so much a part of the broader level of discourse in American society surfaced all too often.

Anonymous Female Artist had begun on a high note, forthrightly taking to task Chrissie Iles, co-curator of the 2006 Whitney Biennial, over the poor representation of women in the show. Anonymity enhanced the cheeky energy of this intervention. But in the months to come a number of themes could be observed in the blogger's posts and the resulting comments. Miss Edna's initial response to the fracas over Ben-Tor's anti-feminist comments on the *Times* panel, "Tamy Been-Torqued," and the comments for that blog posting focused on Ben-Tor's antifeminist views as I had reported them in my own essay.[4] Debates on blogs rage like wild fires and flame out even more quickly. But, while it lasted, the discussion was indicative of the state not just of feminist discourse, but of discourse, period, at this time.

Miss Edna began by noting that "Ben-Tor didn't (and doesn't, to my knowledge) specifically present an anti-feminist viewpoint in her work," something I had myself stressed. She continued,

> Of course, the older female artists (who are all prominent enough to automatically, at least professionally, transcend bitterness) tried as best they could to remind Ben-Tor that they laid the groundwork for her acceptance in the art world. They were shocked and dismayed when she cast them off, and most of what I've read focuses on the fact that she dissed them.
>
> But I don't think that's what she did, or at least meant to do. I don't think that even interests her. That would make her merely rebellious, resulting from not wanting to be associated with feminism's bad rap. Instead, I think she symbolizes a "moving on"—but it's flawed, scary, and all twisted up with issues. It's unsynthesized, and because of that, I think Ben-Tor is rejecting symbolism more than anything.

Thus she seemed to partially applaud Ben-Tor's behavior, as evidence of a new direction for feminism, even though that behavior flouted the very premise of her blog—"militantfeminist." Her comments were contradictory, I think precisely because she was unwilling, as a number of her readers were, to find herself in agreement with a previous generation of feminists—whose work, aspirations, ideas, and even appearance were largely described in the most stereotypically negative terms. Miss Edna continued, "Artists like Ben-Tor don't seem to think existing issues-related artwork is badass *enough*. I think her refusal to align herself with the other women on the panel wasn't because she wanted to react against them (and their ideas), but because she wanted to react against their *art*. She doesn't want to be in their club because she doesn't like their version of cultural commentary. Isn't that what she thinks is 'weak'?" Paradoxically, a male art blogger, "artsoldier," responded to Miss Edna's post on his own site, showing a much clearer understanding of my arguments:

What shocked me the most about Edna's post was how sympathetic she appears to be to Ben-Tor's anti-feminism, especially considering that her "Militant Art Bitch" blog takes a decidedly feminist approach in combating gender discrimination in the artworld. Yet, she writes: "When Schor then poses the question, 'why is it that young women who are not feminists are the ones so often selected to publicly repre- sent their generation in these contexts?' my answer is: because, issues aside, they are making more exciting work." . . . Ben-Tor's stated reason for not being sympathetic to feminism (according to Schor's notes of the event): 'It's fine if it serves the weak but I don't feel affiliated with it. . . . Many women in the world are oppressed, that's where feminism has to struggle, it doesn't have to struggle for me.' Wow. "It doesn't have to struggle for me." It's a good thing that so many women have struggled before her, so that she can feel so unoppressed now.

In general artsoldier articulated a more consistent overall political view-point and consciousness on his site. Miss Edna was distracted into attacks on peripheral art world figures such as Charlie Finch, in much the way that Al Franken used to spend far too much time on his Air America radio show taking on Bill O'Reilly and Rush Limbaugh. On his blog, artsoldier often wrote about contemporary international political events and critiqued the Bush administration, rather than limiting his focus to the confines of the New York art world. This is relevant in terms of noting what constitute political positions at this point in time, and how a clear feminist position may be, perhaps even must be, concurrent with an informed willingness to engage in critical political analysis of culture as a whole.

The discussion on Anonymous Female Artist continued with an ex-change in the comments section about which women artists were femi-nist and which were doing interesting work. The listing of names ended with the following all too predictable development: "Anonymous writes: i feel like your explanation of t.b-t is a little too lenient. your blog name is "militant." i say: if you dont want to call yourself a feminist or dont want to BE a feminist that's fine but if you're just flat out insulting to feminist history then FUCK YOU. and i think that's a more militant stance toward t.b-t."[5]

Here I have to interrupt my reportage to call attention to the language and tone of blogs. On the one hand discussions may reveal passionately engaged people, some of whom are knowledgeable in a substantial manner. On the other hand, many lapse into a more vernacular form of address—"FUCK YOU" was the least of it. I found that many of the women here took on a kind of hip-hop gangsta, feminisma bravura, "badasses," "long-ass," "screw-the-voyeur" kind of thing. OK, that is sort of harmlessly sexy posturing, up to a point, but further, as others have noted, anecdotally and in print, it seems like each conversation online rapidly disintegrates into unflattering comments about other people's dick size.[6] For example, it took only about twelve interchanges in the comments to a May 24, 2006, interview with Miss Edna, which I will discuss a bit later in relation to the issue of anonymity, for the participants to get to the "dick size" discussion. Since we don't know whether the posters are women or men, I guess that at least in this respect we are finally beyond binaries (or that indeed no one has the phallus, which is very small anyway).

Certainly the vulgarity of this level of discourse is enabled by the condition of anonymity: the rules of civil behavior are suspended when you are basically talking to yourself as you type alone and incognito at three in the morning. This posturing style may emerge from the speed demanded or at least enabled by the form as well as influenced by the pervasive influence of hiphop freestyle's flow of language. The Howard Stern shock-jock factor further erodes ordinary courtesy. Blogs encourage relatively unmediated writing. If hard-copy journalism also is written for the moment, there is usually still some kind of editorial or institutional control, whereas the beauty of blogging is that the writer is free of editorial interference—but the writing is only as polished as the writer wants and can accomplish alone. A lot of the writing is good, if a bit loose. Most often it's fairly untheorized. A lot of it is fun, and I admire the energy that goes into writing so much and at such a pace, but some of it comes across as the end of reasoned thought as we know it.

The flip side of "badass" posturing is the highly theorized and academized techno-corporate language that often bedevils online forums such as the Institute for Distributed Creativity's email listserv, which features conversations on topics such as activism and new media. The disembodied language found in these discussions may be one of the factors alienating women participants on the IDC list. An IDC discussion thread in the summer of 2006, "Where have all the women gone?," focused on the problem of the paucity of women actively participating in the email discussion, instead acting as "lurkers," who were theoretically proficient and, in theory, capable of participating, but who were not finding a place for their voices to be heard. One might also suspect that on an art blog, the use of profanity and a low level of discourse would be a reaction formation to the more off-putting aspects of academic discourse.

Returning to the issue of who are the good women artists who are also feminists, the subject came up again in one of the comments to a March 7, 2006, posting of Miss Edna's, "Girl Art Recession," where she mournfully asked, "Exactly why are we in this Girl Art Recession? Are there specific reasons, beyond the subjective, that women do not get equal billing in galleries, museums, collections, and art magazines in 2006?"[7] If the facts are almost tragic, considering all that has come before, Miss Edna's sorrow seemed quite ironic given the ambivalence she herself expressed in her earlier defense of Ben-Tor's antifeminism as a "badass" next-wave feminist gesture. The ensuing discussion was an eerie echo of the Guerrilla Girls' first poster: when dealers began to say that there were no women artists worthy of being exhibited in their artistic stables, the Guerrilla Girls answered with "GUERRILLA GIRLS' IDENTITIES EXPOSED!," from 1989, which listed five hundred women artists. If this poster wittily foiled curiosity about their identities, it also pointed to the existence of a surplus of women artists every bit as accomplished and deserving of exhibition as male artists.

On the Brainstormers blog in 2006, a mission statement announced the bloggers' purpose: "Brainstormers' Report is a performance art collaborative. Founded in March of 2005, we came together to protest the lack of women artists represented in the P.S.1 Greater New York show. Since that time we have been conducting research regarding the representation of women artists in the public sphere. The Brainstormers are Maria Dumlao, Elaine Kaufmann, Danielle Mysliwiec, and Anne Polashenski."[8] Their site included a humorous video on gender discrimination in the New York art world, and they began the process, yet again, of documenting the lamentable statistics of representation and exhibition of women artists in the New York art world of galleries and museums. In making their names and faces visible, they returned to earlier activist models: the artists' coalitions of the Vietnam War era, such as the Art Workers' Coalition (AWC) and the Guerrilla Art Action Group (GAAG), followed by groups involved with bringing the women's liberation movement into the art world, such as Women Artists in Revolution (WAR) and the Ad Hoc Women Artists' Committee, which in 1970, among other projects, famously targeted the Whitney Annual. In all these cases artists, writers, and curators, all named, worked in a multi-tactical manner, incorporating statistical research, letter writing, picketing, protests, collective exhibitions spaces, exhibitions, and guerrilla theater.

While the view of the web as inherently anonymous is problematized by the kind of exhibitionism that the web also facilitates,[9] even if participants are named, one cannot easily verify their identity and the discourse takes place in a undefined space. Although the Guerrilla Girls were anonymous, their posters were plastered on the outer walls or as close to the actual locations of the galleries they targeted. That created a kind of specificity of place—the criticism was in the dealers' faces, anonymity was turned on its head: the criticism worked because the dealers were not anonymous and their neighborhood was defaced. Posting on city walls is illegal and the galleries pursued the miscreants. The Web, at least for the moment, entails less physical risk.

There was very little personal risk for Miss Edna V. Harris and her readers. Her anonymity allowed her to be completely free in her views and style, including how contradictory and sometimes confused she seemed at times about feminism—engaged in feminist action so long as she was not pinned down to an identification with a phantasmatic image of what a feminist is supposed to be, to look or act like. Her anonymity left her unmarked: her "portrait," a drawing like the little sketches that accompanied newspaper bylines in the earlier years of the twentieth century, the Miss Lonelyhearts columnist, a little face with butterfly glasses, was one of the most endearing aspects of her blog site.

She subscribed to the idea that anonymity gave her and others the freedom to express subversive views that might put them at some risk if expressed in their named identity: "Well, if you're someone who might be jeopardizing your career by speaking out (i.e., all women), you can certainly be more honest when no one knows who you are. When women speak up, they are called bitches, or crazy. In the artworld, there are very few female critics who aren't pandering to men. No one wants to believe it, but it's a fact. It's engrained and somehow accepted. That said, my main reason for staying anonymous is that I'm not interested in any sort of recognition. The downside is that people view that as cowardly."[10]

It was in the comments from men (some of them self-identified by name, some also anonymous) that the greatest criticism of her anonymity was expressed. For example, artist Chris Rewalt said: "I still don't think, Edna, you need to be anonymous to do what you do—on the outside" and

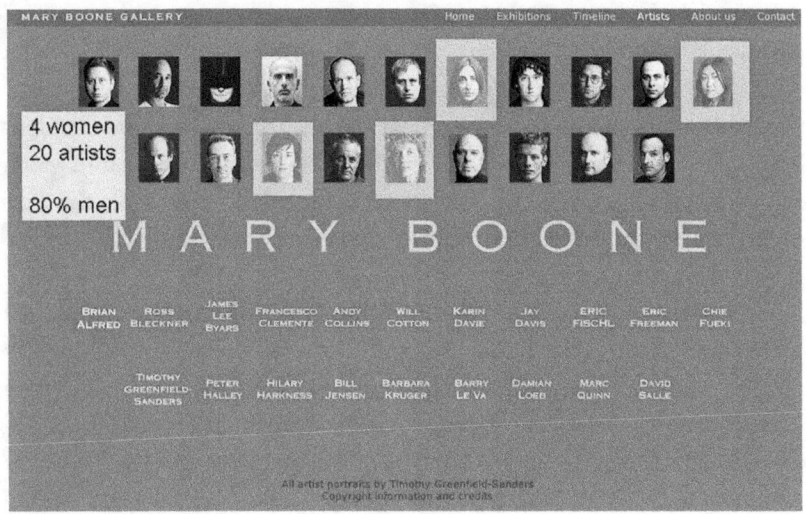

Brainstormers, "Weather Report," 2006. Video still.
© by Brainstormers.

THESE GALLERIES SHOW NO MORE THAN 10% WOMEN ARTISTS OR NONE AT ALL.

Blum Helman
Mary Boone
Grace Borgenicht
Diane Brown
Leo Castelli
Charles Cowles
Marisa Del Re
Dia Art Foundation
Executive
Allan Frumkin

Fun
Marian Goodman
Pat Hearn
Marlborough
Oil & Steel
Pace
Tony Shafrazi
Sperone Westwater
Edward Thorp
Washburn

Guerrilla Girls, poster, 1985. © by Guerrilla Girls,
courtesy of www.guerrillagirls.com.

"Be careful who you pretend to be, because you *are* who you pretend to be."
On the same theme, "Tim" wrote, "And, it isn't a fake personality, just a
fake name."[11] It is interesting to note that "artsoldier," without fanfare or
discussion of potential repercussions, quickly decided to reveal his identity as the artist Jason Laning (although he retained a blog avatar in which
a blurred photograph veils his actual appearance). It would seem that, for
men, identity and name count. However, men may risk less and have more
to gain from identity.

One may wonder what Miss Edna's anonymity masks. Does the actual
named identity of Miss Edna, her "real" persona, voice the same slightly
intemperate and contradictory but basically feminist views when she
functions in the every day world? What is the risk differential if the behavior, in fact, is generally the same? Or, is her public, named behavior *less*
feminist, in order to preserve career viability? If so, does she question the
system that would force her into such a suppression of self?

It would seem that Miss Edna's freedom was in the tactical avoidance of
personal risk, but it may also be a problematic avoidance of public identity
at a time when such a revelation might be as necessary and effective as
anonymous activism was for the Guerrilla Girls in working effectively for
political change. Many of my women students found Miss Edna's "A.K.A.
Militant Feminist Bitch" slogan disturbing. I am not sure what disturbed
them more, the danger of being perceived as a "militant feminist" or the
self-hatred possibly lurking behind the adoption of the slur *bitch* (although some have seen the use of *bitch* as the recuperation of a derogatory term, in much the same way feminists previously sought to revalorize
cunt, blacks have re-marked the word *nigger*, and more recently, women
are said to have recuperated the word *slut*[12]). My own wish is that Miss
Edna would have changed her website name to Militant Feminist Artist
and spoken from her real name and identity.

By July and August of 2006 each blogger had effectively moved on: on
August 2, artsoldier claimed, "This blog is finished, but I shall not leave
thine prying eyes fodderless. I have refocused my efforts elsewhere ("The
End")." He then started a more purely politically focused blog, under his
own name. At the same time, Miss Edna seemed to implode and gave over
her posting to guest bloggers: "About a month ago (when you may have
noticed I stopped posting) I had a small but sustained IDENTITY CRISIS.
. . . Then it occurred to me that I'd created Edna and I could just kill her
off. But how? Just stop posting. It'll be so EASY. Just stop going to the

blog. Who gives a fuck, I thought. LET THE BITCH DIE. And I have to say, I think it was the best decision. I have lots more time now that I'm not crusading against anything. Hell, I hardly notice any problems anymore. Seems like everything's on track. Good-looking chicks under 25 are getting shows. Things are nearly 70/30%. Everything's fine."[13] In 2008 the site included this information: "This is the archive of Anonymous Female Artist (a.k.a. Militant Art Bitch), begun under the pseudonym Edna V. Harris in January, 2006. The blog unofficially ended with the virtual death of Edna V. Harris on Wednesday, July 5, 2006."

Therefore, in the winter of 2007, Anonymous Female Artist's posts were rare and mostly by a substitute blogger, "Rebel Belle." The site did not address major events related to feminist art during this time period, including "The Feminist Future: Theory and Practice in the Visual Arts," a major two-day symposium held at MoMA in January, and the openings of two major museum survey-exhibitions on feminist art, "WACK! Art and the Feminist Revolution: An International Retrospective of Feminist Art from 1965–1980," at the Geffen Contemporary at MOCA in Los Angeles, and "Global Feminisms: New Directions in Contemporary Art," at the new Elizabeth A. Sackler Center for Feminist Art at the Brooklyn Museum. The latter was mentioned on the blog, but peripherally and dismissively, in the comments section on a story about an older and anonymous woman artist in LA deciding to create a fake, younger alter ego with a fake body of work for inclusion in a group exhibition, in response to ageism in the current art market as described on other blogs such as Edward Winkleman.[14]

This implosion of a blog that had begun by boldly staking a feminist identity may have a personal dimension in terms of unknown stresses on the individual known as Miss Edna, but it may also reflect on some of the troubling aspects of anonymity, in relation to feminism and activism. Possibly in the long run public identification would have been a safer, more stable position from which to mount an ongoing feminist critique of repressive, gendered power structures.

We have few public feminists of any stature today. Few figures with a significant national profile as feminists seem to exist as potential talking heads on a variety of issues, or as potential figures to be feared for their point of view. That there are few public intellectuals visible at all, and few Left or even "liberal" voices is perhaps the meta problem. While being identified as a feminist, or as a nonconformist political entity with a feminist view, can have serious repercussions on one's career, at least it creates a genuine identity that might eventually carry enough gravitas to function effectively in a public forum.

This is a moment when activism and political self-awareness is vitally important. Anonymous interventions are still useful, of course, because against a powerful enemy all strategies and tactics are useful. However, if it was necessary in 1970 to use open protest techniques to get women and minorities fairly represented in civic and cultural life, and in 1985 to use anonymity and irony to point to the slippage of such representation within a far more professionalized and hyped art world, I think it is now necessary to re-identify a feminist politics in the public arena.

"I am not now nor have I ever been . . ."

I am not a feminist artist.

Now I've got your attention. I am following a time-honored tradition and taking a page out of Marina Abramovic's playbook. At the MoMA symposium "The Feminist Future: Theory and Practice in the Visual Arts," held at the end of January 2007, she introduced herself that way (as she does at every *feminist* art event to which she is invited) to an audience that included Harmony Hammond, Ida Applebroog, Carolee Schneemann, Mary Beth Edelson, Faith Wilding, and dozens of other major women artists who have identified themselves with the feminist movement, who were not invited to the podium, and whose presence in the room was like a barely acknowledged three hundred–pound Guerrilla Girl.

As the wizard makes perfectly clear at the end of *The Wizard of Oz*, in a spectacle society, you are something only if you are given some visible symbolic proof: the Tin Man gets his heart through an official testimonial. So by the rules of the spectacle I am not a feminist artist, because I was not included in the feminist-art survey exhibitions "WACK! Art and the Feminist Revolution: An International Retrospective of Feminist Art from 1965–1980," curated by Cornelia Butler, at the Geffen Contemporary at MOCA in Los Angeles, and "Global Feminisms: New Directions in Contemporary Art," curated by Linda Nochlin and Maura Reilly at the Brooklyn Museum's Elizabeth A. Sackler Center for Feminist Art. But before you dismiss my argument as sour grapes, please take note that I'm in great company: most of *my entire generation* was eliminated from the history of feminist art by these two major museum shows devoted to the subject in 2007 and 2008. In determining the composition of "WACK!" Butler concentrated on what might be termed the pioneer generation: since this was part of "second-wave feminism," let's call it "Generation 2." In the case of "Global Feminisms," Reilly and Nochlin selected women born after 1960: Generation 3. So a chronological ditch was created into which fell most of the artists born between 1945 and 1960.

Call it Generation 2.5: the first generation whose members were able to embrace feminism as a path in their youth. The generation who really developed most of the tropes we think of as constituting feminist art, often inventing and building them at the same time as their pioneer mentors. Women such as Maureen Connor, Judith Shea, Rona Pondick, Robin Mitchell, Shirley Kaneda, Suzanne Joelson, Joan Waltemath, Zoe Leonard, Rochelle Feinstein, Abigail Child, Deb Kass, Leslie Labowitz, Vanalyne Green, Barbara Kruger, Erika Rothenberg, Nancy Bowen, Pat Ward Williams, Peggy Ahwesh, Beverly Naidus, Terry Berkowitz, Shu Lea Cheang, Nancy Fried, Elise Siegel, Shelly Silver, Valerie Jaudon, Susan Bee, Laurie Simmons, the Guerrilla Girls, Sophie Calle, Jana Sterbak, Johanna Drucker, Lenore Malen, Kiki Smith, Susanna Heller, Elena Sisto, Bailey Doogan, Perry Bard, Lisa Hoke, Elissa D'Arrigo, Elana Herzog, Xenobia Bailey, Nancy Davidson, and Faith Wilding, among many others. Not all of these artists make—BIG SCARE QUOTES—*"Political Art"*—more on that in a minute—but they form a politically conscious cohort.

When Generation 2.5 was getting started in life, feminism was active, visible, and exciting. Women's liberation was a widespread, popular movement. This was a unique historical moment, and it was wonderful, at a formative time in one's life, to understand that one's private fears and dreams were shared by millions of other women, that there were political implications to the personal, and that political analysis of private experiences would take one beyond the personal toward communal and political activism (at least at the level of idealism and desire).

That fascinating artworks by slightly older women artists were for the first time being recognized for their gendered specificities by brilliant art historians and critics, themselves newly transformed by feminism, challenged and encouraged Generation 2.5 to see the potentialities for art in the politically interpreted connection between personal experience, the polis, and art materiality and form. In the 1970s many of us began to develop a strong body of work on gender-related themes, often at the same time or even before our teachers and role models worked on the same subjects.

Nevertheless choosing to ally oneself publicly with feminism was still a rare choice. Generation 2.5 may have grabbed the possibility of a feminist identity almost at the same time Generation 2 was in the process of establishing it, but even at the California State University, Fresno, and Barnard College in 1970, and at the California Institute of the Arts (CalArts) in 1971—schools where feminism was for the first time offered as a legitimate part of the official curriculum—very few young women selected to align themselves with it formally or even informally. Although the widely popular energy of the women's liberation movement made feminism an available and, one might argue, not just a cutting edge but even a trendy direction for a woman artist, the effect of feminist activism on the art world was still in an early revolutionary stage, and there were many incentives for a woman to remain identified with the patriarchal hierarchy of the time. Thus, the young women of Generation 2.5 who chose feminism in the early 1970s were as much pioneers and outlaws as their mentors.

In some cases, the articulation of feminism in our artwork took a little time to develop. One of the brutal realities of the history of feminist art is that only about eight years passed between the first public explorations of feminism in art and the first intimations of new and sometimes radically opposite artistic and political views that would bring an end to the first phase of the feminist art movement. Even the two hundred and fifty years or so since the beginnings of the Enlightenment set in motion movements of individual suffrage and personal liberation do not constitute very much time in the history of civilization for effecting the transformation of human consciousness with regard to gender hierarchies. So eight years is a mere instant for individual women artists to undertake such a transformation in their personal lives and to articulate this in their artistic practice. Even two of the most significant (though dramatically opposite) major works of 1970s feminist art, Judy Chicago's *Dinner Party* (1974–1978) and Mary Kelly's *Post-partum Document* (1973–1979), took most of the decade to execute and were first exhibited toward the end of it. Nevertheless, the canon of 1970s feminist art was set in place by 1980, already ignoring many of the accomplishments of Generation 2.5, and it has proven to be as fixed as the first (male) canon. Who knew when reading *A Room of One's Own* with a sense of pride and momentum in the mid-1970s, that in 2007 "Anonymous" would be a woman artist born between 1945 and 1959?

Curating a feminist art exhibition is a major commitment and a professional statement on the part of the curator, and the more comprehensive and ambitious the curator seeks to be, the more thankless the task. Indeed, it is a truth universally unacknowledged that a woman who wants to curate a historical survey of feminist art will encounter obstacles in finding a welcoming venue and funding, she'll only be able to risk doing it once in her career, she will find that familiar complexities and dilemmas inherent to the topic will bedevil her project, and she will look to documentation of previous such endeavors to shape her own process of historicization.

Future curators and art historians looking back at documentation of feminist art will find much to build on. Feminist art has developed a substantial record of exhibitions, catalogues, books, and theoretical texts. The many exhibitions and symposia on the history of feminist art in America and around the world (as well as on contemporary feminisms) that took place between 2006 and 2008 alone would provide a comprehensive field of information with which to work. One would think that the sheer number of shows during that time would have cast a net wide enough to catch all the significant women artists working in the thirty-five- to forty-year period being studied.[1] Surely, the substantial catalogues for "WACK!" and "Global Feminisms" will inspire new generations of artists and will be influential if not uniquely determinative sources of research for future examinations of this subject. Past art histories write future art histories. Yet, the picture created by these exhibitions is egregiously incomplete.

I don't wish to minimize the contributions to the field of feminist art history of any of the curators of this wave of feminist art exhibitions. Indeed, in "Waiting for the Big Show," an essay I wrote for *Ms. Magazine* in 1996, I noted the difficulties encountered by women curators trying to put together major exhibitions of feminist art in that decade; for example, while working on her video history, *Not for Sale: A Story of the Feminist Art Movement in the U.S., 1970–1979*, the critic Laura Cottingham was turned down by two major museums when she proposed an exhibition connected with her research. According to Cottingham, she had been in discussion for a while with the Whitney Museum of American Art when, as she recalls, "they suddenly came back to me and said, 'Nobody wants to do a feminist show and nobody wants to do an all-woman show.'"[2]

> Practical problems also come into play. . . . *Division of Labor*, for example, was produced solely through the Bronx Museum's operating budget because its granting institutions were already committed to one "women-related" exhibition and would not fund a second.[3] And major art institutions have major sexism built into their pecking order. All the blockbuster exhibitions of recent years at the Met (including Lucien Freud and the Impressionists) and New York City's Museum of Modern Art (Braque and Picasso, Bruce Nauman) have been curated

by men at the top of the museums' hierarchies. Female curators, who crowd the lower echelons, have few opportunities to create exhibitions (feminist or not), and are often given limited space and a less advantageous schedule.[4]

The facts cited in that 1996 text can be updated to the present without any major changes. At the Museum of Modern Art in New York, artists receiving major exhibitions since 1996 have included Willem de Kooning, Chuck Close, and Fernand Léger (1998); Alberto Giacometti and Andreas Gursky (2001); Gerhard Richter (2002); Henri Matisse and Pablo Picasso (2003); Edvard Munch and Brice Marden (2006); and Richard Serra, Jeff Wall, Martin Puryear, and Alexander Calder (2007). At the time of the Serra exhibition it was revealed that the museum had designed and engineered its new building specifically to allow for the installation of Serra's gigantic, extremely heavy steel works.[5] In 2008 the Guerrilla Girls targeted the Eli Broad Collection, newly installed in its own building, the Broad Contemporary Art Museum at the Los Angeles County Museum of Art, for its low percentage of women artists: "Here are the stats: BCAM, the Broad Contemporary Art Museum at LACMA: 30 artists, 97% white, 87% male. Broad Foundation collection: 194 artists, 96% white, 83% male."[6] This one instance is surely not unique and it is likely that the effects of such gendered priorities of major collectors, donors, and museum trustees will continue to be felt despite some encouraging changes in acquisitions of contemporary art in recent years. That most of the conditions, hierarchies, and prejudices I described in 1996 still apply only makes recent curatorial achievements all the more noteworthy and admirable. Such conditions and alarming statistics also should function as cautionary tales for future curators interested in feminist art.

Despite the challenges facing such curators, the erasure of Generation 2.5 does raise a few issues of historical methodology. One of these is the problematic of curating by decades, even if slippage at the borders is always a given. Cottingham's bracketing of the seventies was different than Butler's: she ended that decade in 1979, thereby acknowledging the major radical changes and reversal of aesthetic and political attitudes that became abruptly visible after 1978, whereas the few major women artists from Generation 2.5 who were included in "WACK!" as 1970s artists emerged in about 1979 and more accurately represent the aesthetic philosophy of the 1980s—artists such as Cindy Sherman, for instance. It is certainly interesting to reconsider Sherman's work in the light of 1970s feminism, but at the time it first was shown, it was emblematic of a new and very different aesthetic and political environment.

What makes the women of Generation 2.5 so interesting as artists and as models for how to remain alive as an artist over time, is that we have come into our own at several different points: in the 1970s, in the 1980s, and yet again in the 1990s, and our work continues to grow as we remain awake to changes in the culture around us. The decade approach in traditional historicization and curating misses the richness that intellectually and politically engaged figures can bring to their work as they mature. The hybridity created by our progress through the history of the feminist art movement is the mark of a living synthesis versus a synthetic synthesis of an established menu of already predigested choices, whose initial radicalism has often been significantly altered and even willfully distorted by subsequent historicizations.

Some Generation 2.5 artists can be presented within a decade-oriented survey view: artists such as Laurie Simmons, Barbara Kruger, and Sherrie Levine emerged in the 1980s and can, must, and will be historicized as important figures of appropriation art.[7] But this is not the case for many artists of Generation 2.5. We are often less likely to fit into a standard view of any particular decade of art. Precisely because we were significantly engaged with the major ideas of each of the decades we have worked in from the 1970s to the present, we brought the ideas of each period into the next, like the thread of wool looped over the needle in the process of knitting—a metaphor in keeping with one of the many major tropes of contemporary art that we introduced and developed.

In the 1970s, we were engaged with searching for what would be female or gendered form and content in a range of new media and unorthodox materials. The pioneer generation may have laid the foundations for a number of these tropes—clothing as metaphor, performance of the body, personal narrative, use of materials from the enculturation of femininity—but Generation 2.5 really provided the full elaboration of such tropes, emerging from the nexus formed by feminine experience examined through the conscious lens of feminist politics. We developed the vocabulary and the visual languages—forms and materials—and represented them, often long after the pioneers had faded from active participation in the art world (although such disappearances must be understood as part of the larger problem of continued visibility for any artist,

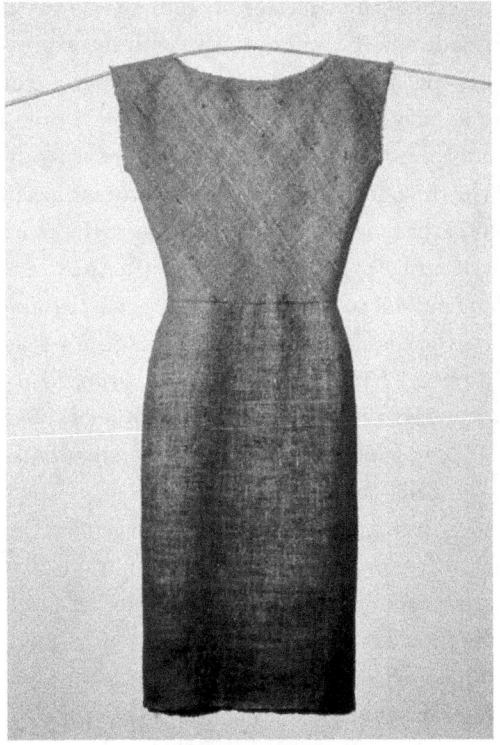

Judith Shea, *Exec.Sec'y*, 1980. Burlap and wood.
42 × 17 × 1½ inches. Private Collection. © Judith Shea.

especially a mid-career woman artist, especially an older woman artist, especially a feminist artist). Thus the tropes of cloth and of clothing may have appeared in works by Mimi Smith from the mid-1960s but this became an extremely powerful area of practice for artists such as Judith Shea, Rosemarie Mayer, Maureen Connor, and, a bit later, Jana Sterbak and Beverly Semmes, among many others.[8] These artists produced images as iconically representative of feminist art as any in the history of the movement, and have been influential through their exhibitions, lectures, and through their teaching.

Many Generation 2.5 artists had been using linguistic analysis and appropriation of cultural signs in critiques of social institutions during the 1970s, before this became a dominant aesthetic mode in the 1980s. But our passage through the process-oriented 1970s gave many of us a feel for materiality that produced a characteristic hybrid art that fused theoretical and psychoanalytic concerns with material embodiment and visual pleasure, as well as the readymade and the appropriative with the expressive and the touch of the hand that greatly influenced the next group of women artists and continues to have relevance for art today.

Generation 2.5's work from the 1970s showed traces of other significant vanguard influences of the time, including Fluxus and process-based post-minimalism. More recently these aesthetic traces appear in the often communitarian, collaborative leanings of some of Generation 2.5's current work. Having been involved in feminist collectives, collective galleries, political performances, and Fluxus-like happenings means that these artists were in fact involved with aspects of relational aesthetics, *avant la lettre*. Examples of this track are evident in the development of artists like Maureen Connor and Faith Wilding, among many others one might note. Connor was not included in "WACK!," though Wilding was.

Connor's work has focused on a number of basic subjects: gender, the body, and conditions of labor, often analyzed within the conditions of a specific architectural site. Beginning in the 1970s she developed in depth one of the major tropes of feminist art: clothing and textiles as the site of social construction, and of memory of the enculturation of femininity. One of her early works on this subject was *Little Lambs Eat Ivy* (1977), in which proper little girls' smocked dresses are deconstructed and reconfigured as a dynamic postminimalist object. In the 1980s Connor continued her examination of the enculturation of the female body by working with assisted readymades, including a sex doll negatively cast in fleshy wax, and she fabricated oversize Duchampian bottle racks adorned like art historical Christmas trees with cow lungs cast in glass. In the 1990s she returned to clothing in combines of assisted and created readymades such as *Thinner than You* (1990), where sexy black lingerie stretches to the limit of the fantastic conflation of desire and impossible ideals of female perfection.

Less well known is Connor's exploration of these themes in a Fluxus striptease that she performed during an evening of celebratory performances at the wedding of George Maciunas in New York in 1978. Connor's own description of this performance recalls the spirit of the times. It also calls attention to the importance of documentation in the history of performance art, crucial to the reputations of feminist artists such as Hannah Wilke and Carolee Schneemann. Future generations of curators and art historians will have to compensate through intensive research for the fact that many great performance artworks during that period were

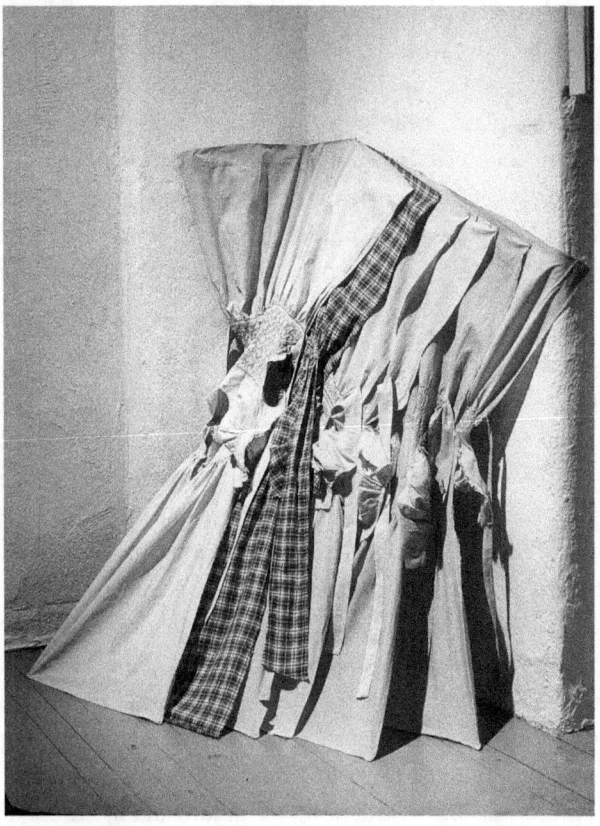

Maureen Connor, *Little Lambs Eat Ivy*, 1977. Smocked dresses.
36 × 55 × 44 inches. Collection of the artist. Courtesy of the artist.

either not documented, during what was a relatively less professionalized time, or documentation was not preserved by the artist herself. Connor did not discover a video clip of her piece until thirty years later. Until then her memory was the only documentation available of a work that, had it been better documented, might have held a more established place in the archive of "seventies feminist" performance art:[9]

> All performances were meant to be erotic and mine was a kind of parody of a striptease titled *25 less* in which I removed twenty-five pairs of underpants, beginning with nineteenth-century pantaloons and gradually paring down to a final pair of lace bikinis. To counter the usual burlesque bump and grind with its gradually increasing exposure

of flesh, I remained covered throughout in a modest, vintage Edwardian dress. Lifting the skirt with my left hand, which also clutched a large bundle of petticoats, I struggled out of the underpants. My right meanwhile, balanced a plate of raw eggs, all to the accompaniment of the surging, staccato, Balinese Gamelan Monkey chant. Only two minutes long, the music paced my performance, limited its duration and made it seem more like a game show contest than a striptease as I raced to finish my task before the sound ran out, all the while steadying the plate of eggs.[10]

Later she created mixed-media installations of the medicalized body, crucial and delicately wrought balances of theory and embodiment, incorporating sound and readymades into installations framed by draped muslin enclosures. In the 1990s she placed closely edited samplings of the engendered representation of women in film within installations mirroring the interior-decorated sites of these Hollywood narratives of gender. In her more recent ongoing project, *Personnel*, Connor continues her interest in architectural spaces and work conditions in art institutions, first explored in site-specific performances in the late 1970s. She now focuses on institutional critique, including analyses of curatorial practices, work conditions in art institutions, and large sociological problems including racism. Her work is always notable for the "femininity" of its manner of visual and exegetic presentation—the delicacy of facture and lightness of narrative hand—and for its continued belief in the transformational utopian goals of the 1960s, but at the same time she has developed her focus from the feminine to a more expansive social context.

Faith Wilding's early work from the feminist art programs at Fresno and CalArts was included in "WACK!," but the development of her work tracks a similar path to Connor's and is significant in establishing the identity of Generation 2.5. Like Connor, Wilding has used and referenced clothing and other textile-related occupations, such as crocheting, which have been coded as feminine, and her more recent work has expanded from intimate examples of the domestic to broader political analyses of working conditions for women in global capitalist society. She too has built on the same utopian and radical politics as Connor has, in a career that has seen her shift from polemic installation art such as *Sacrifice* (1971), the gory and gothic installation of an elaborately dressed but eviscerated bride, to agit-prop theater including her iconic participation in the CalArts Feminist Art

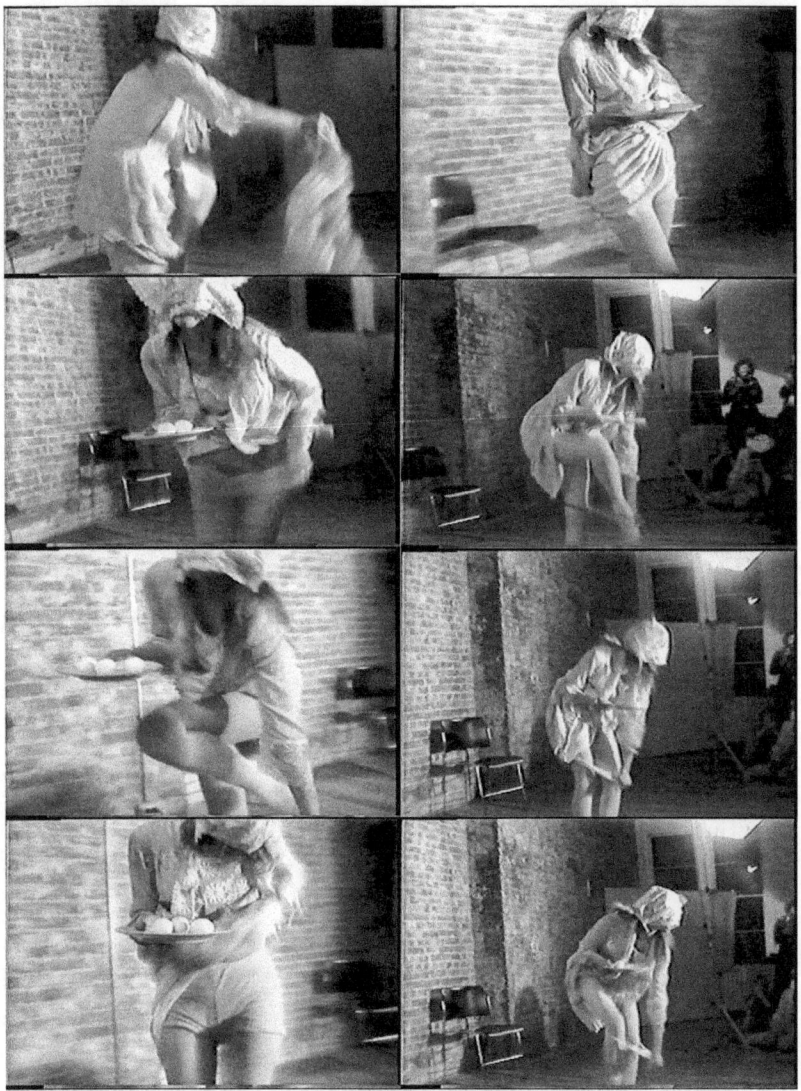

Maureen Connor, *25 Less*, video stills from *Marriage of George and Billy*, 1978.
Thirty-minute color video, footage by Dimitri Devyatkin, Jaime Davidovich, and
Nam June Paik. Video © by Dimitri Devyatkin with Nam June Paik and Jaime
Davidovich; performance and composite image © by Maureen Connor 1978–
2008, courtesy of Maureen Connor.

Program's performances, such as *Cock and Cunt Play*—a Punch-and-Judy play in which dishes and who does them are the springboard for gender warfare—and *Waiting*.[11] In this case, good documentation and distribution have served to assure her a place in the canon but also to limit her image to a single point in time, as has happened for so many other artists. Feminist art history has come to operate just like original (male) canonical art history in reducing an artist's lifetime of work to one image that serves a simplified and linear narrative, erasing the concept of the growth, change, and enrichment of original themes from the standard story of how to be an artist over time.

Waiting could be viewed on a video monitor in "WACK!" but Wilding also renewed the piece as an audience interactive discussion, *Wait-With* (2007), in which she first repeated the text from a tape of her earlier performance—the perceptible gap of memory caused by the time delay enacting but also historicizing the passivity detailed in *Waiting*—and then she invited viewer discussion. Less well known, due to the limited point of view enforced by the decade orientation of such survey exhibitions, is Wilding's more recent work, which emerges from her early involvement with the Critical Art Ensemble, as part of the socially committed performance group subRosa. This work deals with cultural research into cyberfeminism and new forms of female labor and exploitation in a global economy. Again in her artworks a basic commitment to feminist and leftist activism has developed in ways that are both consistent and yet completely different in their visual language and methods of addressing the audience.

Connor and Wilding are only two examples of Generation 2.5 artists who have stayed true to certain basic visual styles and political beliefs while at the same time changing their work radically by remaining vital as artists and politically awake citizens.

But while these artists remain active in their work, the erasure of Generation 2.5 began early: for example, the exclusion of the Feminist Art Program from the history of CalArts began almost immediately upon the departure of Miriam Schapiro from CalArts in 1976, as the history of the school began to be rewritten to favor John Baldessari's students.[12] The current erasure of this generation from the historicization of feminist art is done without apology, in fact without any acknowledgment of the existence of this generation. No curatorial embarrassment or guilt; Generation 2.5's achievements and role in the history are just not there.

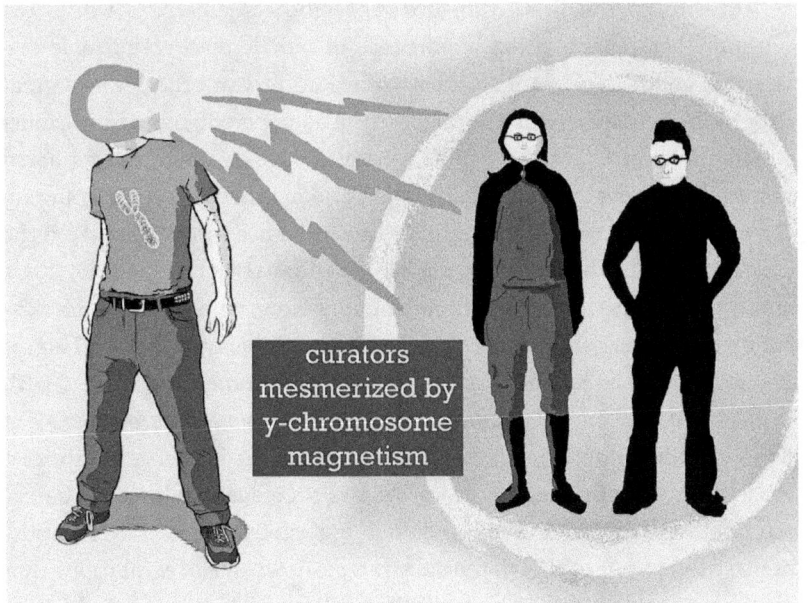

Brainstormers, "Weather Report," 2006. Video still.
© by Brainstormers.

It is much more common to mention the problem of the exclusion of men. You will find *this* issue raised in every curator's statement prefacing an exhibition of feminist art. Some curators have integrated men into their exhibitions: notably, Marcia Tucker and Marcia Tanner, curators of the "Bad Girls" exhibitions of 1994, sought to establish a field of feminism-influenced, gender-focused artwork by women and men.[13] Even when curators eventually choose only women, the "men question" has already undermined the validity and status of the women included by implying that there is something wrong with an all-women show, that it would be truly more important if men were included. That the whole thing (feminist art and art history) got started because women were not allowed equality or, back in the day, even minimal access into the social structures of the art world, and the gender specificity of their interests and concerns was denigrated as inconsistent with the higher, universal goals of modernism, is instantly erased in this concern for the feelings of men who might suffer from being excluded!

Exceptions to my criticism of this curatorial concern would be shows that specifically set out to illuminate the influence of feminist art on male artists: through the direct influence of specific women artists' works, the often deliberately obscured importance of female teachers of male artists who go on to get more critical attention for work that owes a great debt to these women (who the men usually do not credit), and the permission feminist art and feminism has given to male artists to use gendered materials and deal with sexuality and gender in new ways, opening up the normative facade of masculinity. This influence can be seen from the 1980s onward in the work of male artists who use clothing—male attire and women's dresses—to examine and question the production of masculinity: these artists include Charles Ledray, Robert Gober, and Hunter Reynolds (as his alter ego, Patina du Prey), who sometimes worked with the Generation 2.5 artist Chrysanne Stathacos. Other artists, such as Mike Kelley, a student of Judy Pfaff at CalArts, reveal the influence of feminist art in their use of materials and processes previously coded as feminine and domestic, such as knitting and dolls, in their deconstruction of myths of masculine power.[14] The potential strategic downside of exhibitions that would explore this influence is that feminism would be validated for its contribution to the enrichment of art made by men, therefore again subsuming it under earlier gender hierarchies.

Generation 2.5 may also be caught up in a phenomenon some feminist theorists have identified as a boredom factor, where, despite the fact that feminist goals have not been fully met, theory has moved on and declared feminist theory boring. In "The Currency of Feminist Theory," Jane Elliott makes some important observations that have particular relevance for the fate of this generation of feminist artists: "As the repeated declarations of feminism's death in the mainstream media and the academy make clear, the production of the new as the signal intellectual value can be used to dismiss uncomfortable insights, which don't have to be disproved as long as they can be made to seem passé."[15] In a system where there is a "continued affinity for the modern logic that equates the new, the interesting, and the valuable . . . we sidestep the difficult realization that while intellectual work should be exciting, political work may be dull, that things may stay true longer than they stay interesting."[16] The work Generation 2.5 has produced is no more boring than the feminist project is complete, but Elliott's observations offer an interesting point of view on our fate.

Generation 2.5 also suffers from the ageism rampant in the art world today. Ironic, since we were presumably not included in "WACK!" because we were too young in the 1970s, "daughters" rather than "mothers," and because in the 1970s the age of admission into the art world was closer to thirty than to twenty.

The curators of "WACK!" and of "Global Feminisms" were very aware of globalism and racism, but not at all focused on ageism as it especially affects women artists. One might hope that older women curators in particular might be more aware of this problem, but they may wish to be seen as current (young), so they prefer to ignore this issue. Meanwhile male curators who are the contemporaries of Generation 2.5 sometimes find it easier to support the work of much older or much younger women while either taking for granted or feeling competitive with the women of their own generation.

Despite being perceived as too young for "WACK!," already by the 1990s some Generation 2.5 artists were being denied representation in New York galleries because they were considered too old, too experienced. It is rumored that in some cases dealers complained that it would be too much work for their staff to copy these artists' longer CVs and catalogue their more numerous slides![17] According to the curator Robert Storr, a midcareer artist "is the hardest thing in the art world to be: You can be a grand old man or woman or you can be a hotshot kid, but a midcareer artist? To say nothing of a midcareer female artist."[18] The current art world in this decade is more acutely youth focused than ever before: a discussion on Edward Winkleman's blog after the Art Basel Miami Beach Art Fair in 2006 brings this phenomenon into sharp focus. "And one thing that drove us crazy last week (which we don't remember as much of in the past) is the 'how old is the artist' question. I don't know how many times we were asked that and it was the first thing they asked, not what is the process, what is the bio., etc. If you say anything older than 29 (which our artists are) the 'collectors' can't run away fast enough. Very frustrating."[19] A response to this was posted by "artist shabaka": "First it was racism, now it's ageism . . . a whole lifetime of art wasted and never to be seen. Being born at the 'right time' and of the 'right extraction' . . . *sigh*."

Sigh indeed. There is a unique bitterness at the irony of being erased from the history of a movement that critiqued canonicity and that involved career risks from the start.

And it's not as if Generation 2.5 artists are going to be welcomed now when they are in their late fifties and early sixties. No, they are still too young! They have to somehow have the psychological and financial resources to survive into their seventies with their older work in good con-

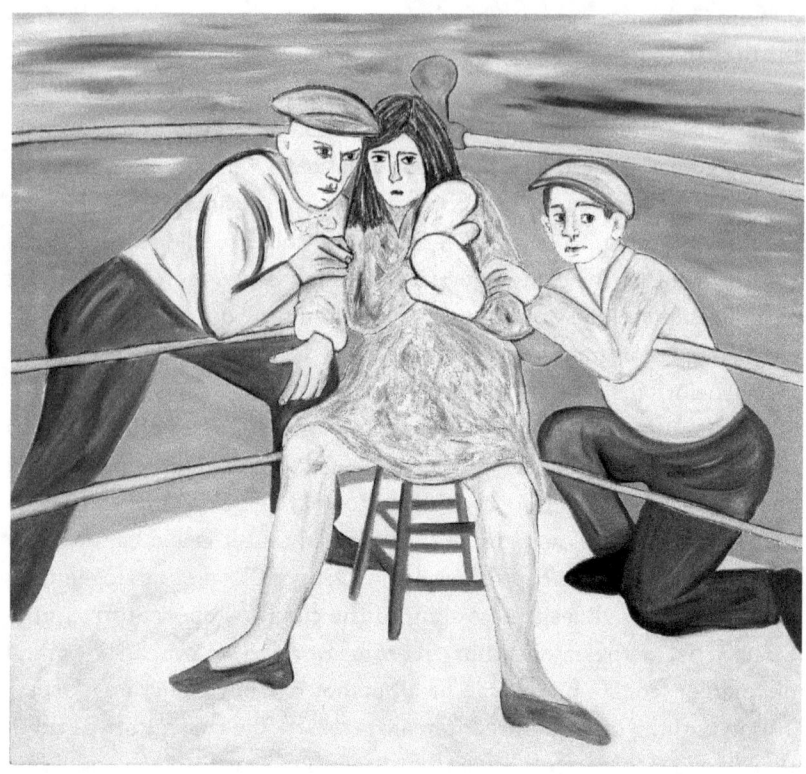

Susan Bee, *Doomed to Win*, 1983. Oil on linen. 50 × 54 inches.
Collection of the artist. Courtesy of the artist.

dition and their inner aesthetic drive intact in order to hope that they will
be "rediscovered" during their lifetime. Then they can fill the soft spot the
world has for eccentric old women artists with powerful personalities and
colorful life histories in addition to great artwork—Louise Bourgeois and
Alice Neel are paradigmatic examples in this category. Martha Rosler referred to this phenomenon as "submergence": "There is a well-noted donut
hole in women artists' artworld 'careers,' when they go from being hot
young artists in the 20s & 30s to disappearance (submergence) in the 40s
through ancient days, when, if we have survived, we are rediscovered (resurgence, re-emergence!) but rarely as WOMEN artists."[20] *Doomed to Win*,
the title of Susan Bee's 1983 painting of a woman boxer, is eerily predictive
of Generation 2.5's complex role and the endurance that it may need for
the fight: the anxious but tough young fighter in a pink dress will need all
the strength and help she can get.

By the way, among the women artists left out of the two exhibitions, one can make a further distinction between Generation 2.5 and Generation 2.75, women who in some cases were born after 1960 but who were also not included in "Global Feminisms" because they were seen as established artists who had been showing since the early 1990s. They include Janine Antoni, Judie Bamber, Ingrid Calame, Renée Cox, Patricia Cronin, Jeanne Dunning, Nicole Eisenman, Andrea Fraser, Renée Green, Mona Hatoum, Rachel Lachowicz, Liz Larner, Carrie Moyer, Portia Munson, Sheila Pepe, Collier Schorr, Lorna Simpson, Kara Walker, Gillian Wearing, Rachel Whiteread, and Andrea Zittel.

If anything, the omission of this group of artists from a series of historical presentations of feminist art is even more egregious, given their success and thus the more evident influence they have had among still younger artists.

Yet some differences in the experiences of and theories available to this other middle generation may be seen as laying the groundwork for recent conditions.

Generation 2.75 emerged after feminism was an established field of practice. This generation of women artists benefited from the openings created by earlier women's political activism in the art world. Career opportunities created by late-1960s and 1970s feminist activism made it possible for these slightly younger women to enter into art careers more smoothly. At the same time, beginning in the early 1980s, in undergraduate and graduate fine arts programs in the United States, standards and techniques of professionalism in career development were more advanced and critical theory was more routinely part of the curriculum, giving Generation 2.75 a helpful jump on "the language."

Many Generation 2.75 reputations were made in the 1990s, a period of slippage back to the essentialized body, as can be seen in some works from that period by Sue Williams and Kiki Smith.[21] Most significantly, although they are chronologically part of Generation 2.5, these only slightly younger women are not as marked by identification with the 1970s, with all the misrepresentations and prejudices that association would command.[22] Thus, they are not seen as "angry"—a designation and identification based on fictive histories ("bra burning"), which are half forgotten yet still deeply entrenched by years of the culture-wide "backlash" against feminism with which Generation 2.75 has sometimes seemed complicit. In the case of each of the aforementioned artists, the works that first won her favorable critical attention and that are her most uncompromising expressions of embodiment and female experience—Sue Williams's kicked and defiled women, Kiki Smith's flayed paper figures—are somehow deleted from her overall image, her brand.

In this light, Generation 2.75 has not suffered the effects of the controversies over essentialism to the same extent that this vexed designation seems to have affected members of Generation 2.5. It serves to marginalize the artists of Generation 2.5 in such a way that they may not get an automatic pass for inclusion in survey exhibition for decades besides the 1970s. Befitting a generation seen as in between post-War pioneers and the first crop of twenty-first-century artists, Generation 2.5 gets it from both sides of the theoretical divide: first tarred as essentialist, then more recently accused of the didacticism and denial of visual pleasure associated with the 1980s, which was in fact more characteristic of the work of those who had termed them essentialists.

Many commentators noted with dismay or bemusement the sheer volume of images of mothers, breasts, and raped and brutalized naked female bodies represented in "Global Feminisms." Viewers were asking, Do these works represent a dominant vein of imagery? Is this what younger women self-selected as feminists consider feminist art, or is this a reflection of the views of the curators? The problem was not the imagery—many of these works are quite powerful and add to the impressive lexicon of feminist art; it was the lack of political or theoretical discourse on the profusion of such imagery.

Here the issue of denial of feminism comes into play. "I am not a feminist or a feminist artist" is the surprising mantra of all feminist exhibitions, symposia, and journal forums since the late 1980s. Read carefully the catalogue biographies of the artists included in "WACK!" and you will see that in each case the curators tacitly sought to justify the inclusion of the artist in a show of feminist art by citing some indication of her public or private identification as a feminist. This proves untenable, however, as further reading reveals that a significant portion of the show's 119 individual artists and artists' collectives are described as having little or no public relationship with feminism, or as denying the identification outright. It is quite interesting to track how many of the women included in "WACK!" were not, are not feminists in any active sense, even if you take into account the differing geo-political contexts and the age of the artist in relation to the benchmark dates of second-wave feminism, and even if you agree that the value of an artist's work to a feminist analysis of representation and form is not dependent on her private politics or intentionality (the age-old struggles between individual creativity and public politics notwithstanding). Consider the following examples from the catalogue: "Many of [Marina] Abramovic's best-known performances from the 1970s stand, in part, as critiques of the traditional role of women in the arts. . . . Despite this, the artist has distanced herself from the feminist movement: 'I have never had anything to do with feminism'"; "[Louise] Bourgeois's relationship to feminism is complex. . . . 'There is no feminist aesthetic. Absolutely not!'"; "[Theresa Hak Kyung] Cha's work is not overtly feminist but . . ."; "Perhaps indicative of her lifelong antipathy to categories, [Jay DeFeo] did not identify herself as a feminist"; "Although [Rita] Donagh was not intimately engaged with the burgeoning feminist discourse in 1970s England . . ."; "While [Lili] Dujourie has recalled feeling marginalized by her primarily male colleagues and acknowledged a debt to feminist film theory . . . she has also rejected a specifically feminist reading of her work."; "[Louise] Fishman too was struggling to resist a movement that had supported her and through which she was able to develop her identity as an artist"; "Although [Catalina] Parra does not identify herself as a feminist artist . . ."; "Although [Katharina] Sieverding does not explicitly ally herself with feminism. . . ."[23]

This politics of denial is familiar: for example, under the covers, as it were, of the qualifiedly triumphant *ARTNews* cover headline "Women and Art: We've Come a Long Way . . . MAYBE" from 1997 were a number of statements by women artists, many of whom articulated the kind of deferral, demurral, anxiety of identification with feminism of the "I'm a feminist *but*" variety: "On the flip side, when it comes to feminism, I'm kind of, Ick, I don't want to talk about it. It's such a scary yucky subject—like any 'ism'" (Nicole Eisenman); "I wouldn't say that my work is 'feminist' in the sense that I have it as a mandate or a goal" (Kiki Smith). In each full statement the woman artist both aligns herself with some aspect of what she thinks feminism is but separates her work from feminism. So, indeed, how far *have* we come?[24]

All artists reject limited readings of their work. But when the work clearly deals with gender and gendered power relations, when it deals with femininity, when it explores female sexuality and the female body, when the work uses the vocabulary of gendered tropes developed by the first generations of the feminist art movement—the ones in "WACK!" and the ones left out of the history proposed by "WACK!"—how is it not feminist art? Why is this identification still such a problem?

Clearly, it is. These denials are a troubling indication that feminism continues to be perceived as a controversial and dangerous identification. Women still don't want to be seen as feminist artists, because that would limit them to being seen as women artists, and no one wants to be seen as a woman artist. *Woman* still denotes second-class status within a (still male after all these years) universal. That this should be, or should be perceived to be, the case only proves that feminism is still a necessary political analysis of society and a powerful tool for mobilizing the production of art that engages with the question of gender and injustice on all levels.

Surprise, surprise, a lot of people in the art world are not feminists, and a lot of people who have power in the art world prefer to deal with people who do not threaten a gendered power system. Feminists are inconvenient, so denying a feminist identity often seems to be the price of mainstream success. This denial ensures that these women artists are more likely to be incorporated into a variety of art histories. It is part of the cost of their ticket of admission into the art market and art history. The feminist art movement did make it possible for *women* artists to achieve big careers in the art world, but not necessarily for *feminists* to achieve such success.

In fact one sub-theme expressed in Butler's, Reilly's, and Nochlin's catalogue writings is that perhaps it is actually better if the artist is not intentionally making feminist art, rearticulating the long-held belief that works done by artists with a conscious political agenda will not have the formal interest *nor even the political power* of artworks done in a more personal and individualistic engagement with form and self-expression. That is the oldest canard in the canon of supposedly neutral high-modernist style—the age-old criticism of political art—as if feminism had not helped make clear that these more "universal" aspirations always have a gendered political dimension.

There is a basic misunderstanding about what "political art" means. Being a feminist doesn't mean your art has to represent cunts and lace. In the current art made by many of the women artists who do not deny feminism, you may not find many obvious markers of a feminist artwork in terms of representation of the sexualized or gendered body, but the sedimentary subtext remains feminist. (This stands in contradistinction to the kind of representation in photography and video installations that dominated "Global Feminisms," a show that included little abstraction or painting but lots of lacerated women's bodies).

One way to get around the embarrassment with feminism as a political position is to dilute its meaning. The word is as inconvenient as the people who don't apologize for it. If only one could get rid of it and keep the societal advantages it has won for women. Meanwhile let's make it palatable by taking "the political" out of the old feminist slogan, "the personal is the political." To say that feminist art is not anything that a woman artist makes, but that it emerges from a political analysis of power and its representations, is just too, well, too *political*.

Think for a minute about the social structure that supports the art market: is it going to support artists who don't pull their punches when it comes to patriarchy? No, and that's where the notion that political artists don't make as good art comes in so handy.

If you say you're not a feminist, then you're not a feminist. But then why would you want to be in exhibitions that have the word in the title?

It really isn't that hard to say you are a feminist: it is a political interpretation of power structures in society. Your work doesn't have to be illustrative of previous tropes. But if you say you are not a feminist artist, don't pretend that you are not engaging in a political act. "I am not a feminist artist" is political speech, with serious effects.

So how will the curators and art historians of the future be able to find members of Generation 2.5? I set about creating a working chart of all the artists included in some of the major exhibitions, films, and books from the nineties to the present that claimed to present a comprehensive historicization of the post-War feminist art movement, as well as those included in a few other significant shows from that period.[25] The chart pointed to figures that by any consensus constitute the feminist canon: Eleanor Antin, Lynda Benglis, Louise Bourgeois, Judy Chicago, Harmony Hammond, Mary Kelly, Ana Mendieta, Howardina Pindell, Adrian Piper, Betty Saar, Miriam Schapiro, Carolee Schneemann, Nancy Spero, and Hannah Wilke are among the selected few. Some Generation 2.5 and more Generation 2.75 artists were suspended in the middle of the table, as they had only appeared either in slightly smaller exhibitions or in the more unfettered spaces of printed surveys such as Peggy Phelan's and Helen Reckitt's *Art and Feminism* and the *M/E/A/N/I/N/G* Online #4 forum, "Feminist Art: A Reassessment."

In feminism as in any other field there are at least two registers, the international consensus of icons and celebrities and the more local or regional community—all politics is local—and every single major survey of feminist art records both registers, as all curators choose from the canon and from a personal index of their more local knowledge base, with personal whims and momentary interests in play. Thus members of Generation 2.5 appear more frequently in smaller exhibitions and symposia organized by fellow artists and individual curators who have more freedom to work experimentally, often in smaller academic or regional institutions where the art market stakes are lesser.

To find the community of women artists that I have lived in since 1971, future generations will have to thoroughly research the résumés of each artist included in any and all of the exhibitions on record of women artists or feminist art. Each woman's résumé would reveal a further web of exhibitions, symposia, and panel discussions that slowly would yield the broader community that is as importantly the face of feminist art as the work of the few artists chosen early on to be in the feminist canon. You would have to look to the participants in collectives, including in the United States—public centers for women's culture such as the Woman's Building in Los Angeles, publications such as *Heresies*, and galleries such Soho 20 Gallery and A.I.R. Gallery, among many others. Laura Cottingham's video *Not for Sale* from 1998 reveals fascinating material otherwise lost to history. The British feminist journal *n.paradoxa* opens a more global perspective.

All this research will require the suspension of belief in one of the prime rules of the spectacle: that only what is seen is valuable, and if something is not seen it therefore either must not exist or not be valuable enough to appear.

A future art historian or curator also will have to return to the potential for radical change in entrenched systems that feminism represented—or presented the hope for in its early days; the feminist critique of the male canon of Western Art was also, or there was the chance that it implied, a critique of canon. It suggested the possibility of other ways of writing history that would be more diverse and that might make it possible to see art as being created in a broader and more inclusive cultural field.

This essay is not the exhaustive survey that I have indicated is needed. Rather, by naming a generation of artists and pointing to the erasure of its contribution to the history of feminist art, and by describing some of the surrounding conditions of this erasure, I am placing a message in a bottle to future curators and art historians.

The inclusive, extensive feminist artist community I have lived in was suggested by the Guerrilla Girls' poster *Guerrilla Girls Identities Exposed* (1989). For this poster, which played with the widespread curiosity about who they really were, the Guerrilla Girls simply wrote to or called up as many women artists, art writers, art historians, and curators as they could think of and asked them if it would be OK to use their names: would they accept the public designation Guerrilla Girl? Feminist? Among the five hundred women on the list, in addition to people I have already named, were artists Emma Amos, Suzanne Anker, Polly Apfelbaum, Andre Belag, Andrea Blum, Jackie Brookner, Ellen Brooks, Emily Cheng, Petah Coyne, Betsy Damon, Leslie Dill, Ellen Driscoll, Nancy Dwyer, Lauren Ewing, Heide Fasnacht, Angelika Festa, Nancy Fried, Cheryl Gaulke, Ilona Granet, Kathy Grove, Mary Hambleton, Jane Hammond, Janet Henry, Rebecca Howland, Nene Humphrey, Silvia Kolbowski, Catherine Lord, Mary Lucier, Ann McCoy, Judy Pfaff, Christy Rupp, Alison Saar, Amy Sillman, Jude Tallichet, Robin Tewes, Gwenn Thomas, Sarah Wells, Millie Wilson, Nina Yankowitz, Jerilea Zempel, Barbara Zucker, "AND MANY MORE," as the list concludes.

This list is no more arbitrary than the rosters of any of the more carefully curated museum exhibitions. It represents through its very arbitrariness or unscientific contingency a real network of women artists at a particular moment in time. It is the exact nature of that network that this essay and the Guerrilla Girls's poster begin to reveal: the community of women artists and art professionals who sustained feminism through thick and thin, its winter soldiers.

But we are not feminist artists.

There is nothing like being the right age at the right time. I still think that to have been thirteen when the Beatles came to New York and appeared on *The Ed Sullivan Show* was the only age to have been. Eight or seventeen wouldn't have been as perfectly suited to the meaning of the moment. So to have been twenty-one, an age when self-definition takes on special urgency, and to have felt the necessity to be a thinking artist, which had already been blocked by a nameless injustice — to have been that age when one hit the wave of a political movement at a point of newness and potential, that was timing that cannot be reproduced or its excitement completely transmitted. I registered to vote in Central Park on August 26, 1971, after participating in a march down Fifth Avenue to celebrate the anniversary of the ratification of female suffrage — we passed Helen Gurley Brown standing at the northwest corner of Fifty-seventh Street watching the mo(ve)ment go by! — and I was in the Feminist Art Program and the *Womanhouse* project at the California Institute of the Arts from 1971 to 1972, "boot camp" for feminist artists when you couldn't get that kind of training anywhere else. To have the inchoate problematics and longings of a short lifetime named and answered at twenty-one was like being Helen Keller at the moment she understood that the tapping and the wet liquid on her hand meant the same thing: W-A-T-E-R; the deeply rooted ancient ideology that limited our aspirations and the revolutionary political movement that would enable us to aspire were tapped onto our hands by the click of feminist recognition described in the first issue of *Ms. Magazine*: P-A-T-R-I-A-R-C-H-Y, F-E-M-I-N-I-S-M.

Frida Kahlo wasn't widely known, Lucy Lippard hadn't published *From the Center*. It seemed that to be a woman artist you had to live alone on a mesa in New Mexico. At first there were only two mesas, one for Agnes Martin, the other for Georgia O'Keeffe, then there were dozens, then hundreds. But much of the artwork that was done in the 1970s is now forgotten, because one of the cruelest ironies of the "success" of feminist art is that the second canon, which was created with so much effort, has turned out to be as limited and hard to intervene into as the first, male canon of art history had been to enter, re-write, discard. The period of the late 1960s and the 1970s was incredibly productive. All the tropes of feminist art were developed for the first time. But not every woman artist who did archetypal feminist art was able to move in from the margins, whether psychological or geographic. And not every woman artist whose brilliant career began as a result of the feminist movement did work that could later be easily categorized as feminist. Abstract painting in particular gets the shaft because it does not *represent*. Even the most advanced feminist theory has been distressingly literal in its preference for representational imagery, albeit photographically based and appropriated rather than created. It is easier to write about. Performance art in this way is also literal, in that a woman stands and performs her body in front of you and this performance can be photographed and narrativized in relation to feminist theory or activism. It may take many more years until a generation of art historians, perhaps just by virtue of the age-old need to find something to study that has not been overexamined to death, will delve beneath the ramparts of this second canon to find equally exemplary or iconic works from the 1970s. Sadly, in just thirty years and as we speak, archives and art works from the period are being lost.

I have no idea what it would be like to be twenty-one now, in a world with Madonna, J.Lo and Buffy, Venus and Serena, the Frida Kahlo industry, GRRLLL this and that, kick-ass female rock stars, and thousands of other famous, powerful, talented, business- and media-savvy women, when the glass ceiling is very high and made of Verilux, transparent and invisible. Young women artists can feel a sense of entitlement unimaginable to the seventies generation. But just check some of the statistics of the international art market, and the glass ceiling drops a bit. And as long as being naked is still one of the best ways for a (young) woman to get ahead (unless making other women stand around naked is an even better way), and as long as women remain chattel in so many other countries and cultures, then we have a problem even if no one wants to think so. For women, still, rights that are not constantly named and fought for can be taken away. Just read *The Handmaid's Tale* for a terrifying blueprint. I don't see much feminism now because I don't see the mindset and habit of political thinking and activism. In the culture at large, the scratching of p-a-t-r-i-a-r-c-h-y and f-e-m-i-n-i-s-m on the wet inside of a woman's brain has again become a silent tapping. But it is there nonetheless. As has happened several times before, the influence of exterior forces that have been enabled by apathy and false security will at some point again amplify feminism's import and urgency, and then we will see the fourth wave and the fifth wave of feminism as transformational political forces.

Joanna Demetrakas's film *Womanhouse* was filmed partly during the run of the site-specific exhibition "Womanhouse" held in an old, deserted house in Hollywood in the winter of 1972 and partly at the end of the exhibition, including the last day while installations were being dismantled.[1] The film was released the following year and shown widely, including at the Whitney Museum of American Art in 1974. It continues to be widely circulated and is often seen in second-, third-, and fourth-generation bootleg video copies. It is used steadily in the teaching of feminist art and excerpts of it have appeared in later documentaries on the subject,[2] and therefore, it has been instrumental in shaping the history of the art project and exhibition.

Womanhouse Is Not a Home was produced by Lynne Littman and directed by Parke Perine.[3] Filmed at "Womanhouse" in February 1972, it was broadcast on KCET, the Los Angeles PBS affiliate, while the exhibition was still open to the public. To my knowledge, it was not shown after its initial network broadcast until I brought it to the attention of Leslie C. Jones, a Whitney Independent Study Program student. She tracked it down and included it in "Abject Art: Repulsion and Desire in American Art," curated by students in her program at the Whitney Museum in the summer of 1993. While abjection was not part of the rhetoric of the women's liberation movement nor of the feminist art movement (as I tried to point out to Jones at the time), nevertheless I was glad to be instrumental in having Littman's film included in the exhibition, if only because the film provides a useful additional take on the *Womanhouse* project and the aspirations of young women artists in the early 1970s.

Obviously Demetrakas's *Womanhouse* and Littman's *Womanhouse Is Not a Home* share much visual content. More curiously they also share a number of narrative devices. Each movie begins its cinematic tour of the house in the kitchen; each movie gives some voice to visitors to the house via "man and woman on the street"–type interviews; each movie validates the work through the introduction of a third party, usually a feminist luminary of the moment. For example in the Littman film, there is an extended interlude in which Miriam Schapiro and Judy Chicago speak with Gloria Steinem. Each movie includes excerpts from the live performances that were part of the *Womanhouse* project and most of the rooms are visited, although each movie does not picture each room.

The Demetrakas film is a much better source for the performances, including Jan Lester's and Faith Wilding's *Cock and Cunt Play*, Faith Wilding's *Waiting*, and the real-time performances of ironing by Sandra Orgel and scrubbing the floor by Chris Rush, among others. These are included at full length as they were performed at "Womanhouse" in front of a live audience, during an actual, scheduled performance at the house. The inclusion of these works in the context of a live performance held in a domestic space, with the audience filmed sitting on the floor close to the performance, is perhaps the Demetrakas film's strongest suit, although the Littman film, in which the same performances are shown performed in a studio, provides alternative points of view and some different material not covered by Demetrakas. The Demetrakas film also includes a wonderfully funny interview with three uptight male visitors to the house who all try to rationalize and control what they have just seen. Asked about Judy Chicago's *Menstruation Bathroom*, the angriest of the three opines that "the lady had a problem or a lot of friends," to which his presumably more scientifically oriented friend adds, "or an IUD." The film also includes segments from a consciousness-raising group meeting of the women who participated in the *Womanhouse* project, which manages to convey a sense of the high excitement, intense emotions, and wild humor of that moment.

The greatest formal weakness of the Demetrakas film is a dated, jazzy, electronic music soundtrack that is completely unrelated to the rock and folk music we actually listened to while working on the house, which would have given a different sense of time and place, marking the film in time rather than dating it. The Littman film concludes with a feminist folk singer accompanying herself on the piano, as the credits roll. The music is earnestly, almost comically of its time, but since it is tacked on to the credits, it does not affect the film itself. Miriam Schapiro does not appear in the Demetrakas film. This is a surprising and, from a documentary and historical point of view, inexcusable omission, although it may have been the unfortunate result of Schapiro's efforts to control the film's content.[4]

As a participant in "Womanhouse," I always felt that, despite the many documentary strengths of the Demetrakas film, it is a shame that the Littman film is not as well known, because it was more sympathetic to the participants, many of whom are accorded long segments in which they speak about their work while standing in "their room."[5] Each woman is articulate and deeply, indeed, given our youth, touchingly serious about her intentions for her piece and also her methodology of production. The interviews with Robin Schiff, about her *Fear Bathroom* and Camille Grey on her *Red Lipstick Bathroom* are particularly affecting. The film's respect for the individual participants and the politically aware, slightly ironic approach signaled by its title are its particular strengths. An extended conversation between Miriam Schapiro, Judy Chicago, and Gloria Steinem is quite fascinating, although for some reason they are filmed reclining on the big pillows that formed the seating for the performance space. This gives the scene a curious atmosphere of the seraglio, with these three powerful and smart women coming across as odd, speaking odalisques.

Taken together these films give a more complete sense of what this signal work in the history of feminist art in the United States was actually like.

*For our last class meeting before Christmas break in December 2005, my col-
league at Parsons the New School for Design Lenore Malen and I asked our
students to come as their alter egos. In order to calm the fear of embarrassment
about masquerade that afflicts some people (including myself!), we said they
could signal this alternative identity by full transformation or by the smallest
of signs. I decided to show a few minutes of an interview with me from* Womanhouse Is Not a Home. *One of the great conundrums of a human life is, am I
the same person I was or have I changed? What would the young woman think
of her older self? How much of her is left in me? Thus my alter ego was myself
as a very young woman artist.*

*In the fall of 1971 I went out to the California Institute of the Arts, in Valen-
cia, California, to get my* MFA *degree in painting. I had heard about the feminist
art program run by Judy Chicago at the California State University, Fresno, in
1970 and 1971 through Sheila Levrant de Bretteville, a close friend of my sister's
who was creating a feminist design program at the newly founded CalArts. I
had met with Miriam Schapiro and Paul Brach before I went out to Los Angeles
and knew that there was to be a feminist art program at CalArts. When I got
there, I had to decide whether I would join the program or not. I did. Although
I didn't know it fully at the time, in making this decision as a graduate student,
I had signed on for a lifelong educational task.*

*The following selections are fragments from letters I wrote to Sheila de
Bretteville and Miriam Schapiro just before I went out to California and, during that first school year, to my sister, Naomi Schor (Nomi), and to friends, including the painter Yvonne Jacquette, my college friend Susan Kinnaird, then
studying art history at the Institute of Fine Arts at New York University, a
young painter Mary Dellin, my high school best friend Michele Moss (Michy),
and her mother Dierdre Moss. I've also included selected fragments from my
student evaluations of the program, which were addressed to Miriam Schapiro.*

*The contradictions that are possible within what sometimes seems like a con-
sistent viewpoint may emerge from comparisons between the conclusions of
these writings from 1971 and 1972 and the views I have expressed in texts like*

"The ism *that dare not speak its name" and "Generation 2.5." What would my alter ego think? I was then twenty-one years old.*

. . .

August 23, 1971

Dear Sheila:

Thank you for your letter though it made me wince. After I mailed my tirade out to you, Nomi arrived with her capacity for making me remember my own experiences and clarifying my ideas and I almost sent you a telegram saying "disregard previous message," though I don't really take anything back! But, from your letter, I gathered that I had sounded even more unaware than I am. I will read S. de Beauvoir and Germaine Greer. I'd also like to read some Doris Lessing. Nomi is a great fan of hers. I've read that January *Art News* on women.[1] Having been an art history student, that subject of forgotten or lost women artists naturally fascinates me and would be a natural course of study for me to pursue at CalArts.

Is that part of Miriam Schapiro's program? I will write to her and tell her the truth: I am very interested in her program—but with all that I've heard I still don't understand the day to day mechanics of it, so that I would like to speak to her and Judy Chicago when I arrive.
[. . .]

The last two weeks in P[rovince]town I was overwhelmed by talk about the movement. God knows I'm interested and have more than one foot in it already but it was as if everyone around me was pushing me to get the other foot off the ground. My friend Pat [Steir] visited us [. . .] and her friend Marcia Tucker (curator of the Whitney) was in town. During a splendid moonrise on the beach Marcia vigorously endorsed the Cal[Arts] program, telling me the movement has changed her life, and that it would change mine, my habits, my attitudes, everything. Granted, I want to change but it is frightening to hear people say that. Already I find going to art school for the first time and to California threats to my identity. I mean, I like Mira, basically, and I don't want her swept completely away, and everyone else was hopping up and down gleefully at the idea!

Also talk about the movement gets almost boring if it is the only subject of conversation not to say conversion.

Obviously it all will seem in proportion when I see for myself, I must say I am truly terrified, Sheila.

August 24, 1971

Dear Miss Schapiro:

Even before and since I was accepted at CalArts as a graduate student I have been hearing a lot about the woman's program that you and Judy Chicago are going to have. Sheila de Bretteville sent me *Everywoman*, which I read and reread and made everyone else read. Sheila has been encouraging me to try to join the program. Recently I met Marcia Tucker and at a beach picnic during a moonrise she gave it, so to speak, a glowing endorsement!

It may sound as if I am being converted to something I don't believe in but that is not at all the case. I am very interested in the program but while understanding its aims and general design I don't fully understand its day to day mechanics; I do not see how it would affect my work (the act of working, not the content), and how it is related to the rest of the school.

I was hoping that if there is still place within the program I might be able to talk to you and Miss Chicago when I arrive in California. [. . .]

I am looking forward to speaking with you,

Sincerely,

Mira Schor

. . .

October 23, 1971

Dear Nomi:

[. . .] Thursday I went to a meeting of the women's group. They were discussing business and at first I got no impressions at all. They were talking about the fact that they are going to lock the doors of their studio which I thought was an awful idea, especially for those people like me who might not be with them but want to know what they are doing. One particularly attractive girl was against it and the question went around the room. Just before it got to me, the girl before me burst into tears, which set me off, and most of the girls in the room suddenly became human. So my very tender feelings changed and when they dealt with me I said I would join them. [. . .] Judy Chicago is short, has short straight black hair, a big nose and wire-rim glasses, a loud voice, is didactic, and in her mind there is no grey.

. . .

November 7, 1971

Dear Nomi:

[. . .] I decided to join the women's group, partly because of my great interest in it and partly because of a pressured sell job. I think that I wrote you just before the night I went to a performance of Judy Chicago's pieces: something I shall one day act out to you called the Cock and Cunt play. There was a huge dinner before and Mimi Schapiro gave me a real hard sell on it. By this time I was so numbed I could hardly react to anything.
[. . .]

I am having my troubles with the group. One by one I like most of the girls in it. But groups have a different psychology than single human beings. Above all I don't get along well with Judy Chicago. The level of intense emotion is high enough without her nervous, driving, egocentric personality. She is especially interested in sort of guerrilla theater and it is one of the things she wants to spend a lot of/most of the class time doing. As you can imagine I can't stand it. I've never liked performing, and her plays are crude and loaded. You must have hated your mother a bit. Well maybe but not enough to do a play about it, which Judy has written. I told her that I was allergic to her and she told me that she felt pretty much the same way about me. I am not an easy person to mold through violent methods although I mold pretty easily otherwise. She believes that she has had the single vision of a liberated woman artist and we must trust her with our lives for the next few months and she will lead us to the Promised Land. I told her that I thought that she was using [us] as tools to create *her* vision and was very upset when we tried anything on our own. She didn't like that too much.

. . .

November 16, 1971

Dear Mrs. Moss:

[. . .] I did join the feminist program. When I first met them I felt such group warmth and good will towards me that I just had to join. But I also had many reservations and they did quite a pressure sell on me. My reservations have not been allayed yet and in fact I am having a tough time within the group. The program is totally time consuming so that I don't have time to cash checks, buy food or do my laundry, or paint! Or think. I have a real personality clash with one of the leaders of the group, Judy Chicago. She's a tough, loud, aggressive, messianic, and insecure woman who demands attention and attracts negative feelings from a lot of people. She did create this program and it is revolutionary and unique in the world really and one must admire her. Every movement must have someone like her. But she is also ungentle, unsubtle. Sheila calls her a primitive. She wants us to give ourselves to her totally and she will lead us to the promised land of independent women artists. But I cannot give my life over to anyone, especially not to a tough person. I can only be molded by gentle means. Also I don't completely go along with her vision of a new woman. She goes too far I think and really wants women to pick up some of the worse characteristics of men, the inhuman driving of oneself beyond one's limits, etc.

• • •

December 7, 1971

Evaluation, Feminist Art Program

[. . .] In a couple of weeks I'm going back to New York. A lot of people there are going to want to know about the program, about what I've been doing, and I have been wondering about what I'll tell them. I realized that mostly I had to tell about personality conflicts, guilt trips, power plays, contradictions. I will also be able to tell them about good people, the house, the catalog, my room [in the *Womanhouse* project and exhibit]. But these seem secondary to the former. And that is not right, that is not the way the program should be; and it is not my imagination. Or rather if it is imagination it is collective, since more than one girl has agreed with me. We have discussed how we feel that certain hang-ups and bitterness are being projected upon us with the ready-made clause that if you reject the projections you're in the mold of the unconscious woman.

To be more specific is to be petty but I must. One small incident was an eye-opener for me. At our last Wednesday meeting we were joking around about how awkward it was when the Ramparts women came and we all had to introduce ourselves. Judy jumped in and said yes, women don't like presenting themselves to other women, so last year the Fresno group had practiced introducing themselves and shaking hands. She then shook my hand to illustrate. Something about that scene didn't seem kosher. Then I realized what was wrong: I don't have hang-ups about presenting myself to other women. I have general hang-ups about touching people, I'm not a huggy/kissy person but it is not unnatural for me to put my arm around another woman or firmly shake her hand. Yet Judy said it as a blanket statement—we all know that women don't like presenting themselves to other women. A light-bulb flashed over my head: maybe that's Judy's problem.[2]

At the same meeting Judy said that she wasn't interested in consciousness raising. She'd done it last year and she'd resolved all her problems about women. She may have rapped a lot last year but before I even met Judy and as recently as this weekend I heard from separate sources that Judy has never been in a strict consciousness-raising group with women she'd consider as equals—as opposed to younger students. I suspect that Judy is afraid of one, afraid of looking at herself. I think that she hasn't resolved all her problems with women. She sometimes seems the most uncomfortable person in the group, her eyes are always so defensive when she looks at you, as if she's afraid of what you'll do next to hurt her. And I think she's afraid of the gentleness within her, of its femaleness. [. . .] There is a quality of gentleness that is sexless or it is perhaps a female quality that some men are fortunate to have. I've found it in a few people, integrated and conscious people, accepting even of their own contradictions. I don't feel that Judy has arrived at that level.

I don't think that Judy has resolved *her* feelings about needing male approval, about ambition to succeed in the (male) art world, about competitiveness with men or women. That is why she projects upon us bitterness and anger about those things, which I don't particularly want to feel, unless I experience them myself. She often says, when we express desires relating to the outside world, "you'll see what will happen out there." Just like our mothers always say, "you'll see," "see what happened," and "I told you so." This kind of vicarious paranoia does not appeal to me. I'm paranoid enough as it is. Also the "you'll see" method of teaching is not so great because—the old cliché says—some nasty things must be experienced. She's not protecting [us] by keeping us in an ivory tower and structuring our time so we can't work on our own, or frightening us so that we are afraid to leave the ivory tower. I believe the world is cruel and crueler to women but not so black as Judy portrays it. I sometimes feel that she is almost cursing those women who have made it as having compromised themselves, or, grudgingly, as being superwomen, freaks who have broken through molds and restraints. That again isn't kosher because I don't feel that my friends who show in New York are either compromised or freaks. They are crazy artists and freaks to that extent. But no crazier than any devoted artist. And no more compromised than any male artist I've ever known.

[. . .] Many of the things I've said can be shot down as being paranoid, as being misunderstandings, misquotes, etc. I think Judy's need for power, fear of it, her contradictions, her use of power are all irritating factors. She did create the program and we owe a tremendous amount to her, but I still think she's terrified of showing weakness, of our getting the program away from her and making it our own.

A postscript: When I saw how beautiful Judy's house is, how delicate and lovely everything was, how afraid she was of our hurting her beautiful cats, I felt I was right about Judy. She has hidden her house side from me at least. No one would be rough with her cats, as she feared. People would be less inclined to be rough on her if she said, as touchingly as she did about her cats, Treat me well, I can be hurt.

• • •

Feminist Art Program Experience Report (undated)

[. . .] I would divide what I have learnt into three parts. First there was the initial exposure and turn on to the ideals of the feminist program, which occurred during the summer before I came out here. Letters from Sheila de Bretteville, the copy of *Everywoman* devoted to Judy Chicago's women, and endless discussions on the subject of feminism crystallized my already strong interest in feminism (or "women's lib"). [. . .] Every new step into feminism is like putting on a new set of prescription glasses and this past summer's set was particularly strong. [. . .] I don't [think] any new prescription will ever be as crucial to my sight.

The next step was my arrival at CalArts, my introduction to Judy, Mimi, the Fresno women and the new women and my formal entry into the program. We were presented with a ready-made project—a house in which each woman would have a room to do anything she wanted in—a fantasy room, which in the ordinary course of life she would never be free to have. The house project seemed more like a super finish to a program instead of a beginning, but at this point I'm glad it'll be behind us instead of ahead. The house project created terrific time pressures, as it [the house] was rented for only three months. It made us even more isolated from the rest of the school than we would have been anyway, since it was in Hollywood. There was also the strain of commuting every day, which meant for me depending on other people for transportation. Finally the house was an old wreck, a vandalized, long uninhabited shell of a house which we had to renovate before we could start our own work. All of this increased the pressure I felt in being in a group. For the second part of what I learnt within the Feminist program consists of the discovery of group process and its difficulties and joys. There were some joys—new friends, funny times, pleasant and moving evenings showing each other our work, scary, emotional, shocking but rewarding consciousness-raising sessions. But, unfortunately for me, there was a great deal of unpleasant stuff. I've found it a tremendous strain to coexist with certain people who I do not like, no matter what I find out about them, to feel pressures on me to be a certain way, to like certain people, to be pleasant, considerate, cheerful, especially while dealing with others' bad moods and unconsciousness. It has been a tremendous strain, once finished with the group shit-work (scraping floors, painting walls) to beg people to help me get materials, and especially lately as I've become more and more involved with my own room, to work in the midst of other people's garbage and noise, to have to feel guilty for my depressions and bad moods, which the house—noise, demands, etc.—only increased. I do not think any of these experiences relate specifically to feminism—but pertain to any group working on such an extraordinary project and in such constant contact. Although this aspect of the program has been very hard on me I do not dismiss it as a learning process. On the contrary perhaps it has been even more valuable than the first, intellectual exposure to the ideas of feminism. *It has taught me good and bad about myself and others.* I think from it I will know better how much I can truly give of myself before I begin to resent giving, before my worst faults and my anxieties begin oozing to the surface—and having been involved in something so consuming, I don't think I'll shy from other, more normal involvements. But—not right away! I need a breather.

This brings me to the last part. I of course feel great pride for the house project as a whole but I think I will be proud of my real contribution to it—my room [*Red Moon Room*]. (I say "will" because as I write, it is about three days away from being finished. When it is I will add slides to this experience report.) I have always worked very small, no more than two by three feet, usually notebook size gouaches. My room in the house has about twenty-five feet of wall space (seven feet high) and when I will be finished, it will be a walk-in oil painting more than a mural, since the painting comes out in [*sic*] the walls onto the floor and door frame. Every inch is painted and the painting is of the room. It is a trompe l'oeil painting of the room continued from actual space into the perspective space of the painting. Within the room (in the painting), there is a woman—looking quite a bit like me—facing the viewer. She is communicating with a red moon, which one can see through an open arcade at the back. This arcade is one of three openings of space in the painting. There is another rising pale yellow moon in a cloudy sky on the left wall and a mountain landscape in a dark sky on the right (these landscapes are continuous).

[. . .] This perhaps sounds like a very negative experience report. That is because I'm worn like a tire from freeway driving, emotion[ally] exhausted, physically in a constant state of interrupted sleep. I'm depressed, homesick, and highly irritable. But if I had it to re-live I'd do it again because I felt I had to be in the feminist program and I know I've learnt a lot—some of which I'll only realize in the months and years to come.

• • •

February 6, 1972

Dear Sue:

[. . .] The opening [of "Womanhouse"] last Sunday was something of an anticlimax. Only six of the art faculty came (if it had been two male teachers and their class everyone would have come, including the L.A. art community, which has totally ignored us), and of those six each one was there by invitation really. Mimi and Judy's husbands,[3] two T.A.s, and Stephan [Von Huene] the teacher I like [. . .].

• • •

February 28, 1972

Dear Michy:

[. . .] I am my usual Cal Arts self, busy, and busy complaining. Yesterday was the last day of the house and it was just insane. We had a sale of a lot of the items in the house and lots of people came and we did sell a lot but especially in the afternoon the people who came were not coming for the sale but just to see the house, which by that time was a total mess. So everyone was disgusted and irritated and tired. Meanwhile a film crew was getting in the way and filming the end.[4] Mimi and Judy began to scream at everybody and Mimi came up to me while I was saying to somebody how stupid and sad it was to film now and she began to yell at me with a vicious expression on her face that I always complain, every time I open my mouth I complain and she'd like to see me run a program like this . . .

• • •

Despite my complaints, I was dedicated to the ideals of the feminist program, as is evident in the following letter to a young painter, Mary Dellin, who had apparently written me in a manner critical and suspicious of feminism.

• • •

March 2, 1972

Dear Mary:

I am sorry that I did not answer you for such a long time, although the way time goes at CalArts it may well have only been a couple of weeks ago. Another reason for my not answering right away was that I am a bit disturbed by your attitude towards feminism and feminist groups. One's attitude is always relative and relative to you I find myself to the left I suppose. That is really ironic because within the Feminist program here I am perhaps the most resistant to group activities and the most doubtful of its value in its present form. However I am in it and I do see the value of having women teaching women (my experience with Manso is enough to keep me on that road),[5] although not forever and not in a restrictive way, which, I must admit, is the way it is being done here. I do believe that groups and political people like Judy and Mimi are necessary. I am finding surprise surprise that I am not yet and may never be that kind of person but such a person, such people are necessary. They pave the way for us. One of the most exciting days this year was the day of a conference of women artists mainly from the West Coast although there were women from all over. There were at least two hundred and fifty women artists in one room for twelve hours [on] Saturday and Sunday, showing slides and slides of work, talking, forming consciousness raising groups and discussing gallery and museum business, hiring practices, etc. It was really an amazing weekend and even more so for the many women there who were older than me or you, who had disappeared into their homes and studios once they were out of school, who had been discouraged, who had been isolated, some of them had never shown their work to anyone for ten or more years. They were really moved. And the work was good. In particular there is a group of painters from San Francisco who is terrific. The L.A. artists are too plasticky for me.

The point of all of this is that such meetings are encouraging and they are unique and they are due to the efforts of such women as Mimi and Judy.

The *Womanhouse* was a similar kind of thing. I was particularly disturbed by your anxiousness that I not get myself associated with a women's group. That kind of feeling in yourself should be examined, I think. I did sometimes feel that way, but it boils down to "what will the men say" and one really should try not to think that way. If the work is good that's all that is important. And the house was quite something. . . . We had a lot of people come to see it, and had a lot of coverage (in particular a TV show on PBS in which all of us were interviewed). Apparently it is known all around the country and similar projects are being planned. And the art world knows what is going on. In a way it is a movement whose time is coming so that one might even join up out of sheer opportunism. Just the opposite of the view you have of it as being a potentially harmful association.

[. . .] In the end I will come out somewhere in between still believing in feminism as I think any intelligent woman would and although I prefer to be on my own pretty much, I would never lose contact with the larger group.

• • •

April 29, 1972

Dear Yvonne:

[. . .] You asked if the program did anything about getting rid of "imposed" values. Yes in a sense it does, it tries to. But many of us feel it only im-

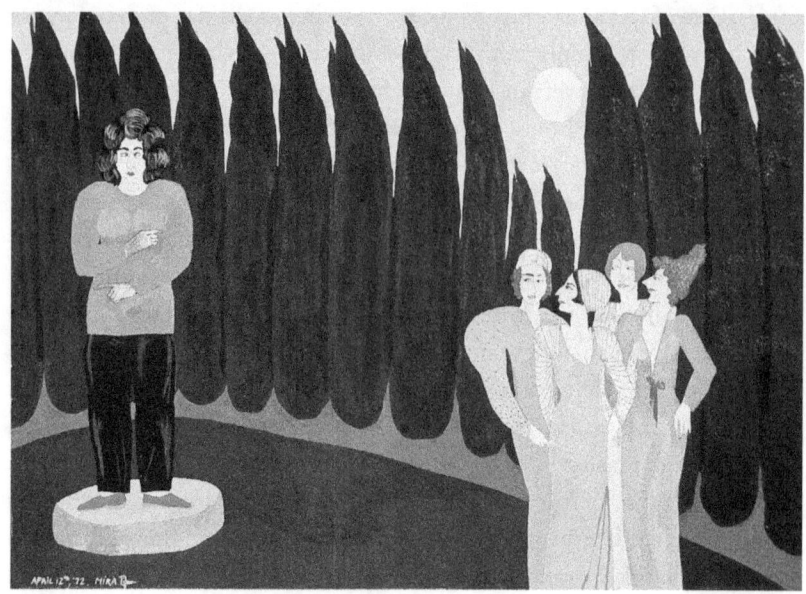

Mira Schor, *Mixed Messages*, 1972. Gouache on paper.
14 × 19½ inches. Courtesy of the artist.

poses others. Judy has her naive obsession about "central core imagery" —
which some of the women swallow. There is a definite bent toward subject
matter.

. . .

May 7, 1972

In answer to Miriam Schapiro's Mentor's Report of April 16, 1972

[. . .] The program, and especially Mimi as we started the drawing and
painting class, has always been more concerned with psyching us out than
dealing with our art. Mimi's Mentor's Report, solely concerned with my
personality, is an example. I cannot stand a totally formalistic approach
but after a while it annoys me to put a painting up and hear *myself* criti-
cized.

[. . .] One of the basic faults of the Feminist program, as it has evolved
this year, is that Feminist ideas took second place to the personalities of
Mimi and Judy and the group dynamics around them. They have generally
reacted to dissidence, independence or doubt as personal betrayals. [. . .]

They were forced to be more respectful of those women outside the program over whom they could have no such power. All of us have a surplus of guilt and that sense of betrayal, as unjust and misplaced as it may be, could not help create guilt in us which robbed us of freedom of action and even thought in some cases. That is not what Feminism ought to create. Isn't Feminism ideally a leaderless movement?

Part Two

PAINTING

SOME NOTES ON WOMEN AND ABSTRACTION
AND A CURIOUS CASE HISTORY: ALICE NEEL
AS A GREAT ABSTRACT PAINTER

Modernism seemed to offer women a fiction in which universals and absolutes could be pursued in freedom from the messy business of gender relations and this prisonhouse of sex.—Griselda Pollock, "Killing Men and Dying Women"

You can't put an abstract painting on a banner. It's less readable when you're flying by in a cab.—Lisa Yuskavage, qtd. in Deborah Solomon, "A Roll Call of Fresh Names and Faces," *New York Times*

Paradox bedevils women artists' access to art historical production and discourse. The status of abstraction versus representation in feminist critical discourse is a case in point.

It may be the case, as Lucy Lippard has suggested, that "the mainstream has always preferred its women artists abstract, and its feminism abstracted, or diffused, defused."[1] Lippard notes as an example the Museum of Modern Art's exhibition "Sense and Sensibility: Women Artists and Minimalism in the Nineties" from 1994—the only thematic group exhibition MoMA has ever dedicated exclusively to women artists. In this show, the body was generally referenced through cultural symbolism in the use of gender-coded readymades, such as eye make-up or lipstick, used as structural components of minimalist artworks that often referenced minimalist artworks by male artists such as Richard Serra.

Nevertheless, in general, representation and more specifically figuration have proved more useful than abstraction for artists wishing to examine gender difference and feminist issues in visual art. Feminist content has been easier to perceive when iconographic analyses of representation and image-based narratives can be brought to bear on the work. Consequently, much to the dismay of women working in abstraction who consider themselves feminists, they are often not included in exhibitions and panel discussions on feminism and gender representation. For example on "The Body Politic: Whatever Happened to the Women Artist's Movement?," a panel held at the New Museum of Contemporary Art in New York in December 1998, not one of the four women included in order to represent four generations of feminist artists—Nancy Spero, Mary Kelly, Renée Cox, and Vanessa Beecroft—was an abstract artist.[2] In their discussion, the subject of abstraction never came up as an alternative feminist practice within the women artists' movement. Conversely, exhibitions or panels on abstraction rarely include women who consider themselves feminists or who refer to feminism as a significant factor in their work. In fact, it was a cry from the heart by a woman artist on a panel titled "Women and Abstraction" at the landmark women artists' collective A.I.R. Gallery in New York City in 1997 that made me begin to think about the subject of women and abstraction in relation to feminist art practice.[3]

To this day, although minimalist abstraction has become the establishment's default style for art in corporate offices or for memorials, representation retains its popularity. Two of the most successful painters of the past decade, John Currin and Lisa Yuskavage, both specialize in representations of half-naked young women, a type of Victoria's Secret catalogue content reformulated and rendered with old master painting high-value and high-finish style to give it aesthetic legitimacy. A full-page, full-color ad of one of Currin's smiling, half-naked girls appeared in the *New York Times* Friday Arts section every week for the full run of Currin's show at the Whitney Museum of American Art (November 20, 2003, to February 22, 2004), exemplifying that in our commodity-oriented era, representation, in particular representation of sexually alluring women, is prized for its efficiency as a tool of commodification. As Lisa Yuskavage has said, "You can't put an abstract painting on a banner. It's less readable when you're flying by in a cab."[4]

The problematics of considering women artists' work in abstraction are ensnared in the subtext of the ideals of abstraction as a universal—ergo, genderless—language as expressed in the hypermasculinist rhetoric of the New York school, and in the dangers of essentialism lurking in any efforts to perceive difference in the work of abstract artists who are women. It is perhaps because of these pitfalls, particularly the last, that I will engage in a paradoxical move of my own in this essay, that of making an abrupt turn away from the consideration of contemporary female abstract artists that would be suggested by my introductory remarks in order to consider the work of Alice Neel from a formalist and also process- or materialist-oriented point of view, to identify the artist as a great abstract painter against the grain of the importance of her work in terms of the visual articulation of a female gaze and also against the grain of her own self-presentation, rooted in autobiography and anecdote.

In order to contextualize Neel's work—which spans from the 1930s to the 1980s—and particularly her experience as a representational painter during the hegemony of abstract expressionism, a general introduction to abstraction and postwar American women artists may be useful.

It has been widely noted by feminist art historians that women artists faced a double problem with regard to painting in the postwar years leading up to the development of the feminist art movement at the end of the 1960s. The utopian ideals of pure abstraction had allowed women artists some kind of entrée into art, since a truly universalist art practice would be gender free; to this day, many women who are successful abstract painters have not specifically noted a desire to create visual equivalents of female experience. The universalizing rhetoric of modernism precluded such content, and practically speaking, to have pursued such a focus would have returned them to the marked identity of a "woman artist" from the privileged identity of simply "artist." The problem was that the universalism of pure abstraction turned out to be a myth that was exposed once theory began to critique the assumptions underlying modernism's notion of universality as put forth by Western white men.

At the same time, the postwar discourse on painting in America associated with the New York school had been particularly aggressive in the masculinity, indeed the misogyny, of its rhetoric. This gendered aesthetic warfare contributed to the efflorescence of feminist art, yet even today it continues to constitute a large part of the mythos about the postwar era. We see evidence of this in major popular biographies, such as Mark Stevens's and Annalyn Swan's recent biographical study, *de Kooning: An American Master*, with its emphasis on de Kooning's sexual exploits. It is also part of common rhetoric: when the usually highly articulate art historian and Museum of Modern Art curator Kirk Varnedoe was interviewed on the *Newshour with Jim Lehrer* in 1999 on the occasion of MoMA's retrospective "Jackson Pollock," he invoked the word *macho* to describe Pollock's work, or at least the way Pollock was turned into an American icon by the mainstream media and art critical apparatus since his time, a masculine model for an American male artist. Varnedoe's characterization evidences the highly complex gendered narratives surrounding this artist, presumably in order to ward off the more feminized or homosexual implications of Pollock's life and art practice, and in a clear reiteration of the anxiety male artists in the postwar period in the United States experienced about the perception of painting as a feminine activity for a man, an anxiety that had to be masked by hypermasculine practices.[5]

The gendered aspects of the work of this period have been the subject of several significant studies by women art historians: for example, just in the last ten years, the work of Helen Frankenthaler and her positioning as a generative but transitional figure between Jackson Pollock and the postpainterly abstractionists Morris Louis and Kenneth Noland has been the subject of studies by Griselda Pollock, Lisa Saltzman, and Marcia Brennan.[6]

Juxtaposing photographic documentation of Pollock and Frankenthaler painting on canvases laid on the floor, Griselda Pollock notes that such juxtaposition might lead to questions such as: "Do Pollock's slashing and throwing of paint, his gyrations around a supine canvas, enact a macho assault upon an imaginary feminine body? Are the traces of paint on canvas the residues of a psychic performance? Is this *écriture/peinture masculine* at its most vivid? How then could we read Helen Frankenthaler's pouring, pushing, smoothing gestures as she stood in the canvas, or knelt near its edge as a surface continuous with her space and her body's large spreading and delicate shaping movements. Is this a feminine modality inviting us to invent metaphors that might link female bodily experience to fluidity in order to account for the sensuousness and lusciousness of her effects?"[7]

Frankenthaler's germinal technique of paint application has long been a vexing issue for feminist analysis. It lends itself to an essentialist reading centered on an analogy between the flowing and staining of paint and female fluidity.[8] Further, Frankenthaler has not endorsed any type of feminist interpretation of her work; she does not associate her work or herself either with feminist art or with feminism. Finally, her technique was quickly appropriated by male artists, in particular the Washington-based artists Morris Louis and Kenneth Noland, who in 1953 were brought by the critic Clement Greenberg to visit Frankenthaler's studio where they saw Frankenthaler's first major work done in this manner, the landscape-based abstraction *Mountains and Sea* (1952). Shortly after this visit they adapted Frankenthaler's technique to abstraction with more standardized systems of form.

Pollock continues, "Something different must occur if the painter who paints with such a body is, in fact, a woman artist, painting from (or to find) 'the creative woman's body.'" But, despite invoking Luce Irigaray's "Gesture in Psychoanalysis" (1985), to wonder whether Frankenthaler's technical "innovation" and relation to painting space, "with stain and soak, with annulling the material distinction between her mark and the canvas's surface by the immersion of the one in the other and the loss of fixed boundaries, [is] the site of an inscription of the feminine dimension of loss and separation," she warns that "this is not to drag in an essential idea about what that body is."[9]

Brennan extends the discussion by examining the meanings of Clement Greenberg's comment that "Helen Frankenthaler served as a 'bridge between Pollock and what was possible.'"[10] Brennan contends that Greenberg used Frankenthaler's work to make a transition from his instrumental reading of Jackson Pollock's all-over painting as a trace of the artist's gestures and body to his later critical support of a non-tactile, optical, and anonymous post-painterly abstraction represented by the work of Louis and Noland, whose visit to Frankenthaler's studio is used as the transitional key not just by the artists in their work but, more importantly, by Greenberg in a shift in his own aesthetic program. The woman artist's "feminine" abstract mark is recoded as "disembodied or otherwise unmarked by gender. Such a privilege was exclusively reserved for her male colleagues." Thus, "formalism continued to derive an idealized conception of masculine artistic subjectivity through a contingent, dialogical relation to the feminine."[11] The stain had been purloined and regendered in an object lesson of the problematics of engaging in a gendered formal analysis of certain tropes of abstraction in the work of women artists.

Greenbergian formalism having emptied the field of the rectangular canvas (and the theoretical ground on which it rested) of all personal, narrative, and literary content and having pushed women artists to the theoretical and critical margins, it stands to reason that when women artists began to try to imagine visual embodiments of female experience, painting was not the logical space for this search. Other, less established media proved more hospitable to women's desire for formal experimentation in the exploration of previously repressed content: sculpture, which had for many years been a troubled discipline but which now was seen as a space that could accommodate both the real and metaphoric abstraction referential to the body, and new media including performance art and video.

Even so, in the early 1970s, feminist artists and critics attempting to theorize a female aesthetic proposed visual organizing principles and images, such as central core imagery, layering, and repetition, as visual embodiments of women's complex and multiple sexual experience and subjectivity. For a moment, at least, abstract art seemed like a privileged locus for feminist art. Important feminist critics such as Lucy Lippard supported a number of women artists working abstractly in the postminimalist movement such as Eva Hesse and Hannah Wilke. "I was looking for sensuous, even sensual, abstraction, an off-center, three-dimensional imagery that shared minimalism's bluntness and presence but didn't cut off all content, all kinesthetic and emotional associations."[12] One of the problematics of considering women artists' relation to abstraction is touched on almost in passing in an ironic subtext of this statement: the fact that artists, male and female and even outsider artists, generally work in some relation to a shared range of stylistic paradigms of their time — and the implication that the feminist critic would look to women's work for a feminine variation on something already done by men. Lippard explains, "In the seventies we talked a lot about 'female sensibility' and 'body identification' in abstraction, about tactility and transparency and layering as ways in which women's work could be distinguished from men's."[13] She argues that the early strategies of women artists were not "a retreat from formalism." "We just left it behind . . . or put it to the side, or relegated it to the bottom layer. Which did not mean *form* was ignored, only *formalism*." Lippard continues, again referring back to what male artists were doing: "Hardcore minimalists also saw themselves as 'antiformalists' in their rejection of composition and a certain seductiveness or 'sublimity' that was associated with 'post-painterly abstraction'; their work was concrete rather than abstract."[14] In any case Lippard gradually moved toward other political concerns and lost interest in writing about abstract art (and in fact about women artists and feminism specifically): "As I became more involved in issue-oriented feminist art from the mid-seventies on . . . I wrote less and less about abstract art because there was less there to get my teeth into, given my own preoccupations. . . . It's just harder to see the subversion and the confrontations in an abstract framework, even when the artist is politically supportive of feminism."[15]

In consciousness-raising sessions during this time, women talked frankly about aspects of their experiences that had not been thought fit for high art, although, in fact, the main topics of discussion — money, sex, family, and power — are the basic subjects of so much art by men as well as by women. Yet, as Anna Chave has argued, most recently in her essay "Minimalism and Biography," the biographical bases of these and other subjects are veiled in a rhetoric of objectivity when it comes to male artists, even when the significant critical texts that serve to place them into the canon are being generated by their female companions, wives, and lovers. "Marxist-informed criticism has largely persisted in depreciating the biographical, in so doing finding common cause at once with much poststructuralist art criticism as well as with the deindividualizing impetus underlying key Minimalist initiatives."[16]

But discussions about family, relationships with men, clothing, one's body, domestic labor—all of these narratives seemingly were most usefully visually articulated within figuration and representation. Here, my personal experience as a participant in the noted early feminist art project *Womanhouse*, created in Los Angeles in 1972, was instructive: twenty-three artists, mostly students at the California Institute of the Arts (CalArts) led by the artists and teachers Judy Chicago and Miriam Schapiro, were given the opportunity to work in a "room of one's own" in an abandoned villa in Hollywood. Only three did paintings, although many thought of themselves as painters or had begun their professional lives as painters. Of these three room paintings, only Robin Mitchell's *Painted Room* was abstract, a walk-in abstract-expressionist painting.[17] But even the representational or figurative painting, including my own self-portrait, *Red Moon Room*, and Ann Mills's *Leaf Room*, were the subject of incomprehension by the viewing public, because they did not meet their expectations for illustrations of the ideas of women's liberation as successfully as installations that included specific reference or incorporation of the real (shoes, lace, wedding dresses, and so on) or as the agitprop performances that hammered the feminist message across as effectively as a Punch and Judy show. Thus I learned early on that within a political (here a feminist) project, abstraction was considered less instrumental than representation, and, at the same time, that painting in itself had a degree of inherent abstraction that made it less useful than the real in the elaboration of a political thematic. Even abstract sculptures such as Hannah Wilke's *Of Radishes and Flowers* (1972) could be interpreted metaphorically and through an allusion to the real, by virtue of their physical presence: latex could be viewed as skin, for example.

Thus, although some of the formal elements developed in the seventies in art and feminist theorization of what a female aesthetic based on female

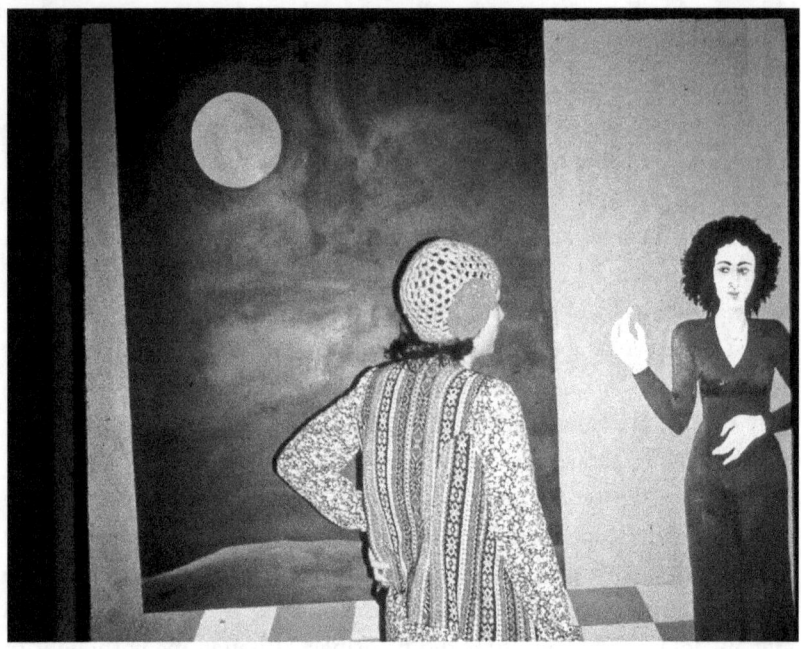

Mira Schor, *Red Moon Room*, installation detail from *Womanhouse*, 1972.
Oil on canvas. 8 × 10 × 4 feet. Courtesy of the artist.

sexuality would look like—layering, multiplicity, repetition—seemed
congruent with abstraction, the early feminist art movement seemed to
orient itself in art practice, art history, and theory, around representation. Women analyzed and identified how the male gaze constructs femininity and how femininity is constructed in accordance with the desire
of the male gaze. Feminist art historians were interested in women who
developed a female gaze, a female construction of the body and subject.
In the 1980s the most successful women artists (and also the most significant of the women allowed into mainstream discourse) were photo-
based artists working with codes of representation of femininity such as
Barbara Kruger and Cindy Sherman. More recently, figurative artists such
as Yuskavage continue to work with codes of female representation in a
painterly style, which, like that of their male contemporaries such as John
Currin, is a hybrid of traditional realism, photorealism, and the simulacral.

At the same time women working within abstraction pose even more
vexing questions for feminist analysis. Stylistic trends cut across gender,

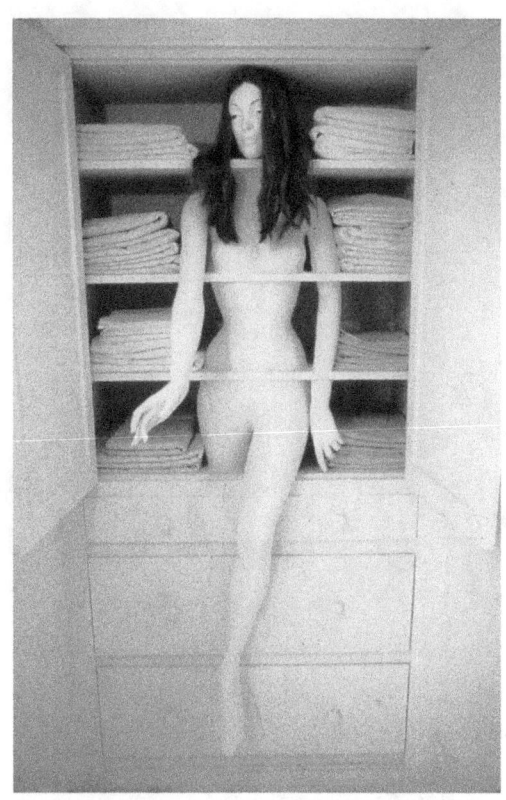

Sandra Orgel, *Linen Closet*, installation from *Womanhouse*, 1972. Mixed media. Dimensions variable. Courtesy of the artist.

Robin Mitchell, *Painted Room*, installation from *Womanhouse*, 1972. Painting and mixed media. Dimensions variable. Courtesy of the artist.

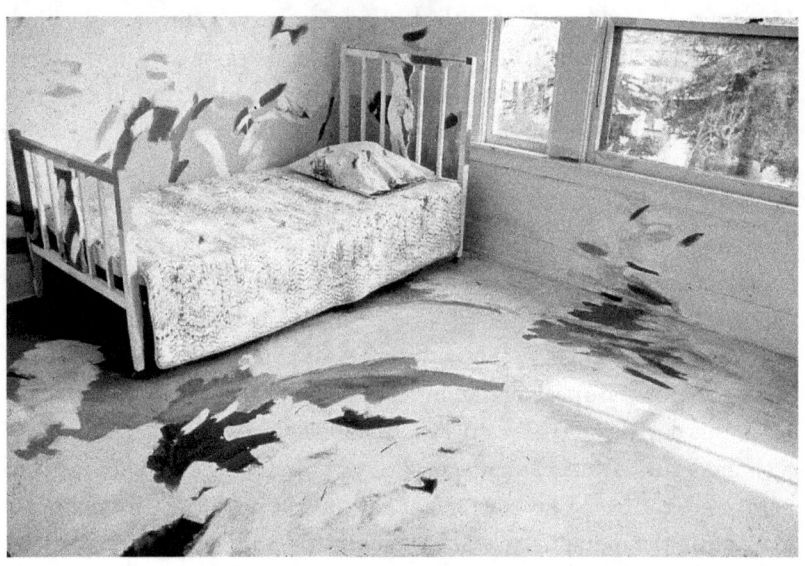

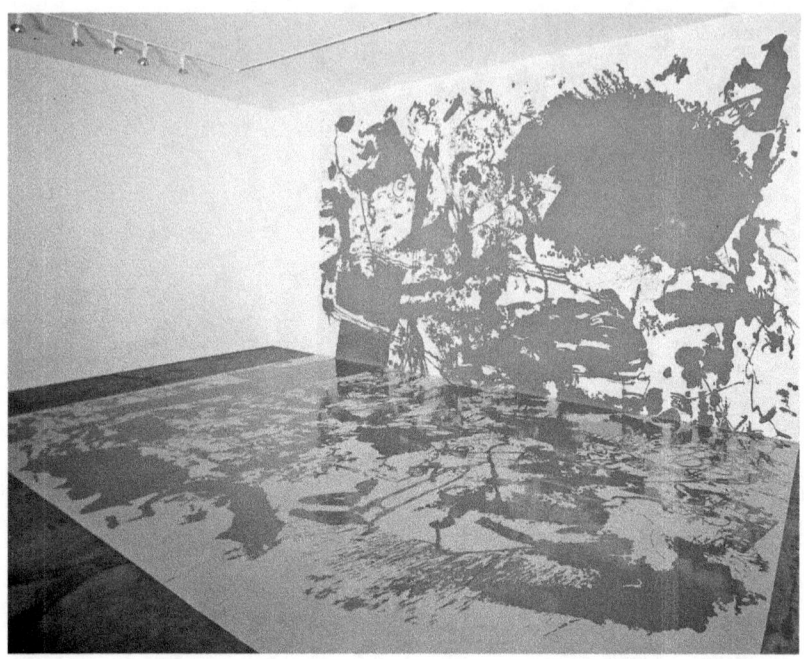

Ingrid Calame, *"b-b-b-, rr-gR-UH!, b-b-b-"*, 1999. Enamel paint
on trace mylar. 29 × 25 feet. Courtesy of the artist.

and essentialist tropes are muddied by transgendered characteristics.
Many of the women working with abstract elements and processes, including spillage and staining, do so today with a high degree of historical consciousness and appropriational awareness (for example, Ingrid Calame's
works, in which found stains in the environment are replicated through a
complex series of tracings and naming, and are painted with a deliberate-
ness that completely contradicts the appearance of spillage). These artists
often reject political content (in this they eerily replicate earlier yearnings
for a genderless universal), while male artists such as Anthony Viti revisit
Frankenthaler's stains, in Viti's case using his own blood and urine, in
radiantly beautiful sheets of translucent bodily substance, to embrace political content and speak metaphorically about AIDS.

To this day, despite the critical and market status of certain schools of
high modernist abstraction, the question of whether the artist of contemporary life can be an abstract artist remains in play. Can contemporary
life endure the metaphoric realm of abstraction or is it too literalist and
information- and representation-based?

It is perhaps because of the continued, fraught complexities of these issues that I embraced the opportunity to give a lecture on Alice Neel at a symposium held at the National Museum for Women during their exhibition "Alice Neel's Women." I was invited to discuss her work from the point of view of "feminist theory," which is an entirely reasonable topic, considering the importance to feminist art history of Neel's oeuvre as a figurative painter, including her many memorable portraits of women in all stages of life and economic strata. I was therefore delighted when the museum accepted my somewhat unorthodox reply, that I would welcome the opportunity to talk about my long held belief that Alice Neel is a great abstract painter!

Alice Neel (1900–1984) began painting in the 1920s, in a realist style influenced at times by expressionism and surrealism. In choosing to remain committed to figuration during the 1950s, Neel overtly disobeyed the dominant legislation of high modernism that, as Griselda Pollock states, "outlawed questions of the social, that is, all ideological baggage that prevented art from saving itself within a capitalist system."[18] Neel's artistic and personal trajectory was perhaps even more extralegal than that of her female contemporaries working within abstraction, women such as Lee Krasner or Helen Frankenthaler: she did not take the road of attaching herself to a famous abstract artist. Thus, though she lived a sexually adventurous life, she did so without the kind of social benefits that such an association would have offered. She had children (two of them later in life and "out of wedlock"), maintained an activist relation to leftist politics, lived in Spanish Harlem rather than in the approved territory of the art world below Fourteenth Street, and committed herself to human subjects who often, especially early on, lived at the margins of established social hierarchies—women, the poor, poets, artists, the elderly, people of color.

Neel's reputation and career grew alongside the development of the feminist art movement, when many young women artists and critics became aware of her work and when interest in representation—fueled by its ability to illustrate gender theories and promote the political message of women's liberation—overcame the marginalization of realist painting that had plagued realist painters during the abstract-expressionist period. Neel herself said that she didn't mind the abstract expressionists: "I'm not against abstraction. . . . What I can't stand is that the abstractionists pushed all the other pushcarts off the street."[19] She elaborates, "All my favorite painters are abstractionists: Morris Louis and Clyfford Still.

I don't do realism. I do a combination of realism and expressionism. It's never just realism. I hate the New Realism. I hate equating a person and a room and a chair. Compositionally, a room, a chair, a table, and a person are all the same for me, but a person is human and psychological."[20]

There is no doubt that Neel's work offers a rich and original field of representations of women: she unsentimentally avoids clichés of standard prettiness or beauty, is a keen psychological detective, and is a brilliant, even sometimes a cruel, caricaturist. She brings all these qualities to her representations of men, and she is one of the few white artists in the history of Western art who has painted with equal sympathy and acuity men, women, and children of color. Neel's work offered images of people as they had rarely if ever been seen before in high art—hugely pregnant naked young women; sophisticated, wily, middle-aged New York art world figures; ambitious young male artists; a Fuller Brush salesman who was a Holocaust survivor; black and Puerto Rican children from the barrio; naked male intellectuals; Communist poets; old women. Her treatment of female subjects stands in contradistinction to the more recent type of female representation by artists from Sherman to Yuskavage, whose appropriational techniques bind them to more standard (male-oriented)—however dystopic—representations of women based on pornography, celebrity culture, and commercial standards of beauty.

However if Alice Neel's paintings are distinguished by her psychological insights, at the same time these insights are interesting as artworks because she draws incredibly well, and uses paint in an inventive and immensely informed and skilled manner—a muscular manner, I might even say, using the kind of gender-coded word usually reserved as praise for male artists. There is inventiveness, a sense of conscious commitment in each paint stroke and an ability to use any type of mark necessary for each individual work.

Neel is as great a painter of abstract expressionist marks as Willem de Kooning or Chaim Soutine, and I tend to look for those marks in her work, as much as I may read the expression and character of the subject. When viewing the paintings in person, I look at painterly details, the weave of the canvas, the importance of what is drawn, what is painted, what is left out, what is sketched, what is impasto. My attention is perhaps not so much formalist, to echo Lippard, as it is cathected to Neel's expressive deployment of painting marks and signs, which are inserted not only as structuring agents of representation but also as references to the history of painting's indexical vocabulary. My perception of her work is that of a painter: each brushstroke engages me in a conversation with the specific painting and with the history of painting. Thus, when looking at a painting like *The Spanish Family* (1943), a portrait of a young Puerto Rican mother and her three small children sitting in front of a wrought-iron fence, I am drawn to the individual brushstrokes that make up part of the baby's diaper, at the top giving a sense of the volume of material of the cloth diaper but giving way to drawing evocative of labial folds, and to the way in which the baby's hands are quickly sketched rather than rendered, creating a sense of the infant in motion right at the center of the painting.[21] And, in looking at what at first seems like a fairly conventional portrait, *Mimi* (1955), my eye is diverted from the strong features of the woman model to the painterly events that frame her, including the painterly strokes of grey that press upon her waist, or, at the upper left, the drift of grey from the pages of one book over the black outline of the cover of the book on top of it. That small painterly event is in no way in the service of any representational program; it is there for the conversation with painting only.

My perception of Neel as a great abstract painter first crystallized in my viewing of an exhibition of her work at the Robert Miller Gallery some years ago when I became extremely aware of how expressively and richly painted the background and details of clothes were in some portraits of children from Spanish Harlem, paintings such as *Two Girls, Spanish Harlem* (earlier titled *Two Black Girls*) (1959). The expression on the girls' faces, one of shyness and tremendous curiosity about this white lady who is painting them, is certainly the principal subject matter of the work as a representational painting, but what makes it interesting as a painting is what is in surplus to that representational content: the completely abstract, painterly strokes of pink and gray that swirl around the two girls, containing them within the rectangle and also separating them from each other, and the separate paintings within the painting of the skirts of each little girl. One could imaginatively construct a sociological analysis that would posit these expressive marks as representative, say, of the turmoil of the subjects' urban environment, but it seems more likely that these are independent painterly responses to the act of the painting and the composition, which also emerge from Neel's awareness of expressionist painting tropes.

Neel was noted for her informative, rather gossipy, and highly entertaining commentaries on the people who posed for her. Many of these

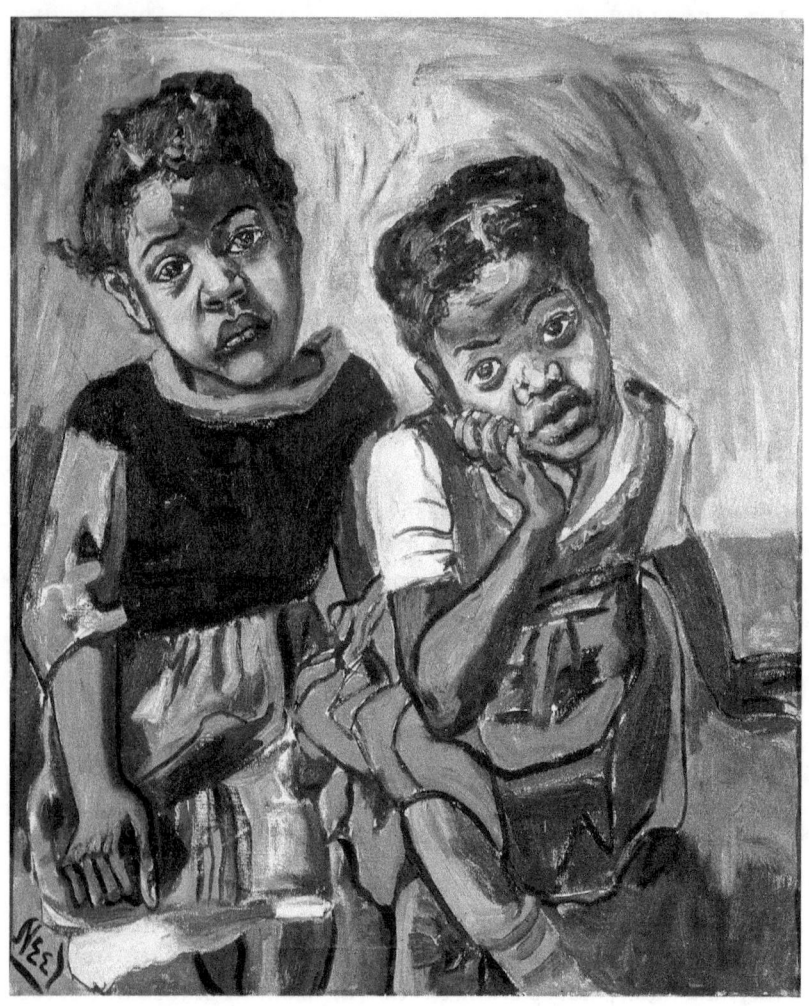

Alice Neel, *Two Girls, Spanish Harlem*, ca. 1959. Oil on canvas.
30 × 25 inches. Private Collection. © by Estate of Alice Neel.

were collected in *Alice Neel*, Patricia Hills's book from 1983, in which many of these narratives first appeared in print. They were important ways of talking about artworks at a time when a formal, non-narrative approach was privileged. Neel had lived an amazing life, several lives, really, and was clearly a brilliant and witty woman. Her rich narratives, filled with pungent asides, astute psychological observations, and personal revelations, in themselves constituted a feminist act in the face of the repression of the personal by much art criticism and art history in the modernist era. The fact that such an anecdotal approach makes an artist seem less significant needs to be critiqued, and, indeed, some feminist criticism has pointed to the discriminatory nature of the opprobrium directed at a gossipy biographical narrative, unless of course it is gossip about an artist such as de Kooning, at which point it becomes myth. Griselda Pollock amusingly notes that she was struck "when researching painting in the 1950s by the wealth of gossip about the artists, their dealers, their marriages and friends. So immense is the wealth of anecdotal detail— interviews, oral history and plain old-fashioned gossip—that I felt I would sink under the unmanageable weight of all the words that rarely touched on the question of the structure, necessity or affect of painting except in lyrical celebrations of the formal innovations that served to celebrate the greatness of the always male artists."[22] There are two types of myth in art: the wild man's stories, which coexist with and enhance his myth as a great artist, and the wild woman's story, which is likely to create a lot of appeal but without necessarily enhancing the perceived aesthetic value of the work. If lurid biographical details are belabored in the many studies of artists such as Pollock or de Kooning, the personal is always balanced by more formalist analysis and much more aggressive art historical contextualization of the artist.

In what might have been a deliberate effort to confront this double standard head-on, Neel was a primary source of the biographical and anecdotal approach to her work, one which has continued to dominate the critical and historical perception of her art, focusing on the character and circumstances of her subjects and of her engagement with them. One might also intuit that this is a familiar mechanism for an artist working from a marginal position, to collapse into biography and the personal in an effort to engage the sympathy of the viewer or the reader. Certainly, this approach is also a function of Neel's way of seeing the world, with a lively awareness of personality and a sharply observant understanding of

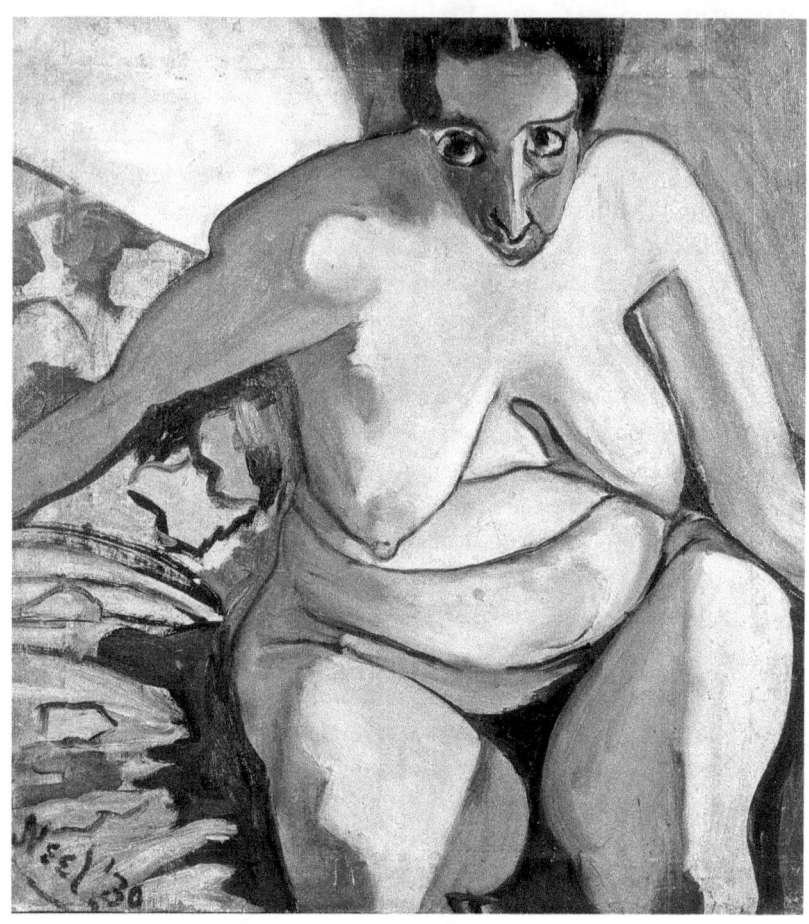

Alice Neel, *Portrait of Ethel Ashton*, 1930. Oil on canvas.
24 × 22 inches. Tate, London. © by Estate of Alice Neel.

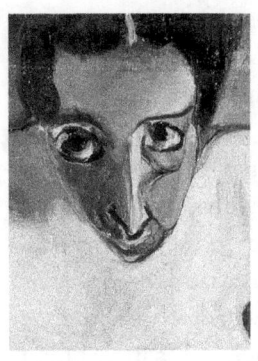
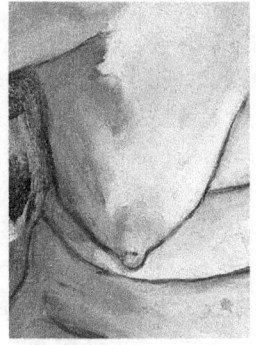
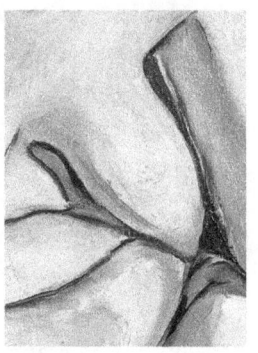

Alice Neel, *Portrait of Ethel Ashton*, details.

the foibles and failings of the human beings she encountered. Neel spoke about her portrait of Ethel Ashton from 1930 — in which the model, a fellow painter, is depicted naked, with big belly and drooping breasts, and a small mousy shadowed face looking up abjectly at the viewer — with the chatty tone with which she typically presented her work: "Don't you like her left leg on the right, that straight line? You see, it's very uncompromising. I can assure you, there was no one in the country doing nudes like this. Also it's great for Women's Lib, because she's almost apologizing for living. And look at all that furniture she has to carry all the time."[23]

Neel would not have felt it necessary to point out certain formal elements of the painting — the way that she replicated the drooping breast shape three times in the work, so that the dark face is only a smaller version of the woman's breasts; the figure sitting in a pool of dark brown that may represent a piece of cloth on the patterned bed, or just the shadow of the indentation created by the heavy body; how her brushstrokes vary so that the face is sketched in quickly with black outlines around key elements such as the nipple-like end of the nose, while the breasts are painted with thicker, wetter pigment. All these aspects add to the pathos, the humor, but also to the abstract, plastic qualities of the work. In fact although I am sure Neel was absolutely aware of all of her skills as a painter and understood them completely, she did not think it was necessary to spell them out. Perhaps it would seem too time consuming and private or esoteric to speak of each brushstroke. They were something she could take for granted in the process of working; it was just something she could do, single out the telling form or sketch in a ground with painterly élan. Perhaps many viewers, tending to overprivilege subject matter as the expense

SOME NOTES ON WOMEN AND ABSTRACTION

of form, also take the visual, painterly inventiveness for granted, engaged and distracted as one can be by the merely literal reading of representational art—where what it is a picture *of* can overwhelm one's ability to see that it is painting first, and a record second.

A second experience that shaped my perception of Neel as a great abstract painter was a conversation I had with the realist painter Raphael Soyer after a slide lecture that Alice Neel gave in Provincetown, Massachusetts, toward the end of her life. She spoke very much as she does in Hills's book, repeating many of the stories and regaling her audience with them. I really enjoyed it and was thrilled to get to hear her; it was in fact fun to hear her tell the same stories I already knew from the book. Nevertheless her self-presentation made me slightly uneasy. I feared that it encouraged a view of her that was consolidated by her very well-received February 21, 1984, appearance on the *Tonight Show* with Johnny Carson as a slightly scandalous but endearingly cute little old lady, a performance that obscured her skills as an artist and her depth as an intellectual.

Neel deserved the attention and at this point in life was entitled to have an audience in the palm of her hands. Since, as I have suggested, there was a revolutionary power to the kind of approach that Neel brought to her presentation of self, my concern is not to eliminate one kind of self-presentation of the woman artist—the biographical, the anecdotal, the humorous, naughty, or outrageous. But what might it have meant for how women artists might be perceived, or how young women artists might imagine themselves, if Neel had also revealed a bit of her more serious aesthetic views, if not on Johnny Carson's show, then in her slide lecture? If the intellectual were allowed in along with the personal, it would build another idea of what a woman artist could be. This would particularly serve young artists at a time when celebrity and thus biography are paramount, while the higher levels of criticism and art history remain concerned with more conceptual issues. Soyer, who had known Neel for many years, and admired her work, must have experienced the same concern because he said to me, "You know she is very intelligent, very well read, a real intellectual," in other words, more so than you might think from the lecture. Neel's reputation is both built upon but perhaps also limited by her own emphasis on her human relationships to her sitters/subjects and the anecdotal approach she brought to the construction of her public identity as an artist. In a late filmed interview she makes it clear that she understood the terms of the stressed duality between autobiography and aesthetic:

"Art for me was more than a profession, it was an obsession and also, long before they talked about being autobiographical, I was, and yet not completely, because there's aesthetics in my work also, it's not *just* auto-biographical."[24]

So in some way I wish to rescue her from her own self-presentation, even though I love the stories and believe they emerge from the impor-tance, perhaps the primacy to her, of her engagement with her sitters as a social contract, an intersubjectivity.

A third experience that makes me interested in drawing attention to the zones of abstraction in Neel's painting goes back to Miriam Schapiro's reference, made in an art history class lecture in the Feminist Art Program at CalArts in the early 1970s, to the theory of the "weak fourth quarter." I'm not sure if she had thought this up herself; it may have been suggested to her by a feminist art historian in those early years of the movement when people were struggling to develop a new field of art history. The theory was that even in excellent works by well-known women artists, one quarter of an otherwise successful, strongly structured composition would inevitably loose compositional integrity, as an unconscious expression of women artists' struggle with gendered visual languages and their unequal access to social agency. For some reason I recall a painting of Berthe Morisot's being used as an example of this theory.

Needless to say this theory was easily disproved, in both directions of the argument: many male artists' paintings are troubled by inert fourth quarters and many women artists, from all time periods, have painted fully animated compositions. What interested me at that time was that this obviously flawed theory nevertheless represented an effort to find a metaphor for the obstacles to full subjectivity experienced by women within the formal visual language of artworks by women. As a young artist, I was interested in developing for myself how a painting could express in its own language the experience of femaleness. Now, I have become particularly interested in the backgrounds in Neel's portraits in which she was able to mobilize the fourth quarter where earlier women artists' confidence on the field of painting *may* have faltered.

A major trope of portrait painting has been the barely differentiated brown soup that lurks behind the foregrounded subject in many old master paintings darkened by time. Neel's treatment of the background goes through a number of phases that trace a movement from realism toward abstraction.

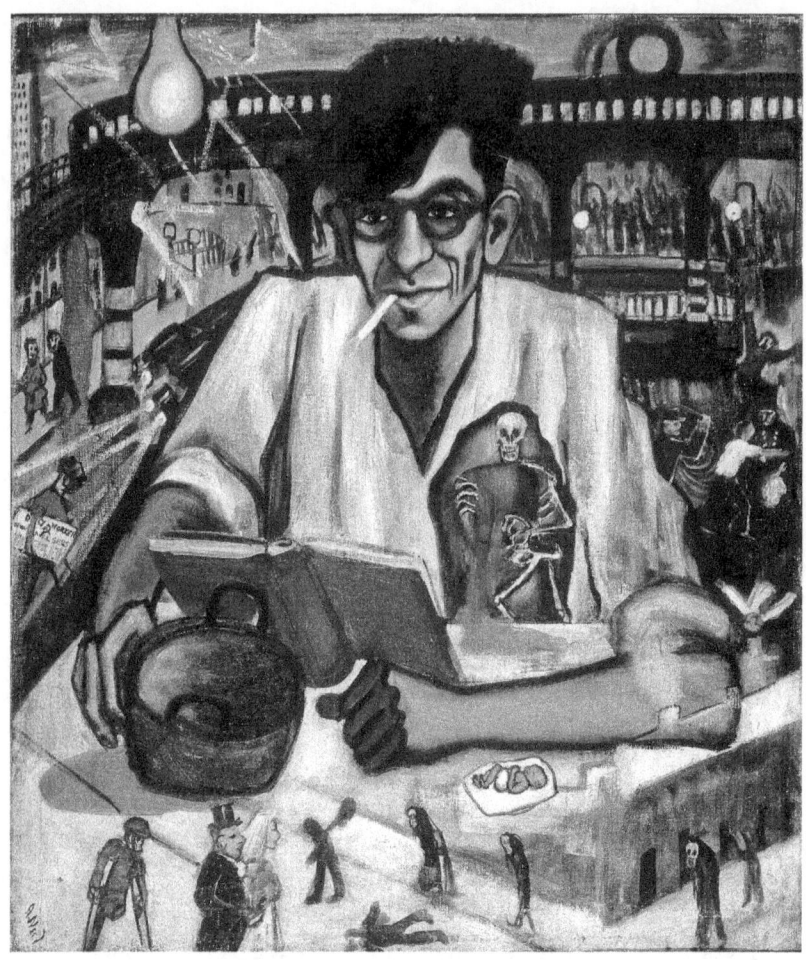

Alice Neel, *Kenneth Fearing*, 1935. Oil on canvas. 30 × 26 inches.
The Museum of Modern Art, New York. © by Estate of Alice Neel.

In her paintings from the 1920s and 1930s Neel generally engages in an imaginative use of peripheral space for additional psychological emphasis and for informative narrative. In a work such as *Kenneth Fearing* (1935), her portrait of the American poet, the background includes a kind of alternate, symbolically biographical representation of the subject, situated in the urban setting of his poetry, with various symbolic references to his work and his personal life surrounding him like a Lilliputian supporting cast.

> In 1935, when I finished his portrait, he said: "Take that Fauntleroy out of my heart," meaning the skeleton. But that was to show that even though he wrote such deadpan verse, he really sympathized with humanity, that his heart bled for the grief of the world. You see, there in the painting is the material of his poetry. This is the Sixth Avenue El that he lived near, and that's the light bulb because he always lived at night. And the figures in the street are characters from his poems. You see the police knocking people down, and a man lies shot on the sidewalk, and one chap is selling *The Daily Worker*. The baby is there because Kenneth's wife just had a baby boy in the hospital. Meyer Schapiro said about this: Ah the empty pot of the Depression.[25]

In this illustrative use of the background, Neel benefited from the permission created by surrealism and the kind of multiple spaces that surrealism adapted from early Italian Renaissance and Flemish painting to suggest more than one narrative space, to include biographical information in the side detail, to suggest internal spaces, and in general to propose more than one reality on one canvas.

In a second phase, in the 1940s and 1950s, her experiences with this unconventional use of the side space of traditional portraiture opened the way for her to reach into the vocabulary of abstract expressionism, placing thick, violently embodied strokes of paint to the side of and to some extent independent of the figure and the conventions of portrait painting. If the style and quality of these marks are similar to marks by expressionist artists such as de Kooning or Soutine (an artist whose reputation was restored by the abstract expressionists' interest in his work as a progenitor of their own),[26] Neel activates the relationship between figure and ground in a manner consistent with the goals of artists such as Barnett Newman and critics such as Clement Greenberg, who emphasized the essential flatness of panel painting. Neel, however, does so within a representational

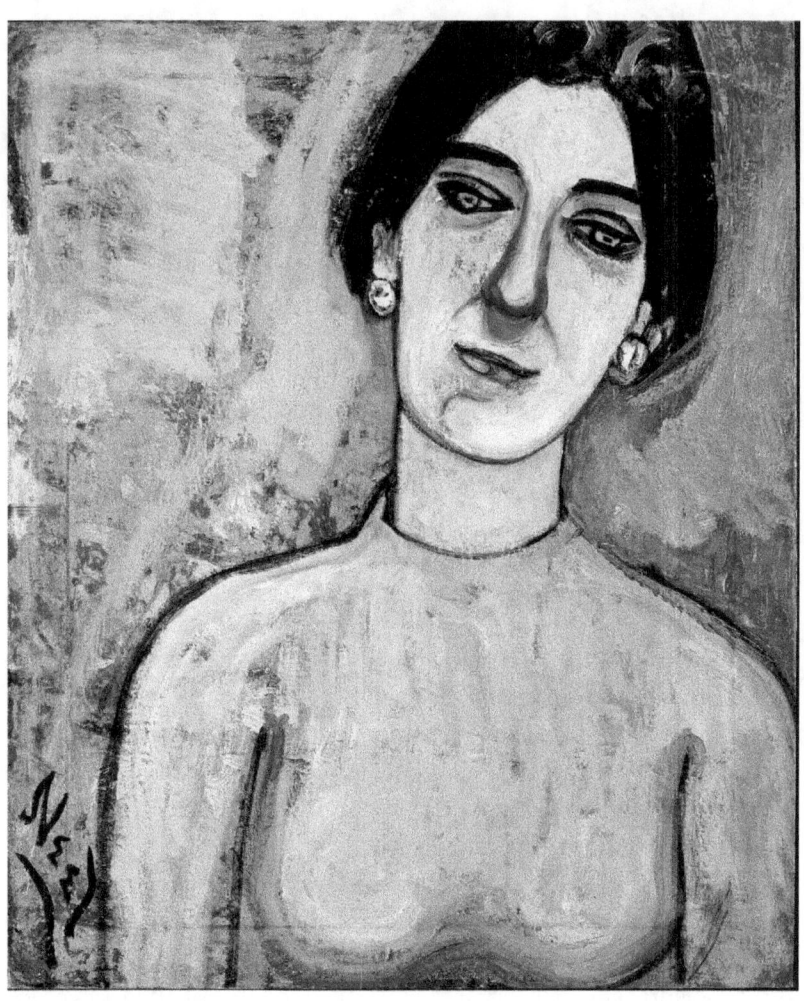

Alice Neel, *Dore Ashton*, 1952. Oil on canvas. 24 × 20 inches.
Collection of the Estate of Alice Neel. © by Estate of Alice Neel.

frame that includes the rendering or referencing of three-dimensional space.[27]

The background in Neel's portrait of *Dore Ashton* from 1952 combines both these trends in an almost didactic manner. Bold, intensely brushed areas of orange, red, and purple crowd the uncharacteristically flat portrait, so that the figure has the sculptural boldness of a Picasso from the same period. But these abstract areas of color may be exactly as narrative and literal as the background images in *Kenneth Fearing*. Ashton was one of the foremost critics of the abstract-expressionist period, married to an abstract artist, Adja Yunkers, and committed to writing about artists such as Philip Guston and Jack Tworkov. It would seem likely that the orange and red marks are representations of a specific painting behind the figure, or a remembered image of such a painting. Certainly this is one work where Neel can overtly, even self-consciously, play with the painterly abstraction that is in fact active in all her paintings.

The excitement of an Alice Neel painting is consistently located as much in the inventiveness and the sense of conscious commitment in each paint stroke and area as it is in the figurative subject. Not only is Neel's portrait of *Robert Smithson* (1962) redolent of his intensity and intelligence, but many a painter could make an entire career from the richness of abstract painting she deploys in the small area of his cheek alone. "He had acne, which for me was *just an interesting surface*, but he was very angry when he saw the painting and made me take some of the blood off his cheek. Another day I went to see him in his studio where he was making papier-mâché Christs all covered with blood. 'Why Robert,' I said, 'you wouldn't let me have even a little blood and look how much blood the Christs have.'"[28] I emphasize the words "just an interesting surface" because they point to the way that Neel abstracted from the real, or, rather, was attracted to the abstract within the real. (At the same time, she understood representational painting as a transubstantiation of the real, highlighted here by the Catholic imagery, which she interposes as one motivation of her focus on embodied painting marks.) Perhaps this is the paradoxical effect of realism and physical presence: because Neel worked from the model, occasionally creating a second painting more liberated from verisimilitude than the first, she could elaborate on pure painting elements. She sometimes worked from memory, which also enhanced her access to abstraction or the life of individual painterly marks.

In her later years her use of the background of the portrait as a space

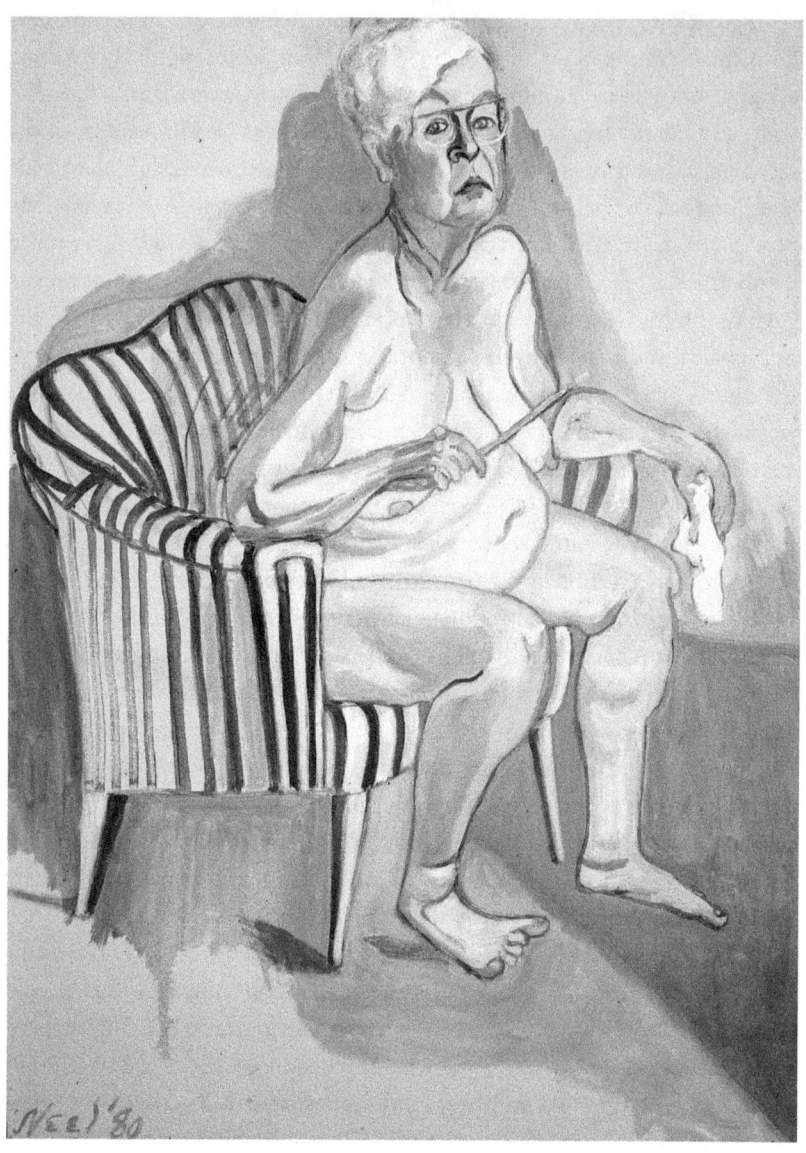

Alice Neel. *Self-Portrait*, 1980. Oil on canvas. 54 × 40 inches.
The National Portrait Gallery, Smithsonian Institution, Washington, D.C.
© by Estate of Alice Neel.

filled with pure painting marks shifts to a confidence with emptiness and telegraphed indications of a site for the figure, with just enough thin color where once was the brown soup of academic portraiture, and where Neel in earlier work might have had symbolic narrative or expressive strokes. In many cases, the ground is white, simply primed canvas and the boldly outlined but barely rendered figure is situated through economically de- ployed areas of color surrounding it at key points. In her portrait of Andy Warhol from 1970, Warhol is posed naked to the waist, revealing the massive scar left by Valerie Solanas's attack. His eyes are closed. The fragility of his body is emphasized by his isolation on a nearly blank canvas. He sits on the sketched outline of a divan that floats into the canvas from the left, and only small areas of blue asymmetrically placed behind his back and to the side of his head and intimations of brown shadow at his feet stabilize his existential quandary.[29] In a portrait of the museum curator Tom Freudenheim, where only the face is at all rendered, the ground is white, with patches of ochre and blue directly behind the upper torso of the figure. Here again, as in the portrait of Dore Ashton, the ground might be an abstract painting on the wall. If so, it is not an intensely painterly one, but, rather, an example of flat, postpainterly abstraction, which would have given Neel the opportunity to sample an artist like Robert Motherwell, perhaps.

Of the paintings from this period, one of the most extraordinary is her *Self-Portrait* from 1980. My memory of Neel's appearance on the *Tonight Show* includes her gleefully showing a picture of this painting and saying something like "and look at those legs, don't they just look like pieces of furniture," eerily reprising her comments on her early portrait of Ethel Ashton. Neel used humor to engage the audience in a painting that achieves something important in the history of representation by foregrounding the body of the woman artist in a stage of life that normally would not be figured in representational art, because it is beyond its use value to a male homosocially structured economy. If the paradigmatic body of the modernist painter is the indexical performing body of Jackson Pollock, whose work leaves its seminal mark and also opens the field of art to the real space beyond the confines of the canvas, then, in that sense, Neel's self-portrait remains a relatively conventional representational portrait: the painter depicted painting, the subject sitting on a chair in a room, in a legible space. Nevertheless, her subject is revolutionary, the old woman's body presented without a trace of abjectness.

In the painting, she sits in the blue striped chair that figures in many of her paintings, against dynamically oriented indications of blue, ochre, and green ground on otherwise white primed canvas. In her left hand she holds a white paint rag that hovers at the edge of the meeting between a few strokes of blue and the white upper right of the canvas, as if she has wiped away the background. The diagonal line created by the meeting of an area of ochre (floor) and an area of green (rug) can be traced directly back to her crotch, suggesting through its formal energy the reserve of sexual potency of this grandmother.

In *Pictures of People: Alice Neel's American Portrait Gallery*, Pam Allara contextualizes these shifts in Neel's composition style and facture within changes in art movements: "Just as in the 1950s and 1960s she had adopted an abstract expressionist facture, so in the 1970s, her paintings became larger and brighter under the influence of pop art and new realism."[30] The spatial emptiness of her later works is also a defining characteristic of the phenomenon of "old-age style," as is evident in the late works by Cézanne, for example—looser, quicker, "unfinished" insofar as areas of blank, primed canvas show through. But these most minimal indications of painterly space are also the most mature embodiment of Neel's strengths as a purely plastic, abstract painter, as well as an astute psychologist and caricaturist. The painting is of course important in terms of what she is depicting: the naked body of the woman artist painting, the older woman's naked body as the subject of the female artist's gaze (a subject rarely seen in the foreground of art, usually relegated to the background of a picture of the beautiful young lady). But it is also important to look at this work as the culmination of the development of the painterly and formal in her work.

What is notable, again, are the "just enough" marks where once was the brown soup of the portrait background, where Neel in earlier work might have placed the enlivened symbolic, narrative, pictorial, or expressive strokes. Looking at the late self-portrait, I am struck not only by the drip at the bottom that recalls Morris Louis but also the abstraction of the diagonally oriented yellow and green floor, perhaps, in fact probably, a faithful notation of something actually visible to her but also an entire abstract painting in itself, a Mark Rothko or Kenneth Noland within a Neel.

The goal of the early feminist art and art history movement, particularly in its American version, was to recover, create, enable, and support great women artists, and the subject matter of great art throughout history is form and materiality, just as much as it is what Meyer Schapiro called the "object matter," that is to say, that which is represented.[31] Thus, to say that Alice Neel was a great abstract painter is to say that she was a great painter whose abilities with drawing and paint, and the risks she took in paint complemented and enriched the other skills she brought to her representation of women and men. Those skills were based on the risks she took in her life. That her interests in art and in the content of representation were coequal is evident in her statement, "I like it at first to be art, you know, so actually dividing up the canvas is one of the most exciting things for me, and then I like it not only to look like the person but to have their inner character as well, and then I like it to expose the zeitgeist, you see, I don't like something in the sixties to look like in the seventies."[32]

Two points in this statement are relevant to my argument: first, the primary importance of formal, here compositional, concerns, and, second, the interest in accuracy to the zeitgeist. My assertion that Alice Neel is a great abstract artist may seem a stretch, given, finally, the obvious representational and narrative importance of Neel's sharp characterizations of individual figures. Yet the zeitgeist is expressed in her work, as we have seen, as much in the period-specific shifts in her methods of painterly application and background composition as in the style of clothing or the body language of her subjects.

Since this essay may seem to the reader like "A Funny Thing Happened to Me on My Way to Writing about Women and Abstraction," I turn full circle to a Whitney Museum of American Art catalogue essay on Alice Neel from 1974 by Elke Solomon, an artist then working as a curator at the Whitney: "Critics writing about Alice Neel seem more interested in her personality than in her painting. They speak of her wit, her biting candor and her sharp intelligence, but not as manifested in her work. Yet it is precisely Neel's ability to tell something both of herself and her sitter that distinguishes her as a portraitist within the academic tradition. To a lesser extent than Gertrude Stein, though similarly, Neel's biographies are autobiographical."[33]

I say full circle because Solomon was the woman artist on the panel "Women and Abstraction" at the A.I.R. Gallery in 1997 who bemoaned the lack of attention to women abstract artists by feminist critics, art historians, and theorists.

As Solomon suggested in her essay, written at the moment when feminists were first turning to Neel's work for its contribution to the new pictography of the female gaze, Neel's painterly intelligence animates her portraits just as much as do her skills as a psychologist or a "collector of souls."[34] Her example is of particular interest at a time when many figurative painters pursue simulacral smoothness or even simulacral "painterliness," without the expressive inflection, variety, or material substance that emerge from the intersubjectivity, with both her subjects and the subject of painting, of Neel's painterly practice. A study of the background in Alice Neel's paintings suggests the continued importance of intrinsically abstract, "surplus" painterly information to the aesthetic and expressive content of representational painting.

Preposterous statements are often hard to refute, especially when they are made about the kind of postmodern artworks that always already contain within themselves a manipulative power over potential criticism. A case in point is the frequently made statement that Lisa Yuskavage paints "like Vermeer." On the face of it, the comparison between the most ineffably quiet, modest, and discrete paintings by Johannes Vermeer and the willfully vulgar, lurid, and grotesque world of Yuskavage is absurd. But because of what it may reveal about some contemporary notions of what constitutes beautiful painting—it is axiomatic in our culture that Vermeer's paintings are beautiful—it is worth giving serious consideration to the perceived resemblances between Yuskavage and Vermeer.

. . .

First, likening a contemporary artist to a recognized master from the canon of art history is an important mechanism of art historical validation, and as I have noted in my essay "Patrilineage" from 1991, traditionally legitimation is established through the father even when, as is the case with many contemporary artists, a "mother's" legacy is not only a historical possibility, but is often patently evidenced by the work itself. Again in "Patrilineage" I noted that to ensure this process of legitimation, it is only necessary to juxtapose the artist with the names of famous male artists, even if the sentence in which the names are juxtaposed establishes a negative relationship, "even if it is in a sentence that begins 'Unlike'. . . ."[1] With this in mind, I was amused by the opening paragraph of a feature on Yuskavage in *Artforum*: "Call it the mind/body problem. If I were preparing a slide comparison for class, I probably *wouldn't pair* Jasper Johns and Lisa Yuskavage. He is a notably cerebral artist who traffics in reflexive visual puns and sets up intricate perceptual conditions. She is all T&A, turning to cultural flashpoints to make her trademark fleshpots. But, just as Johns reveals erotic subject matter on closer examination, a roomful of Yuskavages reveals what you would more likely expect from Johns—meaning of a deeply hermetic sort, much of it linked to formal features."[2]

Yuskavage has been named in the company of old masters other than Vermeer, including Giovanni Bellini, Rembrandt van Rijn, Edgar Degas,

Thomas Eakins, Gustave Courbet, Giovanni Battista Tiepolo, and Correggio, as well as contemporary artists such as Chuck Close, Brice Marden, Ed Ruscha, Mel Ramos, Balthus, Jeff Koons, and John Currin. It is rare that women's names are used in the legitimization of male artists, and thus one should note that Yuskavage is often linked with John Currin in writings about Currin. In writings about Yuskavage, contemporary women artists are named, such as Catherine Howe, Sue Williams, Jenny Saville, and Cecily Brown, but usually these references are there to place the artist generationally, even, one might say, socially, rather than to give the artist the stamp of approval that Vermeer's or Johns's name on her pedigree would provide as an entrance into the canon.

Patrilineage offers financial incentives, adding monetary value to artwork that matrilineage would not. A good patrilineage makes work more collectible. Old master patrilineage increases collectability, particularly by museums. And Yuskavage's own strategic insinuation of a link with Vermeer into the discourse on her work provides her with the ultimate patrilineage: an artist whose work is considered "priceless."

Artists themselves contribute to this art historical mechanism: they set the comparisons in motion by making references in statements and interviews. Yuskavage is a principal source of the "like Vermeer" phenomenon. "'I prefer Penthouses from the '70's,' she said of her artistic sources, 'because the photographs are less explicit. The lighting is so diffuse, like a Vermeer painting.'"[3] "I'm not interested in being ghettoized as a 'woman' artist, or in being didactic. I want to take guilt, politics, and gender out of my work. Plus, I want to play in the larger arena, to associate my ideas and myself with the artists I have admired since I was very young: Degas, Vermeer, Giovanni Bellini."[4] While Yuskavage has the right to assert her intentions, authorial intent ought not be able to stave off political or psychoanalytic interpretations of the emphatically voiced content of her work, which seems to insist on guilt and gender and their politics. However, the repetition of these self-announced comparisons has functioned as a successful meme that moves the artist's strategic self-positioning from artist's statements and studio interviews to art reviews with relative speed and ease. Although the artist's desire to take politics and gender out of her work must be submitted to the test posed by the actual content of her paintings, there is no reason to doubt that Yuskavage's admiration for Degas, Vermeer, and Bellini is genuine, and although we are taught to be skeptical about artists' intentions and assertions, if Yuskavage associates herself with *Penthouse* illustrations rather than with Hannah Wilke or Alice Neel, her word must be taken seriously, particularly if the work confirms such an association. She does not give herself any kind of matrilineage; no interview records her admiration for any women artists. Their works are not part of her discourse. At the level of political discourse, this is significant, given her generation's access to feminist reconsiderations of female representation. She wants to play in the "larger arena" and she is prepared to accept that this is still a masculine domain that marginalizes feminist expression.

. . .

As one critic has written, "There remains something extremely refined about these paintings, with their Vermeer-like treatment of character, light, and sensitivity to feminine finery."[5]

Yuskavage, like Vermeer, depicts women in rooms. In works from the early nineties, Yuskavage's women are posed against colored backgrounds barely indicating architectural space: so, for example, in *The Ones That Don't Want To: Bad Baby* (1992), a pink-fleshed figure, clad only in a pink T-shirt, stands against a hot Pepto-Bismol pink background. Over the years, Yuskavage has been increasing the level of architectural information and of interior decorating in her pictorial field. In *Now You Can Dance* (1998), an indication of the meeting of floor and wall is necessary in order to heighten the horror of the subject: a woman with withered, useless legs that are splayed open; a cornered, floored naked woman, in a red painting. In Yuskavage's most recent paintings, her female subjects are located in luxuriously appointed rooms, often, as in Vermeer's paintings, near a window.[6] This window seems to provide light as an excuse, a narrative device one might say, to emphasize in as prurient a manner possible their naked breasts, ass, stomach, or buttocks. ("The light acts as a voyeur," was the eloquent comment made to me by a woman artist friend upon reading a draft of this essay).[7]

If the appointments of Vermeer's interiors are indicators of seventeenth-century Dutch middle-class comfort and wealth, Yuskavage's more recent paintings are meant to signal great wealth with the most luxurious couches and draperies that money can buy. But oddly they also indicate the way contemporary signs of great wealth are, at a certain level of the culture, barely distinguishable from mass-produced middle-class signs of comfort: the sofas at Crate and Barrel and the Pottery Barn bring a generic standard of design to the suburbs. Yuskavage's women are clothed in lingerie approximating Victoria's Secret ads, in rooms that seem like Martha Stewart's reflections on a Colette-influenced décor. The women lead a life of leisure, but their bordello furnishings are as likely purchased from a catalogue as from a luxury design store. The objects and furnishings depicted by Vermeer were relatively modest in comparison with the treasures and rarities available to the nobility and royalty of his time. Nevertheless the silvery urn in Vermeer's *Young Woman with a Water Pitcher* (ca. 1662) and the other fine things in his paintings are hand-crafted and represent a greater degree of value relative to his culture than any objects or furniture in Yuskavage's rooms have to ours.

The light in Yuskavage's paintings seems to come from a single source, indicated, in her early paintings, by a highlighting of the hair or a body part, just as Vermeer's paintings bathe the female subject in light coming from a single window, indicated by a touch of light on pearl earrings or the tip of the nose. In both Yuskavage and Vermeer there is a certain diffusion of light across the surface of the painting. Darkness and shadow are strong elements in both artists' work. But darkness and light occur differently in Vermeer and Yuskavage. In Vermeer, the depicted light source is the only light source, and the shadows are true to an interior without any other light source but the daylight filtering in from one window or door. Very simply, where light doesn't fall, there is shadow. In Yuskavage's earlier work, the light that creates the gleam on the hair may appear to come from a single source, but the overwhelming impression is that there is no light source in the picture, because there is no air in the picture, and it is air that would allow light rays to enter and move through a space. The figure, already completely artificial because of her sex-doll skin color, dot eyes, and grotesque figure, exists in an equally artificial space in which the light—not even a fluorescent light, that omnipresent flattener that bathes contemporary life—comes from within the pigment that dominates the painting, pink or peach as the case may be. Even in her recent paintings, the existence of a window does not necessarily create the impression of natural light: if a woman's flesh is painted in an intense dark-pink pigment created chemically rather than based on materials occurring in nature, her proximity to a window painted white does not give the impression of filtered light motes illuminating the pale skin of a woman's face as painted by Vermeer. Shadow, in most Yuskavage paintings, is not the soft fading of light, but a harsher, more lurid, pigmented darkness.

. . .

Yuskavage's women, artificially colored and with distorted body parts, trapped in intensely colored rooms, find their sisters in the garish atmo- sphere of artifice of Charles Baudelaire's "Women and Prostitutes," a section of his essay "The Painter of Modern Life" (1863). Yuskavage's figures are often set against lurid colors: "Against a background of hellish light, or if you prefer, an *aurora borealis*—red, orange, sulphur-yellow, pink (to express an idea of ecstasy amid frivolity), and sometimes purple (the favourite colour of canonesses, like dying embers seen through a blue curtain)—against magical backgrounds such as these, which remind one of variegated Bengal Lights, there arises the Protean image of wanton beauty."[8] And the women in Yuskavage's paintings resemble Baudelaire's "Prostitute" more than any woman in a Vermeer painting: "The creature of whom we are speaking is perhaps only incomprehensible because it has nothing to communicate. . . . She is a kind of idol, stupid perhaps, but dazzling and bewitching, who holds wills and destinies suspended on her glance. She is not, I must admit, an animal whose component parts, correctly assembled, provide a perfect example of harmony; she is not even that type of pure beauty which the sculptor can mentally evoke in the course of his sternest meditations."[9]

Part of the difficulty in accepting the comparison between Vermeer and Yuskavage resides at the level of the representation of femininity. (Before one examines subject matter or questions of painting theory as embodied in paint application itself, as I will attempt later in this essay, one should acknowledge that it is by definition impossible to separate the gestalt of an artwork from any of its particulars. Nevertheless, the examination of such components can be useful, as I hope to show.) Both painters do depict women in interiors, sometimes posed near a window. That might imply something about women and domesticity, or the entrapment of women in a domestic or interior world. Every Vermeer woman is in a chamber, often near the window but not necessarily looking out, rather using the light from the window to be seen or to see something she holds in her hand. The domestic environment is refined and modestly luxurious. Only in *The Little Street* (ca. 1658) is a woman shown working outside, but she seems to be a servant, whereas the woman of the house sits sewing just inside the threshold of the street door. The outer world of adventure and enterprise only enters a Vermeer painting indirectly, allegorically, for example in the map that dominates *The Art of Painting* (ca. 1665–1666).

The women in Yuskavage's work are often referred to as "bimbos," even (maybe especially) by writers who support her work: "Yuskavage is a central figure in the we-love-bimbos school of painting;" "Her ghostly, grotesque bimbos seem to rise out of, and recede back into pastel fogs;" "Lisa Yuskavage earned her first fame with paintings of bimbos stepping out of velvety fogs."[10] This appellation is based on their pneumatic (dis)proportions and tiny sex-doll dot eyes. Admittedly, Vermeer's models, though lovely, don't seem all that smart either. They usually do not look out at the viewer with sparkling intelligence and self-awareness. The subject in *Girl with the Red Hat* (ca. 1665–1666), if you look at her with a Yuskavage bimbo in mind, also has little dot eyes, and the gleam around her half-open mouth makes her seem just on the verge of drooling. Only in *Woman Holding a Balance* (ca. 1664) is the subject engaged in an activity that would seem to require skill, as she holds a jeweler's balance in perfect equilibrium. So perhaps the young woman in Yuskavage's *Honeymoon* (1998) really is a sister to Vermeer's *Woman in Blue Reading a Letter* (ca. 1662–1663) or *Young Woman with a Water Pitcher* (ca. 1662–1665). She looks wistfully out a window at a romantic landscape of mountain peaks from a dark purple room in which a pink flower would seem to stand for her innocence and youth. She seems to be all alone at a quiet moment, at dawn perhaps. Her long flowing hair veils her face in much the same way that bonnets mask the faces of Vermeer's young models. One erect dark red nipple the size and shape of her nose pokes its way into the dead center of the painting, ripping through the fabric of pudor and modesty that are the hallmark of Vermeer's painting.

Vermeer's models do seem quite vulnerable to masculine interference: whether as exemplified overtly in *The Procuress* (1656) by the man's hand grabbing the woman's breast through her yellow bodice—significantly this detail of the painting is emphasized in a rather rare use of impasto—or by the sense in paintings such as *The Glass of Wine* (ca. 1661–1662) that the woman is being importuned in some way by the man who is with her. In this painting the woman's face is barely visible, as if she shrinks from the gaze of both her male companion and the artist himself. Yet most of Vermeer's models do seem to give their trust to the painter: they turn toward him, like the girl in the red hat with her mouth slightly open or the young girl in the blue dress smiling slightly as she looks over her shoulder, behind us. Even the figure in *A Maid Asleep* (ca. 1656–1657), who has been interpreted as being inebriated, is represented without the slightest sign of violence. She is as lovely as any sleeping beauty, perhaps only a bit more rosy-cheeked than normal, but nothing like the slatternly figures in works by other northern baroque artists, and absolutely nothing like any of the women ever painted by Yuskavage. Their imprisonment in the home is more brutal: they have no legs, they have huge bodies but tiny feet, they are half-naked, and no one except the viewer visits them. Even the women living in the Martha Stewart environments of the artist's newer work have troll-like features and grotesquely drawn and amplified bodies. Trapped in their world of hyperfemininity and waiting for customers in their fancy lingerie,[11] they are more passive than the hot mamas created by R. Crumb, and they owe a greater resemblance to whores in a Henri de Toulouse-Lautrec or a Jules Pascin painting than to anything in any Vermeer.

124 | 125

There is little political satire or grotesquerie in Vermeer, at least to our contemporary eye, even though the language of carnival was available to him, but there is only grotesquerie in Yuskavage. Indeed the claim for a Vermeer patrilineage undercuts the actual strength of her work. Her work is important even if unpleasantly jarring, because of the sheer rage it expresses at how the female body has been produced by and for the male gaze throughout the history of representation, in both high and low art and other media. A comparison of Yuskavage's depictions of women to those of her contemporary, John Currin, is instructive. Yusakavage's women, in her early works, are featureless, pink inflated sex-dolls, and, in her later work, bulbous half-naked figures waiting indoors for something to happen, trapped in and hypnotized by their own bodies. Currin's women are even more perfectly "pneumatic." As polished, buffed, rosy, and pumped with soma as any young woman in *Brave New World*, they present a cheerful, silly front: after all, as a heterosexual male, Currin gets to enjoy the favors of these bouncy, smiling young naked ladies, whereas Yuskavage has to deal with her own body's inadequacy in relation to the *Playboy* or *Penthouse* ideal. As much as any other, she is a victim of the culture's obsessive representation of the female body as a zone of fear and pleasure and of a regime of domination by impossible ideals of beauty and sexual appeal. It is her insistence on fixing our focus on the most spectacular and abased image of femininity that gives her work its perverse interest and is the reason that it cannot be ignored. The anger and self-hatred surrounding this zone of representation is precisely what links Yuskavage to recent generations of women artists working with these tropes of representation. If Pieter Brueghel, Frans Hals, Otto Dix, Egon Schiele, and James Ensor, as well as Balthus, Hans Bellmer, Fernando Botero, and the artists at *Mad* magazine seem more appropriate patrilineal antecedents than Vermeer or Giovanni Bellini, so too do Jo Spence, Hannah Wilke, Carolee Schneemann, Paula Rego, and Cindy Sherman. But claiming these artists as models would risk placing Yuskavage again closer to the margins than to the center of the arena she desires.

Returning to the mechanism of patrilineage, one can tease another line of succession for Vermeer. First, Yuskavage is not the only contemporary artist who, through word or deed, has directly invited comparison of her work to that of Vermeer. For example, the general sense of quiet, of exquisite cleanliness and pearlescent light, in Uta Barth's out of focus photographs of interiors marked by barely discernible architectural and domestic details, makes it easy to see Barth as part of the Vermeer aesthetic family line. Her works have also been likened to Vermeer,[12] and the artist herself has noted her work's affinities with Vermeer:

> When I hung up the first couple of prints I had made from the interior series in my studio, *Ground #30* (1994) seemed oddly familiar to me. After days of wondering about that, I finally realized that the piece reminded me of a particular Vermeer painting. The only artwork in my home as a child was a pair of small Vermeer reproductions, which now hang in my office at the University [University of California, Riverside]. I brought them to my studio and found that the layout and composition of the space and the direction and quality of the light in one of these paintings was absolutely identical to the photograph I had just made. I think that these images, which I have never grown tired of, have sort of been burned into my mind and I was excited to have aspects of them emerge in my work. It all made a perfect kind of sense; portraiture, light and perception, as well as the discussion of Vermeer's work in relationship to photography, all seemed to overlap in an interesting way.[13]

Barth's comments seem organic to an aesthetic process in which the work's resemblance to Vermeer comes before the patrilineal claim for it. The artist then recognizes this familiar/familial something in her work, makes the connection back to a significant early aesthetic experience, and then acts upon it. A later work from the same series, *Ground #41* (1994), is a photograph of two framed reproductions of Vermeer paintings (*Woman Sewing* and *Woman with a Pitcher*) on a green wall. Because this photograph, like others in this series, is blurred, the reference is relatively understated.

Occasionally the patrilineal argument is deployed for a reverse effect: artists from the past have their work restored to critical attention by being associated with the work of successful contemporary artists. This provides mutual benefit: the historical artist's work gets a fresh lease on critical attention and a boost in market value, while the contemporary artist's reputation is burnished by his or her association with an established member of the canon. So, for example, the later, figurative works by Francis Picabia, for a long time discredited and ignored by art historians in favor of his works that fit comfortably into the formation of the modernist canon, were resurrected in the 1980s because of their use value in giving David Salle's work a canonical underpinning.

However, in the case of Vermeer, if one begins the examination of lineage with the canonical artist, it is not very likely that one would select Yuskavage as the proper contemporary descendant. To examine another contemporary painting with possible patrilineal associations with Vermeer, we might compare Vermeer's *Study of a Young Woman* and Gerhard Richter's *Betty*. These paintings, both portraits of the artists' daughters, are temporal and formal bookends, enclosing between their glances the history of painting. Vermeer's gently smiling young girl in a blue shawl is seated so that her body turns away from us, but she looks back over her shoulder at us from the dark brown background of the history of portrait painting; Betty leans toward the picture plane like a woman leaning on a windowsill about to speak to us, but her attention has been caught by something behind her and she has turned away from the flat ground of the color photograph which is the source of the painting, to look back at that primal ground of painting.[14] The glance of Vermeer's young girl veers slightly over our shoulder, back at the past of the viewer, while Betty looks away from us back at the past. Richter's eerily soft painting style, here in luminescent color, enriched by the softly rendered rich red and white pattern on Betty's sweater, is perhaps the closest equivalent to the softly textured, utterly limpid, and still qualities for which Vermeer is revered.[15]

However, if one reverses the examination of patrilineage by starting with Vermeer, and looks in particular for contemporary artists whose use

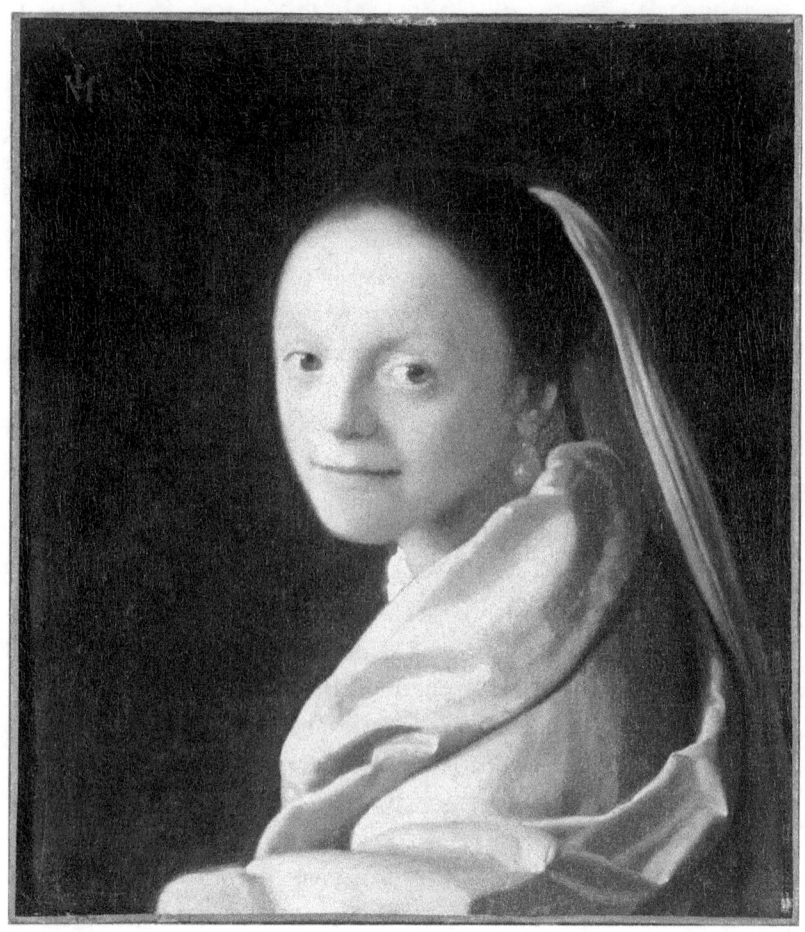

Johannes Vermeer, *Study of a Young Woman*, ca. 1665–67. Oil on canvas. 17½ × 15¾ inches. The Metropolitan Museum of Art, Gift of Mr. and Mrs. Charles Wrightsman, in memory of Theodore Rousseau Jr., 1979 (1979.396.1). Image © by The Metropolitan Museum of Art.

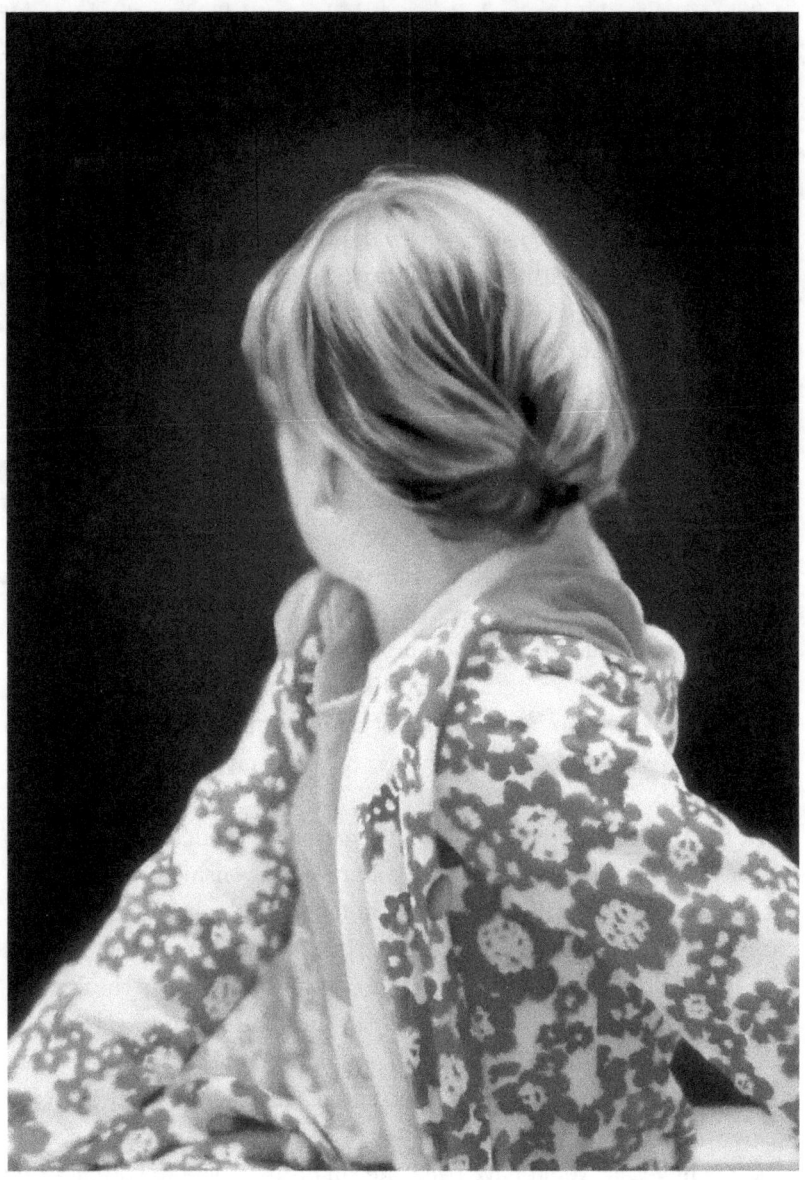

Gerhard Richter, *Betty*, 1988. Oil on canvas, 40¼ × 28½ inches.
© by The Saint Louis Art Museum.

of light might echo his work, one would be more likely to find oneself outside of the discipline and ground of painting entirely, looking at the works of contemporary artists who work with effects of light in actual space rather than with representions of it. The works of James Turrell and Robert Irwin, for example Irwin's *Part I: Times 18 Cubed* and *Part II: Homage to the Square Cubed*, a series of mesh scrim walled rooms installed at the DIA Foundation from 1998 to 1999,[16] would be much more logical contemporary pairings for Vermeer. The "diffuse lighting" Yuskavage mentions is fully realized in these contemporary installation works. Granted these are not figurative paintings, but the fact that they are not paintings, that they are actual spaces in which light is the agent and the human figure is not a representation but an active participant, makes the works fully contemporary. A viewer walking through Irwin's translucent, walled rooms experiences the light in her body, and is the viewer of the other viewers who appear through the filtered light of the scrim walls. They become figures in "Vermeer vivants." The painting is made real. The qualities that once were most effectively presented through the illusionism of painting are now alive in such installation artworks. Even if Yuskavage were indeed presenting women in the "beautiful light" characteristic of Vermeer, it would still be within the confines of an illusionistic painting, while in the development of contemporary art, the light rays have traveled back into the real.

At the core of the statement "like Vermeer" is a claim for Yuskavage as a painter of beautiful paintings with a sincere relationship to the material act of painting itself. It is frequently noted that it is hard to figure out exactly how Vermeer applied his paint. Some have surmised that he used his fingers, which, to the modern reader/viewer summons up the conventionalized tracings of children's finger-painting. In fact, it is hard to distinguish individual brush strokes (or finger marks) in a Vermeer even when you know that a brush must have created a particular line, yet clearly each element of the painting is painted with particularized care. If Vermeer used his finger, it would have been the tip of his pinkie to soften a tiny edge. One can retrace the reworking of areas of wet into wet paint that one can surmise was the consistency of rich butter: it has dried to a velvety surface that thankfully has not been conserved or restored with any kind of glossy varnish: although fur itself is not depicted through the use of any visible hair-thin paint strokes, the overall paintings give the impression of fur seen in moonlight.

Although there seems to be general cultural agreement that Vermeer's paintings are very beautiful, indeed that they epitomize beauty in painting, they are in fact very hard to really *see* in a modern exhibition environment. Recent major exhibitions of his work present the informed viewer, in particular the painter/viewer, with a nearly impossible task of perception and discernment as crowds drawn to the work by media commodification of Vermeer's beauty huddle around the works coded to their audio guide, creating a physical barrier of space, color, commotion, and noise that effectively blocks out whatever might be perceivable behind the protective layers of glass. Works that one could perhaps fully grasp if experienced in the kind of quiet chamber they depict shrink from our perception and understanding in the carnival atmosphere of the contemporary blockbuster art exhibition and the enormous spaces of contemporary museums—environments that Yuskavage's garish colors and controversial sexual representations are tailor-made to conquer. The *ne plus ultra* of Yuskavage's work is that, love it or hate it, you can't miss it. The core of Vermeer's work is that you have to work to not miss it.

At the very least, one can say that Vermeer's pieces are painted by an individual hand in the spirit of sensitized responsiveness to minute variations in the atmosphere, whereas Yuskavage's paint application has a certain mechanistic uniformity, as if one had programmed a computer to paint, for example, with a no. 22 sable bright and so many ounces of medium per stroke mass. However, if you programmed a computer with an analysis of Vermeer's painting style, including surface information plus some suitably codified parameters of the overall impression recognized as "like Vermeer," would a Yuskavage would be the product? And, even if one could successfully program the painting function "Vermeer" into a computer, at best the product would be a simulant. Yet any accusation of simulated painterliness flies in the face of one of the principal claims made for Yuskavage's work, namely that it is sincere, it is real, and furthermore, it is beautiful painting. The insistence that it must be seen as *real* painting clues you in to our actual location as we consider how Yuskavage is "like Vermeer," and that is the realm of the simulacrum as described by Jean Baudrillard:

> To dissimulate is to feign not to have what one has. To simulate is to feign to have what one hasn't. One implies a presence, the other an absence. But the matter is more complicated, since to simulate is not

simply to feign. . . . Thus, feigning or dissimulating leaves the reality principle intact: the difference between "true" and "false," between "real" and "imaginary."[17]

Whereas representation tries to absorb simulation by interpreting it as false representation, simulation envelops the whole edifice of representation as itself a simulacrum.

These would be the successive phases of the image:
— it is the reflection of a basic reality
— it masks and perverts a basic reality
— it masks the *absence* of a basic reality
— it bears no relation to any reality whatever: it is its own pure simulacrum.[18]

Yuskavage is to Vermeer, in terms of aesthetics, methodology, and belief structure, as simulation is to reality, and that is precisely why it is so difficult to refute the assertion of resemblance: Lisa Yuskavage can be "like Vermeer" only when Vermeer, as a sign structure understood at the level of ideology, no longer exists. "When the real is no longer what it used to be, nostalgia assumes its full meaning."[19] Lloyd Bentsen could turn to Senator Dan Quayle in the 1988 vice-presidential debate and say, "Senator, I knew Jack Kennedy, and Senator, you're no Jack Kennedy," because in fact he *did* know Jack Kennedy well enough to call him Jack. But Vermeer cannot be known in the age of the simulacrum. That is not to say that individual contemporary viewers cannot experience the beauty of Vermeer's paintings. But the realm of Yuskavage, a violent and kitsch-based miming of photographic and illustrational mass-media pornography, cannot deliver anything but a simulacrum. Vermeer's work may be a meditation on reality and illusionism, and perhaps daily reality in Vermeer's time could itself never have been exactly "like a Vermeer" (although paintings by his contemporaries confirm the basic outlines of his reality, while pointing to the rare nature of his manner of seeing and painting that reality). But Vermeer does not "mask or pervert a basic reality," does not "mask the *absence* of basic reality," and does not operate in the alternative universe of the simulacrum.

Whereas in the 1980s we all read Baudrillard, now we are naturalized citizens of the simulacrum, where Madonna can indeed be "Like a Virgin," and Lisa Yuskavage, "Like a Vermeer." Without the simulacral fluid which floods our eyes, the work would remain the ultimate reference, and then it might be enough to put a Yuskavage and a Vermeer next to each other and see what the paintings actually say to the viewer. But in the simulacrum, the work is no longer a possible fixed point of reference and meaning.

The confusion between old master paintings — including both the belief structure which created them and their current appearance, often masked by palimpsests of efforts at restoration and conservation — and contem- porary simulants of old master painting is revealed in a vignette about Lucas Cranach–inspired paintings by John Currin, with whom Yuskavage is frequently linked: "John Currin apologized for the drab surface of a new painting in his studio, on the westernmost block of Fourteenth Street — an area dominated by meatpackers which is rapidly artifying along with the gallery boom just to the north, in Chelsea. 'I've been waiting to varnish it,' the artist said. He plucked a brush from a can and made a few strokes on the canvas — a Northern Renaissance–looking picture of an anatomically impossible but convincingly naked young woman with a zany expression. Colors — greenish-brown chiaroscuro background, pale peachy flesh with bluish insinuations — sang. I think I went, 'Ah!'"[20]

In the Currin paintings that borrow subject, composition, and dark background from Cranach, it is the "zany expression" of the "convincingly naked young woman" and the cynical ideological collaboration between critic and artist in the belief that the cosmetic application of a layer of varnish will signify Great Painting to the viewing public that most accurately announce their contemporaneity. "Like Vermeer" is a veneer slathered over Yuskavage's paintings in order to give them the cosmetic patina of greatness while denying them their true value as brutal takes on the continued spectacular production of femininity as a product that warps the lives of girls and women.

I'd like to
put Forward
The motion of
modest painting

I'd like to put forward the notion of "modest painting." It won't put itself forward, because it is inherently resistant to the self-commodification actively encouraged by contemporary culture. Perhaps that is why it is useful to begin in a space foreign to our culture: the traditional Japanese toilet accorded an elegiac description by Jun'ichiro Tanizaki early on in his artistic and ethnological manifesto from 1933, *In Praise of Shadows*: "The Japanese toilet truly is a place of spiritual repose. It always stands apart from the main building, at the end of a corridor, in a grove fragrant with leaves and moss. No words can describe that sensation as one sits in the dim light, basking in the faint glow reflected from the shoji, lost in meditation or gazing out at the garden."[1]

My appropriation of Tanizaki's toilet, which he contrasts to the more hygienic but aesthetically and psychologically brutalizing glare of Western-style white-tiled bathrooms, should not be interpreted as the opening gambit of some desperately nostalgic, phantasmatically Japanophilic checkmate to postmodern Western commodity culture.[2] Simply, in the spirit of Tanizaki, I hope to call attention to a subcategory of Western painting—one whose own preference for "understatement" and "reticence" has hidden it in plain sight,[3] but in the shadows of a culture that denies the existence of any such thing as shadow—in order to suggest some possibilities for painting analogous to turning down the wattage and the amps, for at least a moment, to sharpening our perception of images in a softer light.[4]

Modest painting does not aspire to historical importance through physical domination of the viewer or the room in which it is placed via monumentality of size. Despite the importance accorded easel-sized paintings as uniquely marketable commodities, large scale as a marker of aesthetic ambition and historical significance is an integral part of the history of Western painting. Small paintings, when considered in relation to works that embrace architectural space, and also to smaller works

---

(*opposite*) Mira Schor, *Modest Painting*, 2000. Ink and gesso on linen. 12 × 16 inches. Courtesy of the artist.

within one artist's oeuvre, can be consigned to the realm of "genre" based on their size alone, although this designation is conventionally based on subject matter. And by now it is a commonplace of art theory that genre, including still life, has traditionally been a second class citizen of painting, rendered lesser and therefore also feminized for its attention to the quotidian over the mythological or religious, the historical and military. This hierarchy is part of a critique of painting internal to the practice, rather than a critique of the medium in general for its inability to respond authentically to contemporary media, for its contingent physicality, or for its essentialist aspects.

In *Looking at the Overlooked*, Norman Bryson recalls Charles Sterling's distinction between *megalography* and *rhopography*: "Megalography is the depiction of those things in the world which are great—the legends of the gods, the battle of heroes, the crises of history. Rhopography (from *rhopos*, trivial objects, small wares, trifles) is the depiction of those things which lack importance, the unassuming material base of life that 'importance' constantly overlooks."[5] Bryson focuses on still-life painting as the genre of painting that "takes on the exploration of what 'importance' tramples underfoot,"[6] but even within abstraction, as paintings increased in size toward the architectural scale, smaller abstract paintings were shifted into this zone of shadows, of anonymity, humility, and modesty.

Enormous size certainly intends to call attention to itself, but modest paintings are not necessarily small and small paintings are not necessarily modest. The category "modest" also has an emotional quotient: a character of expressive reserve even if the expressiveness is lyrical rather than stentorian. However, it must be understood that modesty is not synonymous with lack of rigor or ambition for painting. In fact, modesty may emerge from an artist's emphasis on rigor and ambition for painting itself rather than for his or her career. The modest painter may submit the painting to a ruthless criticality that precludes virtuosity for its own sake and, in so doing, risks getting less attention than the painter with fewer scruples about the meaning and integrity of each stroke. But, if rigor and ambition are integral to modest painting, they take varied forms, and are written into history in different manners, so that traditional aesthetic and gendered hierarchies are reinscribed even in the consideration and contextualization of paintings that at first appear to share the rubric "modest."

Does it need to be emphasized that we live in the era of megalography? Exhibition spaces alone cry out to artists, "Supersize me!" The Guggenheim Museum Bilbao, the Tate Modern, and the Massachusetts Museum of Contemporary Art, among others, all are huge spaces that dwarf even the most enormous sculptures and goad artists to envision ever more grandiose schemes[7] — so consider the fate of a small, quiet painting in these spaces and you can imagine the pressure on artists to make artworks that scream for attention and take up as much as space as possible.[8] Occasionally, a small gesture, such as a Richard Tuttle piece hung at knee level in a crack in the wall, may call attention to itself, just like the whispering voice of a woman may force her auditor to lean closer to hear her. But in itself this can be a form of ostentation, and in a museum hall the size of a train station, even this reverse device cannot function.

The pressure to make attention-getting works goes back at least to the Paris salons of the eighteenth and nineteenth centuries and continued to be a factor in the more recent past, even when artworks and galleries were generally smaller and less commercial. Speaking at Skowhegan in 1995, Alex Katz told of going to see his work in one of the first group shows where his work was exhibited: he was horrified to discover that another artist had a big red painting that commanded more attention than his own smaller, grayer one. Like Scarlett O'Hara swearing she would never be hungry again, Katz swore that he would never again allow himself to be eclipsed by another artist. The price of such a vow is the loss of whatever virtue modesty might represent for painting. Today, with so many more artists in the global field as well as at the national and local levels, and with increasingly grandiose spaces to fill, rhopography is clearly a career risk.

By definition, the works I am interested in calling attention to don't have big, blinking neon signs announcing, "MODEST PAINTINGS HERE!," so in trying to define this aesthetic, I have constantly had the sensation of having just overshot a dimly lit driveway along a busy highway. The effort to throw a glimmer of light onto the characteristics of modest painting can be a frustrating experience of *just missing*. The small, the "unimportant," the anonymous, the private and personal, that which has fallen by the wayside of "progress" at the service of another cause more pressing to the individual artist, all of these qualities cast a camouflaging shadow over the work. You have to slow down to see unlit driveways, and the slower I drive, the more I am compelled to swerve into autobiographic narratives when those are imbricated with art histories.

My introduction to painting was also an introduction to modest painting, at home in the workshop of my father, Ilya Schor. This was a space closer in spirit to the shadowy calm of Tanizaki's traditional cedar toilet than to our usual image of what an artist's studio looks like or should look like in order to reflect the importance of the work produced in it. It is important here for me to use the word *workshop*, rather than studio, because of the grandiose expectations that people bring to the concept of the artist's studio these days: big and prodigiously messy, or, sometimes, huge and museum-like in its architectural severity and professional lighting. Megalography is increasingly the order of the day in studio architecture, but my father worked in what had been the "maid's room" of our upper West Side New York apartment, whose architecture accorded the "maid" a prison cell–sized chamber barely larger than the width of one window, barely big enough for a single bed, and with a bathroom the width of a bathtub. In this narrow little room, there were two worktables, and jeweler's, engraver's, and painting tools were arranged on the shelves and walls in an orderly manner. Many unusual treasures, including silver Torah crowns covered with delicately cut out and engraved figures from Jewish life and biblical stories, were created in a space doubly marked as feminine, because of both its domestic associations and the secondary status of craft. He also painted small gouaches that represented and, after World War II, recreated the life of the Hasidic community of his shtetl of Zloczów, in the culturally fertile area of eastern Europe in Galicia in the period during and after World War I. Most of the paintings are about twelve by eight inches and painted with gouache on board, eschewing the very materials that are the sine qua non of major painting, oil and canvas.

Every stroke of paint carries art historical DNA, and in my father's paint stroke there is the influence of the shimmering loosening of local color found in the work of Pierre Bonnard or Édouard Vuillard (modest masters, both), but the humility of traditional Hasidic life is reflected in the reduced style quotient in his work. For example, in the small gouache *Visitor in the Synagogue*, a Jew sits unobtrusively to the left in a small synagogue interior, almost blending into the shadowy woodwork of the house of worship, itself an intimate and modest space. Self-effacement in the house of God is embodied in the way small brushstrokes create a warm, softly lit atmosphere. The painting is suffused with silence and patience. The ego of the artist is there only in the form of respect and tenderness for the subject recollected in memory and for painting itself. His paintings are

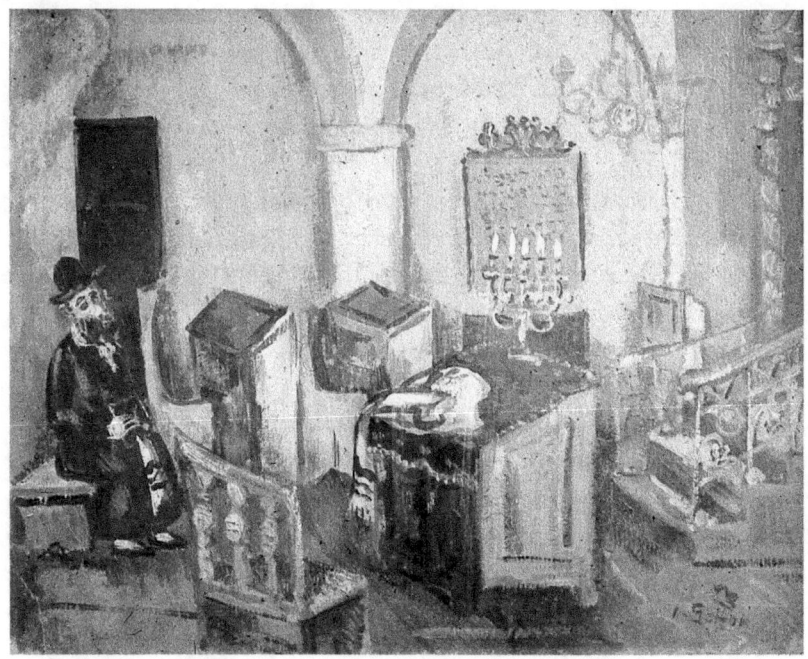

Ilya Schor, *Visitor in the Synagogue*, 1950s. Gouache on board.
8 × 10 inches. Courtesy of Mira Schor.

not expressionistic, unlike the paintings of Mané Katz, a friend and contemporary of my father, who depicted similar figures with a painterliness sharing a kinship with Chaïm Soutine; they are not surrealistic, unlike Chagall's fanciful, gravity-challenged depictions of the shtetl, although these movements inform the work. Occasionally the works shift into a cubist-inspired mode, but the intrusion of modernist "styling" causes them to lose some of the simplicity and authenticity of spirit I find so emotionally and historically compelling. What they may owe to folkloric structures is counterbalanced by sophisticated composition, control over degrees of representational accuracy and abstraction, and in particular, by the deftness of the paint strokes that build up and delineate both form and space.

Some are especially modest in size and, as it happens, these also have the least monetary value not only because they are the smallest—only a few square inches—but also because they do not depict a Jewish "scene" in full narrative mode so that, at the very least, they would have the rela-

MODEST PAINTING

tive value of a genre valued for its ethnic and historical recording of a lost culture. In these paintings, each figure is represented alone, not at the synagogue or in the life of the home, just sitting. In the scale of an image's assault on vision, they are visible at the level of a daguerreotype. Indeed, they bridge the traditions of the portrait miniature and the small-town photo studio portrait from early in the twentieth century. The sitters pose with that eerie lack of guile characteristic of such early photographic models, and the paintings are the size of those photographs: perhaps they are based upon them, but what differentiates them from both the portrait miniature and the photo is the way the figures are composed by and dissolves into small swift strokes of paint of a more painterly nature than the hairbrush marks which build up the smooth image on ivory miniatures.

My understanding of the link between practice and effect was learned by watching my father paint, absorbing the aesthetic and philosophical implications of how he mixed paint on the palette and applied it to the painting's surface. Occasionally I was given a little "painting lesson": this is how you put paint on the palette, in an orderly procession of colors; this is how you mix the paint, with a rhythmic backward and forward stroke of the wrist so as to safeguard the integrity of the small sable brushes; this is how you paint, moving your brush along the surface of the painting and the edge of the figures with swift, mobile strokes. Equal tenderness was accorded the tools of the trade, the image, and the subject. You painted as you stroked a cat, gently, and never against the grain.

Modest Painting: Case Histories

Beyond this immediately domestic arena for instruction, as a child I was surrounded by modest paintings, in the apartments and studios of friends of my parents and in the smaller-scale galleries and museums of the time. There was a world of art to take in, which I did in the way children absorb anything, by gaping at it, taking it in without any of the words that later come to contextualize what you are seeing. What at the time I took to be the private peculiarities of aesthetic ideology belonging to the grown-ups around me turned out to be the basic components of the deeply entrenched consensus of what, during the post-war, abstract-expressionist era, constituted a "good picture,"[9] including traditional concerns for composition enhanced by modernism's imperative for painting to reference the conditions specific to painting—its rectangularity and planarity, and a particularized focus on the authenticity of the brushstroke.

There is, in the few remaining shadows of this overly excavated art historical period, a range of ordinary practice, the journeyman paintings by minor artists that are the true indicators of the prevailing aesthetic consensus of postwar modernism. I am continually intrigued by a quality of many such paintings done during this period which seem to exist in a zone between the utterly familiar and the unknown or ineffable—something in the work that, although you think you know the painting all too well, induces you to take it in again with renewed pleasure. These are immensely livable paintings.

But before proceeding with this subject, it is first necessary to stop for a moment to consider the word *minor*. Every era is determined by the discipline of art history to have its major and its minor artists. A variety of factors are involved in this artist categorization: degree of originality or daring, development of style over a period of time, whether the work was publicized in a timely fashion, craft quality, and quantity of output. At the moment of contemporaneity, it is only partly possible to guess which artists will later be considered major, selected by the processing machine of art history to represent the period, or mediocre, that is, rehearsing the ideology of their time in derivative, uncommitted, or exploitative work. The label *minor* may not adhere to either polarity in a fixed manner: some artists are commonly referred to as "minor masters." Artists from past centuries often surface in art history for their mastery in only one known work. The concept of *mastery* is ubiquitous in art historical terminology: it seems to be the only way language has of marking importance. But some of the works I find intriguing are those that were done—with intelligence, dedication, and a generalized sense of belief in an aesthetic consensus—by artists who, although they were working at the center of the art world of their time, geographically and personally, were considered to be in the second, third, or even fourth rank of contemporary artists, not always even part of the public cadre of "minor" artists, just good painters.

Some of these paintings are abstract, but some are figurative: at forty years remove, it is possible to see how much this "good picture" consensus also affected many representational paintings, including early works by such artists as Alex Katz, Red Grooms, or even Eva Hesse—before they achieved their signature style or found their preferred medium. Such pieces can be found beyond the upper echelons of international art display and in the early rooms of retrospectives of most major figures who first began making art in the 1950s or early 1960s, such as Hesse, Robert Smithson, or Robert Irwin, as well as in the permanent collections of smaller museums. For example, two exhibitions at the Provincetown Art Association and Museum in the summer of 2000, the first a selection of works from the permanent collection chosen to celebrate that artists colony's centennial history, and the second an exhibition of students of Hans Hofmann, provided good examples for the purposes of my research for this essay.[10]

In the first show, there were no works by the major artists of abstract expressionism who might have been included because of their association with Provincetown, such as Hans Hofmann, Franz Kline, or Robert Motherwell. Rather, the installation included small works by artists such as Fritz Bultman (1919–1985), Henry Botkin (1896–1993), and Jim Forsberg (1919–1991), among others, that exemplified the aesthetic consensus's potential for producing "good pictures."

These paintings share a concern with relating to the edges of the rectangular frame and with deploying a kind of searching brush mark. Bultman's painting *Untitled* (n.d.) is notable for very thick impasto that creates the illusion of a much larger scale than would seem likely on its very small surface (3.5 × 18 inches). Two cadmium-yellow shapes, inflected by Naples yellow, one surging out of the lower right corner, the other just skirting the left edge of the painting, join in the middle of the surface where they become the ground for intersecting black lines that form an image of sorts, similar to the symbols for male and female. As is characteristic of most of these paintings, the ground's identity as ground is unstable. Here, as in works by Franz Kline, for example, a white ground visible at the corners begins to intrude into the center, becoming incorporated as a "figure," not the least because it is extremely physical in its substantiality. *Medley* (1962), by Henry Botkin, is an Arshile Gorky–influenced, lead pencil and charcoal pencil abstract drawing on a nested series of colored rectangles painted in a flat oil paint that looks rather like gouache. It is like an abstract painting of a bird's eye view of a traditional still life on a table. The "table," which is the ground of the whole painting, is a grey frame in which is nested the "table cloth," a brushy yellow-ochre rectangle inside the rectangle. A combination of pink and grey rectangles and organic shapes painted in a loose, sketchy, and wet-on-wet manner form the ground for the pencil drawing "still life." The effect is complex and fluid, despite the recognizably formulaic aspect of the entire work. Part of the pleasure of the work comes from one's appreciation of the artist's skill, personal engagement, and even his self-criticality, which are implicit in the many small corrections, within the formulaic.

A bigger work by Jim Forsberg,[11] *Wintersea* (1961), is marked by big, swooping, three inch–wide arcs of palette-knifed color, which open up toward the right side of the painting, creating an asymmetrical drift into an open space. The painting remains relational to the frame and stroke to stroke, but there is an offbeat quality to its relaxed deployment of abstract expressionism's rules, intimating a relationship with more recent works in the lineage: *Wintersea's* big blank areas of whiteness forecast open, asymmetrically composed areas similar to very late de Koonings, for example, or more recent works by Louise Fishman, where, seemingly in response to the anti-compositional influence of paintings by younger abstractionists, she opens up the grid structure of her earlier paintings.

The show of Hofmann students included works by artists such as Larry Rivers and Jan Müller, as well as by relatively obscure artists. These included a pictographic image by Vallie Burlingame (d. 1960), a thickly painted, scumbled but dry-surfaced yellow figure on a grayish-purple ground (*Untitled*, n.d.), which foreshadows the cartoon-based and distinctively painterly works of Elizabeth Murray. The show also included *Untitled* (1959), a small, Hofmann-inspired, freshly painted abstraction by Alve D'Orgeix of a series of very thickly painted and palette-knifed interlocking areas of brown, cadmium red, olive, and dark green, marked by a few small incidents of thickly applied blobs of paint and incised markings, which reveal the brightly colored underpainting. D'Orgeix's piece demonstrates how the work of a disciple can have its own liveliness and integrity.

The provenance of these paintings, which were primarily donations by local artists who most likely had bought or traded for these works from artists who were their friends and colleagues, indicates a significant characteristic of modest paintings: they are often found outside of the primary art market, in the transfer of artworks among artist friends in the form of gifts, trades, and benefit auctions. They are the chips of artistic communication of shared aesthetics and, often, shared fun.

Works of this nature surfaced in a series of exhibitions based on a particular network of artistic friendships from the late 1940s to the 1970s among realist painters, abstract expressionists, pop artists, poets, and art writers, including Rudy Burckhardt, Larry Rivers, Fairfield Porter, and Frank O'Hara, among many others. These exhibitions include "In Memory of My Feelings: Frank O'Hara and American Art," initiated at the Museum of Contemporary Art, Los Angeles, July 11 to November 14, 1999; "Art and Friendship: Selections from the Roland F. Pease Collection," Tibor de Nagy Gallery, July 10 to September 13, 1997; "Rudy Burckhardt," Tibor de Nagy Gallery, June 2000; "Rudy Burckhardt and Friends: New York Artists of the 1950s and '60s," Grey Art Gallery, New York University, May 9 to July 15, 2000; "*Semina* Culture: Wallace Berman and His Circle," Grey Art Gallery, January 16 to March 31, 2007; and "New York Cool: Painting and Sculpture from the NYU Art Collection," Grey Art Gallery, April 22 to July 19, 2008. These exhibitions brought together works, often at an intimate scale, by artists who might not be exhibited together in more "important" circumstances: that is to say, ones who made it into art history and their friends who were good artists too. (The exhibitions' titles often reflected the concept of friendship and community.) These exhibitions recalled a different, more diverse and fluid, more lived and communal aspect of the same art world that has already and so often been pictured in the more iconic histories of the major artistic statements and of their major critical interpretations and revisions.

In these exhibitions were works by artists who combined representational figuration and landscape with characteristically abstract-expressionist gestural brushwork. There is something casual about these works; they seem less about constructing a career through a signature style than about enjoying the act of painting and sharing that enjoyment with another artist. Thus, a quiet academicism is undercut by a thickly painted portrait of O'Hara by Jane Freilicher, or Fairfield Porter's *A Portrait of Roland F. Pease* (1958), wherein Porter's customary awkwardness and understated painterliness adds to the loosening influence of abstract expressionism. In *Rudy Burckhardt Plein Air* (1964), an early Red Grooms portrait (exhibited at the Tibor de Nagy Gallery in June 2000), Burckhardt is depicted painting outdoors, his figure vividly rendered yet nearly dissolving into strong, whooshing strokes of thick paint as bright as the summer's day in Maine when it was painted. Grooms exhibits a full understanding of the abstract-expressionistic brush mark and puts it to work in a relaxed summer picture of a friend painting, done almost anonymously, without any apparent effort at personal artistic style, though fully articulated through a compendium of the visual languages available to a painter at that moment.[12]

These examples of abstract expressionist–era painting often drift off the scope of art history's major narrative. In a curious parallel, they were also less useful as propaganda for the American government, because their small size and intimacy, rather than exemplifying American free- dom of expression, carried traces of a more European tradition of painterliness, which was hugely suspect in the postwar New York art world. The painter and writer Rackstraw Downes writes of this part of the late-1950s and early-1960s art world, in which much of the modest painting at the shadows of abstract expressionism was created. Downes takes care to distinguish this unofficial art's "fresh look" at "past masters" of painting from anything happening in Europe and thus participates in the pioneer rhetoric of American art at that time ("the past was something to *discover*, as much of a frontier as California to a train of covered wagons").[13] Nevertheless, he describes a non-dogmatic art world:

> To see this, the official art of the 1960s, you tramped Madison Avenue beginning at Emmerich and ending with Castelli. But there was another route which some people took, it included Frumkin, de Nagy, Zabriskie, Schoelkopf, Peridot, Graham among others. In these galleries one saw an art which looked awkwardly inexplicable; like so much of the liveliest art of any time it eluded critical dialectic. By the official art world it was virtually dismissed. And so I would call it the "unofficial" art of the 1960s. This was the world which interested me. It was the only art of quality that did not seem stage-managed; it had no party platform, no campaign. It did not bully you into believing that it was "right," a condition impossible to art and which, when claimed by a school or a critic, automatically makes the art seem slightly suspect. . . . In 1964 John Bernard Myers, in an article called "Junkdump Fair Surveyed," called this art "private."[14]

At a lecture at the Wexner Center for the Arts in May 2000, Robert Irwin mentioned the first time he saw some abstract-expressionist paintings in the flesh: from afar he saw a painting by James Brooks, large with big red and green shapes in it, and next to it a little pink and grey scumbled abstraction by Philip Guston. Irwin said that "this little painting blew the James Brooks off the wall," even though, as he noted, Guston's work was considered suspect because it was "maybe too French."[15] This final note represents a significant part of the rhetoric of the time: assertions of what constituted an American Painting. French meant sensual, sensual meant feminine, and feminine meant not masculine, not American. Thus the modest paintings that made up a significant substrata of the era's art were not the type to be used to bolster the image of the postwar American at home or to be shown in an American embassy abroad (where, in any case, they might have seemed as interesting as coals in Newcastle and would not have satisfied European expectations for representations of the America of fantasy and desire).

In the same talk, Irwin said that he came to feel that his own efforts to paint abstract expressionist works were "full of baloney," but in fact his works in this style are as good examples as any of the power of an aesthetic consensus to produce painting of quality. Yet they also contain a certain degree of anonymity precisely because the artist followed the dictums of an established style rather than laying out the parameters of a new one. These early paintings—such as *Pinberries* (1959), an advanced, late abstract-expressionist painting whose flat, greenish, pasty, thickish, slightly scumbled surface threatens to overcome the few and very carefully placed red and green (mostly) horizontal marks—would today still be considered viable, if conservative paintings, with just enough intelligence, toughness, and rigor to keep them from looking like sappy reproductions of a dead style. That this is the case indicates that the aesthetic consensus of abstract expressionism has proved to have a long half-life, but it also may suggest how static and historical that kind of painting has become.

Although histories of the abstract-expressionist era tend to focus on the outsize, often Dionysian personal and aesthetic narratives of such artists as Jackson Pollock and Willem de Kooning, this period also produced major artists who, more consistently than their contemporaries, surrendered artistic ego to a greater cause of an aesthetic, even a moral search. It would be instructive in any consideration of modest painting to look at the work of two highly respected painters from the postwar period, Myron Stout and Jack Tworkov, who, with equally rigorous ambition for painting, produced very different types of work that nevertheless share characteristics of the modest. An examination of how their work has been absorbed into art history will reveal the persistence of familiar hierarchies even within this shadowy subcategory of art.

It would be unfortunate and historically inaccurate to compare Stout and Tworkov in an antagonistic manner, because in addition to being friends and the courtliest of gentlemen, both were deeply and similarly committed to a disciplined private studio practice of abstract painting as both a visually intuitive and a rigorously intellectual domain. Both artists were working at the heart of abstract expressionism's belief in the au- tonomous artwork, the alienated, lone author-hero (or anti-hero—it was the same thing), and the authentic mark. Yet each man achieved, through his search for perfection and control over emotion expressed visually, a refined kind of anonymity and modesty in his work. Form, space, and the stroke are what matter.

At crucial points in their development each artist embraced self-imposed limitations as if they were external imperatives: Stout, the limitation of color to black and white, and of formal composition to centrally and symmetrically placed, flat figures on a flat ground; Tworkov, the containment of the intuitive stroke within a mathematically influenced geometric structure. Both chose to *not* do something: it might have been possible for Stout to move his iconic pictographs into a brighter, larger field, in the model of Adolph Gottlieb perhaps, or for Tworkov to continue his work in the gestural vein of abstract expressionism that he practiced in the 1950s. But neither artist seemed to be able to fully believe in the showier, splashier paths open to him, indeed, not just open but recommended for wider notoriety and success. Their choices suggest that producers of modest painting have a troubled relation to hubris. They know what it is, they may even wish they had it, but they don't, because it wouldn't be right. Or, perhaps it is precisely their sense of justness and their search for truth in painting that is their form of hubris.

Although Tworkov and Stout were modernists who in no way participated in the developing culture of the simulacrum, their work touches on the postmodern ideal of the death of the author, because in some sense they both placed the text—the painting—above the ego of the author. Tworkov writes: "The most creative moments in the painting of a picture occur when the 'I' that's painting and the 'I' that's watching merge into mutual obliteration—when you can say no 'I' whatever exists. It's a toss-up whether one can call that the purest consciousness or the most complete absence of consciousness. Certainly what disappears is 'self' consciousness. Whatever then happens can perhaps be described as the picture taking over as if the painter had no will." [16]

MODEST PAINTING

Despite these similarities of purpose and inclination, their inclusion and contextualization in art history's current versions of their time has been different. For example, Stout's painting *Number 3, 1954* (1954) hung in "New York Salon," one of the exhibitions that were part of "Making Choices," a museum-wide series of internally curated exhibitions at the Museum of Modern Art in 2000. Stout's small painting appeared amidst the usual suspects, such as Jackson Pollock, Robert Motherwell, Lee Krasner, Willem de Kooning, Fairfield Porter, and David Smith. Jack Tworkov's work was not included. It may be useful to examine Stout's and Tworkov's work in order to speculate on why one artist might be privileged in terms of art historical contextualization and the other less so.

Number 3, 1954 is a painting of a slightly uneven, white horseshoe or *u* shape on a black ground. No single brushstroke can be fully traced although one does see some brush work. The weave of the canvas is quite visible, almost irritatingly so. This is a Brechtian device: one cannot get lost in the illusion even of an abstraction without being reminded that this is a painting on woven cloth. It seems to have been painted easily, almost like house painting (with that sort of pill effect of a house-painting roller) except at the edge between black and white, where the black paint is thicker and the endless adjustments Stout made to the edge of the shape are evident although microscopic. These tiny changes, shifting the white shape down on its upper left top, and inside the *u*, are indicators of a heroic struggle, although it takes place within the context of a painting of modest size and simple design. The struggle is "heroic" precisely in that such a small thing as the differentiation of edge matters so much. Stout famously would rework the edges of the shapes in his paintings, often working for many years on the question of a few millimeters. For example, in *Hierophant* (c. 1955) again, as in *Number 3, 1954*, the white three-pronged form has been painted much more than the black. In the black you can see the canvas weave, whereas the white is a smooth surface. There is crackling where the black went over the possibly oilier white; particularly in the crevices of the prongs there is substantial crackling of the surface, like a toe fungus, which is the trace of the overworking that took place at the intersection of figure and ground.

Traces of the hand are sublimated to a rigorous classicism. Sanford Schwartz, writing in *Myron Stout: The Unfinished Paintings*, goes beyond the standard use of the term to speak of Stout's "identification with the stark and unbudging world of classic Greek tragedies." Schwartz con-

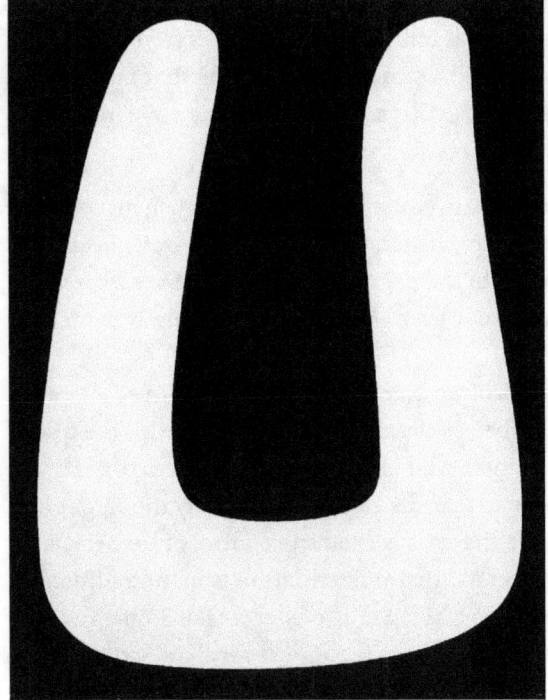

Myron Stout, *Number 3, 1954*, 1954. Oil on canvas.
20⅛ × 16 inches. Philip Johnson Fund, the Museum of
Modern Art, New York (25.1959). © by Estate of Myron
Stout. Digital image © by The Museum of Modern
Art. Licensed by SCALA / Art Resource, NY.

tinues, driving home the way in which a reference to Greek tragedy can
build the notion of the abstract expressionist–era artist as engaged in a
heroic struggle:

> As Stout conceived it, the symmetrical image had to be literally cen-
> tered. So the artist, who worked by being inches away from his given
> painting, building up a shape's contour, then scraping it down, then
> walking back from the easel to see if the shape was taking on the proper
> fullness, now had, additionally, to be measuring every tiny shift on
> two sides. Stout had never used any form of measurement before, not
> even when he made paintings or charcoals that appeared to be about
> straight lines, and the double effort of needing his shape to feel right

and to measure right took its toll. He was drawn to the Greek tragedies for their note of forces held at unbridgeable distances from each other, and he now found himself in a situation resembling that faced by the heroes and heroines of those plays. He had become ensnared by his unrelenting nature.[17]

Tworkov's struggle, in his late years, to contain the brush mark within a classicist frame of geometry, may have been more heroic, because it was more strongly opposed to the painterly strength of his earlier work; there is no evidence that Stout ever worked in a particularly expressive manner.

In painting, classicism is often paired with flatness, hard edges, and a lack of hue; painters described as classicists are rarely afforded the title of "painter's painter," the painter who is thought by his peers to carry the knowledge of how to paint so that the viewer, particularly the viewer who is a painter, can experience the artist's exquisite control of the sensuality of the medium and of the craft. That nomenclature is more traditionally applied to a painterly painter, which Stout was not. Like Stout, Tworkov was also a classicist, as evidenced by his preference for architectonic structure, but given the soft stroke and the subtle colorism that grace even the flattest and most geometric of his works, he is a painterly painter and a painter's painter. Tworkov came to these qualities through his own nature but also through the influence of artists he admired greatly such as Edwin Dickinson, whose subtle tonality of color and surface at the service of representation finds an equivalent voice in abstraction through Tworkov's work.

Stout's work is more aggressive in its signature style. His territory is clearly marked. Tworkov may have less of a signature style than Stout, even though, paradoxically, the trace of his hand is quite distinctive, an undeniable and unconscious signature in every gesture. He is often compared to—only to be subsumed by—Willem de Kooning, a close friend and studio neighbor in the crucial years of the late 1940s and early 1950s, because of undeniable similarities in the works of that period between the artists, paintings composed of sweeping, painterly marks that reflect the frame of the canvas. There are undeniable echoes of de Kooning in Tworkov's work from that period, for example in portraits that parallel the shift from representation to abstraction.

Yet Tworkov increasingly became suspicious of the self-indulgence of expressive automatism. He sought more objective frameworks, and found them in the geometrical underpinning of his later work. Even in his earlier work, he tempered the impulse toward sensuality with an impulse toward reason. The diagrammatic frame for the intuitive stroke also held back any relapses into deeper pictorial space. Oddly, de Kooning's progress was in the opposite direction, beginning with the exquisite control seen in his figurative works and early abstractions, such as *Night* (1948), *Painting* (1948), and *Night Square* (1949), in which stroke and drip are subsumed in a rhythmic, architectural structure, and in which the colors are reduced to black and white, as in Stout's work, so that the compositional rhythms and the meaning of the abstraction can be examined without interference from hue. De Kooning subsequently moved to a complete embrace and celebration of the swashbuckling gesture and the lush, unproblematized stroke. Paradoxically, only old age's blanking out of intellectual control returned de Kooning to a visual discipline in his spare late works, where the sweep of the massive gestural strokes has been drained of oiliness and lubricity.

The difference in Tworkov's work is that on the surface of the stroke, at the very point of its sensuality, there is a constant counter-discourse of control within the pleasurable mark itself. Even in his paintings from the early and mid-1950s that seem the most de Kooning–related, the paint strokes and the overall atmosphere are quite different, softer and more sensitively tuned than in many of the swashbuckling de Kooning works. Rather than appearing muscular and bold, the paintings, even when they aren't grey, affect you like a dense fog of pussy willows (unlike some 1970s and 1980s de Kooning works, which hit you in the face like a plate of heavily sauced, cold linguine). But these are not warm and fuzzy paint-ings; for all their painterliness, the paintings can seem quite remote and intellectual.

In *Idling I* (1969), cascading, irregular rows of dark grey-green vertical strokes descend against a lighter grey field created by broad but thinly ap-plied horizontal paint strokes. The very understated striations caused by the trace of the wide-bristle brushes used to create this shifting horizontal field act against the more concentrated, dripping vertical marks, whose irregular pattern is both clear yet undecipherable, like that of an unknown musical score. It is hard to see where the marks begin or end, and what is the top or the bottom of the work, yet the cascade is always caught back up and the painting never descends into overt expressionism or overstated

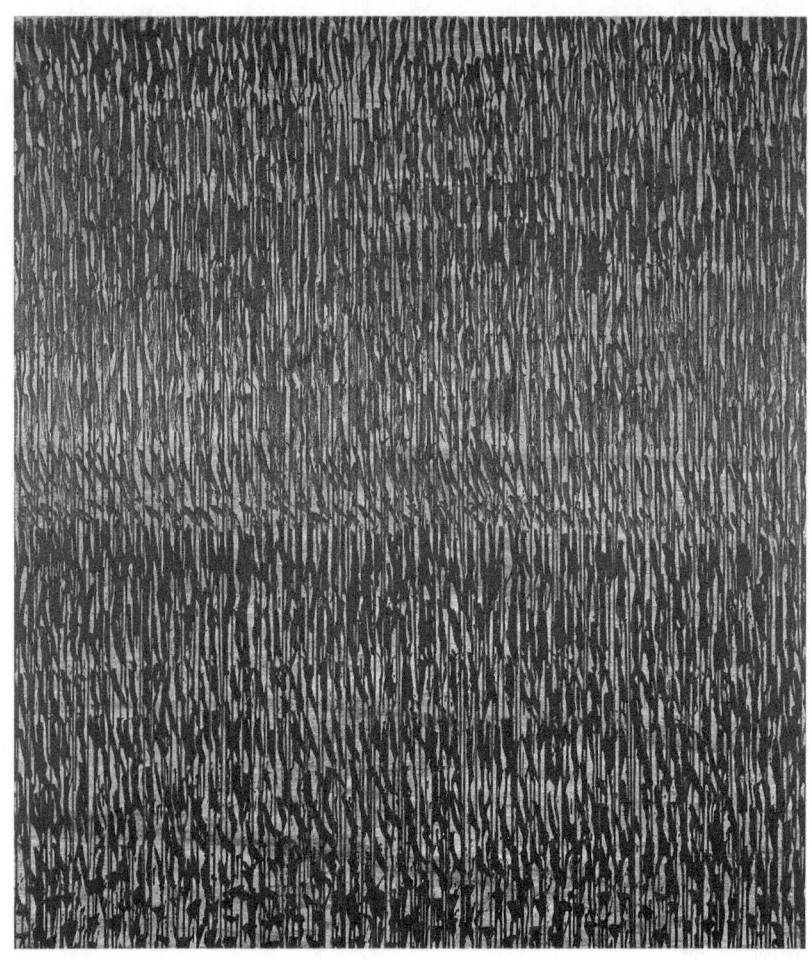

Jack Tworkov, *Idling #1*, 1969. Oil on canvas, 80 × 70 inches.
Carnegie Museum of Art, Pittsburgh, Pa.; A. W. Mellon Acquisition
Endowment Fund and Edith H. Fisher Fund. Courtesy of the Estate
of Jack Tworkov.

brio. Its rhythmic patterns are insistent yet reserved, embodying Twor-kov's goal of containing Dionysian urges within a structured field.

Trace (1966) tricks you into thinking that it is an image created through some sort of older reproduction technology. Looking at this painting, at first you can't quite figure out how it produces its visual effect, or even where it is happening. From afar, it appears as if it might be a giant photo-stat of a drawing; seen up close it appears to be a charcoal drawing. In fact it is an oil painting on canvas simulating the effect of a charcoal drawing. A dense weave of mostly vertical marks, thickened in the center of the work by a core of gestures arcing toward the right, prevents access to the space. Then, just as you realize that it is a painting on canvas, and not a drawing or a photostat of a drawing, you find its beating heart: a tiny red dot off center that refocuses you from a visual drift back into the overall composi-tion. It is a painting that challenges perception, problematizing sensuality even as it deploys it. It is soft, reserved, and profoundly thoughtful.[18]

But Tworkov is undone in the canonical hierarchy of abstract expres-sionism, because, in gendered terms, his work is feminized by a history that prefers bigger and wetter (de Kooning) or more rigid and assertively ascetic (Stout). He is deemed soft, too poetic, too temperate in his discre-tion. Stout's work is like a spectacle of discipline whereas, even in his later, geometric paintings, Tworkov's work is a sonnet to discipline. In Stout's work fetishization of craft can be marketed because it looks obsessional, or rather the product doesn't show many traces of process to the neophyte viewer, so the process can be marketed as obsessional in contradistinction to the final surface, which masks the struggle it took to create it. Stout's puritanical strangeness has in recent years done better as a brand than Tworkov's more painterly poeticism.

Can modesty in painting be linked to modesty as a personal trait? Are modest paintings created by modest painters? To answer in the affirma-tive may be to support a biographical fallacy, although such a connection is a possibility that presents itself empirically—but perhaps it is more a matter of types of ego, not size![19] But it is reasonable to assume that in every generation, no matter what the prevailing ethos of the culture, some set of personal characteristics will exist that may lead to a certain formal approach that would combine aesthetic ambition within modesty of form and scale, continuing through every cultural and historical moment an ongoing dialogue of *mega* and *rhopos*.

Certainly a lot of *small* paintings are being made today. Even as immense museum spaces and art fairs around the world demand the production of very large and also very loud artworks that will, through color, medium, subject, sound, and conceptual gesture command attention among the many, some of the most important cutting-edge galleries operate within marginal and notably small spaces, which encourage small size artworks and conceptual interventions.[20]

In every art center, local "minor masters" or "painter's painters" continue the traditions set in preceding periods. For example, in New York, painters such as Thomas Nozkowski and Andrew Masullo occupy such a position. Nozkowski's small oil paintings are carefully calibrated, hard-edge yet biomorphic abstractions with painterly surfaces—scumbled, brushed, and scraped. The ambition in these works and the pleasure for the viewer is in the project of teasing out innovation of form and materiality on a small field without collapsing into facile repetition. Andrew Masullo also retraces some of the tropes of hard-edge abstraction and related design, and marries them to the gloriously, even ecstatically bright color and inventively luscious surfaces of Florine Stettheimer to produce works whose modesty is marked by joy. Neither artist appears to be working in quite as rigorous an intellectual frame as earlier artists such as Tworkov, or in as spontaneous a manner as Rudy Burckhardt's circle of friends. Neither works ironically. They are not quoting from the vocabulary of art history along a deliberately appropriational model so much as genuinely searching for their own contribution to a known model. Young artists who appear to be working in this tradition include Alex Kwartler, whose subdued small abstractions restrain within a tight composition a mobile process—the dragging of paint developed by artists such as David Diao, Jack Whitten, and Gerhard Richter.[21] The paintings of Tomma Abts also seem to work in this tradition and share certain common traits with the work of Myron Stout: they are small in size and represent strange geometries with intensely worked decisions over small adjustments of line and edge. The seeming modesty of Abts's paintings is oddly inflected by, on the one hand, the paintings' intimation that she has an outsider relation to such histories, and, on the other, by the acclaim accorded to the artist for these works relatively earlier in her career than is usual for artists doing such painting, including the other artists just cited.

Following another branch of the lineage descending from the New York school of both the abstractionists and the Rudy Burckhardt group, the influence of artists such as Luc Tuymans and Mary Heilmann on younger painters highlights the attraction of a loose, informal, unassuming, low-key approach to painting, be it representational or abstract. However, characteristics of these works point to the problematics of maintaining a modest practice in an ironic time.

In her review of Tuymans' work from 1997, Jan Avgikos drives home her notion of the new form that modesty may take in our time: "In the '90s, painting has carved several niches for itself, one of which may be described as 'smartly insipid.' . . . Tactically, this genre favors the average: neither too beautiful, too smart, nor too passionate, its material means are humble and its ambitions seemingly constrained." These paintings are "without a single heroic bone in their body—or so it would seem. The underwhelming impact of Tuymans' work is so carefully managed that it amounts to an ideological position: to dissuade those who expect thrills, inspiration, or the like from painting by making seemingly mediocre works."[22] What is most telling in this characterization is the language of strategy: "tactically," "seemingly." What only time can tell, even more than individual judgment, is whether what is "seemingly" mediocre is actually just *really* mediocre.

There exists as well a variant of painting that at first seems to participate in the modest but that veers toward aspects of the abject: small, "deliberately" bad paintings in the sense of low craft, with clumsy "amateurish" drawing, often representing the psychological abjection of the female subject of the painting. So, for example, consider Karen Kilimnik's paintings about the television character of Tabitha, her own show a spin-off of an earlier sitcom, *Bewitched*. Again, the subject is no longer the "real thing" (even if the real thing was already a goofy television show), but its ironic, teenage spin-off. Elizabeth Peyton's works operate between carefree virtuosity and careless self-satisfaction. Perhaps more abject than her offhand, fashion illustration–influenced style is her melancholic embrace of celebrity culture, notably of celebrities who have been destroyed by some form of abjectness, such as Princess Di or Kurt Cobain. Tworkov's or Stout's struggles with the brushstroke or with the spacing of an edge are replaced by narrative references to eating disorders, drug addiction, and other forms of self-abasement. At the same time, celebrity culture is quintessentially antithetical to modesty, since it is based entirely on promotion of heavily simplified characteristics, so depictions of it, no matter how abjectly presented, mark a desire for participation in celebrity culture.

Continuing in the vein of figuration, examples of what may represent modest painting in contemporary art include the many small representational works with an illustrational character. These include works whose fantasy-oriented narrative derives some of its pleasures from the history of book illustration. In works by artists such as Marcel Dzama, Amy Cutler, and the emerging artist James Franklin, small figures find themselves in situations that range from the banal—strange things happening around a water cooler—to the fantastical, such as fairy-tale transformations affecting young people living in Williamsburg, Brooklyn, or intersections with creatures from the forest of Grimms' tales. The surfaces are carefully tuned, the expressive tone of the narrative is subdued, and there is an element of the childlike in the drawing style. The presumed modesty serves a niche in the market for small works scaled for apartment living and the collector of intermediate means. It may also be an embodiment of a generation's doubts or fears about the expressions of un-ironic emotion and of a contemporary interest in the decorative and the unintellectual—a loss of belief in "isms" at a time when all "isms" are available. However, these works' charm can occasionally verge toward the cute or the smug, with an interesting correspondence to some recent trends in *New Yorker* cartoons: minimally delineated, inexpressive young people in unclear narrative circumstances although clearly privileged situations.

Another type of painting that might be mistaken as modest or, even, and perhaps more significantly, mistaken as abject, has been manifest in recent exhibitions with the most cutting-edge curatorial ambition. In such shows, the overall aesthetic position is a calculated demonstration of the loss of belief or the lack of interest in participating in disciplines or intellectual "isms." Exhibitions of this type have included "Painters without Paintings and Paintings without Painters," curated by the artist Gareth James at the Orchard Gallery in New York City in 2006, and "Beneath the Underdog," curated by the artists Nate Lowman and Adam McEwen at the Gagosian Gallery in 2007.

An example of this new modest/abject painting from "Painters without Paintings" would be *Money Painting (Swiss 20)* (2005) by the collaborative fictional character, Reena Spaulings. This mid-size oil and acrylic painting on canvas is a sort of slacker version of Duchamp's *Tu m'* (1918), and that instance of patrilineage gives their work a context they might appreciate, although the carelessness toward facture, the trend toward abjectness in the way paint is "applied," is in sharp contrast to the complexity, elegance, and painterly skill of Duchamp's work. In "Beneath the Underdog" the exemplar of this approach to painting was a small painting by one of the curators, the British artist Adam McEwen, which presents two Mary Heilmann–esque dark purplish blobs on a thin pink acrylic ground. One might not guess from appearances, but the wall label reveals that the dull blobs are made of chewing gum. (Press releases and reviews of previous exhibitions by the artist explain that these random blobs of chewing gum may represent World War II bomb patterns, in an example of "recipe art," which I define in a later chapter.) The faint trace of a sneaker print on the painting is the final touch, not quite dark enough to be "the subject" of the painting—that honor goes to the chewing gum—but it is just enough to suggest neglect or indifference toward the whole enterprise: maybe the artist or someone else stepped on it, maybe not, but we're going to hang it anyway.

The makers of these paintings are not primarily painters. They are in some cases art historians, in others agents-provocateur conceptual artists working in a variety of materials and modalities. To even discuss their work from the position of a commitment to challenging the problematics of painting through a belief in the discipline, the materiality, or visual pleasures of painting would be to fall into the familiar trap set by one of the conceptual premises of the work. Bring formal or even conceptual painting criteria to bear on works whose intention is to question the "presumption of an immaculate self-identity between the objects that go by the name 'painting' and the subjects given the name 'painter'" and you are sure to miss the point.[23] These are works whose principal interest when using painting is to make manifest the artists' utter indifference toward any ambition for the discipline and toward the history of painting. This phenomenon is amusingly played out in the instances of such paintings being produced by two collaborative groups: "Reena Spaulings," and the artists Joe Bradley and Dan Colen. In their painting exhibited in "Beneath the Underdog," a four canvas construction of a block figure with a chewing gum–encrusted, Jules Olitski–style body and a happy-face head, appropriately entitled *Shithead* (2007), Bradley and Colen prove that today it takes a village (albeit of idiots) to make a painting.[24] We have traveled a long way from the model of one individual painter in a Homeric struggle with line, edge, stroke. Here painting is simply one stop in a kind of intellectual tourism, at best. These artists and curators are engaged in a broader socio-aesthetic commentary with often very sharp and amusing results in other media than painting. Painting is just another thing to toy with when it can yield cultural profit, but these are not even colonists who plan to stay, so they are not likely to ever "go native" in the land of painting.

Possibly these recent works do propose a subversive critique of the market's current embrace of those artists whose seemingly less skeptical embrace of the grand tradition of painting has brought them great success in an art world always on the lookout for a new, young, great painter— here one may think of Dana Schutz for example. Or this kind of work may function as a critique of large-scale paintings such as the red-paint pour paintings by Barnaby Furnas from 2006.[25] But here we are faced with a kind of pincer action of cynicism, since Furnas, with his brand of grandiose showmanship, seems no more committed to the kind of serious ambition for painting exercised by artists such as Stout and Tworkov than these more recent abject "modest" painters. Or maybe even this model of criticality is beside the point of these participants' noncommittal stance. There is a curious counterpoint between abjection and entitlement that may be the current embodiment of a post–September 11 world view in the most privileged sections of the art world: painting is what the trash threw out, but at the best art-world address.

Because of the general cultural atmosphere within which these ironic and skeptical gestures occur, even when paintings do seem to be modest in the first sense I proposed—small in size, with intimacy and formal restraint applied to a deep ambition for painting—the contemporary viewer is affected (or afflicted) by an inculturated suspicion that we are always speaking of "modest," a pose, that the ambition for painting is always bracketed by style, or styling, or self-styling. The burden of suspicion is similar to the experience of watching old movies with our current vocabulary of media tropes: if a woman walks down a street, no matter how innocuous the plot, we expect sudden violence. In the softness of Tanizaki's shadows now always lurks an unknown assassin.

Also, most art made today is appropriative in one way or another: even abstract painting is made with a quotational self-awareness entirely opposite to the equally self-aware but heroic stance of making or battling the authentic mark that was so characteristic of abstract expressionism. Since appropriation is a part of postmodernism's critique of originality, and this critique in part disparages the foregrounding of the author's ego identity, perhaps one could also say that appropriatively oriented works achieve the kind of authorial anonymity sought by artists such Stout or Tworkov. One might add that these earlier artists' effort to not impose their ego on their work had a postmodernist aspect. Nevertheless, their work is marked by traces of a pictorial search, whereas appropriation circumvents search: it can only quote the appearance of search, since it is based on a critique of the abstract-expressionist mechanism of searching for and "finding" the painting through a process of relational brushwork and composition. Con- temporary art doesn't search, it shops and it sells.

If modesty is an instinctive as well as an intellectually and morally based turn away from a histrionic bid for the limelight, then abjectness is a reaction formation to the artist's awareness of the difficulty of obtaining the limelight through painting in contemporary culture at a time when the artist has been taught that getting the limelight is the only excuse for making art in the first place. And, in an era of spectacle, when the painter steeped in postmodern theory is well aware of the painting, and of him or herself, as a commodity, can modesty be anything other than a pose, a face put on the commodity to sell it — **"modest"** in boldface with scare quotes? In his writings, Jack Tworkov noted the moral and logical pitfalls of a stance of modesty: "What will an artist not do for attention — even having his or her behind bared when that was still a novelty. But even modesty is sometimes no more than a ploy. And the mien of utter integrity is often no more than a mask for frustration. No pose is likely to be more false than that which takes obscurity and poverty as the stigmata of probity and integrity."[26] Today, resistance to (self-)commodification in the pursuit of such now fraught or antiquated values like truth, be it for an outer precept or an inner drive, is more and more difficult to sustain.

Contemporary, self-consciously modest, deliberately "seemingly mediocre" paintings may, by admitting to the futility of the effort to paint in the face of more spectacular media, be the truest painterly expressions possible, or they may be seen as symptoms of retrenchment, markers of a reduced confidence in what painting can express or perhaps even more, what there is to be expressed about contemporary life.

Tanizaki looks to the use of gold in traditional Japanese lacquerware and fabric design and the fate of that gold when the glare of electricity hits it:

> And surely you have seen, in the darkness of the innermost rooms of these huge buildings, to which sunlight never penetrates, how the gold leaf of a sliding door or screen will pick up a distant glimmer from the

garden, then suddenly send forth an ethereal glow, a faint golden light cast into the enveloping darkness, like a glow upon the horizon at sunset.

I have said that lacquerware decorated in gold was made to be seen in the dark; and for this same reason were the fabrics of the past so lavishly woven of threads of silver and gold. The priest's surplice of gold brocade is perhaps the best example. In most of our city temples, catering to the masses as they do, the main hall will be brightly lit, and these garments of gold will seem merely gaudy.

A phosphorescent jewel gives off its glow and color in the dark and loses its beauty in the light of day. Were it not for the shadows, there would be no beauty.[27]

Modest paintings are garments of silver, even harder than gold ones to make and to perceive in the gaudy bright lights of contemporary culture.

Very late at night, unable to make the effort of getting up so that I can get ready for bed, I run my remote through every channel of digital cable and chance upon the following scene: a young German officer in a World War II uniform is painting the landscape he sees from the window of his moving train, putting up his brush in the characteristic gesture of measuring scale and proportion. Then the camera swings around to show his painting—the perfect representation of a blurred landscape! This sight gag, from the comedy *Top Secret!* (1984), indicates the degree to which the blur has become an utterly familiar and ubiquitous trope, and it almost renders pointless any serious consideration or further use of the blur as a distancing visual device. Yet the juxtaposition of a German officer's uniform and the painting of a blur is at the core of a work from the history of postwar high art that allows us to also examine the meaning of the blur in contemporary art. Indeed, a focus on the blur is in order in the face of this now common trope.

. . .

Why does the past have to be represented as grey and out of focus in visual art? Do irony and lack of affect as the preferred emotional markers of postwar art find their roots in the Holocaust? And do these characteristics now perform a destruction of subjectivity to which, in earlier instances, they may have seemed the most appropriate response? Gerhard Richter's painting *Uncle Rudi* (1965) acts as a portal into considering these questions as they are posed and answered in a range of postwar and contemporary practices.

The conceptual clarity and formal acuity of Richter's use of the blur in *Uncle Rudi* makes it a perfect point of entry for considering the historical, moral, and affective dimensions of the blur, which has become an established convention of contemporary art in painting and photography, both in works about the same historical moment as *Uncle Rudi* and in works about contemporary culture.

If your family photo album includes Uncle Rudi, what are you going to do? You may feel a duty to at once acknowledge and de-heroicize him. Painting from a snapshot, retaining the grey of the photograph so as to

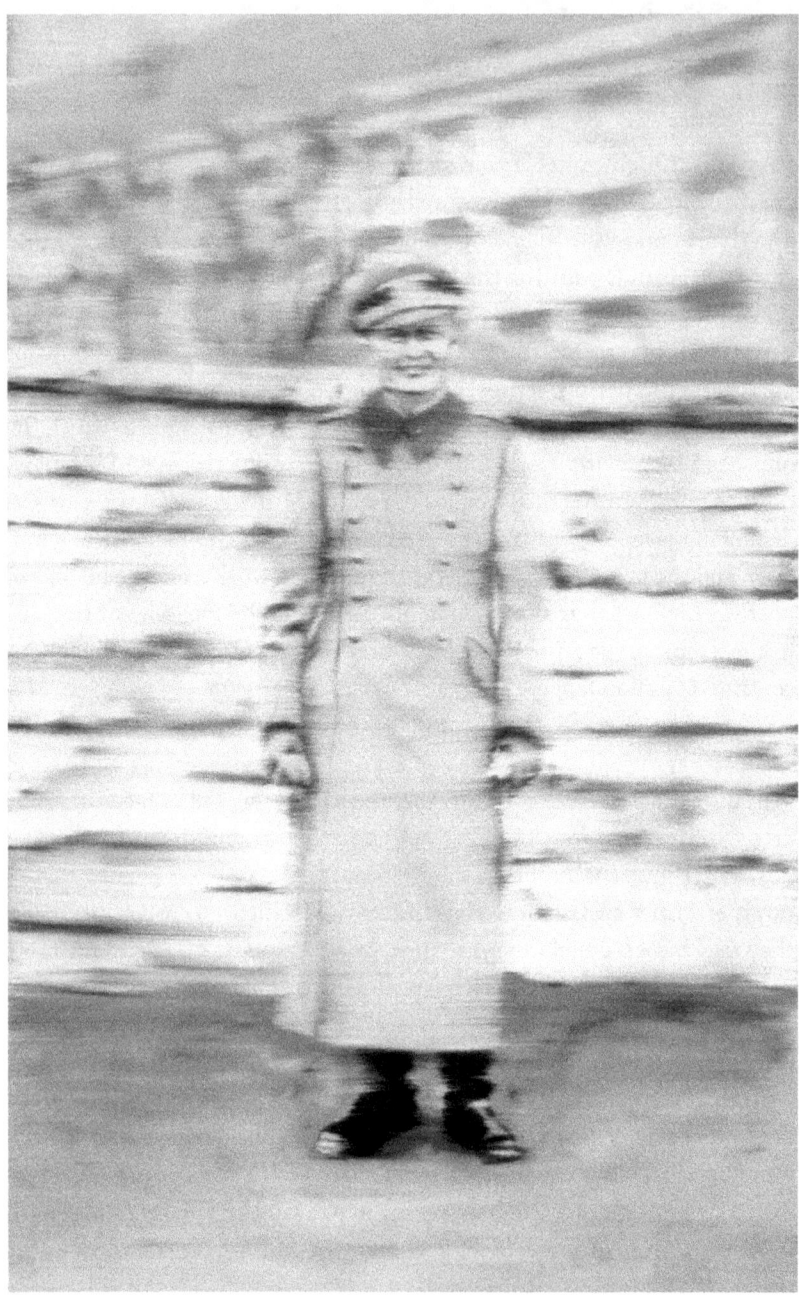

Gerhard Richter, *Uncle Rudi*, 1965. Oil on canvas, 34½ × 19¹¹⁄₁₆ inches.
Czech Museum of Fine Arts, Prague, Lidice Foundation.
© by Gerhard Richter.

deny the subject the vitality of color, and blurring the image all might provide useful distancing mechanisms. You wouldn't want to paint him with any other affect than ironic objectivity, which the photographic matrix presumably ensures. Richter argues that you *couldn't*. He writes, "I first paint the pictures very precisely from the photograph, sometimes more realistically than the originals. That comes with experience. And the result is, of course, a unendurable picture from every point of view."[1] The intervention of the blur provides a necessary distance from the unendurable. Similarly, in Richter's early work grey provides a note of negation and indeterminacy: "I have a special relationship with grey. Grey, to me, was absence of opinion, nothing, neither/nor."[2] And, "To me, grey is the welcome and only possible equivalent for indifference, noncommitment, absence of opinion, absence of shape."[3]

Although an artist's intentions can only form one contribution to the interpretation of the work, Richter's writings have been as influential as his paintings in terms of interpreting the blur and the affective stance ascribed to the blur. Richter's comments on what he paints and why he has chosen photography, grey, and the blur do reveal a desire to take a neutral stance in relation to an overly fraught historical narrative. "I blur things to make everything equally important and equally unimportant."[4] (It should be noted that in recent years Richter has tempered, to the point even of disavowal, the deliberate moral indeterminacy, posture of affectlessness, and implication of random subject matter choice that characterized these often quoted statements from the sixties and seventies.)[5] Nevertheless, to comment on "the destruction of subjectivity" within totalitarian regimes and under the generalized amnesiac regime of the Society of the Spectacle, it is necessary to have visual strategies that will properly enact "lack of affect," including, to quote Benjamin Buchloh, "the glacial and anonymous style of the photographic simulacrum," which will mirror "the collective lack of affect, the psychic armor with which Germans of the postwar period protected themselves against historical insight."[6]

But why should artists working from a different position in relation to this same history submit to the aesthetic imperative suggested by the historical and aesthetic importance accorded to Richter's work? Or, to put it another way, why would I want to blur my Uncle Moishe?

Uncle Rudi stands in front of a wall; behind it, a block of apartment buildings, painted in a cool grey blur, runs along the upper right of the painting. Now imagine that as the bird flies, you find yourself on the other

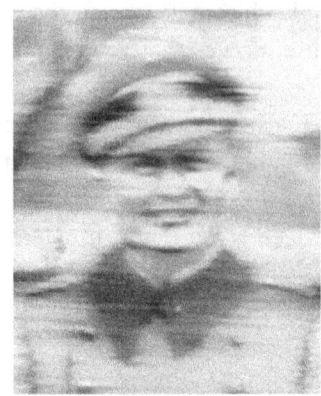

Uncle Rudi, detail.

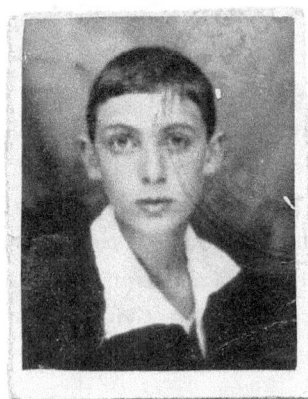

Moses Ajnsztajn (Einstein) (b. 1921,
Lublin, Poland; d. ca. 1942, Treblinka
or Auschwitz), the author's maternal
uncle, Warsaw, mid-1930s. Photograph courtesy of Mira Schor.

side of the buildings, in a darker toned black and white photograph. At the left of this picture is a block of apartments, slightly blurred, as they are at a distance from the figures that are the subject of the small photograph. It shows my grandmother Fajga Brucha Ajnsztajn, née Weisman, and her two sons standing together on a street in the Warsaw ghetto in 1938. They are my uncle Schloime (Solomon), on the right, and my uncle Moishe (Moses), on the left. These figures, exposed to the de-oxygenated air of pre-invasion Poland, are the repressed of the painting *Uncle Rudi*. Metaphorically, in terms of the history to come for all these figures, *Uncle Rudi* stands just behind those buildings, in his fine new uniform, and my family stand behind my critical practice in this instance.

My Uncle Moishe's existence is kept alive by a few pictures that reside in a plain wood box, like a tiny pine coffin, in the upper shelf of my mother's bedroom closet, along with a small, decorative box Moishe gave her when she left Poland in 1938, and by my mother's memory, all now entrusted to me.[7] The nature of oral history is significant here: Moishe's story was told over and over, and, although memory may have blurred much, what remains is what has stayed in focus. It was related in bold strokes, with sharp, telling details that make the story live in a vivid manner.

An episode toward the end of Art Spiegelman's *Maus II* illustrates the effect of such a box in a parent's closet and of such memory, in which a running narrative provided in accented English is imbricated within a series of precious, though frayed, black and white photographs from interwar Europe. Spiegelman's father, Vladek (rendered, like all of the Jewish characters, as a mouse), suddenly materializes with a box. Vladek tells his son: "Below my closet, I find these snapshots, some still from Poland."[8] Spiegelman depicts the urgency with which these narratives were transmitted in his father's retelling by overlapping pictures of these old family photographs on top of the comic-book sections. Sometimes the photo crowds the window under it, so a picture of a handsome, bow-tied young mouse squeezes to the side and nearly covers the explanatory text: "*This* brother of Anja, Josef, he was a sign painter, a commercial artist, always she said you resemble." The stories and the photos multiply, until they drift onto a pile on the "floor" of the page: they are large and closer to us, and behind, Vladek mourns, "Anja's parents, the grandparents, her big sister Tosha, Little Bibi and our Richieu . . . *All* what is left, it's the photos." And of his own family, "It's *nothing* left, not even a snapshot."[9]

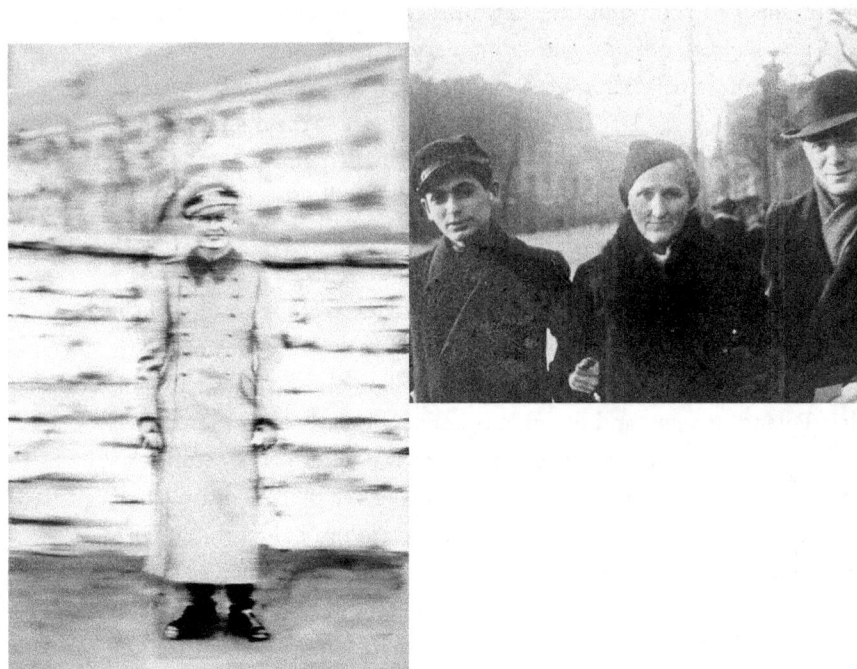

Mira Schor, *The Uncles*, 2008. Composite image of Gerhard Richter's *Uncle Rudi* (1965) and a photograph of Moses Ajnsztajn, Fajga Brucha Ajnsztajn, née Weisman (b. 1889, d. unknown), and Salomon Ajnsztajn (b. 1911, d. unknown), in Warsaw, Poland, ca. 1938–1939. Courtesy of the artist.

Spiegelman breaks the visual program of his book when, toward the end of the tale, after the reader has gotten to know both the horrors that Vladek survived and the impossibly difficult figure he had become, Spiegelman suddenly reproduces an actual photo of Vladek, taken just after the war, in a "photo place what had a *camp* uniform—a new and clean one—to make *souvenir* photos."[10] There is enormous power in this one image of a Jew as a human being, not a mouse, even if he has chosen to "dress up" in a stripped camp uniform in a performance of his recent experience. The black and white photograph is as significant a tool for Spiegelman as it is for Richter, but in this case, instead of providing only the initiatory matrix of distantiation and objectivity, the photograph is used at a crucial moment and as a unique intervention so that the alert and defiant survivor can address us directly, no longer through the recording of his words, but in his eyes meeting ours.

Christian Boltanski's installations of blurred photographs, small lights, and reliquary-like objects, such as *Archives Purim* (1990), re-create the mysteries of dark recesses in ancient Catholic churches more than Jewish sites of worship, a strange effect considering the Holocaust-related subject matter. But, in fact, this quality makes the work in some way familiar and even easy to understand and like. These works have contributed as much to the trope of the blur as Richter's, but because they do not necessitate the specific painterly skills required to articulate a response to Richter, they may serve as a model for artists for whom Richter is too skilled, or too intellectually rigorous and forbidding. Boltanski's visual tools—dimly glowing lights in a darkened room, illuminated spectral blurred faces— create an atmosphere of melancholic prettiness that allows one to feel sad rather than outraged or devastated, partly because the lights are so much more visible than the photographs that often disappear into the darkened wall. But the feelings "how sad" and "how beautiful" do not enact the contemporary value of the "antiredemptory" monument posited by James Young in his book about late twentieth-century Holocaust memorials, *At Memory's Edge*. On the one hand, the pathos that is incorporated into the particular visual pleasure offered by small lights in a darkened room and the loss of specificity engendered by the blurred photograph can sentimentalize an expression of mourning. On the other hand that pathos can seem like just another form of lack of affect, the binary other of cooler, less sentimental examples.

The conceptual softness of Boltanski's memorial projects is clear when compared to the anti-Nazi activist Serge Klarsfeld's documentary project *French Children of the Holocaust: A Memorial.*[11]

For Klarsfeld, "True emotion comes from precision."[12] Klarsfeld compiled a list of names and gathered, from sources around the world, photographs of over 2,000 of the 11,402 Jewish children under the age of 18 deported from France during World War II. For each child, the documenters recorded the location of arrest, if different than that of permanent residence; the age of the child at the time of deportation, and similar information on siblings and parents; the precise convoy number to the concentration camp destination—and then one learns their fate. Klarsfeld emphasizes the importance both of documentary detail and of representational clarity: "I wanted to create a children's book that would make an original contribution to the literature on the Holocaust. I believe this has now been done by bringing together the children's *names*, with precise personal information; *places*, their addresses at the moment they were arrested; and *faces*—as many photos as possible of the deported children. We have been able to identify in this book the faces of more than 2,500 of these children."[13]

The research is so heartbreakingly thorough that in one case the effort to trace the fate of a child, Bernard Dziubas, was resolved "by reconstructing a phonetic name that a child of 5 might produce. We found him under 'Jubes, Bernard' on convoy 49."[14]

The photographs are extremely varied. Some are barely scraps, tiny fragments of paper; in some cases these have been placed under glass in some kind of funerary monument and the reproduction in the book is the photograph of the embedded photograph. A tiny horizontally-oriented oval under glass on a stone shows us Israël-(Noël) Artszejn "born in Poland on September 20, 1928. He was deported with his mother Sara, on convoy 15 of August 5, 1942."[15] On another commemorative stone plaque, for a little girl named Ida-Yvette Berneman, her older sister, and their mother, who were deported in convoy 20 on 17 August 1942, Ida is represented by a tiny, scratched little fragment of a photo of her head. Encaustic portraits of Coptic youths have survived death better and longer than the only surviving image of this little girl. Some photographs are carefully posed and show some evidence that the photographer really looked at the child closely and had the ability to control site and light. Some are family snapshots taken in happier days before the war. Sometimes one can deduce from the child's date of birth that the picture was taken when the war had already started.

Most of the children whose photographs have been collected by Klarsfeld died before they reached adulthood. Many died shortly after the photograph was taken. Among these are the studio portraits of small children, often dressed in elaborately hand-knit clothing, made with love but undoubtedly itchy: the child has been placed on a chair, a table, a bench, with a toy or a flower, and looks off to the side, at the parent just beyond the photographic field. So, we open the book and come upon a little toddler with tiny little teeth, who looks off to his right, laughing. He is "*Claude ALEXANDER . . . born on January 18 1943, in Lyon. He was deported from that city by the Gestapo when he was 18 months old, on convoy 78 of August 11, 1944.*"[16]

Although this project is intended as a documentary project, not an artwork, it is consistent with contemporary art's many forays into archiving and documentation,[17] which serve to blur such disciplinary distinctions. Perhaps some of the moral issues raised by Adorno's injunction against "poetry after Auschwitz" are bypassed by the Klarsfeld work, because he does not set out to make "poetry."[18]

The Klarsfeld text achieves a kind of universality through its meticulous effort to restore specificity to each victim. Certainly this project is intended as a historical memorial, not an artwork. However, it is consistent with what James Young describes as the first Jewish reaction to the problem of memorialization: "In keeping with the bookish, iconoclastic side of Jewish tradition, the first memorials to the Holocaust came not in stone, glass, or steel—but in narrative. The *Yizker Biker* (memorial books) recall both the lives and the destruction of European Jewish Communities according to the most ancient of Jewish memorial media: the book."[19]

The interpolation of text and narrative are crucial to reversing the distantiation created by the beauty of the photographs or the curio factor of pictures of another era. Instead of an anonymous blurred photograph of a child being allowed to stand alone and dilute mourning into beauty, as is the case in Boltanski's work, Klarsfeld's use of narrative information grounds the soft-focus generality of something lost sometime in the past into a cruel specificity. Take for example this picture of a baby smilingly raising himself on his little pudgy arms.

Without text it has a certain timeless quality. But he is not just any baby, or every baby, an ur-baby, he is: "*Alain BERR* [who] was not yet

2 years old—he was born on May 27, 1942, in Nancy (Meurthe-et-Moselle), where he lived at 16 rue Christian Pfister—when he was deported on April 13, 1944 on *convoy 71*. He was deported with his mother, Léa, who came from Buenos Aires, and his father, Ernest, from Thoul (Meurthe-et-Moselle)."[20]

Instead of bathing gently in a softly lit, votive, almost romantic atmosphere of sadness, the Klarsfeld text follows you onto the street and the subway. Each child was photographed as they were, in the ordinary safeness of an average childhood, or in the intensified charade of safeness their parents composed for them as danger was imminent and anticipated, and so, suddenly you sit on the Lexington Avenue subway in New York City looking at each infant or toddler reaching out from his stroller to her mother for her bottle, toy, shoes, crackers, and imagine what it would be if that particular mother and child were arrested and taken to their deaths, for being Puerto Rican, or Chinese, or African American. Klarsfeld's project thus functions almost as a virus of historical awareness, infiltrating one's daily vision of ordinary life.

Perhaps the most interesting image in the book with respect to our era's privileging of mediation is the portrait of Elisabeth Apelgot, represented by a poor-quality photo of a poor-quality, thinly painted portrait, which is clearly taken from a photograph. It is realistic but done with no particular artistry—not primitive by any means, just not beautifully rendered or skillfully blurred like a Richter. Elisabeth was thirteen years old when she was deported on convoy 71. Her older sister, Sonia, survived and sent Klarsfeld the photograph with the following letter: "[Here] is the picture of my sister Elisabeth. When I returned from the camps, I found practically none of our possessions and the only photographs left were moldy. Through a friend I found a painter who copied the decaying photos. From these I then had photos taken."[21]

This process of mediation, described so matter of factly despite such tragic circumstance, is remarkably similar to the process of mediation engaged in by the Los Angeles artist Amy Adler in *What Happened to Amy?* (1996). In this work, Adler made colored-pencil drawings based on photos taken of her when she was a teenager, in a mail-order illustration course–style that itself conveys an affectless emotive stance. Adler photographed the drawings, which she then destroyed along with the original photos, leaving only the last step of the mediation chain. Thus, in our culture, the authenticity of the indexical trace is always already troubled and erased;

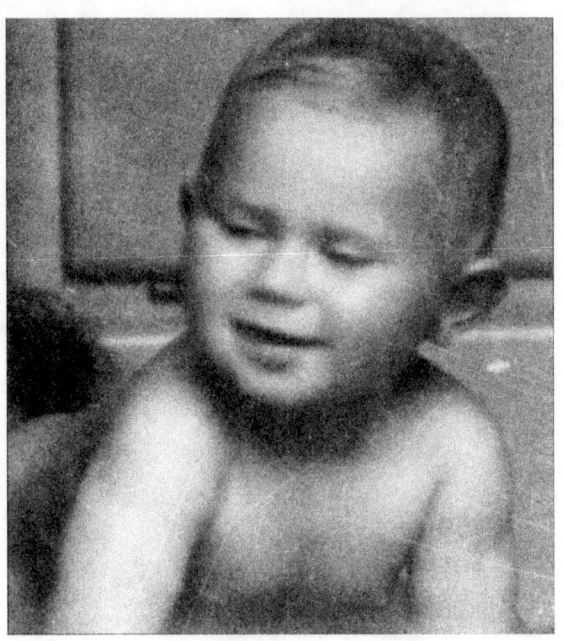

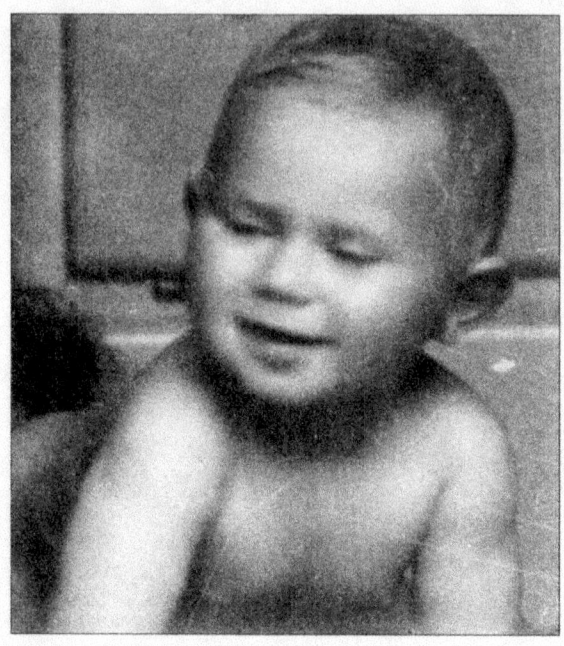

Alain BERR was not yet 2 years old—he was born on May 27, 1942, in Nancy (Meurthe-et-Moselle), where he lived at 16 rue Christian Pfister—when he was deported on April 13, 1944, on **convoy 71**. He was deported with his mother, Léa, who came from Buenos Aires, and his father, Ernest, from Toul (Meurthe-et-Moselle).

(*above and overleaf*) Photograph of Alain Berr. From Serge Klarsfeld, *French Children of the Holocaust: A Memorial* (New York: New York University Press, ca. 1996), 624. Courtesy of Serge Klarsfeld and the Beate Klarsfeld Foundation.

only the mediated trace is "real." Adler's trail of distancing mechanisms narrates a kind of loss, of innocence perhaps—her Brady Bunch figure, posed at the fringe of child-porn, has a sinister undertone—whereas Elizabeth Apelgot's image engages the macabre, as she is eternally trapped, guileless, and incapable of mediation, in her smiling effigy. Sonia Apelgot did not dispose of the contemporary artist's luxury of surplus or deploy Adler's distancing of aesthetic commentary: she commissioned a chain of mediation out of the desperate need to salvage any record of a trace she would never willingly destroy. It is as if, face to face in a mirror, these two nearly identical processes of mediation from photography to painting to photography demonstrate how lack of affect has mutated. Its evolution can be traced from its first apparition as the emotional quotient of a highly strategized mechanism of destruction (the Holocaust) to its contemporary incarnation, embodied here by Adler's work, as a highly strategized aesthetic and affective mechanism of representation.

The work of David Levinthal seems to speak for the generation James Young describes as "post-Holocaust," which can only experience "the Holocaust as vicarious past."[22]

How is a post-Holocaust generation of artists supposed to "remember" events they never experienced directly? Born after Holocaust history into the time of its memory only, a new, media-savvy generation of artists rarely presumes to represent these events outside the ways they have vicariously known and experienced them. This postwar generation, after all, cannot remember the Holocaust as it occurred. All they remember, all they know of the Holocaust, is what the victims have passed down to them in their diaries, what the survivors have remembered to them in their memoirs. They remember not actual events but the countless historic novels, and poems of the Holocaust they have read, the photographs, movies, and video testimonies they have seen over the years.[23]

According to Young, Levinthal "takes pictures of *his* Holocaust experiences—that is, recirculated images of the Holocaust." His work is said to be in keeping with a generational "fascination with the ready-made simulacrum." The reality depicted is not the reality of the Holocaust, something impossible for an American Jew born after the war, but "a particular kind of reality—that of the cultural icon and myth." Although Young is careful to note the historian Saul Friedlander's caution on "'fascinating fas-

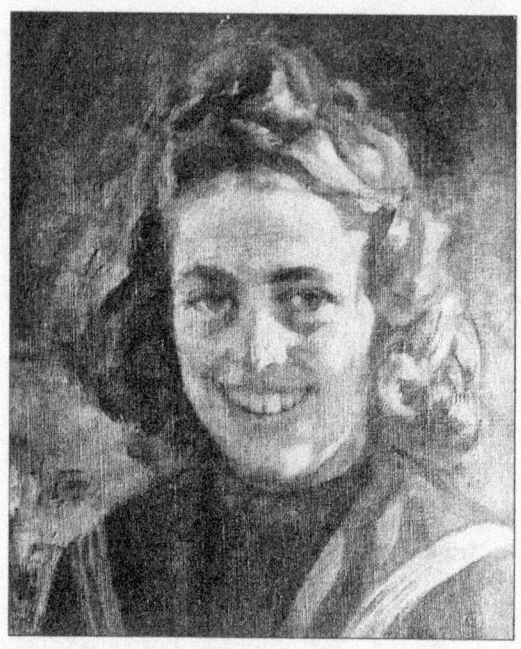

Elisabeth APELGOT was 13 when she was deported on **convoy 71** of April 13, 1944. She had been arrested in La Bachellerie (Dordogne) with her mother and her older sister, Sonia, 19. Sonia survived deportation and wrote: [Here] is the picture of my sister Elisabeth. When I returned from the camps, I found practically none of our possessions, and the only photographs left were moldy. Through a friend I found a painter who copied the decaying photos. From these paintings I then had photos taken. . . . The publication of these pictures seems to me a good idea. A face is more than a name.

Painting of a photograph of Elizabeth Apelgot. From Serge Klarsfeld, *French Children of the Holocaust: A Memorial* (New York: New York University Press, ca. 1996), 443. Courtesy of Serge Klarsfeld and the Beate Klarsfeld Foundation.

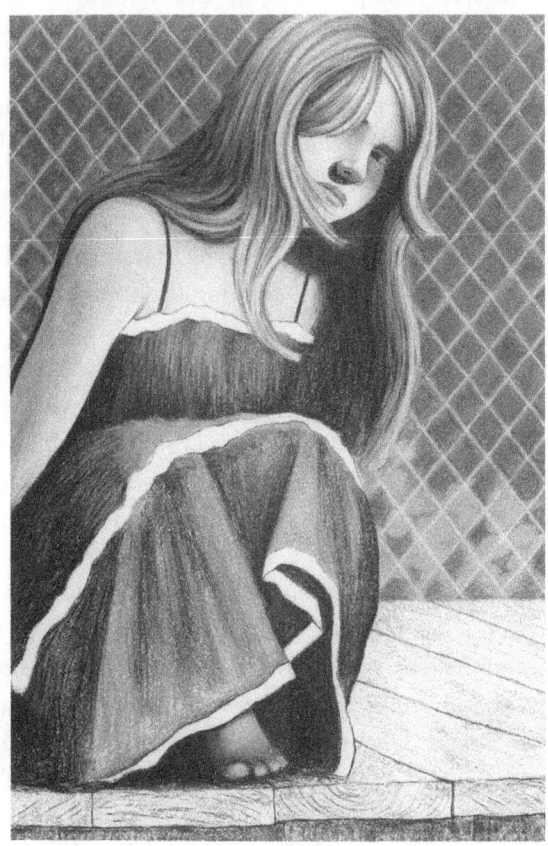

Amy Adler, *What Happened to Amy?*, 1996.
C-print photograph. 20 × 16 inches. Courtesy
of the artist and ACME Gallery, LA.

cism,' in which Friedlander wonders whether an aesthetic obsession with fascism may be less a reflection on fascism that it is an extension of it," he also seems to consider viewers who might feel "unease" with some of these types of works to be "those less at home in the languages of contemporary art."[24] Take, for example, the responses of outrage elicited by works in the Jewish Museum's exhibition "Mirroring Evil: Nazi Imagery / Recent Art" from 2001, in which contemporary artworks that may in fact just have been silly and shallow to many of those "at home in the languages of contemporary art" were exhibited in a context such that elderly Jewish people were provoked to look even sillier for getting so upset.[25]

The work in this exhibition was in keeping with some of the major themes of Young's influential text, and the ideas expressed in the text are as significant as the works in defining the contemporary canon of Holocaust-related artwork.

Young refers to Levinthal's "intentional ambiguity," which allows the viewer to "make [his or her] own story."[26] The blur is key to the creation of this ambiguity: it alters the scale and lends Levinthal's tableaux the possibility of realism — the viewer remains uncertain whether, if refocused, the picture would show the purported subject, or instead reveal the actual objects Levinthal works with, toys. At the same time, the blur maintains the suspension of disbelief and postpones the triviality that the toys might bring to mind. At some level one might perceive a perhaps questionable equalization between the war play of boys and fascist militarism. A boy is a boy for all that. In American art, "fascination with fascism" is joined by fascination with childhood, its cultural artifacts, and, especially, its dysfunctionalities. The conjunction of these two fascinations may have a disconcerting effect in the face of something like the Holocaust, but conversely, the toy's quality of magical belief may lend the historical subject a special poignancy as well as a salutary distance to which the blur provides a further aestheticizing gloss through its meaning as the universal sign for the past — signaling it and distancing it.

For Young, the blur has a dual use for the contemporary artist: "What used to be called 'soft-focus portraiture,' a fountain-of-youth technique by which photographers could obscure the flaws of mortality and the lines of age, has been radically extended by a new generation of painters and photographers to turn the camera into a tool of mimetic doubt and insecurity, not certainty. On the one hand, the blurred paintings of Gerhard Richter or Ed Ruscha suggest to critics like Donald Kuspit a certain collapse of authoritative meaning in our culture at large. At the same time, such fuzziness also prompts the viewer to work harder, if a little less confidently, toward finding meaning, which now exists in the tug-of-war between image and viewer, not in the image or viewer alone." He further remarks, in his discussion of of Levinthal's *Mein Kampf* series, that "the cool studied polish of these images constantly reminds us of their aesthetic intervention between then and now. They are staged to look deliberately staged, choreographed to show their choreography. All rawness is gone, all innocence put to flight. Resonant with our own corrupted traces, these photographs show us how far away from events the icons of our culture have taken us."[27]

Simulacra, cultural icons, deliberate ambiguity—themes naturalized in Levinthal's work are reproblematized in a photographic work by the sculptor Marsha Pels, *I Like Germany and Germany Likes Me*. In this image, used as the show card for a group of works about the fetishization and aesthetization of fascism, *The Hitler Vitrines* (2001), she tries something on. She grafts the Führer's appearance onto her own face and body. In contrast to the casual ease and pride with which Uncle Rudi wears his new uniform, Pels looks uncomfortable, even slightly preposterous. Her masquerade is dangerous and fraught in a number of ways: it is the double imposture by a woman of a man, and by a Jewish woman of the instrument of her destruction, and also of the work of a major German artist, Joseph Beuys, by a Jewish American woman. Her title, *I Like Germany and Germany Likes Me*, is based on the title of a Beuys performance installation piece executed in New York in 1974, *Coyote: I Like America and America Likes Me*. One could argue that Pels's masquerade of masculinity in putting on the image and uniform of Hitler may point to the extent to which Hitler's image is itself an imposture of masculinity, a hypermasculinity that can be seen as a perversion. Pels risks ridicule, which, it should be stressed, would not fall upon her if the image were blurred, because the imposture and her own discomfort, and therefore the potential for ours, are only really evident due to the sharp focus. Levinthal's theater of blurred play-war is frequently reproduced and eminently reproducible, whereas Pels's image is perhaps too raw and controversial to be as successfully integrated into popular circulation as similar works by appropriation artists of her generation, and thus remains relatively unknown.

In researching this essay I was prompted by my sense that Richter's blur was a ubiquitous influence. But in some ways Richter's work has been hard

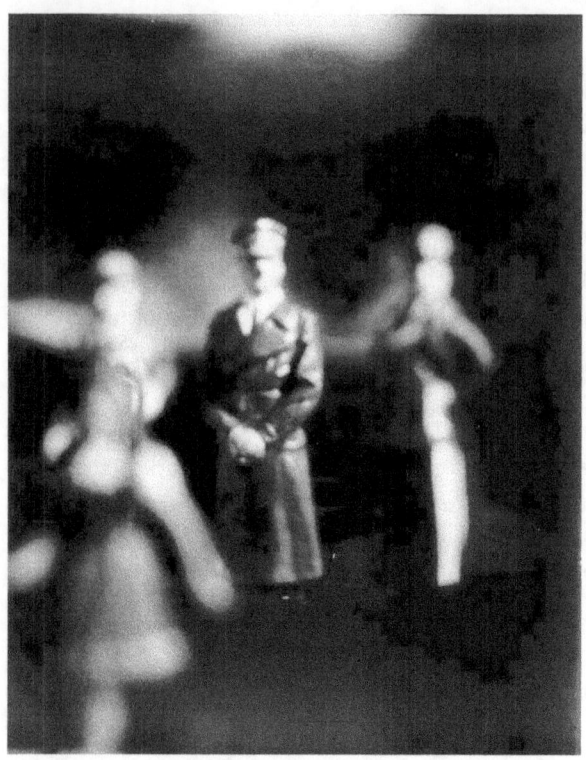

David Levinthal, *Untitled from Mein Kampf*, 1993–1994.
Polaroid Polacolor ER, film print. Courtesy David Levinthal
and Paul Morris Gallery.

to duplicate, or rather what has been hard to duplicate is what I would call
Richter's trifecta. There are other artists who share at least some of the
same historical context or his desire to address a particularly unrepresentable history. The appropriation of the photographic image is a major
category of late-twentieth-century art. The blur effect as an instrument of
distantiation has been a trope since the history of early cinema. But bringing all this together within a painting project is hard to replicate with any
level of effectiveness. It requires "dazzlement of skill" to do what Richter
does—just what he sought to avoid by the gesture of using photography
as his subject.[28] Richter's stated reasons for blurring are usually framed
in terms of his desire to avoid virtuosity, but of course, Richter's blurring
is itself dazzling as a painterly effect despite the fact that such painterly
mastery is not his primary intention. He has written, "I don't create blurs.

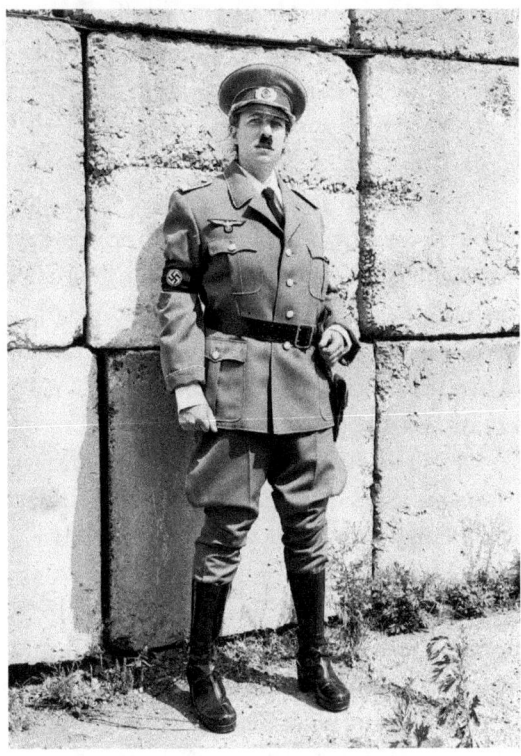

Marsha Pels, *I Like Germany and Germany Likes Me*, 2001. Photograph. 26 × 20 inches. Courtesy of the artist. Photograph by Andrea von Lintel.

Blurring is not the most important thing; nor is it an identity tag for my pictures. When I dissolve demarcations and create transitions, this is not in order to destroy the representation, or to make it more artistic or less precise. The flowing transitions, the smooth, equalizing surface, clarify the content and make the representation credible (an *alla prima* impasto would be too reminiscent of painting, and would destroy the illusion)."[29] However, out of his hands but under his influence, blurring takes on the nature of that which is "too reminiscent of painting" — *his* painting. It may just be too much of a trademarked visual language for anyone else to get away with it in painting. Also, certain ideologies adhere to photography including that it is a more mechanically or technologically based art form so that technique is less trademarked and more democratically available. Finally it is important to keep in mind that the critical apparatus that first produced our understanding of Richter was profoundly hostile to painting. Thus appropriation of photography and blurred focus have spilled back into photography. Even Richter blurs his photographs, as one can see in details from his major archival work, *Atlas*.[30]

But why does the *present* have to be blurry and out of focus? Contemporary artists have accepted the blur as an aesthetic vehicle for nostalgia, memory, and mourning without necessarily sharing the historical context that may have constructed some of Richter's early motivations for using the blur. Artists as diverse as Uta Barth, Bill Jacobson, Sharon Harper, and so many others apply the blur to a variety of subjects—interiors, landscapes, still lives, illness, spiritualism,[31] pornography. Additionally, the blur denotes speed and movement, phenomena also related to the passage of time and to loss, via an imaging method that implies physical and emotional distancing. In many cases there is indication of the direct influence of and the paying of homage to Richter by the younger artist.

For example in Uta Barth's black and white photograph *Ground #39* (1994) the blurred black and white image of bookshelves seems to directly reference Richter's *Cell (Zelle)* from the series *October 18, 1977* (1988), which was painted from photographs of Andreas Baader's prison cell after his death. Barth has zeroed in on only the bookshelves, which occupy the right side of the Richter painting, creating a more formal, all-over composition. A diffuse blur creates a less spectral, even a less Gothic atmosphere than the vertical pull of *Cell*'s paint surface. In the purely aestheticized images of Uta Barth, the blur, "generated by focusing the camera on an unoccupied ground,"[32] gives renewed interest and a postmodern twist of indecipherability and unfixed identity to the highly modernist aesthetic of the pre-blurred image—the plane of a blank wall, white curtains on a white wall in an empty room, a few rectangles on a green wall, the red of a traffic light oozing into the space around it. "The lack of clear focus in her images results not from an urge toward romantic ambiguity, which Barth strongly resists, but rather because she focuses her camera on the absent subject in the foreground, thus rendering the resulting 'background' images indistinct."[33] Avoiding a particular narrative or image is key, both through blurring and emptiness or shifting of subject matter. While beauty is a constant in Barth's work, so too seemingly is a willed desire for a noncommittal stance, for which blurring is the visual stand-in.

In Sharon Harper's work, *Flug (flight)* black and white photographs of the German landscape as seen from a train use the blur, described as "selective focus," to indicate speed, boredom, distance, displacement.[34] Harper's process assures unintentionality of composition to the photograph, since "at high speed on a train, she cannot see exactly what the camera frames at the moment of exposure."[35] The blur creates a kind of gorgeously romantic charcoal drawing effect, while at the same time the landscapes themselves refer to an already known code of generic landscape already referenced by artists such as Richter, among many others.

Bill Jacobson's photographs push the blur to the limits of visibility in portraits of ghostly figures and landscapes that vanish into whiteness. Jacobson writes: "They are about personal desire and collective loss, as well as the tentativeness and vulnerability of life in the age of AIDS. My intent is that they refer to those known and unknown, and to the fading of our memories and the recurring of our dreams."[36] While documentary photography, in focus, would be effective—for example, in showing the physical manifestations of illness—Jacobson's blur performs erotically cathected loss and the instability of memory. If representation almost by definition is an effort to bridge the gap between what was and what is, the blur takes that basis in lack a step further. Unlike Richter who still has some faith in the truth, perhaps even in the superior truth of photography, Jacobson's work has been interpreted as indicative of our loss of "faith in its precision or exactitude."[37]

In other contemporary photographic works, blur is the visual analogue of the fluidity of gender identity. Jack Pierson's photographs, of young men or beautiful places where such young men might hang out, are said to represent "post-sexual desire": "Post-sexuality versus sexuality is photographing a partial, transitive sexuality that never settles into a category. Whatever subversive power these pictures have does not come from representing some sort of sexual marginality (as in Nan Goldin's work), but from diffracting and atomizing all sexual models, authoritarian or not, mainstream or marginal, for the sake of post-sexual fluidity." And this is accomplished via the blur. "Pierson has absolutely no interest in sexuality as soon as it takes on a sharp, clear form."[38] For other artists, blurring is proving to be popular method of updating the nude, either stereotypically aestheticized or stereotypically pornographic. So, for example, in the work of Thomas Ruff, blurring is used mainly when the subject is a nude, as in his *Nudes* series from 2000 of images downloaded from porn sites on the Internet, blown up and blurred. (As if it were not entirely obvious in any case that most work has a patrilineage, and nudes have been the currency

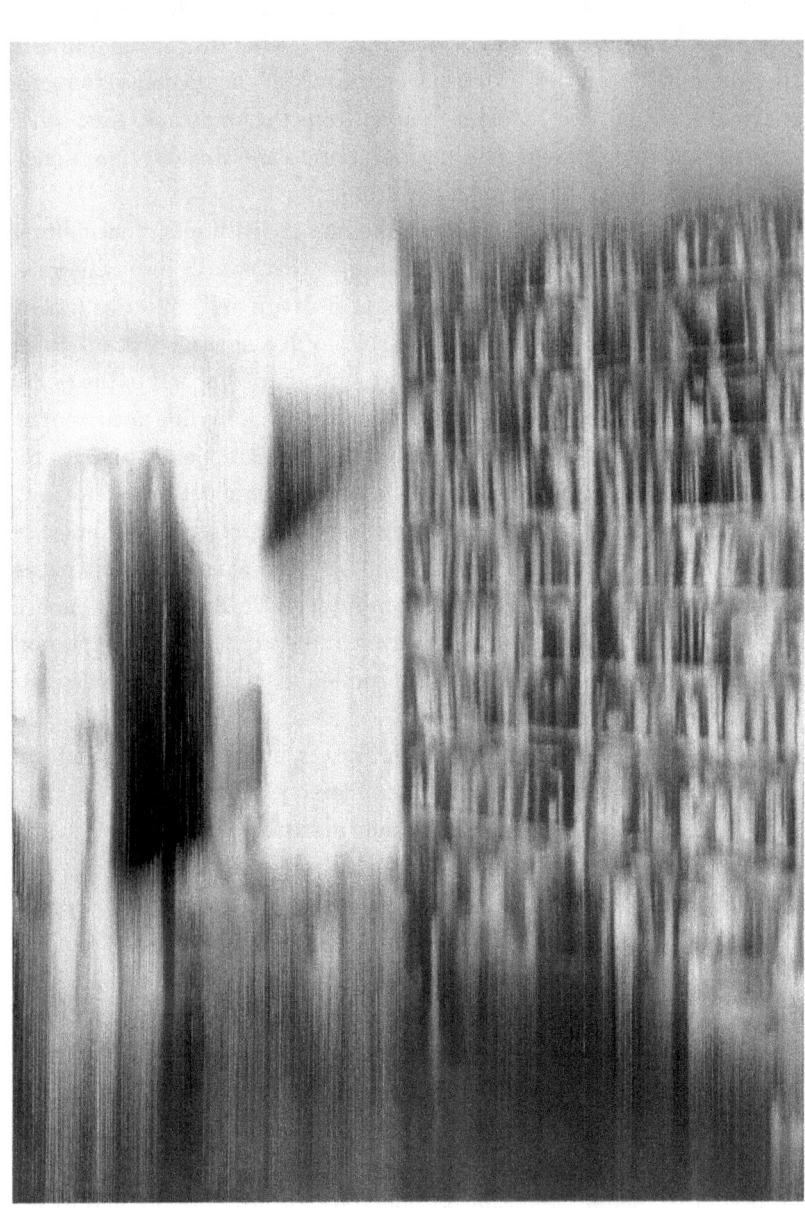

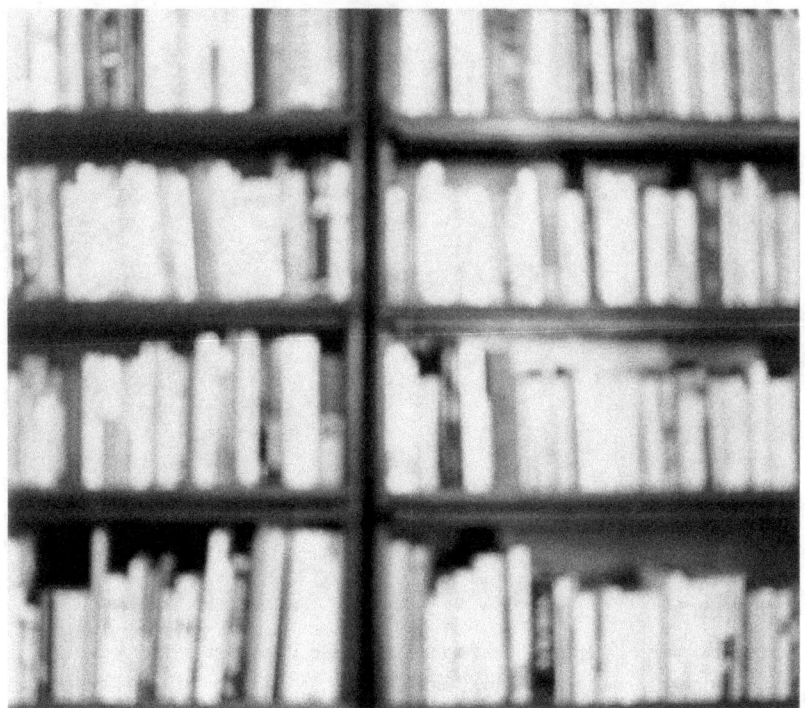

Uta Barth, *Ground #39*, 1994. Black and white photograph mounted on panel.
13¾ × 16 inches. Courtesy of the artist and Tanya Bonakdar Gallery, New York.

(*opposite*) Gerhard Richter, *Cell (Zelle)*, from *October 18, 1977 (18. Oktober 1977)*,
1988. Oil on canvas. 6 feet, 7 inches × 55 inches. The Sidney and Harriet Janis
Collection, gift of Philip Johnson, and acquired through the Lillie P. Bliss Be-
quest (all by exchange); Enid A. Haupt Fund; Nina and Gordon Bunshaft Bequest
Fund; and gift of Emily Rauh Pulitzer (169.1995.m), the Museum of Modern Art,
New York. Digital image © by The Museum of Modern Art/Licensed by SCALA /
Art Resource, NY.

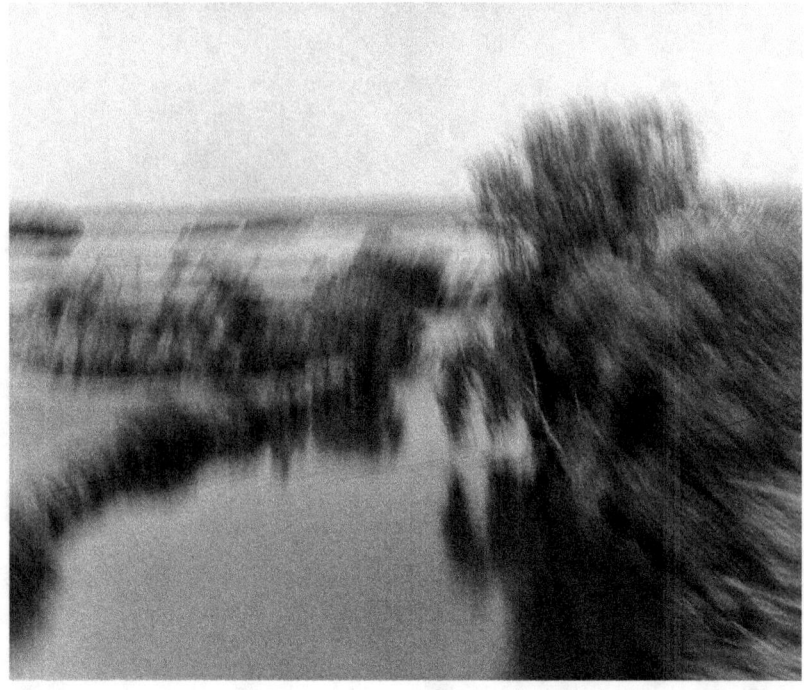

Sharon Harper, *Flug (flight)*, *Germany vi*, 2000. Gelatin silver print.
20 × 24 inches. Photograph © by Sharon Harper.

of high art since the Renaissance, these blurred porn images pay obei-
sance and take on the legacy of Richter's initial grey blurred porn images
from the early 1960s.)

The blur in these artists' work relies on a shared cultural memory of
a certain type of generic black and white snapshot. Many of these artists emphasize the techniques used to "defocus," or get a "bad" picture,"
whereas in the history of amateur photography blurring generally has
been considered an unfortunate accident.[39] Technological advances have
sought to eliminate any opportunity for such human error in order to
make photography "foolproof" by developing increasingly accurate lenses,
sensitive film, and, for the amateur in particular, autofocus, "point and
shoot" cameras. In these contemporary works, perhaps blurring represents a form of resistance to technology, an assertion of human frailty. On
the other hand, the blur is now codified in the settings of digital-imaging
software programs and is built into digital cameras themselves. The blur
is just one of many given effects based on received ideas about the repre-

sentation of the past, memory, and sentiment. Adobe Photoshop offers a number of subheadings to its "blur" filter, including "Average," "Blur," "Blur more," "Gaussian blur," "Lens blur," "Motion blur," and "Smart blur." In a euphemistic blurring of the word "blur," the Canon Digital Elph camera I bought in 2002 offered a "photo effect" setting entitled "Low Sharpening."

The insistence on the overdetermined nature of the process of blurring raises questions about the problematics of intentionality. Returning to Young's analysis of Levinthal's work, for example, the blur is seen as important because it creates an undetermined image and "the more ambiguous, underdetermined, and oblique the image, the more it seems to invite the viewer's own narrative. The sharper the image, the more repellent it is of multiple readings, for it crowds out the reader's projected story with the clutter of its own detail."[40] However, one might also recall Roland Barthes's dismissal of intentionality in the case of the *punctum*: "Certain details may 'prick' me. If they do not, it is doubtless because the photographer has put them there intentionally."[41] In contemporary photography the blur is always intentional and thereby may also be highly overdetermined (especially to a viewer like Barthes), just the opposite of the creative ambiguity ascribed to the blur by Young and others.

These blurred images assert a deliberate blindness. They are also a blind: they blur something in order to prevent one from seeing that there is nothing to see in the first place. As a larger instance of contemporary utterance, they emphasize a kind of withholding of *punctum*, punctum denial. What is often masked by the blurring mechanism is the utter ordinariness and lack of historical import of the photo, or the memory. Most people today do not count a Nazi or a serial killer among their family photo album. The blur is there as a pretense, in lieu of a past. It implies that if only one could see it clearly, something would indeed be there to be seen. But the blur in photography prevents the apprehension of the *punctum*, as defined by Barthes: "Very often the *punctum* is a 'detail.'" And if the undifferentiated, fogged-over field of vision withholds from us the traction of the punctum, it also withholds the informational aspect of the *studium*.[42]

The denial of punctum is an active process that is not benign in its physical effect on the viewer. Many who write about these blurred photos emphasize the effort that one has to make to see better and compare the experience to trying to see without one's glasses. At its limits this effort can be painful, as one almost instinctively does try to see in focus. In these moments, denial of punctum is a species of sadism, a somatized deployment of indifference. And this has become just another style that has penetrated the academy, the MFA stream. Because appropriation is the method most validated by the highest echelons of critical reception, an unbroken cycle of an affect of indifference is engendered and promoted. This essay demonstrates my desire to at least trouble that cycle, which I experience as vicious indeed. The blur challenges the viewer to strain to see . . . perhaps nothing. Ultimately the viewer must resign herself to a kind of double blindness, her own and that of the artwork.

But the blurred work is itself possessed of a look that creates an emotional effect that brings me to a consideration of the relationship between lack of affect as a postwar reaction formation and lack of affect as a primary mechanism of the original "banality of evil" performed by Germans during World War II.[43] In *Survival at Auschwitz*, Primo Levi expresses curiosity, in the most serious meaning of the word, about the ability of one particular German to not perceive someone else as a human being:

> When he finished writing, he raised his eyes and looked at me.
>
> From that day I have thought about Doktor Pannwitz many times and in many ways . . . above all when I was once more a free man, I wanted to meet him again, not from a spirit of revenge, but merely from a personal curiosity about the human soul.
>
> Because that look was not one between two men. . . . One felt in that moment, in an immediate manner, what we all thought and said about the Germans. The brain which governed those blue eyes and manicured hands said: "This something in front of me belongs to a species which it is obviously opportune to suppress. In this particular case, one had to first make sure that it does not contain some utilizable element."[44]

I am not suggesting that an artwork or a critical aesthetic framework can be compared to a Nazi, yet the collective impact of Richter's influence or, rather, the general consensus that "lack of affect" or "indifference" are the only appropriate stances in the face of contemporary culture, enshrines "psychic armor" so that it no longer functions only as a self-protective mechanism against historical insight within a "German modality"[45] (or only as a critique of that mechanism) but also as armament against the sensibilities of those whose personal losses have rendered them incapable of endowing themselves with such self-protective armor. If it is generally the case in criminal situations that the victim is left to sustain affect which the murderer is able to suppress or never felt in the first place, it becomes a bit more serious when lack of affect seeps beyond its historical root to permeate postmodern attitudes.

It is one thing if a person won't look at you as a human being. It is quite another, and almost as painful a matter although certainly not an actual danger to life and limb, if an artwork presents an affectless face. (In this regard, style is immaterial; thus, I am not equating minimalism or reductivism with lack of affect.) Richter's use of lack of affect is authentically formed by, and representative of, a doubly fraught experience of German history, whereas later artworks that insist on "anomic banality (even if given only as a posture)" may have the capacity to kill me as a viewer and as a historical subject.[46] That is to say, my own historically grounded emotional reaction—to the textual exegeses of *Uncle Rudi*, Richter's early statements about subjectivity, and the same network of art and exegesis surrounding some of the work of Richter's artistic descendants and critical acolytes—is denied validity as a critical response by such later artworks' deliberate "posture" of indifference, thereby denying me an equal place as a historical subject. The death of the author is now the death of the viewer, not through fire but through ice. In the killing of the subjectivity of the viewer, the cult of anomie is just another modality of the Society of the Spectacle. The problem is with the shifting of rhetorical meaning and with what happens when a language that makes sense for one person in one historical condition is picked up by others in a different, unrelated historical condition, and, further, made into a dogma and a commodity. If the balance between deadpan and fury is tipped too far on either side, we are left with empty emotionalism or false rebellion on the one side—for instance, the neo-expressionist art that repelled both Richter and Buchloh—or heartless cruelty on the other. Richter has tried to come to terms with the Holocaust or, at least, the tragedy of the German character, on the most serious of terms, but the enshrinement of lack of affect, or the choice of an affect of indifference articulated through visual means (such as the blur) as the correct strategy for dealing with the Holocaust, may try to counteract or critique this phenomenon yet it risks re-creating the same effect it sets out to critique. The circle is unbroken: anomie works to repress collective guilt, historically determined psychological anomie gathers to it aesthetic imperatives and these become the legitimated model that enacts, performs, and enforces itself not only upon the descendants of the murderers but of the murdered, and, further, on people who have no history at all but have adopted anomie as "posture."

The possibility of artworks having, if not historical ambition in the grand sense that one can ascribe to Richter, then at least a desire to create a historically induced yet nonheroic portraiture of a destroyed culture is suggested to me by the work of my father, Ilya Schor.

Clearly it may be impossible for me to take an objective critical stance in relation to such work, thereby by some standards invalidating my argument, yet insertion of his work is at the heart of it. And who will argue against the verity that most art historical judgments have at least some personal basis and are hardly neutrally axiomatic no matter how much the goal or the rhetoric is one of objectivity?

Born into the shtetl Hasidic culture of Eastern Europe, my father studied painting at the Warsaw Academy of Fine Art. He went to Paris in 1937 and came to New York in 1941. Beginning during the war and particularly after he arrived in America, his work turned to his early memories of his small village of Zloczów in Galicia. His paintings are modest in their temperament. They allow a momentary impression of not just the appearance but something of the soul of a world that had been eliminated, a world in which, as Abraham Joshua Heschel wrote, "history was only an intimation," and where "what was apparent to the mind [was] but a thin surface of the undisclosed, and [the Hasidim of Eastern Europe] often preferred to gain a foothold on the brink of the deep even at the price of leaving the solid ground of the superficial."[47]

There is perhaps a folk aspect to my father's work. It seems far from modernity and part of that distance is evidenced by the very sweetness and unwordliness that seems to have been a characteristic of this lost world.

These paintings avoid the tropes of heroic painting in general and of portraiture in particular, despite their centralized composition; their models are anonymous Jews from the shtetl, who even when they are located centrally and frontally within the composition, avert their eyes from the viewer looking toward a spiritual world of study of Torah. They are subsumed to a religion of humility; painted in an unpretentious style, they are small, and they are in gouache rather than oil—all the traditional markers of "importance" are lacking. In relation to Richter's *Uncle Rudi* my

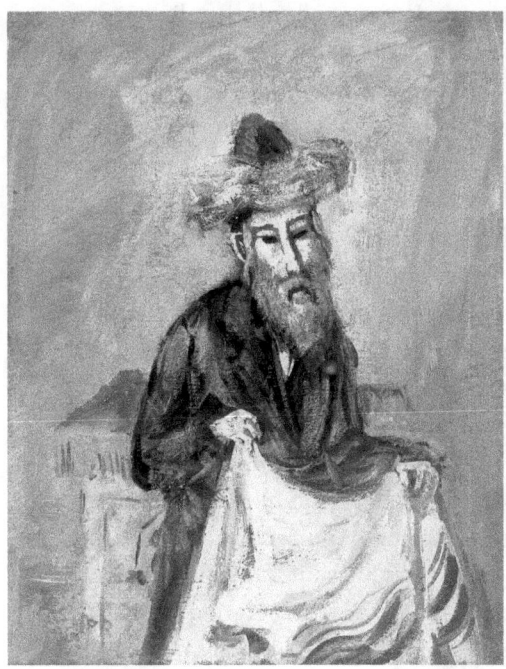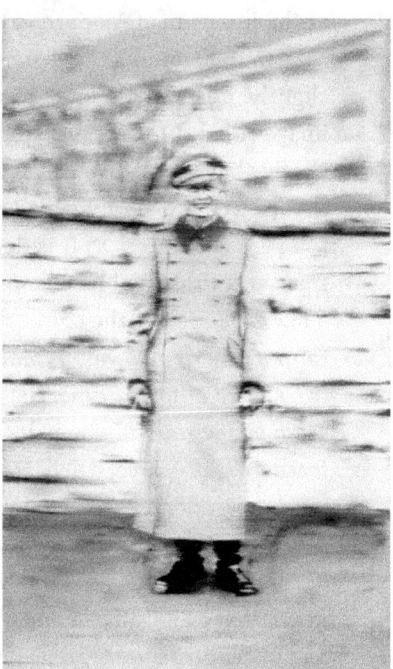

(*left*) Ilya Schor, *Folding the Tallis*, 1950s. Gouache on board. 9½ × 7½ inches. Courtesy of Mira Schor. (*right*) Gerhard Richter, *Uncle Rudi*.

father's Eastern European Hasids of pre-War Europe are truly the "unrepresentable subject of history."[48]

If one was to consider portraiture on a spectrum, with anonymous folk paintings at the left and official portraits of Napoleon, Hitler, or Stalin at the right, my father's small gouache portrait of an early-twentieth-century Eastern European Hasidic Jew folding a tallis is close to the left and *Uncle Rudi* is closer to Napoleon's portraits, edged there in part by its own historical ambition and by the machine of art critical reception. While what my father called the melody of Eastern European Jewry has been stilled, in history and in art, Richter's critique of heroicism in painting and memory has become heroicized via the installation of Richter as exemplar.

• • •

I finally saw the painting *Uncle Rudi* at the exhibition of Gerhard Richter's work, "Gerhard Richter: Forty Years of Painting," curated by Robert Storr at the Museum of Modern Art in 2002. It is a small painting, lighter grey than in the reproductions of it which all seemed to have blurred the image slightly. Certainly Richter has subjected the appropriated photographic image to a process of blurring: evenly horizontal traces of what appears to have been a bristle brush drag the image out of focus. But these traces themselves are very visible and crisp—let us say that they are sharper than the blur effect as it is deployed in later works by Richter where the trace and thus the blur is more diffuse and poetic. In addition there are a few dark areas—the shoes, the eyes, lips, collar, cuffs, and the horizontal midline of the wall—that are sharply delineated by fine dark brush marks of a different type. The clear flicks of dark grey and the black boots seem to levitate off the painting surface. The vertical line of the coat is feathered, it is a very delicate painting mark, and therefore doubly outrageous, under the circumstances. All of these non-blurred marks serve as visual *puncta* to the painting, anchoring our attention. *Uncle Rudi* is brash, ironic, young, exuberantly objective; it is almost giddily humorous in relation to its subject and to the method of representation the painter had at that time newly developed. If it is a critique of heroic portraiture, nevertheless it has the energy of a large historical statement arrived at early and almost all of a sudden, and this reflects back on the subject in such a way that it is less about the negative aspects of Uncle Rudi's historical identity than it is about its own identity as a triumphant gesture in the history of painting.

My assertions are that much contemporary art is engaged in a stance of indifference; that the visual device of the blur is one of the methods by which that stance is realized in visual art, although of course a whole other essay could discuss the affect of indifference in many other types of twentieth-century artworks. I have indicated that sometimes blur reaches for sentiment but also can transmit moral equivalence. Also that art whose stance exudes lack of affect, or an affect of indifference, may in some way create in the viewer who has been unable to secure the "psychic armor" of indifference some emotions that parallel (although certainly don't equal) the effect of a Nazi's look, a look that denies the viewer's subjectivity or desires for that denial. I point to a great irony of contemporary art—that because the great horror of the Holocaust is perhaps fundamentally unrepresentable and because overly emotional expressions can seem either unequal to that reality or even historically compromised, what has won out is an emotional temperature of coolness and a romancing of mediation and distantiation that can at times share the hard heart of the horror, except attenuated to a survivable constant.

Richter's use of the blur has been a triumphantly successful device, in his work and as a widely imitated gesture. Uncle Rudi the man may have died and the Nazis may have been defeated, but *Uncle Rudi*, as an artwork and an art idea, won the war.

OFF THE GRID

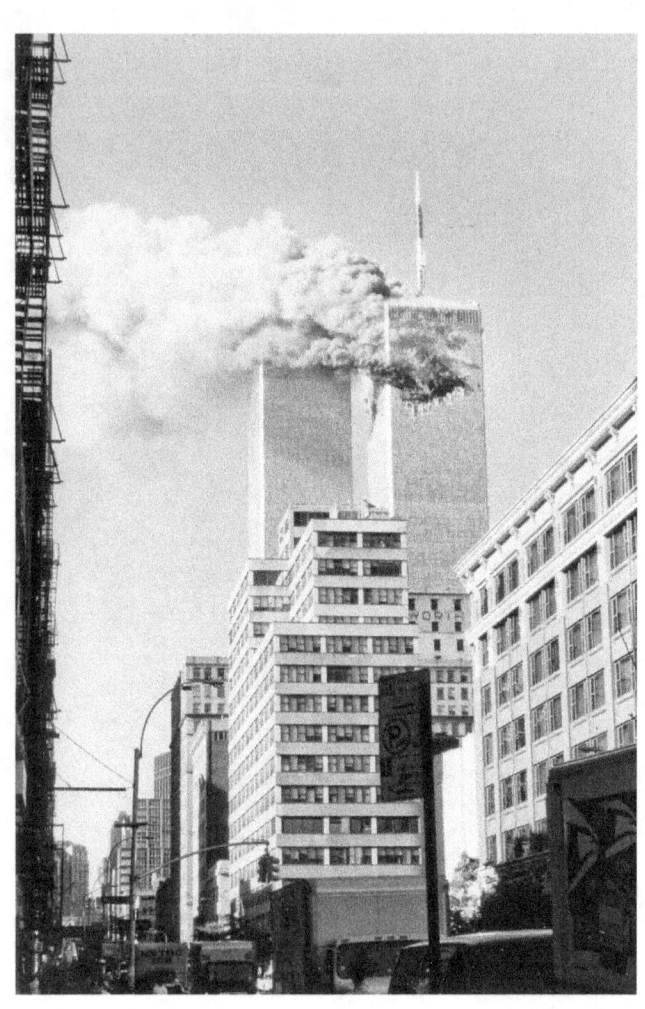

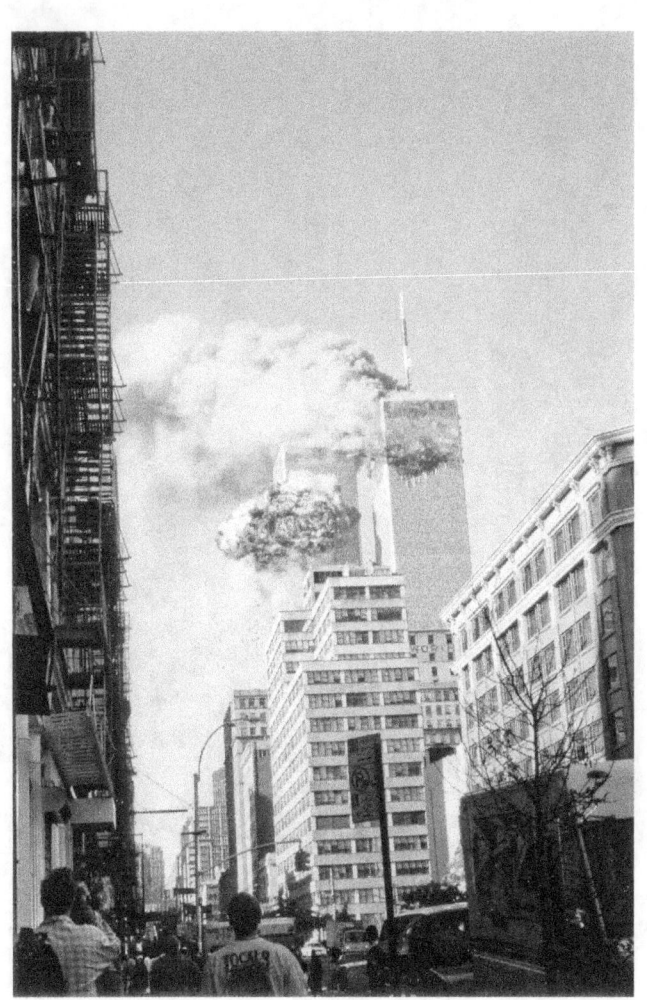

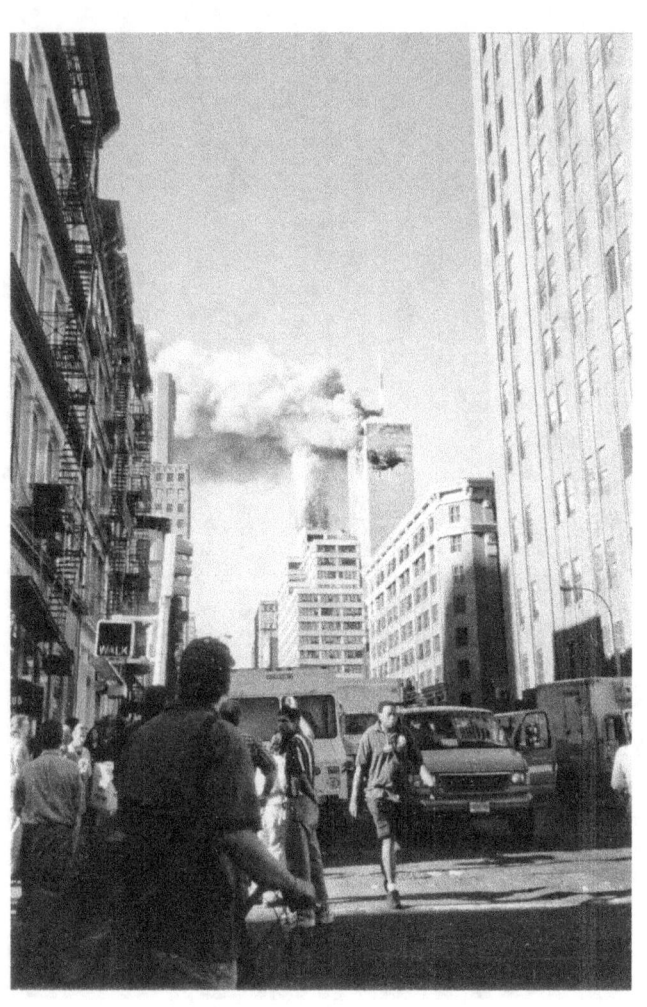

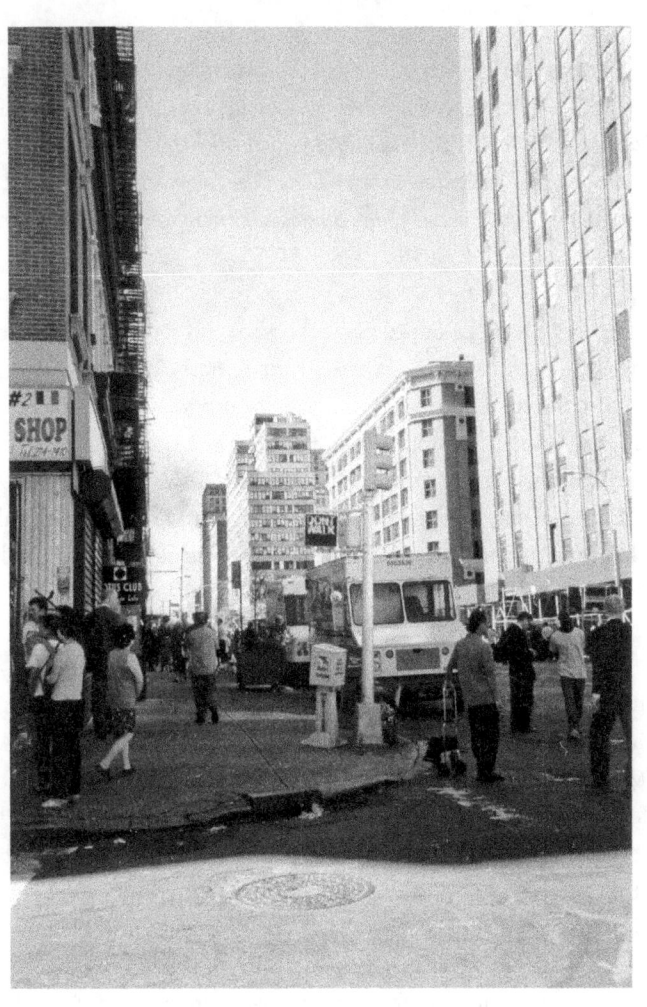

This text began as an email composed in the days following September 11, 2001. In those days, writing it was my principal occupation, and I wrote to preserve the details of each day. There are many records like this. Mine made its way to other countries, and, my name dropped from the forwarded message, it eventually was emailed from Europe to my downstairs neighbor.

. . .

The evening of Monday, September 10, 2001, rainstorms moved through the New York area from the west. At 7:00 PM, a brief, intensely heavy downpour scoured the streets of Lower Manhattan. Just then, a friend who was delivering my computer and paintings from Provincetown called from her van parked in front of my building. I went downstairs and we stared at each other, me in my lobby, she in her van, as torrential sheets of rain kept us from moving. A Yankees game was delayed and finally postponed.

. . .

I live in Lower Manhattan on Lispenard Street, which is one block south of Canal Street, fourteen blocks north of the World Trade Center. At about 8:45 AM on the morning of Tuesday, September 11, I was still in bed and had just turned the radio on to WNYC, the NPR affiliate in New York City.

I heard two sounds, some kind of muffled roar and then a thudding crash. This neighborhood is incredibly noisy, so it could have been a truck crashing into something on Canal, but the noise was notable enough that it crossed my mind that it might be a building collapse in the area. After the interval of time it took for that image to cross my mind, within less than a minute of the sound, an announcer on WNYC yelled that there had been an explosion at the World Trade Center. I rushed into my clothes,

---

(*previous pages*) World Trade Center, views south from the corner of Lispenard and Church Streets, September 11, 2001, at 9:01 AM (EDT), 9:03.30 AM, ca. 9:20 AM, ca. 1:30 PM. Photographs © by Mira Schor.

grabbed my keys and my camera, ran out the door, and got to the corner of Lispenard and Church by about 8:57 AM. This is the corner from which the video of the first plane crashing into one of the buildings, which I would call the "money shot," was filmed. In this brief clip you may notice firemen and wonder what they are doing there.

They were investigating the report of a possible gas leak in front of my friend Jack Whitten's house. Jack saw the whole thing from the moment one fireman looked up at the loud noise from the low flying plane. On the tape, after the plane hits, someone says, "Holy Shit." That was Jack.

I stood with neighbors and passersby and we gaped at the black gash, flames, and smoke at the top of the building. I felt sure that I could see a person waving a white cloth from a window at the top right corner of the first tower. I could not hear any sirens. Although I know now that even in that brief time emergency vehicles and the mayor had already arrived on the site or were speeding toward it, it seemed as if this was happening and no one was doing anything.

In the sequence of pictures I took from the moment I reached the corner, between the sixth and the seventh picture there is a gap which represents perhaps twenty seconds. In this interval, an enormous explosion on the left side of the South Tower expanded and engulfed the entire top half of the building in a giant ball of flame before subsiding into flames and smoke. During this time I forgot I had a camera.

We couldn't see the plane from our vantage point and I was stunned when I found out several days later that everyone watching TV at that moment had seen the plane hit the building in real time, "live."

As more people gathered, and people passed us walking uptown, we watched the smoke and fire in both buildings. We all reassured each other that the buildings were built to withstand the impact of a plane. Perhaps because of this belief, I went home to call family and thus I only saw the collapses on TV as I spoke to a friend who was looking from her window on Franklin Street at the debris from the second tower falling toward her. I felt no fear for myself but I had lost all realization that I could go out and see what was happening. I feel deep regret that I didn't see the collapses with my own eyes, no matter how nightmarish, because it seems like it would help me understand the reality.

About forty minutes after the collapses, knowing the city was being closed down, I decided to go out to get food and cash. It was a beautiful day in New York City, clear, mild, and dry, the kind of day when the postcard pictures are taken and when the air is most pleasantly compatible to the inner temperature of the human body. Where the towers had stood the sky was a gorgeous blue with just a low movement of the ochre-gray dust toward Brooklyn. Completely surreal, unreal, nuclear.

A few blocks north at the Gourmet Garage, people were beginning to arrive to buy as much food as they could carry. One lady was standing with a small container of raspberries and one other small item. I said to her, "Lady, you're not really prepared for an emergency, are you?" She said, "Oh, my husband will be back from New Jersey later." Exit and access to the city had already been blocked off. I said, "Your husband isn't coming back from New Jersey tonight." Now *that* sounded like an emergency to her.

On the street in SoHo, I flinched slightly when I heard a fighter jet above, and looking up I also saw, silent and silvery, very high up in the sky, perhaps on its way to Canada, probably one of the last jets to fly over New York for days.

At the corner of Spring Street and Broadway, the streets already emptied of all traffic, a guy had pulled over his SUV and turned his radio up. A crowd of about thirty people listened. In the midst of all the confusion, a lady took the time to warn me that my bag was open. I took pictures. In one picture, a tall, large man stands apart, looking back downtown. His suit is covered with ash. I realized later that no one spoke to him.

I returned home against the moving tide of people walking uptown, some wet from sprinkler systems, some covered with dust, some intact, all calm and quiet, and I prepared to hunker down.

I went out again at dusk: on Broadway the sunset was backlighting the cloud of dust and the Woolworth Building with a glowing pink. At the corner of Church and White the temperature suddenly rose about ten degrees. The closest I could get to the World Trade Center site was a barricade on Franklin and West Broadway. A few blocks down, the vista narrowed and it looked as if the world ended there in a dark grey cloud.

That night was very scary. Cable TV went out at 7:00 PM (paradoxically, for the next three days, during major media coverage of a real story that for once affected me directly, I only had access to the local CBS affiliate and grainy BBC coverage on an old black and white TV). The neighborhood was deserted. We were twenty blocks south from the line of demarcation above which some sort of normal city life apparently continued.

We feared another building collapse or gas explosion. I packed a small bag with absolute necessities: passport, wallet, money, flashlight, the little of my mother's jewelry that I had, a zip drive with my computer files, medication, my keys. What else could I take? I grabbed the negatives from my time at Bellagio as a memory of great beauty. I looked around my studio at my work but realized the futility of taking even an album of slides with me. I placed slip-on shoes near my bed and lay down half-dressed: I wore a T-shirt and panties and left a pair of pants at the door near the bag, figuring that I could always put them on in the street!

THE NEXT DAY, I found my street behind police barricades. There was no traffic for miles. After hearing it was open, my neighbor Olga and I ventured as far as the Gourmet Garage. I bought flowers: freesia for scent and yellow-centered sunflowers for joyful color. The wind changed direction on Wednesday around noon and that second night terrible, acrid smoke filled my loft, especially my small bedroom.

THURSDAY I was desperate for the *New York Times* and walked up toward Fourteenth Street, which was the line of demarcation. In 1950s movies, the aftermath of WWIII might be indicated by a vacant Wall Street filmed at 5:00 AM on a Sunday morning. That's what the streets of SoHo looked like. You could have shot a cannon down Grand Street and lain down to sleep in the middle of Broadway. Looking south the sky was white with smoke. At every major cross street there were police checkpoints. In the Village there was a slightly greater sense of peacefulness although very few food stores were open; there were no cars and few people.

Suddenly at Fourteenth Street there was a Hollywood version of a New York traffic jam, with buses, cars, and emergency vehicles, and sidewalks crowded with people. I was afraid to cross to the other side for fear I would not be able to get back home, so I doubled back through the East Village, empty except for a few restaurants with people sitting out and eating: the air was hot and increasingly heavy with the acrid smell of smoke. At Astor Place a newsvendor had a few *New York Times* issues salted away behind a crate. I stopped at Dean and Deluca on my way and enjoyed an iced coffee and the beauty of a row of some kind of red bottled liquid arrayed on an upper shelf illuminated by the bright lighting in the store. I asked workers there to wet a paper napkin for covering my face so that I could breathe as I walked the final blocks home. I cleaned my house and washed the bedroom floor, changing the smoky sheets, and putting a fan in it. That night another intense rainstorm befell the city, thunder and enormous lightning bolts humbling the scale of the city. If ever a rainstorm could be said to be apocalyptic, this was the one.

FRIDAY Susan B. came back downtown. On Tuesday she had been on the subway going down to her studio on Canal Street. The train moved at a crawl and the conductor only said that the delay was due to "police action at Cortland Street." She had no idea of any of the things that had already happened when she finally got out shortly before 10:00 AM and found herself in a crowd of people looking at the towers burning. Just then the South Tower fell.

We had lunch at Lupe's. I had felt nauseous but ate ravenously when the food was put in front of me. I walked to the Village through light rain, again to get the paper, which this day I found a bit closer, at Eighth Street. At Washington Square one of the many impromptu memorial walls had sprung up, with flowers, candles, letters, and signs for the missing. Through the arch looking north I could see the Empire State Building's elegant needle to the sky, to the south, only a great gap where the towers once had been my beacons homeward.

SATURDAY, the line of demarcation came down from Fourteenth Street to Canal Street, bringing with it a great human circus. I met Susanna H. for lunch and more friends joined us on their way down to volunteer with the Salvation Army. There was a crazy looseness to such impromptu socializing in a city where everything is always planned far ahead and friends no longer even speak on the phone; rather, just thinking of someone qualifies as a visit. The streets were crowded with flotillas of work vehicles and spectators finally able to come closer to where *it* had happened. In sci-fi movies there is always a moment when the monster or flying saucer is destroyed, and people gradually come out from hiding to look at the mangled and smoking remains or wreckage. If they stare in awed silence, security and order have returned to the world and it is the end of the movie. If chaos and revelry ensue, more havoc is yet to come.

Canal Street's circus included both elements. People who finally could get closer to the disaster crowded at places with a clear view downtown to stare somberly while a marching band of black students from Oakwood College in Huntsville, Alabama, marched east on Canal, continuously playing the Star Spangled Banner and the Battle Hymn of the Republic. The melodies and the physical vibration of the drums made my neighbor and me cry briefly. This was good since in general I felt like I had suffered an emotional lobotomy. But there were also people in funny hats hoping to get on television.

I walked downtown, eventually getting as far as Reade Street. In the frozen zone, the streets were silent and deserted, except for emergency vehicles, trucks filled with debris, Verizon and Con Edison trucks, and the occasional temporary deposits of completely destroyed cars. I now know what steel-thread tires are, because often the threads were all that had survived in the wheel casings. The closer you got the eerier it was, because there was nothing to see but a few smoldering, jagged ruins enveloped in dark smoke.

But the beautiful cast-iron buildings of TriBeCa were remarkably intact. The streets and the buildings had been washed down, not just by Thursday night's rain, but also by department of sanitation trucks, so that they sparkled. At the corner of Hudson and Duane lovely old Dutch-style buildings' clean windows caught the light of the clearing late afternoon, and the intersection glistened like a street in a Vermeer painting. But a block south were the National Guard, Salvation Army disaster relief trucks and storefronts, police, and temporary above-ground cables snaking along the gutters.

The site is said to be indescribably enormous and terrible, the TV miniaturizes it. The relief work is incredible—the people who run New York turn out to know what they are doing. People in the neighborhood also speak of girders covered with blood and workers vomiting on the site. One artist went to his roof after the first plane crashed and found it covered in blood, fragmented flesh, debris, and paper. I repeat these things not to exploit their horror, but because this repetition is part of what it means to be a New Yorker now. We always have to be experts, so now we are experts on the details of horror. What seems ghoulish relish is really one of the myriad ways in which we are trying to get a grip on understanding what happened.

In those first few days, my neighbors and I felt very isolated from the rest of the city. We felt fortunate that we had power and water, relatively unaffected phone service and that we were able to stay in our homes unlike many of our friends a few blocks closer to the site. And somehow it felt right to be close to "ground zero," in an abnormal place.

When I had been at Bellagio that June, our comings and goings from the Shangri-La on the hill through the ornate cast-iron gate was the cause of envy and curiosity. Now my photo ID gave me a new privilege, of being an inhabitant of the zone nearest hell. And it felt like a privilege to be here. I even have a strange longing for those first few days when we had the sense, disturbing yet comforting, that we were the last people on earth. We were alone, yet we were together. We felt a tremendous solidarity with our neighbors and our neighborhood. In fact, in a neighborhood besieged by millionaires, the only people around seemed to be a very few of the longest-term artist residents.

I ran into Nancy Davidson and her husband, Greg, just as they came out of their place on Duane Street. Nancy had a show up at the Robert Miller Gallery. The opening had been scheduled for September 11. They had been home during the crashes and collapses six blocks away and stayed in their loft, though without power and phone (but with water and gas).

They stayed because they were afraid that if they left, their landlord, who has been trying to get rid of them, would take the opportunity to claim the building was structurally damaged so that they could never return and he could gut the building for luxury lofts. Near such devastation, I could only wonder, who else but artists would chose to live in such difficult physical circumstances?

Many of us have lived here for over twenty years, with the towers looming above us as a constant, familiar, and beautiful presence. Do I exaggerate? After all, now I can't even remember where they were and from where I could see them. But they were, from afar at any rate, as glorious as Chartres Cathedral, in that verticality represents the essence of human kind's desire for transcendence from "this mortal coil." So their destruction not only represents unimaginable loss of life, but also the very murder of this human desire to defy gravity and the contingency of flesh.

I did not see my students for more than a week. I wondered what I would say to them about the repercussions of this event on artmaking, because that is what we do and will go on doing. Perhaps irony will not look like such an easy option now. What we saw "with our own eyes" looked like a movie; we couldn't believe what we saw, and we don't believe anything we didn't see with our own eyes, so what is the nature of the image?

The event was marked by the usage of new methods of communications—cell-phone calls from the victims, video recorders and cameras all over the area. There was also the primacy of the real, of flesh: the victims' families listing their birthmarks and what they were wearing, being asked to bring tooth and hair brushes for DNA samples; the sheer mass of matter that must be removed by hand to rescue anyone and to clean that immense space. Yet just because one saw terrible things, doesn't mean that these have to enter one's artwork literally. In Iran listening to Britney Spears might constitute rebellion. Here some of my friends sought relief in Marx Brothers' movies. I was first able to feel human compassion when on Sunday I lay down and listened to my favorite record of Dinu Lipatti playing Chopin waltzes. You never know where the political really resides in art.

That being said, the first Sunday afterward I did a fourteen-foot-high drawing of the letters that make up the word *trace*, destroyed, burnt, deconstructed, falling. It needed its twin, which I finished a few days later, making it a bit shorter than the first, as the South Tower was to the north. My ceiling is only nine-and-a-half-feet high so the paper spilled onto the floor.

. . .

HURRICANE BOB had cut a path across Cape Cod on August 19, 1991. It was composed primarily of dry, high wind that drove salt spray from the bay and ocean onto the summer vegetation. By the next day everything green had died. For the rest of that summer, one's footsteps crackled on autumnal dead leaves in hot, bright heat unrelieved and unfiltered by what would have been the cooling shadow of richly leafed trees in an ordinary August.

If this weren't depressing enough, the storm had disturbed beehives, wasps' nests, and yellow jackets from miles around. They buzzed angrily, not only in the streets and gardens, but even on the beach, where they hovered over a vast expanse of foul-smelling seaweed. These homeless, angry bees came to my mind after September 11. In the 1980s we had become accustomed to street people—such as Barbara the bag lady who haunted the phone building at Church and Lispenard, and howled deprecations in Polish through the night outside my bedroom window—but this crazy cast of characters had disappeared many years ago.

On Duane Street, near the National Guard encampment, I passed such a young man, tall, handsome with curly short dreadlocks, in shorts, dust-covered, barefoot. If his mind was lost within itself before, imagine what it might be like to be barefoot, homeless, and crazy five blocks from a sudden holocaust in streets now occupied by men with guns.

EVERY ONE of us is a maddened bee. The commonplace complaint is that we can't concentrate. That isn't exactly true, we are concentrating "like mad," constantly replaying in our heads what happened, what we saw. It is all we can talk about; every conversation overheard in the street is about it. It is exciting, in the truest sense of being pushed from being somnolent to being awake.

Each person's buzz is a reflection of who they are. So the ecologist wants a gas mask, the fashion plate wants one too that fits—as if those kinds of preparations could help: despite my carefully prepared emergency bag, a few nights after September 11 I heard a constant loud noise outside at night and ran out to the stairwell . . . in my socks. (It was just a garbage truck.) Nancy B. volunteered with the Salvation Army on the fourteenth and the fifteenth and made her way to near ground zero where she handed out hamburgers to rescuers for hours. She says she just wanted to see what she could see, but I think it was her Mother Teresa side.

My sister is angered by the stream of emails from her fellow academics taking the Noam Chomsky and Susan Sontag line of anti-Zionism and anti-Americanism. Sontag's piece in the *New Yorker* seemed rather hard and arrogant in tone even if it said some true things. I guess it was her job and her madness to not give in to the temptation of sentimentality, but at what point does she imagine that she is not part of Enlightenment philosophy? But all of us are just bargaining with, for want of a better word, God, trying to make sense of horror and assuage shock whether by action, madness, or finger-pointing at the victims.

My madness is that I think I can interpret the buzz of the other bees, but don't see my own symptoms (if you don't count insomnia, nightmares, and teeth so tightly clenched I practically had to pry open my mouth with my hands).

MONDAY the seventeenth I went uptown to see my mother. It was the first time I had strayed north of Fourteenth Street, and my first time on the subway. I thought I was calm, "normal," but her neighborhood was "normal" enough to make me realize how crazed I really was. The crowds at Zabar's shopping for the holidays made me scream with impatience. The subway ride up had been quick and simple but the ride back down was terribly tense, the old A train was very crowded, but when we slowed down every few minutes in some tunnel or other, the car was silent except for the babbling of toddlers. At West Fourth Street it was announced that the train was going to be diverted, so I had to walk home from the Village with my groceries. The conditions in my neighborhood were intense: police barricades, the rescue effort vehicles, the epic-scale recovery and repair work, the smoke. God knows what we were breathing, but I found the Upper West Side's relative normality disturbing.

I read once that people who lose their parents as children always have a certain attitude called "and suddenly." This sensibility affected my first reactions. I couldn't believe what I was seeing, but there was also a sense of inevitability as the tower exploded. Believe me, that my parents were refugees and had fled Paris and then Europe with only their lives and the clothes on their back, and the fact that they had lost all their families, and the fact that my father then died when I was eleven, have not made me embrace change but rather have caused me to cling to stability. I have particularly staked a lot on living out my life in New York City, in Manhattan, where my parents found welcome, where I was born and which I love deeply. At the same time shocking loss seems familiar.

PEOPLE BEGAN to move more freely around the city. Downtown people were walking so that the atmosphere reminded me of the festive aspects of some transit strikes. Yet faces were off, contained, stricken, stunned, serious, guarded, chastened. Slowly the level of chatter and ordinary behavior returned but not the same as it was. Life gradually seeped back toward the south: on the first Saturday a little Chinese mailman in Bermuda shorts appeared with mail that had already been in the station on Tuesday but had never been delivered that day; on the first Monday, Wall Street was opened for business and pedestrians were allowed down during the day, then some UPS trucks; after about nine days I didn't need to show my license to get home; finally the *New York Times* was delivered to my home again.

ON THE SECOND WEDNESDAY, I finally felt that I could turn off my air conditioner and open the window only to be woken in the middle of the night by another wave of sickening, frightening, acrid smoke permeating the loft. The WTC site is still smoldering but as the smoke subsides, the hole in the skyline gets bigger. Friday, September 28, the sky was marked by enormous cumulus clouds that, like the lightning of the night of the 13th, dwarfed the city, reminding its citizens that we exist on a planet. The visibility was great. From every corner from here to midtown I look downtown and think, *could I have seen them from here*? It is the opposite of the phenomenon of the missing limb, amputated but still sending messages to the brain of its existence. Here we cannot re-place or recall its enormous dimension. *They* are gone. At night, klieg lights mark the spot and the plume of smoke, still as tall as the average high-rise.

I have been down near the site a few times. I could see the great standing ruin of the South Tower, a magnificent trace of modernism, Piet Mondrian's *Boogie Woogie* meets Robert Smithson's "Monuments of Passaic, New Jersey," the grid undone. After looking for a while a friend said, "It's something else." And that is exactly it, you see something, but what you see bears no relationship to what was. You think, if I get closer, if I get on top of it, maybe then I will understand, and yet even what I did see I couldn't understand. I constantly come back to the first moments at my corner. My amazement begins even earlier, with something unbelievably simple: that I had understood that something significant had happened and got from bed to street so uncharacteristically fast is as much a subject of wonderment for me as anything else that happened that day. I was completely disconnected from the human reality of what I was seeing: just, "Look at that big hole in the building." Many were already dead but that hundreds of people were no longer even physically there did not penetrate my consciousness. I see myself standing on the street seeing the giant fireball. Even as I stood there, I saw myself standing there, with utter detachment. Something amazing was happening and my mind was a perfect blank.

. . .

The art world has begun to stir. Susanna, Nancy B., and I met at Nancy Davidson's opening on the 28th, where we would have all met on September 11. Everyone there was very happy to see each other. As for many of us, it was the first time I was out in the city after dark, other than standing at Lispenard and Church. We had a nice dinner, although all we talked about was *it*, from every angle of conversation possible. At about 10:00 PM as we crossed Ninth Avenue at Twenty-third Street we heard sirens. A motorcade approached as if for a visiting dignitary: an unmarked black police car with red lights flashing on its roof stopped downtown traffic in mid-intersection. Three motorcycle cops, then at least six more, passed preceding an ambulance, which was followed by a state police car and a NYPD police car. When they find the body of a policeman or fireman, they give the ambulance trip to the morgue an honor guard of three motorcycles, so this seemed even bigger, and yet it wasn't even anything that would ever be on the news.

Today, October 2, it is three weeks since — "the attack," "the incident," "the bombing," "the unfortunate activities in Lower Manhattan," "the catastrophe," "the tragic events of September 11, 2001," "nine-one-one," "nine-eleven." I measure time by The Tuesday, The First Wednesday, The Second Saturday. Today I have a "to do" list and my email from astrology. com says: "As the intensity drops, reasonable expectations rise. Gemini is free to take care of simple business that was neglected during those days of glory. Be patient with strangers, and really listen to their point of view."

. . .

CODA (May 2002): "In the years to come." This is the irritating narrative device used by the writers of the *American Experience* programs on PBS this season, including their history of New York City. It gives the narrator an omniscient yet melancholic tone. Using this device one can place oneself at the inaugural of the memorials that will inevitably be built at the site—in all likelihood safe and unimaginative. Or one can imagine yet a further moment: *In the years to come the destruction of the World Trade Center became a distant memory, as the people of New York adjusted to the new streets and buildings that replaced the behemoths that once had anchored the great skyline of New York.*

"In the months to come," life returned to "normal" in New York City. But. . . .

The weather continued balmy. Part of a pattern of drought afflicting the Northeast but a blessing for those of us for whom the cold wet winds of fall would have been one more unbearable misery.

On October 11, I saw a man cry on the subway. A handsome, dark-skinned man in workers' overalls got on the downtown IRT. He was sobbing uncontrollably but silently, ineffectually dabbing at his face now and then with a handkerchief. He was crying like I've often seen women cry in public places, but I had never before seen a man cry in public. He cried even as he got off the train.

One began to have to avoid the staggering lurch of inebriated men in the street early in the day. Then homeless and disturbed men returned to the streets in the greatest numbers since the early 1980s, making it difficult to stop in the street to talk to a friend without being accosted. The National Guard and city and state police stationed at either end of Lispenard Street were removed one night in early January. "In the weeks to come" violent, random street crime made its return to Lower Manhattan, with rapes and shootings in the Village and around Houston and Canal Street.

On October 31 the burning smell returned one last time. Then the fires that, according to Fire Commissioner Thomas Van Essen, had burned "hot red" were finally out. A few days later the Red Cross made vouchers for air filters more widely available to neighborhood residents. Later that winter it was rumored that, until the fires subsided at the end of October, residents in Lower Manhattan had been breathing unprecedented levels of pollutants, even compared to pollutants produced by such ecological catastrophes as the oil-well fires set during the Gulf War. The terrible poisonous smell would emerge late at night, a nocturnal miasma apparently propelled by mini-climactic air currents that shift throughout the day and night in the streets of the city.

On the weekend after Thanksgiving Day I stretched some new canvases and got ready to paint. On November 25, yet another warm day, I took a rapturous walk down Fifth Avenue from Fifty-third Street to SoHo. The strangely empty city was beautiful in a timeless and mystical way. At the northwest corner of Madison Square I was alone with an early evening's cobalt-blue sky and the glorious lit golden roof of the Met Life Building and the prow of the Flatiron Building ahead. My beloved city was still there. I felt I could begin to get back to work.

"AND SUDDENLY." On November 30, my sister, Naomi Schor, suffered a massive cerebral hemorrhage. She died on December 2. Her funeral at Swann Point Cemetery in Providence was on December 5, a day as beautiful and nearly as warm as September 11, astonishingly mild and clear. Thus the most beautiful days now always carry for me both the threat of total reversal of human fortune and the poignancy of the profound discordance between human emotions and natural phenomena.

People's expressions of sympathy to me have often included a comment on what a terrible year I'd had, first September 11, then my sister's death, but I steadfastly have refused to see the two losses as related or equal. One had not happened *to me*, the other had. And yet the two do exist in a curious tandem. On the one hand, I feel some comfort in the knowledge that others are grieving a sudden loss. On the other hand, their grief is historical and newsworthy, mine is the private grief that affects any family that endures loss. Yet ultimately they are also alone with their grief, and I know from losing my father when I was a child that, like the Towers themselves, which loomed larger the further one got from them, the impact of personal loss grows in time rather than diminishing. There are other differences: the towers were in one place, and several times everyday I find myself walking downtown toward where they were and doing the strange mental work of trying to reconstruct their position and how big they were, using landmarks such as the Western Union building over which the first plane flew to assist me. I must have a body memory of where they once were, but you can't see what isn't there. My sister did not occupy one fixed place, she permeated my whole life, and thus I don't need to consciously resurrect her image; she is as the left side of my body.

If September 11 rocked my sense of security in the city of my birth and temporarily knocked me off my creative track, who I will be and what my art can be after my sister's death is a much more complex question. I have only done two paintings since September 11, both of the word *joy* painted in the most contingent of colors, shit brown and scrapped flesh. This dark, painterly embodiment of *joy* has been my first means of re-entry back into artmaking after the loss of such a primal figure in my life.

A LAST THOUGHT . . . FOR THE MOMENT: Yesterday, walking in the Village, just as I was wondering if many people had already forgotten, three young people passed by, a guy in a flashy robin's-egg-blue suit carrying a boom box, a guy with a film camera, and a girl following along. Suddenly the guy in the blue suit put the box down and broke out into a perfect Mick Jagger imitation, complete with jerky dance movements, on the lawn in front of the Picasso sculpture at the NYU houses on LaGuardia Place!

The annual phenomenon of NYU film students fanning out in the Village to work on their spring projects!

The divine silliness of the moment served to reinforce my suspicion that for many people the Titanic-like disaster was just a blip on the screen of their youth, and that only those already immersed in loss in their own lives and histories would keep this terrible memory in their hearts. And perhaps that inexorably forgetful energy of youth is the truly necessary movement forward of joy.

Part Three

TRITE TROPES

Old styles never die, they just continue to permeate the substrata of American art, lurking under the radar of the mainstream art world. Mutating and merging, they form new subspecies of styles with recognizable characteristics and a persistent life of their own. Yet, made up of clichés from styles whose original radicality, purpose, and lineage are lost, they are unconscious of their own existence as specific and historically based style types. In the same way that television signals leave earth and stream out into the universe, so that *I Love Lucy* doesn't just live on in cable reruns but also slowly makes its way to be picked up on some planet in another galaxy where ditzy red-heads may become goddesses of a new cult, so too art styles go out into the universe of art practice at the ground level of art schools, through the media of art magazines, books, and, most importantly, teachers who keep on teaching the ideology of their youth, from every vintage since the 1950s, finding sometimes eager or, more likely, helpless adherents among the young. Like nuclear waste, old styles leach out from under the lead and concrete bunkers that avant-garde criticism has built to protect the new from their pollution and to deny their continued existence. These styles are insulated from the rest of the art world, or change at a slower pace, while the centers of the international art world cling to the belief in constant newness, which despite the recent rhetoric of the post-historical, still pertains.

The one-hundreth issue of *October* magazine is devoted to the concept of obsolescence. It includes a forum of artists' statements on the subject of obsolescence as a potential site of resistance. In it, the artist Christian Philipp Müller asks, "How far removed into the past does an artistic style need to be in order to obtain this bonus of being recycled?"[1] Indeed, such a question may legitimately be asked when there is a constant process of stylistic recycling going on in art, not unlike the recycling of "decades" in the world of fashion: fashion designers and magazines regularly feature revivals of everything from 1890s' leg of mutton sleeves to 1980s' recycling of 1940s' shoulder pads. It would be interesting if *Artforum* ran a similarly open survey of the range of artistic styles currently obtaining "the bonus of being recycled"—something like "minimalism is in this year!" (This is done of course, but usually more covertly in order to maintain the illusion of the new and the sanctity of the old.)

But I am interested in something else—not the artistic style that is instrumentally recycled at the right moment to speak to present concerns while burnishing the patrilineal credentials of the new generation, but the phenomenon of many artistic styles continuously living a half life in a space just adjoining the art world that *October*, *Artforum*, and other major art publications recognize, champion, or envision. Just as the near past may be obsolete, the near art world is obscured, but if it is like the dust that follows a comet's ball of ice, the tail of the art comet is much larger than its head, and there may be some value in studying it.

The persistence of styles can be attested to by anyone who teaches art at the undergraduate or graduate level, who visits art schools around the country, or who serves on slide juries for schools, artists' colonies, or state or private grants. The subject of this essay first occurred to me while I served on one such a slide jury in 1999. Typically during the preliminary round of a slide jury's review, jurors may look at anywhere from four thousand to eight thousand slides in one day, in groups of four or five images in fifteen- to thirty-second intervals. Slide—Slide—Slide—Slide. After the first few hours, things may get a little silly. Jurors can't help but notice patterns, some of them inane: there may be an inordinate number of paintings of pears or bears or sheep. As the tenth sheep appears, helpless hilarity may ensue.[2]

However, a fly-on-the-wall glimpse into and a deconstructive exegesis of such sessions, which always are confidential and take place in darkened rooms, would certainly be worth a year of graduate school. First, they would reveal the existence of an established knowledge base of art codes widely shared by jurors who are usually selected to represent disparate aesthetic and social views. Jurors hope for an individual voice to emerge from the artist's conversation with art history and contemporary art. One hopes for someone who has something to say and who is at the same time engaged with the language of form. But this is the rarest thing. So jurors look for familiarity with and competence in the chosen style. They know the basic vocabulary and clichés of each genre. The criterion is how well the familiar is deployed and articulated. They feel duty bound to choose the best of styles they don't personally work in. Democracy does reign. At the same time, the fly on the wall would see a predictable range of known styles from the last one hundred years, which can be summarized instantly in shorthand descriptions: "Trite and Trippy!"[3] "Pearlstein on acid!" "Slacker Guston!" The panel nods in agreement, and groans when the artists evidently couldn't decide which trope they wanted to address and threw too many style references into the pot; what were they thinking?

This range of clichés is not a new phenomenon. My most treasured memory from a slide jury is of the moment when, during a graduate-admissions committee meeting at the Nova Scotia College of Art and Design in the mid-1970s, after about the twentieth submission of work incorporating branches, twigs, hay, and stones, one of my colleagues turned to me and said in a snarly whisper, "What's that, some kind of Paleolithic sandwich?" It is indicative of the persistence of styles and clichés that although this pithy comment was made over thirty years ago, twigs and branches still make regular appearances whenever, because of their interest in the environment, or as a reaction formation to factory-produced minimalism or commodity fetishism, artists want to reference Nature.

Jurors look for the level of newness of the chosen style. In effect, there are clichés and there are clichés. As remnants of every style since the early Renaissance make their appearance, and they all do, often in the same work, the jurors—even if they cling to belief in independence, originality, and veracity of personal content, even if they have more conservative tastes—find themselves judging work not only by the artist's skill in his or her chosen style, but also by how relatively recent their chosen style is. Has the artist picked up the most recent message from earth or the one sent out into the ether fifty years ago? Thus, being adept at creating an unexamined, tenth-generation version of a Robert Motherwell painting will yield the applicant poorer results than being adept, or even inept, at cloning Mary Heilmann. Evidence of newer influence, or of recycling the correct, hip, sufficiently past style, as suggested by the *October* discussion on obsolescence, in the end looks better than sincere, though deadened rehearsals of older styles, even when one despises facility or pandering to art market trends. Revealing the influence of Heilmann or Jenny Saville, Matthew Ritchie or Matthew Barney, Banks Violette or Rachel Harrison, at least marks the artist as being engaged with current ideas and contemporary culture.

I am using the word *style* in a broad sense, which includes the formal, representational, and narrative codes of each major *ism* of modern and contemporary art history, as well as a variety of more recent tropes that may not neatly fit into the confines of the terms *style* or *material* or *genre* but are nevertheless also fully encoded.[4]

In order to study the zone of persistent styles, I had to search for images in sites available to the general public, since when you are on a slide jury you can't take pictures of what you are looking at and you can't take the slides home with you. The conflation of these various stylistic categories and the institutional enshrinement of this ongoing multiplicity of styles are demonstrated in the organization of another one of the art-world spaces in which, like the jury, a wide range of artists can present themselves in a democratic situation: Artists Space's Irving Sandler Artists File Online.[5] A pull-down menu offers a choice of:

abstract
allegorical
architecture
assemblage
autobiographical
biomorphic
cartoonesque
color field
conceptual
constructed
decorative
didactic
documentary
domestic/family
environmental
erotic
expressionistic
fantasy
feminist
figurative
functional
futuristic
gender/sexuality
geometric
hard-edge
humorous

illusionistic
interactive
ironic
kinetic
kitsch
landscape

light reflective
linear
literary
lyrical
minimal
narrative
nudes
optical
painterly
political
popular imagery
portraits
primitivistic
process oriented
psychological
religious
representational
romantic
serial
shaped-format
sociological
spiritual
still-life
surreal
symbolic
technological
trompe l'oeil
urban

Here art historical movements such as expressionism, impressionism, and surrealism are mixed with "styles" that are in fact different media or form types, or are associated with political movements and identity politics (although there are also separate pull-down menus for "Media" and "Materials").[6] Although these categories are listed separately on the menu, they in fact are fragmented in confusing ways: "abstract" is a category that can include "biomorphic" or "hard-edge," and also "spiritual" or "process-oriented"; "assemblage" is a technique associated with a number of art historical movements including cubism and Dada; "didactic" is a subcategory of "political" and "conceptual" (while also continuing to be a value judgment); "feminist" indicates a political intentionality and hints at the likelihood of certain types of representational content as well as certain types of materials and form sources. Nevertheless, in the pull-down menu, each category telegraphs a set of predictable appearances; the whole purpose is to make it easy for a curator to find what she is looking for.

Indeed, artists are encouraged to cross-reference themselves when they enroll their work in the online file so as to achieve the widest possible coverage for the curators who may be searching through the file. For example, an artist might choose the following labels: ironic + kitsch + sculpture + popular imagery, humorous + political + representational, minimal + hard-edge, narrative + feminism + illusionistic, narrative + popular imagery. These labels are a useful way for artists to be found amidst the crowd: in July 2007 there were 6,098 artists on file.[7] The site offers a prefab set of codifications and branding techniques, for the purpose perhaps of discourse but more certainly of commodification. Curators can find the work they are looking for through these pathways of association and labeling, but the system also reflects the arguably rather depressing fact that artists can be and in fact must be pigeonhole-able in such a manner: the variety of choices masks an incredible process of homogenization. Both parties work in tandem: artists choose from the menu the clichéd style most appropriate to their expressive needs and the few keywords that will define them, and curators go shopping for "hard-edge," or "didactic." They are shopping for artworks that they already have imaged in their heads, and they will find them, since everyone participates in the coding.

My comments do not reflect on the quality of specific works by individual artists that are available in the Artists' Space Online File or selected for inclusion in various juried situations. This is true of all the types of work I describe. Within any given category there are extremely able and sincere artists, and any of the styles and substyles mentioned can still be viable if the tropes are genuinely problematized and can be productively reinvested with new references and personal necessity.

I am also differentiating the persistence of styles from the necessity of tradition and of historical knowledge and awareness on the part of the artist. An expression not of one's time, in an unrecognizable language will not be understood. As Roland Barthes writes in *Writing Degree Zero*, "It is not granted to the writer to choose his mode of writing from a kind of non-temporal store of literary forms. It is under the pressure of History and Tradition that the possible modes of writing for a given writer are established; there is a History of Writing. But this History is dual: at the very moment when general History proposes — or imposes — new problematics of the literary language, writing still remains full of the recollection of previous usage, for language is never innocent: words have a second-order memory which mysteriously persists in the midst of new meanings. Writing is precisely this compromise between freedom and remembrance."[8]

In our time it is fashionable to assert that the artist can choose his or her mode of writing, painting, or whatever from a kind of "non-temporal store of forms," the postmodern mall of free-floating signs and signifiers. It is axiomatically impossible to work outside of established codes, even if the relationship is adversarial. However, many artists labor under a misapprehension that is itself encoded into these persistent styles and that is curious under the circumstances: they continue to believe in the rhetoric of originality (despite postmodernism's critique of authorship and originality). So, for example, as a representative case history, one artist represented in *New American Paintings* with paintings that clearly replicate Brice Marden's loop paintings states, "These paintings come from within my subconscious. . . . What I try to do is set up a process that will produce a beautiful and mysterious work of art that communicates (to me, and hopefully others) the debris that stirs deep within my subconscious mind. I think there is truth beneath the surface of consciousness that can be communicated through form and image."[9] The problem with this very common argument is that the artist cannot consciously rely on the subconscious; by definition it operates without one's conscious volition. And what is not recognized in this statement is that the unconscious or subconscious "debris" is the debris of painting history.

Certainly working through influences represents an established stage of an artist's development, and the ability to revitalize past tropes is an important aspect of a successful work. In discussing his generation's relationship to abstract expressionism, for example, Chuck Close writes, "Art students unabashedly worked through other people's work. I mean it was *not* with any sense of irony, it was not 'appropriation.' We knew we were students and that was the way to learn—to *be* de Kooning, *be* whoever it was, and just devour them and then move on to another artist."[10]

It is important also to state the generative value of a pluralistic aesthetic atmosphere. As a young artist I experienced first hand the prescriptive influence of late New York School formalism on higher art education and was fortunate to benefit from the expansion of formal means and appropriate content that occurred in the "pluralist" 1970s as a result of a variety of insurgencies against the dogma of Greenbergian formalism. The permission for—in fact the emphasis on—appropriation and sampling following the late 1970s indicates still another critically sanctioned usage of aesthetic traditions. In calling attention to this new kind of standardized pluralism of trite tropes, clichés, and the persistence of styles, I am singling out something other than the potential richness of artistic influence or the critical usefulness of appropriation.

I collect stylistic tropes. It is how I can bear going through the acres and acres of art fairs and biennials: I trawl for tropes. In addition to the ubiquitous blur that I discuss in "Blurring Richter," a host of other familiar tropes pertain. On one jury in which I participated, we decided that a moratorium should be declared on family photos, cartoons, waifs, underwear, childhood, dresses, birds and bunnies, blobs, and hair.

But actually all of these are recent and current tropes, and our moratorium pertained to some of the work we *did* accept. What about the style types of works we rejected, the degraded, unconscious, and unnamed stylistic hybrids, many of which we often see in other parts of our professional practice?

These styles are the subject of this essay as stated at its outset. But here I find that I avert my descriptive eye, reflecting the literally repellent nature of much of the work in question: these are the works about which jurors indicate, through a zero on their chart, their absolute lack of interest in ever seeing them again. They never even get into the second round where the speed is slightly slower: slide—slide. These are the bad yet eerily familiar works that form the déjà vu-all-over-again feeling of teaching. We are all familiar with abstract paintings where the paint is still being "pushed around," pretty pictographic paintings where lots of little images of dresses, birds, or cartoon figures are drawn on a diagrammatic ground that nevertheless cannot resolve itself fully to flatness because it too is painted in a variegated manner; installations of hundreds of scraps of paper pinned to the wall, with squiggly doodles, childlike drawings, teen-age cartoons, or porn drawings on them; old family photographs of the artist's African American, Korean, Cuban, Japanese, Chinese, Polish, or Irish grandparent, often obscured by some digital distancing effect (such as a blur), framed by symbols of Santeria, Buddhism, or Catholicism, and by handwriting of biographical testimony, going around the image or over it. But do these ring a bell? Stylized Picasso-esque figuration; street scenes that make John Sloan look postmodern; tenth-generation Edward Hopper. And also gloomy academic realism, bored nudes — paintings where everything looks bored, even sneakers, lamps, apples, pears; compositions that call attention to nothing; representational paintings based on snapshot photography but where the nature of photography is not the subject of the work, and the photographic sourcing is masked in a clumsily deployed rhetoric of observation-based painterliness. Desperate boredom — not the cool ennui that propels the purposefully banal, emotionally uninflected works of artists who occupy and influence the high end of the spectrum of art production. Just boring boredom.

Where do these style types come from? Why are they stubbornly resistant to change? How does one address such works individually when the strangest thing about them is their lack of individuality? Are there underlying meta-categories of these persistent styles?

One key to many of these works, particularly the figurative or representational ones, is that their meaning is over-determined: the artist is trying to appear interesting or to be *seen* as saying something. In other words the desire for meaningful expression may be completely sincere, but maybe it isn't quite as sincere as it wishes to portray. Deer heads in an upside-down bathtub, dramatic staircases to nowhere, self-portraits as clowns. Clearly all the young (usually male) artists who continue to image themselves as clowns have never read Benjamin Buchloh's critical analysis of this imago of the artist in the abject role of jester to the bourgeoisie. In his essay "Figures of Authority, Ciphers of Regression" from 1980, Buchloh writes: "The Harlequins, Pierrots, Bejazzos, and Pulcinelles invading the work of Picasso, Beckmann, Severini, Derain, and others in the early twenties . . . can be identified as ciphers of an enforced regression. They serve as emblems for the melancholic infantilism of the avant-garde artist who has come to realize his historic failure. The clown functions as a social archetype of the artist as an essentially powerless, docile, and entertaining figure performing his acts of subversion and mockery from an undialectical fixation on utopian thought."[11] If they had, they would think twice . . . or would they? (Think of Paul McCarthy's imago of the artist as a disgusting clown and all the artists influenced by it.)

What is so disturbing and intractable about this sort of work is that the more the artist wants to express something meaningful, the more predictable and generic the forms. The work screams that it is trying to say something, it emotes and declares individuality, and yet the works are without individuality, not only in terms of content, but also at the molecular level of brushstroke, color, paint application, and form, so that even *self-portraits* by different artists all look alike. The overly dramatic dorm-room/student-apartment/late-at-night-in-the-school-studio scenes: why is it that in all of them, and there are so, so many, the figures all have the same nose? In works where people are so desirous of indicating personal expression—and here identity politics and ethnic tropes are the most problematic to critique because formal criticism can be misinterpreted as racism or sexism—there is no hand of the artist. Literally: no matter who did it, the handwriting around the ethnic family photograph is always the same.

This phenomenon subverts a principal definition of style. Once upon a time each era was dominated by a pervasive set of conventions for the representation of human beings, space, and architecture as well as a set of stories that were generally understandable to the majority of the culture that might have access to those works. The range of types of work was small: from the Renaissance to the mid-nineteenth century, there was history painting (replacing religious painting as the most important type of art work), and later genre painting and still-life painting (typically of cows, flowers, mothers, and children), each with the dual function of depicting commodities and mores with a symbolic component that retained religious meaning, while also functioning as a laboratory for pure form. In this economy of subject matter, to speak of style was to refer overall to collective characteristics of a particular era, and, further, to the individual artist's unique and largely unconscious way of articulating the overall set of representational conventions of the day, the unintentional specificity of the individual hand, which is the means by which connoisseurship is established—how, for example, a Carlo Crivelli can be identified by the oddly long and spiky conformation of the toes. But what is so puzzling is that this naturally occurring individual specificity does not obtain in the over-determined contemporary works, despite their cry for individuality.

One of the dilemmas for a teacher faced with such works is that you can't show the students the other works that are identical to theirs, be- cause, quite simply, there are no consciously formed collections of reproductions of bad art. It would be unethical and possibly illegal to accumulate a collection of the images screened by juries and admissions committees. And the mission of slide libraries and art historical surveys is to present the relatively few works that have been determined through the consensus of art historical canon formation to be the best and most historically significant. They are unlikely to reproduce or archive mediocre works by secondary artists: or, rather, there are plenty of mediocre art works in such collections, however these inclusions are inadvertent, and the mediocre works are by artists considered to be primary initiators of major movements. Conversely, art history has obscured very excellent bodies of works by supposedly "secondary" artists, much to the detriment of a complete, lived sense of an aesthetic movement, and to a full history of particular movements and styles.

Stylistic sleuthing through the history of academic art instruction as well as regional variants of style within such instruction would surely reveal complex generational pathways back to significant art schools such as the Art Student's League in the 1950s, the Hofmann School in the 1940s, 1950s, and early 1960s, or even influential but less noted schools such as the art department at the California State University, Northridge, in the late 1960s. The influence of certain key teachers in specific locations would clarify stylistic sub-lineages. This detective work might highlight something that is usually obscured: students (and probably also their faculty) think they are looking to the initiatory major artists for influence but most likely they are more closely influenced by artists who, though famous, are essentially secondary, even academic figures in comparison to the major twentieth-century figures who influenced their own work. In the late 1980s, teaching one semester at the University of California, Berkeley, I was amazed at the surprisingly non-Oedipal admiration some students felt for earlier Bay Area artists of note, rather than for the artists that these regional artists had looked to: thus, for example, Henri Matisse was experienced only indirectly and often unconsciously as a trace memory in some work by Richard Diebenkorn, as taught by someone for whom admiration for Diebenkorn in his or her own youth was a formative experience.[12]

Returning to an examination of the wide range of persistent styles, two major tendencies emerge: the popularity of surrealism and the continued struggle to adapt desire for representation, particularly figuration, to the spatial flatness developed through the history of twentieth-century abstraction.

That both surrealism and the formal tenets of modernism are still in play throughout the full range of visual culture is a testament to the durability of the basic philosophies and representational desires they stand for in the history of representation. It is also an ironic commentary on the problematic role of surrealism within the narrative of abstract expressionism. These two movements are intimately bound through linear influence; consider the role played by surrealist techniques such as automatism and the interest in biomorphic forms for artists like Arshile Gorky and Jackson Pollock. They are also interlinked through opposition: the abstract expressionists thought that the surrealists' hyperrealism, in the words of Barnett Newman, "inevitably must become phantasmagoria, so that instead of creating a magical world, the surrealists succeeded only in illustrating it."[13] These two movements continue to clash today, often no longer knowingly.

The legacy of surrealism is paramount. Surrealism privileges an irrational, violence-oriented unconscious. It allows for figuration, narrative, symbolism, and theatricality; it fosters creepiness and horror. It appeals to and allows for the visualization of basic tropes of embodiment, fear of contingency, the body, death, sexuality, blood. It accommodates the desire many artists have to speak individual stories, and the desire to speak strange and scary things, to be WEIRD, that is particularly resonant with so much popular culture, much of which is itself an emanation of surrealism: horror movies, animation, the infinite vocabulary of absurd juxtaposition afforded and multiplied by digital processes. The permission to use sources such as folk art, Asian art, Gothic art, early Renaissance art, and outsider art all flow from surrealism's reiteration and privileging of forms and spatial organization typical of and influenced by these styles and histories. Even popular genres of abstraction (biomorphic abstraction, mutant anime, the styles of Takashi Murakami and Marimekko designs, the turn to flat and bright, cute and weird) also flow from surrealism as much as from other decorative and pop practices. The narratives and images in our dreams have been fed into and back out of surrealism to such an extent that we experience our dreams as surrealistic art events. Again, what is so notable in the persistence of styles is the generic quality of such tropes, the homogenization of quirkiness, so that the common phenomenon of throwing in extra symbolism in order to be creepier and more expressive than the next guy seems like a kind of anxiety that also reads as false speech, a sense of the unimaginative hidden behind the excessively imaginative.

Surrealism, like expressionism, another style with continued appeal for its ability to visualize angst, provides many examples for intense stylization of the figure, in particular elongation of the body and angular linearity of depiction. This typology of form, which traces back at least to a Gothic antecedent that continued to echo through early Italian Renaissance art and into Northern Renaissance art, appeals to the theatricality that is seeking a home in these stylized styles that rely on particularly exaggerated forms or distortions of form. It has had particular resonance for women surrealists and their followers (think of the recurrence of elongated figures in works by women artists who were particularly committed to representing private narratives of female sexuality and experience, including Lenore Fini, Remedios Varo, Leonora Carrington, and Florine Stettheimer, as well as Charlotte Salomon).[14]

Stylized styles in general are more useful to "branding," and are more likely to be appropriated for commodification than critically problematized. Thus scholarship on these women artists tends to focus on biographical narratives, just as analysis of Max Beckmann's stylized figuration is likely to focus on exegeses of symbolism and historical context. It does help to know the work of Albrecht Dürer and of the Northern Renaissance limewood sculptors to appreciate the place of Beckmann's style in the lineage of a certain Germanic typology of formal expressionism, but also it is useful to be critically aware that sometimes there can be something very dated in his figurative stylization, even though he is a very great artist. Similarly the stylization of almost all of the variants of Picasso's figuration, from the early skinny, elongated clowns to the bulbous figures in *Guernica*, are in some ways as deeply problematic as they are stylistically emblematic. Certainly they are problematic as artistic, stylistic models. But since these issues are rarely raised, young artists don't get the idea there might be something there to think about, to imitate consciously and for cause, or possibly to not imitate.

Now consider the importance of regional sub-influences and you begin to see how these familiar stylized styles form into hybrid sub-styles that have recognizable appearances but complex provenances: the style type of the too much alizarin crimson, dorm room photo–based painting of stylized twenty-somethings who all look like each other doing weird things is an American hybrid creature composed of the influence of Chicago-based artists (such as Hollis Sigler and the Hairy Who), Florine Stettheimer, Max Beckmann, Otto Dix, and so on back to Rogier van der Weyden, Hieronymous Bosch, and Giotto, via Edward Keinholz, Philip Pearlstein, and Norman Rockwell. And in most cases every single ingredient has been predigested and naturalized; usage is either unconscious or almost proudly unproblematized.

Nevertheless, the struggle to integrate imagery within abstraction without betraying the movement in modernist painting toward pictorial flatness has animated many artworks, including paintings by de Kooning and many West Coast artists, such as Emerson Woelffer and David Park, as well as early paintings by Alex Katz. Artists returned to this task in the mid-1970s, moving away from the flatness and appropriative nature of pop art, the impersonal nature of minimalism, and the abstraction of post-minimalism, bringing back to painting some of the narrativity and imaging that had moved from the emptied canvas into performance and video. This was the movement presented in the Whitney Museum of American Art's "New Image Painting" exhibition in 1978.[15] "New Image Painting" articulated the problem of how to combine an image (some sort of illusionistic picture or representation, usually other than the photographic) with the flatness of modernist painting; how to accommodate, retrieve, or salvage the figurative and representational within the flat anti-illusionist field of modernist painting as codified over decades, particularly in North America, through the imperatives of Clement Greenberg and his acolytes. It is perhaps significant that this exhibition, although it launched major careers such as that of Susan Rothenberg, was generally seen as a failure, a last gasp of modernism and of art values such as authenticity before the major change toward appropriation and institutional critique that took over the art world beginning in 1979 with early shows by David Salle and Sherrie Levine, among others. Yet the project of incorporating rendered representation into flat abstraction continues to be attempted or reenacted many years after the art world, in part, decided that the New Image was a wrong turn up a dead end, and, in part, recuperated it for the kind of juxtaposition of imagery and flatness characteristic of some 1980s painting, such as works by Salle, Troy Brauntuch, Thomas Lawson, and Jack Goldstein.[16]

One persistent style that has emerged since the advent of the monochromatic, flat abstract painting is the pictographic painting, which allows an artist to have her cake and eat it too by placing an image of some sort on a flat background. This style was popularized by artists such as Stephanie Brody Lederman in the 1970s and more recently artists such as Squeak Carnwath. In works of this style type, the background is usually *almost* flat: the diagrams, pictograms, and words are placed on a ground that may be geometrically framed but also painted in an atmospheric, variegated painterly or textural manner. These works owe a great debt to Paul Klee's introduction of a pictographic vocabulary into cubistically organized flat space. His references to the childlike and the "primitive" in relation to previous types of representation are a historically situated philosophical intervention within an aesthetic imaging system rather than a style chosen without thought or struggle. For some reason Klee can get away with it—I am tempted to add, or can he? I ask that mischievous question only because the proliferation of such pictographic paintings throws a poor reflection back onto Klee, which only can be eliminated by looking at actual works by Klee, which usually retain their formal rigor and the charm of the lyrical and whimsical pictorial elements. (A variant of this mode of the pictographic is the one enabled by Cy Twombly's later paintings: a few loosely scribbled or graffitied marks, pictographs, and words on a scumbled, *almost flat* expressionistic ground. In this case, I am of the opinion that even Cy Twombly can't get away with it; nonetheless it is a very popular substyle.) Again, I'm merely emphasizing the need for both conscious awareness on the part of the artist of the earlier and vanguard work in a chosen genre, and some ability and willingness to analyze such styles critically. The pictographic style in America also has antecedents in "The Ideographic Picture"—the title of an exhibition at the Betty Parsons Gallery in 1947, which included works by Hans Hofmann, Pietro Lazzari, Boris Margo, Ad Reinhardt, Mark Rothko, Theodoros Stamos, and Clyfford Still. Many of these artists, as well as artists like Adolph Gottlieb, went through a phase of pictorially reconciling surrealist-based pictographic representation and rigorously flattened pictorial space.[17]

Everything has been absorbed but not necessarily understood. People speak languages without knowledge of their etymologies. Because artists are largely unconscious of the hybrid traditions they are working with, their work suffers. It lacks the critical address of the conventions of such traditions that would be the signal feature of a work that would move the language of art forward.

But works by artists who are able to successfully articulate visual languages also pose problems that are not exactly the same yet are parallel and interconnected in their effect on the overall social and formal characteristics of much contemporary art. I have so far looked at the paradigm of trite tropes, clichés, and persistent styles from the angle of the worst artworks made within it. But predictability and historical iteration are as, if not more, prevalent and intractable in work that is considered successful in the contemporary art market. I examine such formulaic tendencies in recent artwork in the next chapter, "Recipe Art."

What makes an artwork look contemporary? This is an important question because the acquisition of this knowledge and the skills to act on this understanding are key to market success, and also to successful intervention in the status quo of received ideas.

Nevertheless this is the wrong question because the contemporaneity of an artwork today preexists one's sighting of it; it is established by language, by how efficiently and commodifiably it can be described. There is no point in describing what makes an artwork look contemporary, because that quality of the contemporary changes all the time, and, to complicate matters, may even include the use of aged, decrepit materials. Yet one knows contemporary art when one sees it or, more accurately, when one hears it described:

> Most impressive is the *life-size Zamboni* (the big gliding machine that restores the ice of a hockey rink) *constructed out of rigid pale green insulation foam* by Chris Hanson and Hendrika Sonnenberg.[1]

> A *chandelier made of 14,000 tampons* by the Portuguese artist Joana Vasconcelos.[2]

> "I am trying to make *gravel* out of *Play-Doh*," explains Tom Friedman helpfully. . . . A tiny *self-portrait carved on an aspirin*, a *color-field fresco* rendered in *aqua toothpaste*, a nearly *life-size figure* of himself fashioned entirely from *sugar cubes*.[3]

> It was a 12-foot-tall replica of a *church*, or more accurately the charred beams and gables left standing after a church had been burned. Instead of wood, however, the *entire structure was made from salt*.[4]

Embodied in the high-concept, one- or two-sentence description, the recipe ingredients usually include something from the real cleverly juxtaposed with something else from the real, or something made with a material from the real not ordinarily an art material; something that references the real; something made from something else (e.g., a minimalist sculpture made of chocolate, a similarly monumental cube made of millions of wooden toothpicks, Richard Serra–leaning-plates made of red lipstick, etc.). Recipe: something from popular culture + something from art history + something appropriated + something weird or expressive = useful promotional sound bite. The work is selected for review because it can be written about efficiently. It is not necessary to see the piece.

The Jewish Museum's exhibition, "Mirroring Evil: Nazi Imagery / Recent Art" from 2002 provided classic examples of the genre, including Zbigniew Libera's *Lego Concentration Camp Set*, and Tom Sach's *Prada Deathcamp*. The titles already contain the recipe ingredients: "It's a pop-up deathcamp. It's a sort of best-of-all-worlds composite, with the famous Gate of Death and Crematorium IV from Auschwitz. I made it entirely from a Prada hat-box. . . . Prada mainstreams hipness. . . . I'm using the iconography of the Holocaust to bring attention to fashion. Fashion, like fascism, is about loss of identity."[5]

My point here is not to rehash the much belabored moralist reviews of "Mirroring Evil." And the inanity of specific artists' comments serves only to underline one principal characteristics of recipe art: the works that get the most attention, because their ingredients can be condensed into a provocative sound bite, are frequently the least interesting in person. After I went to see the show, my then ninety-one-year-old (Holocaust refugee + artist) mother, who had not seen the show but had read everything about it, asked me what I thought about Alan Schechner's Buchenwald Coke can piece. I realized that I hadn't seen it, although I still can't figure out where it might have been placed that I would have missed it, but the point is that, based on one reproduction in the *New York Times* and several descriptions of it, only two paradigms (in three words) are relevant to the mechanism — *Buchenwald + Coke can* — and these were enough to make the work memorable, sight unseen. Any work whose description would be longer or more complex is too long and *too* complex and therefore probably not a good contemporary artwork, because it would not display the economy of content that is the partner of recipe art.

However if you do see the work, its components can easily be broken down and encapsulated into a recipe. For example, my notes scribbled on a show card: "Take a cement block, put cake icing on it."[6]

This is conceptual art adapted to the market age. Consider the instructions laid out by Lawrence Weiner in his "Untitled Statement" (1970):

1. The artist may construct the piece.
2. The piece may be fabricated.

3. The piece need not be built.
Each being equal and consistent with the intent of the artist the decision as to condition rests with the receiver upon occasion of receiver-
ship.
Tried and True[7]

• • •

All things being equal, when conceptual art was new (or re-newed,
given the precessionary model of Duchamp), it was not necessary to
physically realize the work; the idea was the work. As a typewritten sheet
of paper pinned to the wall of MoMA, Weiner's statement in the museum's
exhibition "Information" from 1970 was a conceptualist manifesto akin
to Martin Luther's "Ninety-Five Theses" nailed to the door of the Castle
Church in Wittenberg. (There is also an interesting connection that can
be made between Luther's critique of the purchase of indulgences and
Weiner's implicit critique of the monetary value afforded by conventional
art objects.) Now, in recipe art, while the verbal describability of a work
may matter more than its physical manifestation in terms of its circulation through the media into discourse, the current conditions of receiver-
ship are such that it is apparently again necessary to make the work, contrary to the original, radical implications of Weiner's formula, because this
conceptual work is being done with the market as its goal. The conceptual
quotient operates primarily as a marketing device: "Watch as David Cole
uses *excavators* to *knit the world's largest American flag*."[8]

Recipe art is a changeling, the offspring of conceptual fathers and
Hollywood huckster fathers. There are no mothers here, although many
of the most successful practitioners of recipe art are women, in part because feminist art brought into high art a variety of non-art materials and
techniques such as lipstick, wool, clothing, knitting, and cooking. These
reinvigorated traditional practices but rapidly became easily available
tropes.

Sculpture is as plagued by the same range of clichés as painting (and
much successful recipe art is object-based, since most often one ingredient is an appropriation of something from the real). While in slide juries
one sees every variety of polychrome, craft fair–related object, figurative
and abstract, that ever could be imagined, as one enters the zone of recipe
art, one finds that new trite tropes have quickly adhered to all new media,

performance video, and sculpture. In her article "The Kudzu Effect" from 1996, Joyce Kozloff mercilessly skewered all the clichés that had already accrued, in a relatively short period of time, in the type of politically correct public-art projects that were developed in order to counter the oppressive nature of earlier tropes of public art (the big figurative or abstract stone or metal monument plunked down someplace without any awareness of societal context). It is tempting to quote the entire text of "The Kudzu Effect (or: The Rise of a New Academy)," because it is so funny and the tropes so instantly recognizable, but two of the "Ten Most Popular Art Projects in the '90s" give a general idea:

> 3. Junior High School Geography Project
> There is a terrazzo map on the floor, depicting the place where we stand. An arrow points to our exact intersection because one cannot assume that people know how they got there. There is a clock indicating what time it is, followed by a series of clocks showing what time it is everywhere in the world. Additionally *trompe l'oeil* murals represent this street as it once appeared before all the landmark buildings were destroyed.

> 5. Kids "R" Us
> The artist has gone into the local schools and invited hundreds of children of maximum ethnic diversity to draw a picture of their neighborhood or family. These drawings are then fabricated on ceramic tile or baked enamel, depending on the budget, and installed in a subway station with the kids' names prominently displayed nearby. A press conference is called, and all children are invited.

Having pointed a devastatingly accurate finger at the field of public art (which the artist had at that point decided to abandon), she wonders, "How it is that projects like these have emerged, like kudzu, all across the country, executed seemingly independently, by an array of different artists?" She also takes responsibility for participating in this system of clichés: "In these times, we want to be supportive and positive, but we also must remain self-critical. Who among us has not created, or at least proposed, a variant of one or more [of] these 10 projects? For an older artist, it is at best a dubious distinction to have become a pioneer of clichés."[9]

The major lineages that dominate the substyles I described earlier can be traced even to the top of the food chain of contemporary art practice.

Surrealism continues to be a favored style, evident in the extravagant imaginary creatures populating Matthew Barney's *Cremaster* series; the new Goth sensibility of David Altmejd's "bejeweled werewolves"—Keinholz + Sephora; Chloe Piene—Blair Witch in underwear; Banks Violette's black versions of Barney's Vaseline, organic/orgasmic, gym/torture-chamber sets; the return of psychedelia; a general fascination with a kind of dungeons-and-dragons, teenage-boy fantasy world in one variant, or a pseudo-cosmological fantasy world in another; fairy tales narrative scenes, from dark and lurid to cute, from Kiki Smith and Sue de Beer to Amy Cutler.[10] And currently all blob-like forms are Surrealist-rooted formations, whether in the crisply delineated biomorphic forms of digitally influenced, pop-colored, Hello Kitty–Murakami abstraction—Dalí on Prozac or Ecstasy—or the excremental lumps of the base materialism, "formless" branch of the surrealism family tree.

. . .

When an artist learns his craft too well he makes slick art.
—Sol LeWitt, "Sentences on Conceptual Art"

The rules of modernism still apply. Good recipe art is formally flawless: all visual languages used are fully understood and cannily re-articulated. Success depends on the canniness of the re-articulation, the knowing manner of juxtaposition. You always know what is being done to what is being quoted. Whereas, at the "bad" end of the scale of trite tropes the artists will often have gotten something wrong, made some small mistake of expression, a fudging of a line, the mottling of a flat space, or there will be the fatal appearance of a stray cliché from another adjacent style from some other point in the vast history available for unconscious consumption. Perhaps it isn't a mistake at all, but a deliberate deployment based on an equally deficient mastery of the tropes of appropriation art and other postmodern visual strategies. At the recipe art part of the scale there will be no errors of appropriation. "In 'Tower of Babel' the Swiss artist Corine Borgnet covers a *sculptural ziggurat* with *thousands of handwritten notes on Post-Its* and scraps of paper, most of which she *gathered from offices at the United Nations.*"[11]

Despite the prevalence of formal economy, another characteristic of recipe art is that the premise of the work can seem very *recherché*, or what the French call "tirer les vers du nez" (to pull worms from the nose, a difficult job). You need to know a lot to understand the work, or the work may be visually pleasing, and the premise may have validity, but the connection between the two is obscure to the viewer who has not read the accompanying, or precessionary, text.

The recipe art that is most seamless formally, including work that is about revealing sutures, is work that cannot be fitted into a sound bite even though all the ingredients are in place. Here, the example of Rauschenberg is paramount, in particular his manner of introducing old, scrappy, and new, pop-culture found objects into flawlessly elegant, three-dimensional re-articulations of abstract expressionism's version of Western painting's compositional rules. This influence is operative, for example, in the work of Jessica Stockholder and in more subtle ways in the works of sculptors such as Rachel Harrison, Evan Holloway, and Isa Genzken, who were included in "The Uncertainty of Objects and Ideas: Recent Sculpture" at the Hirshhorn Museum in 2006 and "Unmonumental" at the New Museum in 2008.[12] If the general rule of recipe art is that it must take physical form in order to participate in the market but also be formulated for quick verbal consumption for marketing purposes, all the ingredients are present in this movement's work—appropriated elements combined with abstract ones in untraditional materials—yet a coherent sound bite cannot be established a priori, therefore it does rely on being seen. The formal ingredients cohere: shinier surfaces and a slacker attitude to formalism and to appropriation serve to give the work the look of newness, and yet the basic modernist principles can be collapsed back into Rauschenberg's innovations. And in many 3-D installations of this style, if you squint, you can optically collapse them back into a 2-D modernism that is something closer to a Motherwell composition than you might expect. Thus the newest versions of postmodern works contain traces of modernist stalwarts, proving the continued importance of modernist formalist compositional rules to current artworks' success, as well as pointing to the underlying conservatism of some work presented as most emblematic of this moment's version of modernity.

The works I have singled out have distinguished themselves by the skill with which their artists resynthesize formal and narrative tropes. (Recall how my slide jury rewarded the iteration of the newest familiar styles.) There can be considerable pleasure in the ingenious and imaginative conjunctions of familiar elements and the skillful manipulation of art and craft vocabularies. It is the instrumentally formulaic aspect of the mechanisms of recipe art and all the clichés and persistent styles at the high end of art production that are the focus of my critique, not individual works that may be produced within the formula.

Part of the source for the proliferation of trite tropes, clichés, and persistent styles lies paradoxically in inadequate or non-existent early art education and in art historical instruction that is often summary, even cursory. Certainly the concepts behind the appearance of styles are not taught sufficiently if at all. Also students often do not get to see enough real artwork: how many students perpetuating surrealism have ever actually seen a Max Ernst or an early Dali in person? They may be shocked at the small scale, the delicacy, even at the formal simplicity, and at what is still the true strangeness of some of the real works, the way they refuse even now to fold back into the known. Or artists may not know the deeper past of art—how many hours does anyone spend in the back galleries of the Met anymore? Who has time anyway? And, if they accept the market's focus on what is in art magazines and Chelsea galleries now, they still may not even know much about the near past of fashion: the artworks in those galleries five years ago might have better luck being known if they were prehistoric. Thus they mine a shallow lode. Alternatively, some young artists *only* admire old art and cannot accept even the radicalism of forty years ago. This is a reality in the culture at large. In a July 2005 article in the *New York Times* about an avant-garde theater festival at Lincoln Center, Margo Jefferson gave basic instructions on how to experience modern theater, including being prepared for the lack of continuous narrative. Her guidelines indicate the degree to which people, even though they live their everyday lives in the disjointed spaces of postmodernity, have still not learned to accept it when they see it articulated in an artwork.[13]

Most art teachers I know work hard to remain responsive and responsible to new movements; it is in fact one of the reasons to teach — the necessity that teaching imposes to keep up to date. However, they may not be able to compensate for other gaps in contemporary aesthetic education and market conditions.

While the persistence of styles may be fostered by those art teachers who teach what they learned in the two years of their own schooling, gradually transforming art philosophies into sets of visual habits while being overwhelmed by the increasingly corporate academic frame, recipe art emerges from the complicity of some fine-art departments and schools with the values of the art world and art market. In fact such complicity is a prerequisite of success for the institution, whatever its actual impact on art. Rumor has it that in Columbia University's MFA program, currently one of the most successful graduate programs in the United States, faculty are evaluated for contract renewal by their ability to network successfully for their students' careers. A couple of years ago, one of the institutions I teach at sent out a card announcing a panel on "self-promotion for artists and designers," "The Brand Called You." A 2008 course offering, "Internet Famous," is described as "the first class in the history of academics where software awards each student a grade based on a quantitative measurement of their web fame," or whether they are "famo."[14] Many MFA programs have professional practices courses, in which students hone their skills at, for instance, "the elevator pitch," where they have to condense a spiel on their work that will last no longer than an average elevator ride with a prospective collector or dealer. These are certainly practical and realistic studies in the current cultural economy. But one of the effects of this pressure is to encourage the formation of work that *can* be boiled down to a few words: recipe art. Then the art world grabs the graduate-school product most likely to rely entirely on the clever recycling of currently appropriate, obsolescent styles. The predictability of the work produced in this system creates an undercurrent of nihilistic cynicism that is expressed in the often extremely nasty, dismissive tone of the comments on websites that discuss recent artwork.[15]

The continuing, basic formal and narrative categories, such as those Western civilization has termed Apollonian and Dionysian, expressionist, romantic, or classical, are in fact perhaps as embodied as basic human character traits — we all recognize, sometimes ruefully, sometimes with pleasure, recurrent character types in the people we meet throughout our life. So too in art. This continuity is a form of cultural storage and may be constitutive of civilization. What I am talking about is the point when the structure of this system of legacy and continuity becomes so commodified and trivialized that the rats start biting each others' tails in frustration.

I'd like to return to Chuck Close's comments about his unashamed working through of other artists' work: "We knew we were students and that was the way to learn — to *be* de Kooning, *be* whoever it was, and just devour them and then move on to another artist." He continued, "And we all knew that it was student work, it could not be confused with mature work, and nobody thought twice about it. You could not leave graduate school and take the paintings you did at graduate school and go to New

ADD
2 CUPS OF
WARHOL
AND
A STICK OF
NAUMAN
AND
SERVE!

Carl Pope, from the *About Bad Art* poster
series, 2008. Letterpress broadside. 17 × 26
inches. Courtesy of the artist.

York and get a show."[16] Students frequently express tremendous anxiety
at the idea that their work displays any influence. But, paradoxically, the
pressure to produce consistent and "original" product disrupts the kind
of carnivorous, instrumental, and instructive process of imitation that
allows an artist to come to a more genuine personalized intervention into
art language, and instead insures the deadly familiarity of much work.

Unlike the process of consumption of influence described by Close,
market pressures disable artists from moving through stages of influence
at the pace each individual might need. Only the most facile, the quickest
studies succeed in the short run, freezing into formulaic product what
might in the past have been just a stage in the movement toward more
individualized work. Market success makes one stubbornly resistant to
change. And who am I to argue with success? Or, put differently, the young
artist can think to himself, who is *she* to argue with *my* success? The art-

ists who have learned to deploy the most current tropes are likely to be showing their work and even selling it, and it is hard to critique artists at such (usually fleeting) moments in their career. "Natalie Frank, the only Columbia student in the group . . . currently has a solo show, her first, at the Briggs Robinson Gallery, in Chelsea, and she is not worried that early success may pose a threat to her artistic development. 'I started taking drawing classes three times a week when I was ten,' she said. 'This has been my goal for some time. I feel ready.'"[17]

In the seasons of 2005 and 2006 the *New Yorker* and the *New York Times* launched a series of articles focused on the art school–celebrity nexus. First in this series were Nick Paumgarten's October 17, 2005, feature article, "Salesman: Days and Nights in Leo Koenig's Gallery," which portrays the adventures and business deals of the well-born, young German gallerist and his stable of artists—mostly young and male, and Mia Fineman's January 15, 2006, article, "Portrait of the Artist as a Paint-Splattered Googler," about the very successful, twenty-nine-year-old Columbia MFA graduate, painter Dana Schutz.[18] These were followed by Calvin Tomkins's "Dept. of Precocity, Artists in their Youth" from February 27, 2006, a short piece in the *New Yorker*'s Talk of the Town column noting the phenomenon of MFA students exhibiting their work in commercial galleries to great interest from collectors, in this case in a show called "School Days," at the Tilton Gallery uptown, "featuring the work of nineteen graduate art students at Hunter, Columbia, and Yale." Tomkins's March 13, 2006, piece, "The Creative Life: The Pour," discusses the making of a large poured-paint artwork by Barnaby Furnas, an artist showing with Marianne Boesky. The *New York Times* picked up the "Dept. of Precocity" story, with Carol Vogel's April 15, 2006, front-page article, "Warhols of Tomorrow Are Dealers' Quarry Today,"[19] followed by Jori Finkel's "Tales From the Crit: For Art Students, May is the Cruelest Month," an article synergistically driven by the recently opened movie, *Art School Confidential*, by Terry Zwigoff and Daniel Clowes.[20]

Next came Mia Fineman's *New York Times* article "Looks Brilliant on Paper: But Who, Exactly, Is Going to Make It?" about a two-tiered class structure developing in the art world between A-list artists such as Paul McCarthy and Mariko Mori and artists who graduated from B- and C-list MFA programs.[21] In these less prestigious programs, the second group learned the technical skills necessary to make gigantic and enormously expensive projects like those conceived of by the A-listers, but their execution, in fact their aesthetic character and realization, often have only the sketchiest relation to the A-listers' work. Dorothy Spears's article "The First Gallerists' Club" depicts the ultimate success that the young MFAs picked up by the Tilton Gallery are led to expect: the power to unceremoniously ditch the gallerist who supported their career from its inception in order to go to the biggest dealer they can snag, with the most money and most international market access.[22]

Arguably, there is more than a dash of satirical intent on the part of the writers of these articles. However there's very little coverage of other types of artist, dealer, curator, or art practice. These articles perform a number of functions related to the success of the new academy of recipe art and that mark them as part of the machine of the Spectacle: they obscure the existence of other, less market-oriented or market-attractive aspects of art practice; they undermine the very real, formal, and conceptual interest of so much artwork, including work that is successful, that addresses major issues of our time — from ecology to technology to war — within a substantial formal investigation; and they promote within the world of high culture the values of late free-market capitalism. Many of these articles focus on painters, even though the art world as a whole has largely shifted its attention to other media — painting remains a primary, easily recuperated commodity. They impress on the reader the often seemingly disproportionate sums of money involved in these transactions, from graduate students selling paintings for more than their teachers are paid, to mid-career artists such as John Currin selling paintings for up to a million dollars. In Tomkins's "Dept. of Precocity," the author describes the gallery owner Jack Tilton, who "hove into view, a youthful-looking man in an open-collared white shirt. Asked about the perils to young artists of showing so early, he said, 'we're thinking of doing a think-tank session here in the gallery. Get a diverse group of older and younger people, give them a good dinner, and talk about this. If you have a strong enough philosophical base you're not going to get knocked off your feet by greed and capitalism.' He continued, 'you have to act more as a muse. You're not forcing capitalism down their throats. It's more, let's get together.'"[23]

In fact you don't *have* to *force* capitalism down the throats of young artists who have been bred into an unquestioning acceptance of its rules and recipes, even if they will in most cases ultimately be among its many victims. There have always been business savvy artists and there have always been very rich, socially ambitious collectors. The media has always participated. The difference is found in the scale of money, amount of artists, and the lowering of the age of entry. Most importantly, this generation of art students was formed during the Reagan-Bush era, during which anything resembling true critiques of authority and power was methodically ridiculed, demonized, or erased, creating a cohort that is surprisingly obedient and conformist, when not imbued with a sense of hopelessness. As Calvin Tomkins reported, "After a few more slatherings of paint [Barnaby] Furnas was ready to knock off. His wife and [Marianne] Boesky's husband, Liam Culman, were expected any minute. 'My husband is a total philistine,' said Boesky, whose father is Ivan Boesky. 'Liam is a Wall Street trader, but he loves Barnaby, and Barnaby loves the bourgeois life my husband loves. They play squash together at the Racquet Club.'"[24]

Each of these articles contains a few quotes from highly reputable art world notables, including Chuck Close and Rob Storr, who sound a note of warning about the dangers of this cradle-robbing system, but it is simply a fact of life that young people can never be effectively warned about dangers to come; they always think whatever it is they're being warned against won't happen to them, and the very existence of the articles in which these disclaimers appear would seem to undermine their warnings' credibility. Nevertheless most contemporary critics who even attempt a critique of the obscenities of the market conclude that it is naive to imagine one could avoid it. So in the guise of a rather fatalistic realism, we are always returned to the market's axiomatic presence, its existence as essence. The nature of what might be an alternative system is not given the time or space by mainstream art media. "*Artforum*/Karybdis," the whirlpool that regularly swallows up all those who cross its turbulent waters, operates according to the dictates of a commercial calendar that does not allow attention to ideas and artworks that are not immediately part of a specific market economy. In fact, when something does appear in print without a commercial hook-up, you look for one anyway because it seems impossible that it could be there just because it is interesting.

Though it may always have been so, when read against the backdrop of incipient global war over resources and religion, with a tremendous toll on not only the poor of the world but also the educated middle classes and women, the triviality of much of this artistic and commercial discourse has been hard to countenance. The jarring effect of a trite-trope, recipe-art, celebrity-youth art industry was strongly felt when artists ventured back to Chelsea in the weeks after September 11 and were startled by the disjuncture between what they had just experienced and the art on exhibition. Since then, the international situation has worsened, and although many artists have seriously engaged with the importance of the major struggles that confront us, the acres of recipe art still displayed in the proliferating art fairs and the attention to recipe and celebrity are even more disturbing—and boring.

Recently, my students read various standard texts on appropriation and simulation, including Hal Foster's "The Expressive Fallacy." In an effort to reinforce the link between seminar readings and studio practice, I asked them to make two art works on the same subject, the first using appropriational techniques and strategies, the second working expressively. The results were disappointing. At first I felt that their use of appropriation was timid and inept, which seemed strange considering the pervasiveness of appropriation in the culture at large. Next it occurred to me that the real difficulty might lie in doing something expressively, with any authenticity or necessity at the level of the image, the story, the stroke, the line, the object. It is a strangely complex paradox: self-expression and authenticity form the bedrock of the rhetoric of art practice, yet the critique of authenticity and originality has been so effective (even when the artist is uneducated to theory), and simulation, conventionalized commodification, and sampling are so present in every day existence, that the hardest challenge for an artist today is to make an authentic mark that represents personal or formal investigation. My students' predicament suggests that current cultural conditions are such that recipe art may be the only solution for a majority of artists who are trapped between a surplus of cultural quotation and the present loss of access to anything passing for an "authentic" artistic gesture.

"Come Saturday it will look as if a tornado had picked up a Prada store and dropped it on a desolate strip of U.S. 90 in West Texas. That is where Prada Marfa, a permanent sculpture by the Berlin artists Michael Elmgreen and Ingar Dragset, will be installed. . . . The sculpture is meant to look like a Prada store, with minimalist white stucco walls and a window display housing real Prada shoes and handbags from the fall collection. But there is no working door."[25]

So, I walk into a studio and I see something I've seen a million times before, at best the successfully articulated latest model of the latest style. I walk into a gallery, and I see—the same thing I just saw in the studio, a *mise-en-abyme* of cultural reference, yet another endless loop of appropriation. The work was made to be incorporated into the market and the discursive stream of the academy. That its originality is homogenized is part of its ethos. It may be chillingly, even heartlessly proficient, but that proficiency is a good indicator that we find ourselves in the Neo–New Academy.

For the inaugural exhibition of its satellite location in Williamsburg, Brooklyn, the artist Emily Katrenik is eating the wall that separates the gallery's exhibition space from the bedroom of its director. . . . Video of her ingestion is included in the exhibition; she also removes some of the plaster and bakes it into loaves of bread, which are available for gallery visitors to sample.—Mia Fineman, "The Munchies," *New York Times*

What really matters, I mean, *really*, beyond the rhetoric of it mattering, is having something to say that can truly reinvest familiar materials and forms with cultural energy. What makes something at least temporarily uncategorizable in relation to history and to ambient cultural language may require a self- and other-criticality that for some artists takes decades, not months, to achieve. Yet now there is no time for the slow aesthetic growth that used to be one of the standard tales of origin. Meanwhile every stroke, blob, or pixel has been analyzed, recycled, branded, as every trope has been trumped.

The question is where to look for the work that really alters your world, not just the work that tells you why this world is so mutantly oriented to the commodification of tropes. Or, having had my methamphetamine, my hit of the latest re-articulation of the near-past and the "next-modern," I need something I would describe as real food. I walk into a museum and have an intimate relationship with a random artwork or artifact from the past that suddenly speaks to me—if I am in a museum that still allows for private experience. Or I take advantage of the exit conveniently gnawed open by the artist ingesting or regurgitating the possibly toxic confines of the spaces of art, step outside, and turn to other modes of expression and cultural action than high art.

In the years bracketing the 2004 Presidential election, I was most compelled as a consumer of culture and a spectator of visual interventions by animated political cartoons, "viral videos" that came into my computer through emails and political blogs like Daily Kos and Raw Story. Since the 2004 election, I have spent much of my time in these forums, as well as listening to or watching Rachel Maddow, Al Franken, the *Stephanie Miller Show* on Air America, Amy Goodman on *Democracy Now*, the *Daily*

Show, and later, the *Colbert Report*: comic sites and news outlets that created stepping stones to help me get through the perilous and depressing landscape of each day in the American body politic of that time. The viral videos I discuss here circulated in the immediate pre-YouTube era, so there was a less centralized or named aspect to their effect and their dispersal. They were made out of political exasperation and the desire to communicate this through humor, not to appear on YouTube in order to become "famo."

I tried to track down one such video that had been sent to me in March 2001, "A Night at the White House," which featured a sing-along with the (animated) Marx Brothers: "Dubya, oh Dubya, say have you met Dubya, the wag from Texas? Dubya, oh Dubya, don't let I.Q. trouble ya." I googled "Dubya," which led to a treasure trove of comic material, much of it at the Peace Candy and Angry Candy blogs.[1] For example, in the video "Asleep at the Wheel," Bush, snoring all the way, crashes his U.S.-shaped motorcycle into everything he encounters, waking only briefly amidst the wreckage to say, in his real voice, "God Bless America." The best part is that the snoring doesn't stop until you remember to close the browser window.

Sometimes these animations are crudely drawn, such as those from Scott Bateman's year-long project of creating an animated film a day, which showcase President Bush, drawn as a spinning and bobbing death head, and Stoner Dude, his heart in the right place but, well, stoned since the 1960s, among other characters real and imaginary.[2] Yet, unlike the slightly cartoon-like, quasi-narrative drawings by artists such as Marcel Dzama, Royal Art Lodge, and their many followers, which were all ubiquitous at major art fairs during the same time period, no cultural institution asked me to think that Bateman's work was great drawing.

Political art and even more so political cartoons are said to have a short shelf-life, while fine art's more metaphoric approach and the complexity of its referential languages may outlive the details of a limited polemical moment. Bateman's project may have been the most overt in its ambition to discursively stay on top of the news, and not all of the videos and animations I enjoyed appeared in such instantaneous relation to current events, but the general motivation was to respond to the political moment. The pieces were about the election when that was part of our collective experience; they address the war and the villainies of Bush, Rumsfeld, and Cheney, as well as revel in whatever colorful characters and outrageous details emerged from the political narrative stream.

These works are not earnest. They exude a blithe joy that occasionally eludes political art, highly committed and equally necessary as it may be. They are not particularly beautiful or original—the humor often comes from the alteration of highly recognizable and beloved cultural entities like Star Trek or Dr. Seuss. Among my favorites are the brightly colored, boldly black-outlined caricatures by "Citizen Twain" at toostupidtobe- president.com. For example, "Star Trek: The Wrath of Condi," in which the August 6 PDB (Presidential Daily Briefing), which famously begins, "Bin Laden Determined to Strike in U.S.," is placed in a Star Trek–themed cartoon: "Petroleum, the final reserves. These are the voyages of the Star Ship Enron's Prize. Four-year mission: to explore pristine worlds, to lay pipe amid old civilizations, to boldly drill where no man has drilled before. Captain's Log, Star Date August 6, 2001." The text is like a bad play: all exposition and no action, read by anonymous actors who sometimes sound like they are recording the whole thing in a bathroom, or a tin can, but always like they are having a lot of fun. In a bored voice, "Condi," as Uhura, says, "Captain, I'm picking up a transmission from Israeli intelligence to the CIA. It says buildings that symbolize American government, military might, and commerce are at risk of kamikaze attacks using hijacked U.S. planes." The captain leaves the mess for his cronies to fix while he vacations on the Holodeck. In "How the Bush Stole the Election," a cartoon in two parts, the story of the 2000 election is told in a parody of Dr. Seuss, in terms of representation style, voice, and rhythmic composition. Another cartoon, "Get Stupid," riffs off of James Bond movies and their cultural take-offs, such as *Get Smart* and *Austin Powers*, while addressing the secret planning of the Iraq Work Group. In "McClellan," hanky panky at the White House literally takes place in a series of untoward appearances behind the press secretary, who refuses to answer questions about "ongoing investigations" into matters completely visible to an increasingly horrified White House press corps.[3]

Some of these works share techniques with artworks by Christian Marclay or Douglas Gordon, such as rhythmic film and sound-clips montages, but in the moment I preferred the sedition of Camp Chaos Entertainment's "Read My Lips," in which slightly slowed-down moments from George W. Bush's and Tony Blair's joint appearances, set to Lionel Richie's "Endless Love," highlight the homosocial, erotic subtext of this nefarious international alliance. When they stare into each other's eyes, the effect is quite convincing. "Gay Bar by Electric 6 (Lo)" pushes the relationship further.[4]

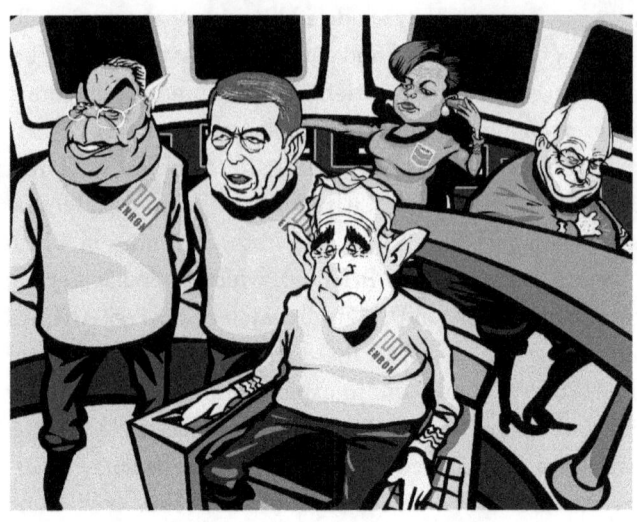

Citizentwain, "The Wrath of Condi," 2002. Animated cartoon.
© by Citizentwain.

Googling "Dubya" also led me to "Don Knotts Is Dubya," a short film put together from clips from Don Knotts movies such as *The Shakiest Gun in the West* and *The Incredible Mr. Limpet*.[5] Knotts's movies, which turn on his signature persona—a quivering coward—placed into situations that call for machismo, turn out to be a treasure trove of *uncannily* apt opportunities for satirizing George Bush: the composite character is named George, has a "spunky" mother and a war hero father, avoids the military, and lands on an aircraft carrier. My favorite moments emerge from Knott's trademark quavering delivery of his lines: "I have been called brave. [voice cracks] What is brave?," and, drunk in a saloon, "Failure, failure, failure, failure, failure, failure, failure, failure, that's the story of my life, you know." The cherry on top of this filmic appropriation is that, while beneath Bush's macho image and hypermasculinist policies of preemptive war lies his own avoidance of combat, Don Knotts, on film the epitome of pusillanimity, was actually a decorated WWII veteran! Suddenly I am dying to Netflix his movies and think he should replace Jerry Lewis in the hearts of the French.

These works are not art because they don't chose the context of art. Their context is a field of communication potentially as large as the Internet itself, thus with an audience that far exceeds any that might go into an art gallery or museum, but they are also shared as private correspon-

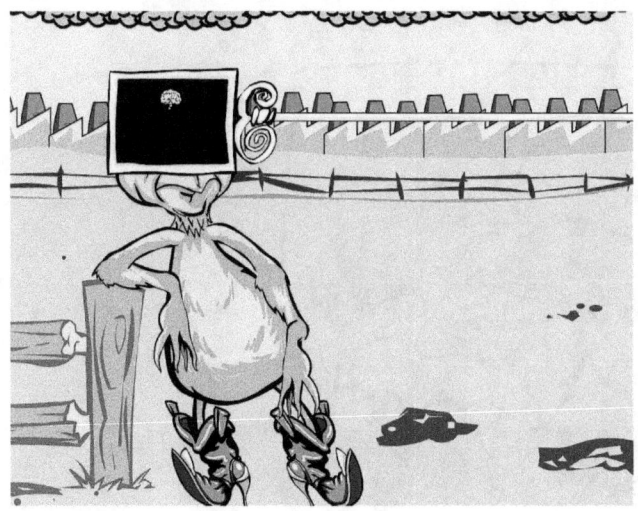

Citizentwain, "How the Bush Stole the Election," 2001.
Animated cartoon. © by Citizentwain.

dence between friends. Yet there are interesting similarities between the Peace Candy website's Fake State of the Union Address, an actual speech edited to revealing effect—"Every year by law and by custom we meet here to threaten the world"—and Maria Friberg's memorable video *No Time to Fall*, shown at the Team Gallery in 2001, in which the artist edited everything out of Bush's State of the Union speech except the standing ovations and Bush's preening reactions.[6] Similarly, two of the funniest videos I saw in 2004 and 2005 were Tamy Ben Tor's *Women Talking about Adolph Hitler* (2005), at P.S.1, and Ze Frank's "Red Alert" (2004).[7] Ben-Tor is able to convincingly capture the vocal intonations, the appearance, point of view, and assurance (despite their often absurd points of view) of a variety of stereotypical characters you immediately recognize even if you had never considered them before. The most priceless moment of the video is when the woman sporting a tidy little Hitler mustache word-lessly adores a framed photograph of the Führer. In his video, Frank por-trays a relentlessly cheerful young man from "Wakeesha, Wisconsin" who helped design the Homeland Security Advisory System ("HisAss") "to let the general public know how close they were to dying." Frank's and Ben Tor's differing career tracks indicate the importance of someone's cultural address yet the randomness and perversity of reception. Both are terrific actors who are able to use and alter their appearance and intonation in

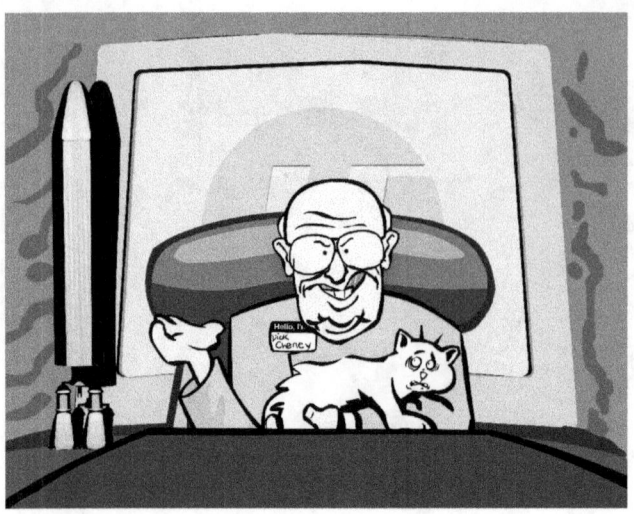

Citizentwain, "Get Stupid," 2003. Animated cartoon.
© by Citizentwain.

order to brilliantly portray a wide range of social stereotypes for political effect. But Ben Tor placed herself in the art context, and the art world immediately singled her out for stardom, while at first suggesting that she'd do wonders for *Saturday Night Live* (although the politics of her content is much too intense and idiosyncratic for such a popular context). Frank did not chose the art world, may be too independent to work as a regular actor, and apparently did not come to the attention of Jon Stewart or similar impresarios of contemporary political satire.

The art world does occasionally provide a home for acts of *détournement* involving hegemonic power structures—for example the interventions of the Yes Men, recently included in the exhibition "If It's Too Bad To Be True, It Could Be DISINFORMATION" at Apex Art in New York. Their work usually takes place in the world of international media and finance and has actual, if temporary, effects on corporate malfeasance, but they do not need the art world to support their practice.[8] Nor does Will Ferrell, reprising his great *Saturday Night Live* impersonations of Bush during the 2000 election cycle, or Andy Dick in his video "Harlan McCraney, Presidential Speechalist," a high production-value comedy short whose premise is that a guy actually wrote Bush's mangled English, including, as his greatest accomplishment, Bush's . . . *silences*.[9] (At one point during the 2004 presidential debates, Bush appeared to be waiting for audio instructions to be piped in through a mysterious box visible under his suit; here, the "speechalist" *instructs* him to *not* answer for inordinate amounts of time.)

It's obvious by now that I don't want these works to be considered art, or "non-art," or even "un-art"[10] even though I reflexively am led to consider them in relation to art, because art has been my context. I want to protect them from art's pretensions, its high priests, and its zero-sum game of success or failure. I am even loath to call them agitprop because that term has its own marginalizing, art historical baggage. These videos are joyful acts of generosity by people who have had *something to say that must be said* about an outrageous, absurdist, dangerous political moment.

My enjoyment does not change my professional appreciation for much contemporary art, but the intensity of my consumption of this alternative news analysis and humor indicates that, in a world where there are few if any dissenting voices in the center of the media, I need somewhere to feel at home. These works address pressing concerns and relieve my sense of political isolation. The people who have created many of the political satires I have described seemed to be working in a non-branded section of culture—relatively anonymous websites, which one mostly stumbles upon, and which in many instances are not a major source of fame or income for their creators, including independent animators like "Citizen Twain"—and have cathected cultural experience by using forms, media, and a mode of distribution that suit the necessity of the time.

Can they transform the body politic? We are haunted by the contested legacies of 1960s political activism and cultural revolution. The Reagan-Bush regime, curiously echoing Baudrillardian visions of no-exit hegemony, has done such a good job of destroying both social progressiveness and belief in political activism; that everyone seems to turn away from activist models from that earlier era fosters the idea that political activism is futile. But these short comic interventions and their means of infiltration through the Internet, acting synergistically with courageous alternative journalism and with other forms of comedic political commentary, form part of a *pushing back* whose cumulative effect can be seen in stirrings of political courage at top levels of government and media. This is one of the new faces of political activism.

I walk into a room in a museum and a man speaking Arabic in a video says, "I won't starve you to death," and he blows me a kiss.

. . .

In the time frame of the 2004 presidential election in the United States, I proposed the temporary solution of taking a break from Art in favor of more contingent popular political humor. Here I will leave intact the timeline and point of view I outlined in "Work and Play," but by reflecting on some new works since that time, I will bring my reader closer to the "present."

. . .

The flow of short-form political satire continued to the end of the Bush regime. But as the 2008 election approached, humorous satires of Dubya yielded to inspirational pop videos such as Will.i.am's impeccably elegant, black and white "Yes We Can" video, in which, with gently rhythmic musical accompaniment, a succession of young white and African American musicians and actors echo a speech by Barack Obama. The counterpoint of simultaneity and slight disjunction of speech add to the political impact.[1]

The boundaries and crosscurrents of influence between entertainment, political satire, TV news, home video, and museum video installation have become ever more fluid. Inevitably, the war infiltrated high art, although it took time for its tropes to develop. Because the vision of a self-perpetuating system of tropes and recipes that I have outlined might well leave my readers wondering how one can get past the temptations or even the seductive inevitability of recipe art, I will consider a few such war-related works, some of which play out the aesthetic politesse of recipes while others step outside those lines. In particular, I would like to end this book by discussing a work that I am struck by and love, *Not a matter of if but when: brief records of a time in which expectations were repeatedly raised and lowered and people grew exhausted from never knowing if the moment was at hand or still to come* (2007), a work by Julia Meltzer and David Thorne, which was included in the 2008 Whitney Biennial.

This thirty-two-minute video, divided into five parts marked by fade-outs to black, features the Syrian performance artist and director Rami Farah. Thorne and Meltzer worked with Farah in Damascus during the period of 2005 to 2007, with the war and civil war in Iraq and turmoil in Lebanon as the immediate background, inviting him to improvise from simple prompts of suggested subjects.[2] Farah, a thin, dark-haired young man, is seated in front of the camera against an unmarked white background, and is seen in close up: only his head, hands, and shoulders are visible. He speaks in Arabic, his words translated in subtitles. The formal elements of the video are minimalist and minimal, but the speaker is the opposite of minimal. The close camera focuses on every detail of his darkly stubbled face and intensely expressive hands and black eyes. His narrative also is the opposite of minimal, as he tells vivid stories about the experience of living in a country overcome by war.

Politically or historically, it may be of some importance that Farah speaks in Arabic rather than in English (or American) — especially in comparison to another Iraq War–related work in the biennial, Omer Fast's *The Casting*. But from the point of view of emotional understanding, it does not matter at all; even without subtitles, he is the very essence of expressivity. His eyes burn and flicker with intense emotion, fear, horror, love, hate, and compassion for the person he is speaking to. His hands, face, and shoulders are actors in their own right; his voice, sometimes whispering, imploring, is urgent, intimate, and soft. A new Scheherazade, he embodies storytelling where wonderment and horror mix at will.

He describes a murdered child turning into a crow and the wolf who ate his remains crushed on a road; he tells of the villagers who, instead of succumbing to its effects, become addicted to the poisoned bread and jam they are fed. In the most remarkable sequence he looks at his palms and through his fingers, and, with one eye peering out in horror at us, the [American] viewers, he foresees a war coming. It comes. His body is exploded. The body parts are scattered in the bloody street. After a few moments they seek to reassemble, but now each one wants to be on top:

> I see a long life [. . .] Yes, with many tragedies and much happiness and sorrow . . . and luck [. . .] lucky man! But . . . yes, I see it. . . . There is . . . there's war! [. . .] Look—a war! I don't want any war. A war is going to happen. A bomb will fall on us. My body will be blown into pieces, and each piece will land in a different place. The pieces begin looking for each other. "Here we are!" The head is shaking around, saying, "I am

here!" The torso is crawling around trying to reach the other parts. The legs are walking here and there, searching. . . . All the pieces are searching for each other. They all gather together by chance and begin to put themselves in order once again. [. . .] The legs say, "I saw you all first because I am the tallest." [. . .] But the torso responds, "I felt all of you. I knew where you were, I came to you." They reach out to each other and start to put themselves back together. But the legs suddenly decide to be on top so they climb on the head and stand there. [. . .] The arms are wrapped around the head, the head is stuck between the legs, and the torso is at the bottom. [. . .] The head looks up at the legs, and says, "No, this is my place, get down. . . . You can't see from the top." [. . .] The torso climbs up to the top saying, "No that's mine, I'm the one who stands here. I'm the one who most feels you all." [. . .] The arms, legs, head, and torso are spinning around each other . . . trying to arrange themselves, one moving up, another down . . . each of them wants to be at the top, alone on top. Why can't they all be on top? All next to each other in a single row? They try, it doesn't work, they change positions, one moves up, another down. [. . .] The head begins to eat itself, slowly . . . it eats itself, slowly . . . The legs are trampling themselves . . . and the torso is feeling all of it . . . and it is enough.[3]

It is horrific and absurd and Farah paints it with his words, his eyes, his hands, his whole body. Here is necessity, the necessity to tell the tale, to imagine the horror for us; it is the righteous outrage of the innocent.

We have seen these images before. This soliloquy recalls the twisting bodies of *Laocoön and His Sons*, and maybe this is the moment to recall that Laocoön was punished, condemned with his sons to death by a host of snakes, for attempting to expose the ruse of the Trojan Horse — that is, for telling the truth.[4] Other images come to mind: the base materiality of Théodore Géricault's paintings of severed legs and arms; Philip Guston's tangles of body parts, shoes and legs rolled into grotesque balls against a livid ground; or the pile of innocent noncombatants, the top figure lying upside down, so that the legs indeed are on top, in one of Francisco de Goya's *Ravages of War* etchings. But is it necessary to recall Art? This is a specific new voice telling an old story and, like Géricault, Guston, and Goya, for now it is enough.

In another segment, Farah gets up, leans into the camera to breathe on the lens. A white haze blossoms, then his image slowly reappears, temporarily polarized by the remainders of condensation, but as close as a secret or a kiss. He moves his body in and out of focus range, but blur is always succeeded by deeply detailed and emotional scrutiny: the lens focuses on him but he is focusing on us.

Fast's *The Casting* (2007) also deals with the Iraq War, skillfully inter-weaving four scenarios or narrative settings in a four-channel installation with two double-sided projection screens: a plump, pink-faced, corn-fed American soldier posted to Germany dates a self-mutilating girl with a comically perfect Aryan family; a highly stylized series of tableaux en-acts the accidental shooting of one member of an Iraqi family stopped by American soldiers on the road; the soldier narrates these events to the filmmaker; in a reenactment, the "soldier" tells his story to the "artist filmmaker" against a sterile background at what appears to be an audition in LA. The filmmaker (and the "filmmaker") says to the soldier (and "sol-dier"), "We'll call you." His story may not pass the audition of spectacular culture.

The diegetic frame of the audition provides the ironic imprint of America's luxurious distance from the violence perpetrated in its name, as the spectacle's response to the soldier's traumatic stories or stories of trauma is aesthetic and critical. The manner in which Fast focused on the American soldier's experience, and in which the war narrative is bracketed, framed, and distanced with a sophisticated, state of the "Art," technical gloss, ends up seeming hegemonic in terms of politics (including art world politics). Certainly the narrative is presented in a manner consistent with the way we are conditioned to accept information today: through techno-logical proficiency, spectacle, story, framing, and the flat, affectless tone of the American youth who has suddenly been confronted by violence of a non-virtual nature after growing up on video-game violence. Such trau-matized testimonies, presented with less artistry or distancing devices, are available on YouTube, for example in the documentation of *Winter Soldier: Iraq and Afghanistan* (2008), produced by the Iraq Veterans against the War.[5]

There are also art videos that represent an American experience of the Iraq War with a differently aimed, ironic style. In Guy Richards Smit's short, single-channel work *Hot Body Robbin' G.I's* (2008), two American soldiers, one male, one female, enter a bombed-out house.[6] As in *The Cast-ing*, the setting has a certain approximation of verisimilitude that is real-istic enough yet too sanitized to be anything but fake. The soldiers come upon a charred body with a gleamingly undamaged Rolex on its wrist. Each in turn tries to grab it off the body but it is too hot. Like two monkeys trying to figure out how to get a banana, they look at each other, they look at the watch. They ponder in silence. This work is far less sentimental than even Fast's heavily bracketed narrative and therefore more damning.

Significantly, *The Casting* was more prominently placed in the Whitney Biennial than *Not a matter of if but when* (which was located in a small room in the furthest back corner of the fourth floor), and Fast was awarded a great deal of critical attention, as well as the 2008 Bucksbaum Award for a work in the biennial. Yet Meltzer and Thorne, by modestly withdrawing the traces of their own mediating role, made their work a vehicle for Rami Farah's poetic, emotionally complex, and generous voice, a voice of the Other, the innocent sufferer of violence, which we have rarely if ever heard or been allowed to hear in the United States during this war committed in our names.

The two principal qualities that allow an artist to get beyond the seductive but predictable trap of recipe art seem too simple to even mention, yet they are surprisingly hard to find in such vital combination: necessity, and having something to say with an investment in the formal means you use to say it. Nothing in *Not a matter of if but when* was predictable or easily integrated. This piece was part of the pushing back against a decade of negative thinking—expressive, imaginative, enchanting, and unsparing.

In developing the essay "Blurring Richter," I focused on Richter's use of the blur, and found that it would be too cumbersome for the essay to also contain considerations of his use of grey. I merely noted that "in Richter's early work grey provides a note of negation and indeterminacy: 'I have a special relationship with grey. Grey, to me, was absence of opinion, nothing, neither/nor.' And, 'To me, grey is the welcome and only possible equivalent for indifference, noncommitment, absence of opinion, absence of shape.'"[1]

Richter's use of grey is valued because it is seen as the emblematic color of an anti-ideological position, which would nevertheless be valorized as moral in the light of the ideologies that had turned Richter against ideologies: fascism and Soviet totalitarianism. Rob Storr writes,

> At one level then, gray is a symbolic mid-term in a context where many are prone to seeing things in black and white. The keynote of an anti-rhetorical style, it not only distinguishes his work from the neo-Expressionist painting prevalent at the time, it fundamentally alters our appreciation of the tradition of chiaroscuro painting, which *October 18, 1977* updates in unanticipated ways.
>
> Combined with various *un*painting procedures, gray thus operates as the agency and emblem of doubt, in a situation where doubt is intolerable to many if not most of those with the deepest involvement.[2]

However for Primo Levi, "the gray zone" is the zone of moral ambiguity (or morality lost in a situation of traumatically brutalizing amorality), which Richter's paintings may perform even outside of their desire to do so. Levi notes the moral ambiguity enforced by the Lagers, the degradation of the victims, and the "gray zone of collaboration," in his chapter, "The Gray Zone," from *The Drowned and the Saved*.

> In contrast to a certain hagiographic and rhetorical stylization, the harsher the oppression, the more widespread among the oppressed is the willingness, with all its infinite nuances and motivations, to collaborate: terror, ideological seduction, servile imitation of the victor,

myopic desire for any power whatsoever, even though ridiculously circumscribed in space and time, cowardice, and, finally, lucid calculation aimed at eluding the imposed orders and order. All these motives, singly or combined, have come into play in the creation of this gray zone, whose components are bonded together by the wish to preserve and consolidate established privilege vis-à-vis those without privilege.

It remains true that in the Lager, and outside, there exist gray, ambiguous persons, ready to compromise. The extreme pressure of the Lager tends to increase their ranks; they are the rightful owners of a quota of guilt (which grows apace with their freedom of choice), and besides this they are the vectors and instruments of the system's guilt.[3]

Memories may be fragmentary, they may well be false—at the very least they are highly subjective constructions. At the cellular level, the very process of remembering, of articulating a memory, is thought to be a process of instantaneous chemical re-creation of the memory that has just been taken out of "storage." Just like a drawing taken in and out of a drawer gets frayed around the edges, a VHS copy loses resolution, and a computer file gets corrupted by tiny misfires, so memories are rebuilt from scratch each time they are used and thereby they are subtly altered.[4] But once recalled, memories are experienced more like "snapshots" of the computer desktop image, tableaux of an emotionally significant event, or images caught in a bright, phosphorescent flare of light to which a narrative adheres and accretes than a messy blur of misremembered facts. Even if superficially trivial, what remains in memory is likely to be something that mattered deeply, something that shattered the blur and also the greyness of our average daily consciousness. Events and things that for each one of us represent life and death or hatred and love concentrate the mind and memory.

Philip Roth suggests as much to Primo Levi in a comment about the second of Levi's three books about his Holocaust experience, *The Reawakening* (in Italian, *La Tregua*, "The truce"): "What's surprising about *The Truce*, which might understandably have been marked by a mood of mourning and inconsolable despair, is its exuberance. Your reconciliation with life takes place in a world that sometimes seemed to you like the primeval Chaos. Yet you are so tremendously engaged by everyone, so highly entertained as well as instructed, that I wondered if, despite the hunger and the cold and the fears, even despite the memories, you've ever really had a better time than during those months you call 'a parenthesis of un-limited availability, a providential but unrepeatable gift of fate.'"

Levi responds to this suggestion, "A friend of mine, an excellent doctor, told me many years ago: 'Your remembrances of before and after are in black and white; those of Auschwitz and of your travel home are in Technicolor.'"[5]

Despite Levi's comment, the use of *grey* to denote the past is a recognized trope of contemporary art and popular culture. In his analysis of Gerhard Richter's *October 18, 1977* paintings, Robert Storr notes the accepted code: "Gray was also a way of showing that he was painting the past, and a signal that he had opted for a style belonging to *his* past."[6] A friend of mine, when she was a child, used to refer to black and white movies as "grey." Steven Spielberg's decision to film *Schindler's List* in black and white seems partly based on this trope. This choice is an example of the way in which black and white is seen to give an artwork the imprimatur of the past and of a kind of deep significance and pious respect.[7]

Grey legitimates an artwork as an act of mourning, although it is an accident of technological development that black and white film was the only widely available type until well into the 1960s, resulting in a black and white visual record of much of the past; still, we accept that as the chromatics of memory. In fact it is the contention of Jean-Luc Godard that black and white photography was an artificial construct purposely chosen and retained for its specific relation to mourning: "We should analyze the fact that when photography was invented, it could have been color from the very beginning, it was possible. But if it was in black and white for such a long time, it's not by chance. There should be a moral aspect since in the European, Western world black is the color of mourning. So we were taking the identity of nature out of painting and killing it in a certain way. . . . And I add that the first Technicolor, and Technicolor still today, is more or less the color not of real flowers but the flowers on funeral wreaths."[8]

The black and white photography of *Schindler's List* also gave Spielberg the opportunity to "cheat" on his own scheme in one specific moment of poetic license where the use of one spot of color furthers the narrative and provides an explanation for the actions taken by the hero. As he looks down from his horse onto the raid of the Krakow ghetto, Schindler's eye is caught by an artificially created *punctum* in the black and white cinematic field. A beautiful little girl dressed in a red coat escapes from a group of Jews being herded down the street at gunpoint. She is seemingly unnoticed by the Nazis yet she is noticed by Schindler, for our benefit, because of the selective apparition of red within a black and white picture (although if you try to figure it out, it makes about as much sense as a sci-fi movie plot: did Schindler, like the audience of *Schindler's List*, actually *see* in black and white?). The purpose of the red is in the reappearance, later, of the red coat in a pile of corpses that, in Spielberg's narrative construction, crystallizes Schindler's otherwise nearly inexplicable effort to save "his" Jews. In fact, this vignette from an Aktion in the Krakow ghetto in 1942 is taken directly from Tom Kennealy's book *Schindler's List*, based on the rec-ollections of "Schindler Jews," upon which Spielberg based his movie. The little girl is Genia, a three-year-old who arrives in the Krakow ghetto after being hidden by Polish peasants. "She had her vanities, though, and like most three-year-olds, a passionately preferred color. Red. She sat there in red cap, red coat, and red boots. The peasants had indulged her passion."[9] Spielberg's movie is quite faithful to Kennealy's book, except that the scar-let coat does not reappear on the pile of corpses in the Plaszów concen-tration camp. So it is only this second notable appearance of the red dress that is an instance of poetic license. One wonders if it is this particular spot of color in the book, in the "true" story, that caused Spielberg to use black and white in order to highlight this significant episode and use it to help establish "motive" in an extraordinary story. Black and white is used for the center part of the narrative, the "Holocaust" section, which is framed by color. Although grey clearly is used to denote the past, the film is bracketed by two color scenes. The opening credits are in color, of Sabbath candles: when these are snuffed out, we fade to "grey," and then at the very end of the movie, color returns to indicate, if not the present (since the movie is always already a record of something that has already happened) then the continued survival of Schindler's Jews and their de-scendants. So current reality is in color. For Godard, Spielberg's chromatic artifice goes beyond this spot of color: "*Schindler's List* is a good example of making up reality. It's Max Factor. It's color stock described in black and white, because labs can't afford to make real black and white. Spielberg thinks black and white is more serious than color. Of course you can do a movie in black and white today, but it's difficult, and black and white is more expensive than color. So he keeps faithful to his system—it's phony thinking."[10]

The equation grey=the past, that is to say the past of movies, can occa-sionally be done with campy humor. One of the characters on *Star Trek:*

Voyager constructs a "Holodeck" entertainment called "Captain Proton," a program that emulates the visual style and the narrative structure of old Flash Gordon serials. As the regular characters enter this Holodeck fiction, which is in black and white, they "become" black and white themselves. In one episode, the black and white space is used to trouble the timeline between past and present, as "Captain Janeway" finds herself on a journey through non-linear time as her ship is riven by temporal displacements.[11] The Captain Janeway of an earlier time finds herself "meeting" crewmembers and plot lines the audience is of course familiar with. Entering the Captain Proton program, she notes with interest "a monochromatic universe." In this narrative frame, her knowledge of this play-embodiment of the past is in her future.

But the use of grey in art, particularly in painting, has not always connoted memory and history and has not always referenced photography.

Grisaille has a dual lineage, a realist and a romantic one. Grisaille's first significant appearance in painting was in the guise of referentiality to sculpture, just at the point when figuration in painting as well as in sculpture had reached a certain verisimilitude of three-dimensionality. Examples of grisaille used for this purpose include Giotto's figures of Sins and Virtues at the bottom of the Scrovegni Chapel cycle, and the outer panels of Jan Van Eyck's *Ghent Altarpiece*, a tour de force of painterly virtuosity as well as a practical way of suggesting architecture and sculpture while maintaining the portability and light weight of panel painting.

The next significant deployment of grisaille, in some works of Jean-Auguste-Dominique Ingres, presents perhaps the closest moment of communion between grisaille and photography in the nineteenth century, before Richter's photo-based grey paintings in the twentieth century. These paintings occur nearly simultaneously with the development of photography but in fact just before it. These sharply focused but monochromatic painted renderings of images that Ingres also painted in full color seem to recall, but in fact anticipate, the look of mid-nineteenth-century photographs such as those by Nadar. It is almost as if Ingres's grisaille versions were an attempt to replicate photographic reproduction, but actually they forecast this imaging process. So, for example, *Odalisque in Grisaille* (1824–1834), surely done as a less expensive duplicate of the Odalisque in color,[12] seems to provide a way of making a replicant for sale without sacrificing the uniqueness of the original work of art. Its uniqueness, in relation to the accuracy of the grey-scale in black and white photography, is evi-

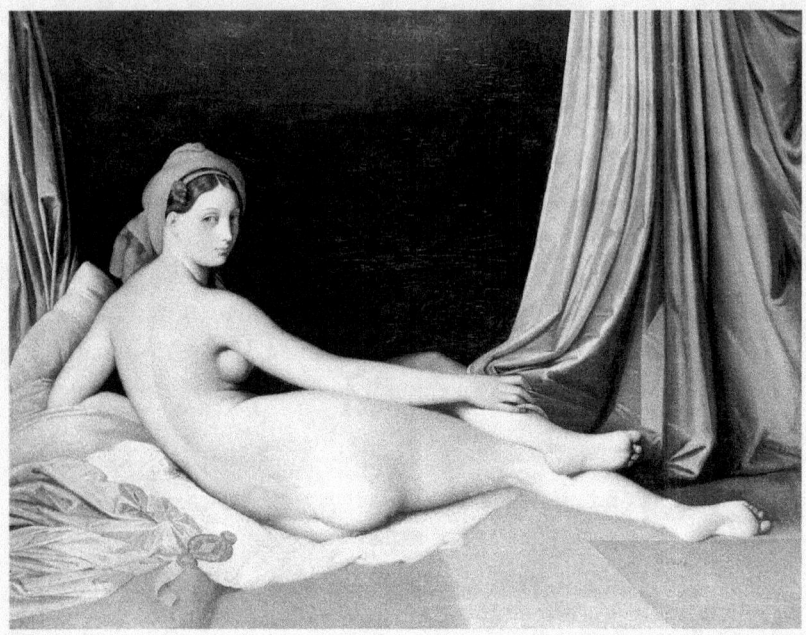

Jean-Auguste-Dominique Ingres and Workshop, *Odalisque in Grisaille*, 1824–34. Oil on canvas. 32¾ × 43 inches. The Metropolitan Museum of Art, Catharine Lorillard Wolfe Collection, Wolfe Fund, 1938 (38.65). Image © by The Metropolitan Museum of Art.

denced in the shifts from warm to cool in the painting, most visible when the viewer gets close to the painting. From across the room to about six feet away, the illusion of the photographic in grisaille is perfectly convincing. But upon closer examination, the Odalisque sits on a cloth, painted in an unfinished manner, which is warm grey on almost a Naples-yellow under-painting. Some of the rest of the cloth is cool grey. Her skin is cool grey, particularly her legs, but her back and ear have a pink tinge. The shifts from warm (yellow) to cool (blue and violet) tip the image into its identity as a painting.

In the twentieth century, grey is often a virtuosic act and an academic one, showing an artist's ability to work every aspect of a discipline, in this case every aspect of chromatic reference in painting. It marks also painting's liberation from the responsibility of representation of the real. Painting no longer must be in color. Painting now can do what it chooses.

It may choose to be influenced by photography. It may choose to elaborate one small aspect of plasticity.

Beginning in the nineteenth century there is another family of grey-ness, a more romantic one, beginning perhaps in the silvery tones of Jean Baptiste Camille Corot's landscapes, where grey appears more to evoke a lilting emotional state much like the notes of a Chopin *Nocturne*. In the twentieth century, this lineage of grey is articulated in works by Edwin Dickinson, Jack Tworkov, Walter Murch, Vija Celmins, and Jasper Johns. A soft pastel-like touch even in oil, a buttery atmospherics of fog creates a link to the use of grey as connotative of remembrance and loss, loss of the visual spectrum. Grey appears in works by these artists in order to evoke death as well as natural beauty, a sadness of memory recollected in tranquility except that the materiality of these works, the velvety softness of pastel, the burnished physicality of oil, lead, or encaustic, the shifting lines and dot patterns created by charcoal on paper, exist by definition in the viewer's embodied present. These works often are the embodiments of what I have called "modest painting": paintings that have a quiet affect while painted with willed self-abnegation and discipline that underscores a rigorous ambition for painting.

Even Richter's use of grey, non-committal and almost scientifically exact with no trace of his technique left for the viewer's eye to rest in, and whose critical validation is based on its relation to photography, has a romantic aspect in the truest use of the word. Romantic in relation to the romantic movement — it dips into the romantic by virtue of its classical coolness and with a stance of negation that finds its philosophical roots in the romantic movement, especially in Germany: "I did have a special relationship with grey. Grey, to me, was absence of opinion, nothing, neither/nor." "To me, grey is the welcome and only possible equivalent of indifference, noncommitment, absence of opinion, absence of shape."

These various greynesses all share a containment of carnality, a stepping back from blood and flesh and death. If they all share a certain aspect of memorialization and marmoreality, it is nevertheless a reference to death that includes the poetics of presence.

Preface

1 See Naomi Schor, *Reading in Detail*.

Introduction

1 Saul Ostrow used this expression in a conversation several years ago to describe our shared hybrid practices.

2 "Nextmodern" appears in Paul Greenhalgh, "Paul Greenhalgh's Welcome," http://www.nscad.ns.ca/about/presidents_mes.php (accessed 2002). This opening page to the Nova Scotia College of Art and Design University's website was accessed before Greenhalgh was named to become president and director of the Corcoran Gallery of Art and Corcoran College of Art and Design, in Washington, D.C. See Trescott, "British Art Scholar Named Director of Corcoran Gallery." *Washington Post*, December 1, 2005, C1. The Greenhalgh statement can no longer be found online.

3 Mayor Michael R. Bloomberg's imperious compulsion to erase eccentricity from New York City in favor of rationalized urban planning is the only force that could interrupt the flow of traffic down this several-hundred-year-old pathway. On May 24, 2009, as I was completing revision of this book, the mayor shut off car traffic on Broadway between Thirty-third and Thirty-fifth Streets, and from Forty-second Street to Forty-seventh Street at Times Square, as part of his goal of diminishing overall traffic volume in that area of Manhattan. In the early days of this change, tourists sat around in the street on cheap lawn chairs and the scene suggested a parking lot filled with refugees.

4 Benjamin, "H The Collector, [H1a, 1]," in *The Arcades Project*, 204.

5 Benjamin, "Exposé of 1939, C. Louis Philippe, or the Interior, I," in *The Arcades Project*, 19.

6 Section headings in Baudelaire, *The Painter of Modern Life and Other Essays*, 1–40.

7 Section headings in Buck-Morss, "Mythic History: Fetish," in *The Dialectics of Seeing*, 78–109.

8 Mira Schor, "She Demon Spawn from Hell," *M/E/A/N/I/N/G* Online, January 13, 2006.

9 Jack Tworkov, journal entry, October 9, 1962. See Tworkov, "Journals and Diaries, 1947–63," in *The Extreme of the Middle*, 139.

10 Tworkov, qtd. in Mira Schor, introduction to Tworkov, *The Extreme of the Middle*, xvi; Tworkov, "Journals and Diaries, 1947–63," in Tworkov, *The Extreme of the Middle*, 71.

11 Tworkov, journal entry, January 11, 1979. See Tworkov, "Diaries 1979–80," in *The Extreme of the Middle*, 395–96.

12 Buchloh, "Divided Memory and Post-Traditional Identity," 62–64.

13 "The Art of Nonconformist Criticality," was delivered February 14, 2006, as part of a lecture series on art criticism at the School of Visual Arts in New York. It is archived at http://www.artonair.org/archives/j/content/view/1648).

14 "The Crisis in Criticism" was held at the School of Visual Arts, New York, on March 25, 2004. For further reflections on the state of art criticism emerging from this panel discussion, see Rubinstein, ed., *Critical Mess*. Michael Duncan's contribution, "Buggy-Making in Tulip Time," is particularly relevant to the issue of negative criticism.

The ism *that dare not speak its name*

This essay originally appeared in *Documents*, no. 15 (spring/summer), and was republished in *M/E/A/N/I/N/G* Online, January 2006, http://writing.upenn.edu/pepc/meaning.

1 In an interview in the mid-1990s, Lucy Lippard spoke about the Ad Hoc Women Artists Committee, started in New York in 1970 "primarily in order to protest the paucity of women in the *Whitney Annuals.*" She said, "We started the Women's Registry [in 1970] so when institutions told us, as they constantly did, 'there are no women who . . . (make sculpture, do conceptual art, work with technology, etc. etc.),' we could throw a huge batch of images of them and say, 'Oh yeah? Take a look at this.'" Stoops, "From Eccentric to Sensuous Abstraction: An Interview with Lucy Lippard," 27. In 1989 two posters by the Guerrilla Girls, *WHEN RACISM & SEXISM ARE NO LONGER FASHIONABLE, WHAT WILL YOUR ART COLLECTION BE WORTH?* and *GUERRILLA GIRLS' IDENTITIES EXPOSED!* listed hundreds of women artists in response to similar "there are no women who . . ." statements from major figures in the art world, proving that not much had changed in two decades, despite everything that seemed to have changed. See Schor, "Just the Facts, Ma'am," in *Wet*, 87–97. The statistics gleaned by the Brainstormers, discussed in "Anonymity as a Political Tactic" in this volume, support Spero's comments that the statistics of female representation in the art world remained remarkably unaltered by feminism, though there are much signs and rhetoric to the contrary, and in fact that the situation may have worsened since a high point in the 1990s.

2 These and other quotations are transcribed from my audiotapes of the panels discussed in this essay. I have chosen to faithfully record the words of people for whom English is a second language.

3 These were "Women and Abstraction," moderated by Elke Solomon; "Realities of Feminism and/or Activist Practice," moderated by me, with comments by

Johanna Drucker, Elizabeth Hess, and Peggy Phelan; "Committing *Heresies*: Ideas and Battles behind a Unique Women's Magazine," moderated by Carey Lovelace, with panelists Mary Beth Edelson, Elizabeth Hess, Joyce Kozloff, and Lucy Lippard; and also a roundtable on the Women's Action Coalition (WAC).

4 The Woman's Building in Los Angeles was a major center of feminist activities, including the Feminist Studio Workshop, founded in 1973 by the artists Judy Chicago and Sheila Levrant de Bretteville and the art historian Arlene Raven, all of whom had previously taught in the feminist art and design programs at CalArts. For a complete history of the Woman's Building, see http://www.womansbuilding .org; for visual archives, see http://www.womansbuilding.org/wb (both sites accessed May 13, 2009).

5 FAWS, "Journal Notes from F-word Symposium Week at CalArts" (Santa Clarita, Calif.: FAWS, 1998); FAWS, "Working Papers for Themes and Topics" (Santa Clarita, Calif.: FAWS, 1998).

6 See Schor, "Medusa Redux: Ida Applebroog and the Spaces of Postmodernity," in *Wet*, 67–81; and Schor, "Backlash and Appropriation."

7 The fall 1999 issue of *Documents* included "Schism-ism: Thoughts on Intergenerational Feminisms," by Liz Barrett, Catherine Hollander, and Andrea Richards, three members of FAWS. This piece describes the circumstances and reasons for the formation of FAWS and both indirectly and directly responds to the present essay as well as to Faith Wilding's essay about her experiences working on consciousness-raising sessions with FAWS, tellingly entitled "Don't Tell Anyone We Did It!" (Wilding's essay was published in the same issue of *Documents* as "The *ism* that dare not speak its name.") Barrett, Hollander, and Richards took issue with what they perceived as my pessimism about the feminist will in younger women. In "Schism-ism" they mention many of the questions raised at "The F-Word," including "Is the personal still political—how and when? What is the political? . . . What are the risks of identifying oneself and/or one's work as feminist? . . . What is a woman? What is a body?" (42–43). They note, "The anxious cry of 'Why are there no (young) feminist artists?' posits another self-fulfilling and blind prophecy. We do exist, though we may not be recognizable through the lens of a monumental feminism. We can and do spell out feminism, we write it in many ways, and we write it in the now" (42). They conclude, "The schismatic and mutating feminisms we profess is akin to blasphemy—a perpetual blasphemy that assures no unified field or established ideology by constantly contesting its own definition" (45–46). In other words, in response to my conclusion to "The *ism* that dare not speak its name," they asserted a commitment to feminism, albeit in a problematized and shifting form. In spring 2007, in conjunction with the opening of "WACK! Art and the Feminist Revolution: An International Retrospective of Feminist Art from 1965–1980" at the Geffen Contemporary at MOCA in Los Angeles, a new group of CalArts students organized "Exquisite Acts and Everyday Rebellions," an exhibition and a symposium, on March 10, 2007. Their

website (http://alum.calarts.edu/~feminist/home.html) and reports from symposium participants, such as Faith Wilding, indicate that the event had a different, more open atmosphere than that of "'The F-word."

8 For an extended discussion of "the language" as it is deployed here, see Schor, *Wet*, ix.

9 Barbara Crossette, "An Old Scourge of War Becomes Its Latest Crime," Week in Review, *New York Times*, June 14, 1998, 1, 6.

10 Paul O'Donnell and Lucy Howard, "Capitol Hill: Shoe Show," Periscope, *Newsweek*, October 26, 1998, 8. In reporting on the 2008 presidential campaign from the summer of 2007, a similar issue was made of Hillary Clinton's revelation of some cleavage.

11 Susannah Breslin, "Designer Vaginas," *Harper's Bazaar*, November 1998, 130. According to a press release for Dr. Virginia Braun's April 15, 2009, lecture, "Cosmetic Surgery, Commercialization and Culture: The Case of the 'Designer Vagina,'" "The so-called 'designer vagina'—a term used to refer to various forms of female genital cosmetic surgery, usually performed by plastic surgeons or gynecologists—appeared in public discourse about a decade ago. Since that time, this area of cosmetic surgery has been identified as 'the fastest emerging growth trend' in cosmetic surgery, itself a field which has expanded exponentially over that time. It seems more and more women are, apparently, having their genitalia altered for aesthetic purposes." Lecture given in conjunction with the exhibition "I am Art: An Expression of the Visual and Artistic Process of Plastic Surgery," curated by Dr. Anthony Berlet, MD, Apex Art, March 28 to May 9, 2009. See http://www.apexart.org/events/braun.htm.

12 A National Public Radio "Morning Edition" report on abortion rights (on January 22, 1999, the twenty-sixth anniversary of Roe v. Wade) noted the high median age (around fifty-five) of women actively involved in fighting for the maintenance of abortion rights against substantially successful efforts to restrain access by anti-abortion forces. In the years since I wrote the first version of this essay, the war against women's rights has continued its deliberate erosion of rights to abortion and access to birth control. For example, see "Indiana R's Seek to Criminalize 'Unauthorized Reproduction,'" a posting on the Daily Kos website by the contributor "Hunter": "'Unauthorized Reproduction?' 'Gestational Certificates?' Legal 'Petitions for Parentage'? No, it's not something out of *The Handmaid's Tale*, or a reference to a now-defunct European fascist regime. It's the focus of a new law currently being drafted by Republican lawmakers in Indiana, seeking to limit fertility treatments solely to married women who have successfully petitioned the court for state authorization. . . . According to a draft of the recommended change in state law, every woman in Indiana seeking to become a mother through assisted reproduction therapy such as in vitro fertilization, sperm donation and egg donation must first file for a 'petition for parentage' in their local county probate court. Only women who are married will be consid-

ered for the 'gestational certificate' that must be presented to any doctor who facilitates the pregnancy. Further, the 'gestational certificate' will only be given to married couples that successfully complete the same screening process currently required by law of adoptive parents. . . . As the draft of the new law reads now, an intended parent 'who knowingly or willingly participates in an artificial reproduction procedure' without court approval, 'commits *unauthorized reproduction, a Class B misdemeanor*'" (posted October 5, 2005, on http://www.dailykos .com). On the same website, see also "Wisconsin Attempts to Ban Birth Control," posted by "A Hidden Saint": "College campuses have emerged as the latest battlefield in the nation's war on women's reproductive rights. Wisconsin has passed a bill entitled UW Birth Control Ban-AB 343. This bill prohibits University of Wisconsin campuses from prescribing, dispensing and advertising all forms of birth control and emergency contraceptives" (posted August 2, 2005). Additionally, see Chincoteague, "The War on Women—Ladies, Start Your Engines," the Daily Kos website, March 25, 2006, http://www.dailykos.com. Among the stories noted in this online article are the refusal of the FDA to approve over-the-counter sales of "Plan B"; South Dakota's law banning all abortion; the "American Pharmaceutical Association [passing] a resolution called the Conscience Clause," which recognizes the right of individual pharmacists aligned with the Religious Right to "exercise conscientious refusal"—used to "deny not only RU486, and Plan B, which they consider abortifacients, but also birth control pills"; and the closing of abortion facilities, forcing (poor) women to drive hundreds of miles for such services. And this is just in the United States. The revival of the Taliban in Afghanistan and the imposition of religious prohibitions in Iraq, a previously secular nation, are well documented but generally not considered important enough to affect foreign policy. See also "The War Against Women," editorial, *New York Times*, January 12, 2003, sec. 4: 14.

The issue of inequality and discrimination at the highest levels of the art establishment and their effects on the physical and mental health of women art professionals is specifically addressed by Anna Chave in her essay "'Normal Ills': On Embodiment, Victimization, and the Origins of Feminist Art." Chave wonders whether "the market's present attentions to photogenic young female artists will lapse during their later years" and, alluding to the effects of the backlash against feminism in the United States, states that "as long as the feminist project may not be said to be concluded outside of an 'art world' that has at last begun taking a full world of practitioners and audiences into its purview, neither can the feminist project be considered to be concluded within it" (135–36). Chave points to the problematic equation made in much popular culture between feminism and victimization, yet also notes many of the very real instances of victimization of women around the world, as documented by institutions of record, including the United Nations and the justice department of the United States. She also notes, "Nearly every woman artist and art historian I know well enough to know

NOTES

such things about them (and relatively few of the men) have endured serious, often persistent ailments: especially autoimmune diseases (nearly 80 percent of whose victims are women); migraines and chronic pain (which disproportionately affect women); debilitating anxiety and depression (about three-quarters of all psychotropic drug prescriptions are written for women); gastrointestinal and eating disorders; breast cancer; diseases or dis-eases of the reproductive systems, ranging from cancers and other growths, to infertility, to the sometimes extreme effect of PMS and menopause; and osteoporosis" (143). Chave concludes that "far from occupying a reasonably level, communally human playing field—as some deluded postfeminists imagine—women still face huge and systemic problems, especially problems hinged to their corporeality, problems from which 'bachelors' are ordinarily exempt" (145).

13 The conference attendees were not completely blindsided: the Fresno State and CalArts feminist art programs member Chris Rush had regaled the opening night audience with the story of Judy Chicago dragging the "Cunt Cheerleaders" to the Fresno airport in 1971 to greet Ti-Grace Atkinson, who, according to Rush, was not amused by this display! In *Through the Flower*, Judy Chicago recounts the same story but, she says, the "cuntleaders" did this "much to my chagrin. Although I loved it, I also felt embarrassed at such overt expression of womanly pride" (107).

14 This has been said better before. I return often in my mind to the passage from Virginia Woolf's *A Room of One's Own* that begins: "One goes into the room—but the resources of the English language would be much put to the stretch, and whole flights of words would need to wing their way illegitimately into existence before a woman could say what happens when she goes into a room" (91).

15 In my extemporaneous remarks at the opening reception of "The F-Word" symposium, I asked a blunt and overdetermined question: "Young woman, if given the choice of identifying yourself as a feminist or having a show at Deitch Projects in New York, what would you do?" So I was interested by the first sentence of Inka Essenhigh's artist's statement for her first show at Deitch Projects (January 7 to February 13, 1999): "My paintings present an apolitical world." This assertion seemed unnecessary, not to say egregious. To say the work is apolitical is in itself a political statement since it calls up the discourse of the political: if the work is truly apolitical, why bring up the subject? Additionally, the statement was at cross-purposes to the work: the paintings depicted little dick-headed homunculi engaged in samurai-like behavior and disposed along dynamic vectors on strongly colored, enameled flat backgrounds. Given the undercurrent of violence in the work, it would seem that the artist's statement was intended as a passport into Deitch Projects—"let me in, I'm not political."

16 See "The *Womanhouse* Films" in this work.

17 See Elenna Mann, "Exquisite Acts and Everyday Rebellions: Notes from the Trenches" (2007) online on the comprehensive website organized for the ex-

hibition "Exquisite Acts and Everyday Rebellions." http://alum.calarts.edu/~feminist/home.html.

18 In retrospect, compared to Ben-Tor, Beecroft seems more ambivalent toward feminism. She was at least aware of it as a political position, however absurd she made it sound.

19 For an expanded retelling of my series of encounters with this representative of the negative aspects of patriarchy, see note 5 of "Miss Elizabeth Bennett Goes to Feminist Boot Camp" in this volume.

Anonymity as a Political Tactic

This essay first appeared as a chapter in Karen Frostig and Kathy Halamka, eds., *Blaze: Discourse about Art, Women and Feminism* (Newcastle upon Tyne: Cambridge Scholars Publishing, 2008).

1 More recently two Guerrilla Girls outed their identities in a lawsuit, as a sad coda to the history of their collective. However, this partial unveiling arrived long after the most significant and risky part of their intervention into art world politics. See Toobin, "The Bench: Girls Behaving Badly," 34–35. See also Schor, "Just the Facts, Ma'am," in *Wet*, 87–97. In much the same manner that the long awaited revelation, in 2005, of the identity of the Watergate figure "Deep Throat" as the former FBI official Mark Felt was anti-climactic, the revelation of the two Guerrilla Girls' identities did not really penetrate the public awareness of the group as a political entity. See David Von Drehle, "FBI's No. 2 Was 'Deep Throat,'" *Washington Post*, June 1, 2005, A1.

2 See at http://www.writing.upenn.edu/pepc/meaning.

3 The *M/E/A/N/I/N/G* online material was de-archived in 2004 when Artkrush sold its name to another online art-related magazine.

4 "Tamy Been-Torqued," Anonymous Female Artist blog, anonymousfemaleartist.blogspot.com, January 23, 2006, with comments through January 24.

5 All quotes from Miss Edna V. Harris, "Tamy Been-Torqued," and reader comments, on the Anonymous Female Artist blog, http://anonymousfemaleartist.blogspot.com, January 23–24, 2006; and by "art soldier" at http://artsoldier.blogspot.com, January 24, 2006. Jason Laning closed the artsoldier blog on August 2, 2006. His last post on his next blog (http://friendlyagitate.net) was around April 2008. He shut it down completely in July 2008 (email correspondence with Laning, May 18, 2009).

6 Charlie Brooker, "Supposing . . . There's Only One Thing Worth Debating Online," *Guardian*, Friday June 2, 2006, 32. The *Guardian* columnist Charlie Brooker, writing about the blogosphere response to one of his columns, concludes that, "The internet's perfect for all manner of things, but productive discussion ain't one of them." In particular, he notes, "In the debate sparked by my gibberish outpouring, it wasn't long before rival posters began speculating about the size of their

opponents dicks. . . . Anyway, if we must debate things online, we might as well debate that. It's not like we'll ever resolve any of that other bullshit, is it? Click. Mine's bigger than yours. Click. NO it isn't. Click. Yes it is. Click. Refresh, repost repeat to fade." On the PainterNYC blog, "Painter" (the host blogger) asks why the level of discourse isn't higher: "It seems that you're satisfied with a blog full of mostly lazy, immature, and uncritical comments — the status quo being exemplified by such witty banter as 'this sucks' or 'i love it' or 'this is lame.' Thoughtful, engaging comments are rare, although I'd guess that most who participate here would be capable, if pressed. Is this representative of how NYC painters discuss painting away from this blog? Perhaps this explains why so much bland painting continues to be made. Why not raise the level of dialogue here by somewhat directing the conversation to a higher critical plane. Or, at the very least, you could set a rigorous, knowledgeable example with your own comments that would not only serve as a positive model for others to follow, but would also be a discouragement to navel-gazing blog saboteurs whose only goal is to impress themselves with name calling and circle-jerking (hint: they become bored and tend to go away when ignored)." To this, another "anonymous" blogger answers: "jeezus christ, critics, it's not SCHOOL — why does everything have to be an 'improving' 'higher' conversation? do we ALWAYS have to raise the fucking bar? cant you conceive of something between a circle jerk and a seminar? what i like about this blog is you can get on and say what you'd say to a friend while walking down the street as you leave the gallery. ok it's not the middle or end of the conversation, but just a first hit. havent you left galleries and turned to your friend, and said, that sucks? or wow that was great. this blog is just a first hit. maybe get a small conversation going. i for one dont need an mfa discussion everytime i come on here." "Cheyney Thompson," http://painternyc.blogspot.com, posted March 3, 2006. See also "Damien Hirst Apparently Has the Smallest Dick Ever; But We Kinda Knew That Already," Anonymous Female Artist blog, http://anonymous femaleartist.blogspot.com.

7 "Girl Art Recession," Anonymous Female Artist blog, http://anonymousfemale-artist.blogspot.com, posted March 7, 2006.

8 When I accessed the website again in May 2008, the wording of their introduction had been changed slightly although the substance was the same and the participants' identities remained public. "Brainstormers is an art collective that, through public performance, exhibition, publication, internet, and video, has forced discussion on a topic that most would rather avoid: gross gender inequities in the contemporary New York Art World" (www.brainstormersreport.net).

9 See Alan Finder, "When a Risqué Online Persona Undermines a Chance for a Job," *New York Times*, June 11, 2006, 1, 30. Employers have learned to look up prospective young employees on sites such as Facebook and MySpace, where "college students often post risqué or teasing photographs and provocative comments about drinking, recreational drug use and sexual exploits" (1).

10 John LeKay, "Edna V. Harris Interview II," in *Heyoka*, an online magazine with art, music, and other cultural features, with a high production value and a slight new age tilt. *Heyoka*, spring–summer 2006, http://www.heyokamagazine.com.

11 Quotes from comments to "*Heyoka* Magazine Interview," Anonymous Female Artist blog, http://anonymousfemaleartist.blogspot.com, posted May 24, 2006.

12 See Stephanie Rosenbloom, "The Taming of the Slur," *New York Times*, July 13, 2006, G1; and Maureen Dowd, "What's Up, Slut?" *New York Times*, July 15, 2006, A15.

13 "So Here's the Deal," Anonymous Female Artist blog, http://anonymousfemaleartist.blogspot.com, posted July 5, 2006.

14 Rebel Belle, "She's Not Taking This Shit Anymore," Anonymous Female Artist blog, http://www.anonymousfemaleartist.blogspot.com, posted March 25, 2007; Edward Winkleman, "Something (Slightly) Naughty; Something Very Nice," the Edward Winkleman blog, http://edwardwinkleman.blogspot.com, posted December 22, 2006. See also "Generation 2.5" in the present work.

Generation 2.5

Portions of this essay were published as "I am not now nor have I ever been . . ." in the *Brooklyn Rail*, February 2008.

1 Among the events that occurred from 2006 to 2008, many coordinated under the aegis of the Feminist Art Project, were a number of thirty-fifth anniversary exhibitions and celebrations: of Judy Chicago's Feminist Art Program (FAP) at California State University, Fresno; of the Mary H. Dana Women Artists Series at Rutgers, the State University of New Jersey, originated by Joan Snyder; of the exhibition "Where We At," organized by Faith Ringgold and other African American women artists; of the publication of Linda Nochlin's signal essay, "Why Have There Been No Great Women Artists?"; of the formation of the landmark women artists cooperative New York gallery, A.I.R.; of the Feminist Art Program at CalArts and of its 1972 installation project, *Womanhouse*; and of the foundation of the Woman's Building in Los Angeles and the Women's Caucus for the Arts at the College Art Association. In addition to "WACK! Art and the Feminist Revolution" and "Global Feminisms: New Directions in Contemporary Art," among the many other exhibitions around the United States were: "How American Women Artists invented Postmodernism, 1970–1975," curated by Judith K. Brodsky and Ferris Olin at Rutgers University; "One True Thing," curated by Dena Muller at A.I.R. Gallery; "From the Inside Out: Feminist Art Then and Now," curated by Claudia Sbrissa at the Dr. M. T. Geoffrey Yeh Art Gallery at St. John's University in Queens; "Re:Generation," curated by Joan Snyder and her daughter, Molly Snyder-Fink, a show of eighteen emerging women artists held at Smack Mellon Galleries in the DUMBO area of Brooklyn and the Kentler International Drawing Center in Red Hook, Brooklyn, for the thirty-fifth anniversary of the Women's

Artists Series at Douglass College; "Women, Art, and Intellect," curated by Leslie King-Hammond, at the Ceres Gallery; "Women Artists of Southern California Then and Now," curated by Bruria Finkel at the Track 16 Gallery in Bergamot Station, Santa Monica; "Exquisite Acts and Everyday Rebellions," a symposium and exhibition organized by students at CalArts in March 2007; "The Feminist Future: Theory and Practice in the Visual Arts," a two-day symposium that was at MOMA in January 2007; and a day of panels that are part of the Feminist Art Project, held at the CAA annual conference in New York in February 2007. In February 2007, Susan Bee and I hosted a *M/E/A/N/I/N/G* Online forum, "Feminist Art: A Reassessment," which included statements by a cross-generational grouping of women artists, curators, and art historians. Exhibitions in Europe included "Kiss Kiss Bang Bang: Forty-five years of Art and Feminism," curated by Xabier Arakistain at the Bilbao Fine Arts Museum in 2007. These exhibitions and events were accompanied by major catalogues, art magazine reviews and articles, as well as more spontaneous blog and email responses. These activities and exhibitions continued into 2008 as "WACK!" opened at the P.S.1 Contemporary Art Center in New York in February and more panel discussions were organized in the New York area by the Feminist Art Project, P.S.1, the *Brooklyn Rail*, and the Brooklyn Museum's Elizabeth A. Sackler Center for Feminist Art.

2 Cottingham discussed this aspect of her project when presenting early cuts of *Not For Sale* at the A.I.R. Gallery in 1998. See Laura Cottingham, "Not For Sale: Feminism and Art in the USA during the 1970s," apexart website, 1998, http://www.apexart.org.

3 "Division of Labor: 'Women's Work' in Contemporary Art 1970–1995," curated by Lydia Yee, Bronx Museum of Contemporary Art, February 17 to June 11, 1995; Museum of Contemporary Art, Los Angeles, September 1995 to January 1996.

4 Schor, "Waiting for the Big Show," 72–73.

5 There were some major exhibitions of women artists, notably "Focus: Elizabeth Murray," curated by Robert Storr (October 19, 2005, to January 9, 2006). Also during this period at MOMA there were a number of smaller exhibitions of women artists as well as exhibitions where important younger artists were featured, particularly in the Projects series and in the video department (senior curator, Barbara London). The situation I've described is endemic to the institution, and these precedents create the future of curating, particularly curating from within the institution's collection, an attractive direction for many museums in times of economic problems. Others share this concern. On May 28, 2009, Jerry Saltz posted the following statement on Facebook: "The Museum of Modern Art practices a form of gender-based apartheid. Of the 383 works currently installed on the 4th and 5th floors of the permanent collection, only 19 are by women; that's 4%. There are 135 different artists installed on these floors; only nine of them are women; that's 6%. MOMA is telling a story of modernism that only it believes. MOMA has declared itself a hostile witness. Why? What can be

done?" He corrected his figures within the hour: "I made one mistake. There are not nine women artists installed on the fourth and fifth floors of the permanent collection. There are 10. That's seven percent." He vowed to mount a campaign to get the museum to reframe its presentation of pre-1970 modernist painting and sculpture to include more women artists. See Facebook threads on Jerry Saltz's Facebook wall, May 28 to June 2, 2009.

6   Email from "Kathe Kollwitz," February 13, 2008, linking to the Guerrilla Girls' Eli Broad poster on their website, http://www.guerrillagirls.com/posters/dearest elibroad.shtml. The Broad Collection's response, written by Joanne Heyler, the director and chief curator of the Broad Art Foundation, stressed the foundation's support of political art in general including by women artists and claimed that "since 1995, of the 43 new artists added to The Broad Art Foundation's collection, 14 (33%) are women, and nine of those are collected in depth." http://www .guerrillagirls/com/posters/dearestelibroad.shtml, accessed May 16, 2009.

   As the Guerrilla Girls pointed out, "It's misleading to count all 49 of Cindy Sherman's photographs to prop up the percentage of work by women in the show when there are only 4 women out of 30 artists."

7   In fact, these artists first made significant art works beginning in the mid-1970s. The exhibition "The Pictures Generation, 1974–1984," held at the Metropolitan Museum of Art from April 21 to August 2, 2009, made clear how many iconic works by these artists were produced in the late 1970s, even if their fame developed in the 1980s.

8   In my statement for "Feminist Art: A Reassessment," *M/E/A/N/I/N/G* Online #4, (http://writing.upenn.edu/epc/meaning), I write of my own work, beginning in 1974, with the image of the empty dress as a vehicle for expressing femininity as both an unstable signifier and a reminder or remainder of embodiment.

9   See my comments in "The *ism* that dare not speak its name" (in this volume) about Annette Hunt's story about the near loss of all the hours of tape from the history of the Women's Building, and Sue Maberry's experience of having to chose only 1,500 out of 10,000 slides of early feminist art to be digitized with the help of a Getty grant.

10 Maureen Connor, "(Con)Testing Resources," 251.

11 Judy Chicago wrote *Cock and Cunt Play* in 1970 and 1971, and Faith Wilding and Jan Lester rehearsed and performed it first at the Feminist Art Program in Fresno. They then took it to *Womanhouse* in 1972. Faith Wilding wrote *Waiting* in 1971 and first performed it at *Womanhouse* in February 1972.

12 See Jones, "Faith Wilding and the Enfleshing of Painting," In notes 24 and 25 to this article, Jones touches upon this process of erasure and forgetting: "The most egregious specific examples of this strategic forgetting include the 1987–88 catalogue and exhibition celebrating the history of California Institute of the Arts *CalArts Skeptical Beliefs* (organized by Susanne Ghenz of the Renaissance Society at the University of Chicago . . .), which almost completely excludes the Feminist

Art Program" (Jones, note 24). The FAP and the women artists who emerged from it are cursorily dismissed from Richard Hertz's book about Jack Goldstein, *Jack Goldstein and the CalArts Mafia*, which also functions as a kind of unofficial history of the early years of CalArts.

13 See Tucker, *Bad Girls*. It should be noted that two edited volumes on feminist art, Cornelia Butler's and Lisa Gabrielle Mark's *WACK!* and Peggy Phelan's and Helena Reckitt's *Art and Feminism*, also included some men, but only when they were essential collaborators with women artists, such as Peter Wollen with Laura Mulvey, or Ulay with Marina Abramovic.

14 The fact that feminist art helped open up what could be art and what art could be about is discussed, for example, by Tom Knechtel in "Sexy, Glamorous Feminism!," in *M/E/A/N/I/N/G* Online #4, http://writing.upenn.edu/epc/meaning. See also Jones, "Lari Pittman's Queer Feminism." The particular impact on gay male artists of feminism's permission to deal with gender and sexuality leads to some other ways in which Generation 2.5 got passed over that are touchy to discuss from a politically correct viewpoint. Feminism was in some ways quickly superceded as a major political movement by other liberation movements, and in the changed cultural atmosphere of the post-1970s era, gay male artists were able to benefit from feminism while at the same time bringing to their career the advantages that still accrue for men in a male-dominated culture, whether they are gay or straight.

15 Elliott, "The Currency of Feminist Theory," 1700.

16 Ibid., 1701.

17 More currently, many dealers require that their gallery websites provide the only online access to the artists they represent: for a young artist this may preclude inventiveness and experimentation in their self-presentation, but for an older artist such a rule may be even more damagingly restrictive, since most gallery websites give very minimal information and provide a limited number of images of recent work for sale. An artist with a history of thirty or more years of practice and some movement within their work may be more interestingly represented with a more complex personal website. Awareness of such artists' contribution to art (and feminism) could be seriously diminished by the kind of market-oriented regimentation imposed by dealers. A mature artist is more likely to resist such a regime than a beginner, so that also may make an older artist with a history and a developed sense of self seem like a more difficult commodity to work with.

18 Storr, qtd. in "Show and Tell," 181.

19 Anonymous comment to Edward Winkleman, "Fair Fatigue," Edward Winkleman blog, http://edwardwinkleman.blogspot.com, posted December 15, 2006. This comment was discussed further in this comments section and also in "Rebel Belle, What's Age Got to Do with It Anyway?" Anonymous Female Artist blog, http://anonymousfemaleartist.blogspot.com, posted December 18, 2006.

20 Martha Rosler, email to the feminist listserv FACES, "Conversation: [faces] Women Artists / Submerging Artists," April 27, 2008.

21 Williams and Smith are also Generation 2.5 members who were not included in "WACK!" or "Global Feminisms."

22 In the case of Williams and Smith, for example, they are part of Generation 2.75 despite the fact that they are also part of Generation 2.5 and were active during the 1970s, because they are perceived as having emerged later. This only proves the complexity of art practice and unsatisfactory nature of curating by birth date or decade.

23 Butler and Mark, eds., *WACK! Art and the Feminist Revolution*, 210, 220, 223, 226, 229, 231, 236, 280, 299.

24 Carey Lovelace, "Weighing in on Feminism," 140, 145.

25 I went through the check lists of "Bad Girls," an exhibition curated by Marcia Tucker at the New Museum, New York, part 1: January 14 to February 27, 1994, and part 2: March 5 to April 10, 1994; "Bad Girls West," curated by Marcia Tanner, UCLA Wight Art Center Gallery, Los Angeles, January 25 to March 20, 1994; "Global Feminisms: New Directions in Contemporary Art," organized by Maura Reilley and Linda Nochlin, Brooklyn Museum, March 23 to July 1, 2007; "In the Lineage of Eva Hesse," curated by Barry A. Rosenberg and Dr. Marc J. Straus, Aldrich Contemporary Art Museum, Ridgefield, Conn., January 23 to May 1, 1994; "Sense and Sensibility: Women Artists and Minimalism in the Nineties," curated by Lynn Zelevansky, Museum of Modern Art, New York, June 16 to September 11, 1994; "Sexual Politics: Judy Chicago's *Dinner Party* in Feminist Art History," curated by Amelia Jones at UCLA at the Armand Hammer Museum of Art and Cultural Center, Los Angeles, California, April 24 to August 18, 1996; "WACK! Art and the Feminist Revolution," organized by Cornelia Butler, Museum of Contemporary Art, Los Angeles, March 4 to July 6, 2007, P.S.1 Contemporary Art Center, Long Island City, New York, February 17 to May 12, 2008, and Vancouver Art Gallery, October 4, 2008 to January 18, 2009.

Email to a Young Woman Artist

This essay first appeared in *Gloria: Another Look at Feminist Art of the 1970s* (New York: White Columns, 2002), a newspaper-format catalogue of an exhibition of the same name, organized by Catherine Morris and Ingrid Schaffner at White Columns in New York, September 13 to October 20, 2002. *Anonymous Was a Woman*, a book put out by the Feminist Art Program at CalArts, ca. 1974, contained many "Letters to a Young Woman Artist" by leading women artists of the day. Now, in 2002, in the age of cyberfeminism, we do email.

The Womanhouse *Films*

1 Demetrakas conducted an interview with me at CalArts in front of my work from "Womanhouse" after the exhibition had been dismantled and parts of my painting torn off the walls of the small, windowless room in which it had been installed and painted onsite. This interview was not used in the finished film, and I only appear, but do not speak, in group scenes of a consciousness-raising session held about the experience of "doing the house."

2 E.g., Laura Cottingham, *Not For Sale: Feminism and Art in the USA during the 1970s*, video essay, 1998.

3 Lynne Littman went on to direct feature films and documentaries, often with political and feminist content. She received the Academy Award for Best Documentary Short Subject in 1976 for *Number Her Days*, which addresses the work of the anthropologist Barbara Myerhoff.

4 See Levin, *Becoming Judy Chicago*. "Chicago heard that Johanna Demetrakas had completed her film on *Womanhouse* and that her colleague's hassling had caused its maker to leave Schapiro on the cutting-room floor. 'Mimi could never learn to trust women & so always tried to dominate them,' Chicago reflected. 'In return, they turned on her. Johanna & I would both have honored her, but she couldn't trust either of us.'" (237). The likelihood of this version of events notwithstanding, the omission of Schapiro from the film is historically inaccurate and understandably infuriated the artist.

5 The interview of me in my room is interesting for me, because I am able to see my "alter ego," Mira Schor at twenty-one, sophisticated and yet excruciatingly naive. I still remember the wide-eyed expressions on the faces of Littman, her crew, and other CalArts Feminist Art Program members, all crowded into the doorway during the interview, as, quite unaware, I assumed the hand gestures of the self-portrait figure behind me.

Miss Elizabeth Bennett Goes to Feminist Boot Camp

1 This was the issue where Linda Nochlin's essay "Why Have There Been No Great Women Artists?" was first published.

2 I do not recall who the Rampart women were. I do, however, recall that incident vividly because I quickly absorbed the lesson of this moment: the difficulty that women do have in putting their hand out, both literally and metaphorically, and saying, Hi my name is ——, and I am an artist. I have used this story in my own teaching of feminism almost from the moment I left the Feminist Art Program at CalArts, despite my first reaction of dismissing the situation Judy described as absurd.

3 Miriam Schapiro was married to Paul Brach, a painter who was the dean of the

School of Art at CalArts and whose support of the Feminist Art Program was crucial. Judy Chicago was then married to the sculptor Lloyd Hamrol.

4 See "The *Womanhouse* Films" in this volume for an extended consideration of the film being shot that final day at the house, Joanna Demetrakas's film *Womanhouse*.

5 Leo Manso (1914–1993) was a painter in New York and Provincetown with whom 278 | 279 I engaged in a sporadic but nearly thirty-year-long political and pedagogical battle. He taught at the Cooper Union and, from 1959 to the late 1970s, ran the Provincetown Workshop, a summer art school in Provincetown with the artist Victor Candell. The school had a New York School, Hans Hofmann–inspired aesthetic program. I had known Manso since my childhood: the first summers I spent in Provincetown with my parents, we lived across the street from Leo and his wife Blanche. When my mother bought a house in the East End in 1969, a block from Leo's school, I applied for admittance for the 1970 summer season. My friend Mary Dellin, who was a student at the Cooper Union, also applied. At the time, I was doing small ink and watercolor works representing young women in 1920s-style clothing with pointy-featured faces and wearing pointy shoes in strangely lonely cityscapes or landscapes, in a style related to the work of the Chicago-based group the Hairy Who (there were other influences but this would be a pertinent contemporary reference from the time). Mary was pouring paint on paper in a manner indebted to Lynda Benglis's early works. We went together to meet with Leo at the beginning of the summer. He did not accept me. He told me that I was very intelligent but that I would never be an artist. Mary, on the other hand, was a real artist, he said, and she was accepted. The next year I went to CalArts, having been accepted on the basis of the very same quirky little watercolors, and I joined the Feminist Art Program there. In the years that followed, after this letter to Mary Dellin was written, I got my MFA and, shortly after, a teaching job at the Nova Scotia College of Art and Design. While still in my twenties but emboldened by these accomplishments and also newly informed by the responsibilities involved with teaching, I approached Leo at an opening and said, "You know, you told me something that one should never tell a young person. You told me that I would never be an artist." "What? Me? No I never said that." At the end of the summer, proving that he had been thinking about it, he cornered me at a cocktail party. "I never said that you would never be an artist, I said that you'd never be a painter." After I began to exhibit in New York, he took some credit for it, saying he had given me a kick in the pants that had worked. This experience was formative in terms of my own teaching. I may be quite critical but I keep my crystal ball about my students' future as artists to myself, knowing full well that you cannot predict who will have the drive to continue, or indeed who will succeed, no matter the early promise, talent, or performance of a student. The rest of the story, with its enactment of the workings of the male universal

under the rubric of the word *humanity*, is related at the end of "The *ism* that dare not speak its name," in this volume.

Some Notes on Women and Abstraction

This essay originated as a lecture titled "Alice Neel as an Abstract Painter," which I presented at the "Alice Neel Symposium," held at the National Museum of Women in the Arts in Washington, D.C., on November 19, 2005. A version of it was published in *differences* 17, no. 2 (2006); another, shorter version was published in *Woman's Art Journal* 27, no. 2 (2006).

1 Lippard, qtd. in Stoops, "From Eccentric to Sensuous Abstraction," 31.
2 I describe this panel more fully in "The *ism* that dare not speak its name" in this volume.
3 "Women and Abstraction" at the A.I.R. Gallery on November 21, 1997, was one of three events that complemented "Generations," an exhibition of small works by women artists at the gallery. This show and the related events were part of a celebration of the twenty-fifth anniversary of the gallery. I moderated the second panel, "Realities of Feminism and/or Activist Practice," held November 12, 1997, with the panelists Johanna Drucker, Peggy Phelan, and Betsy Hess. The moderator of "Women and Abstraction" was the artist Elke Solomon, and panelists included the artists Marcia Hafif, Stephanie Bernheim, Lenore Goldberg, and Rebecca Quaytman, and the art writer and critic Lilly Wei. (The panel had originally been advertised in a gallery press release of October 1, 1997, for an earlier date and as including the artists Rochelle Feinstein and Pat Steir and the art historian Harriet Senie.) The final panel was "Committing Heresies: Ideas and Battles Behind a Unique Women's Magazine," held on November 25, 1997, and moderated by Carey Lovelace, with panel members Mary Beth Edelson, Elizabeth Hess, Joyce Kozloff, and Lucy Lippard.
4 Lisa Yuskavage, qtd. in Deborah Solomon, "A Roll Call of Fresh Names and Faces," *New York Times*, April 16, 2000, sec. 2, 35.
5 The report by Jeffrey Brown was titled "Jack the Dripper" and was broadcast on January 11, 1999, on PBS.
6 Pollock, "Killing Men and Dying Women"; Saltzman, "Reconsidering the Stain"; and Brennan, "How Formalism Lost Its Body but Kept Its Gender," in *Modernism's Masculine Subjects*. Brennan does not reference Pollock. Lisa Saltzman does acknowledge Pollock's essay as a text she became aware of "since [her] essay first took shape" (Saltzman references Pollock's essay "Killing Men and Dying Women" and Anne M. Wagner's "Pollock's Nature, Frankenthaler's Culture" in "Reconsidering the Stain," 381 n. 3). It is impossible to entirely keep up with the new scholarship in any field, but my extended consideration of the comments of Lippard, Brennan, and Saltzman on abstraction is generated by my sense that

feminist art history and criticism seems more endangered than other disciplines by a lack of collective memory. A collective and constant reiteration of germinal feminist texts would serve as an effective counterdiscourse to the critical hegemony enacted by almost all art historians whose field is modernism: to this day there is no text on modernism that does not deal extensively with the writings of Clement Greenberg, just as there is no text by someone associated with *October* magazine that does not extensively refer and defer to at least one other Octoberite. My research on women and abstraction revealed a number of texts that have dealt with this theme yet often without any significant reference to each other.

7 Pollock, "Killing Men and Dying Women," 247–48.

8 See Luce Irigaray, "Volume-Fluidity," in Irigaray, *Speculum of the Other Woman*, 227–40.

9 Ibid., 258, 250.

10 Brennan, *Modernism's Masculine Subjects*, 116.

11 Ibid., 131, 133.

12 Lippard, qtd. in Stoops, "From Eccentric to Sensuous Abstraction," 26.

13 Ibid., 31.

14 Ibid., 29.

15 Ibid., 31.

16 Chave, "Minimalism and Biography," 387.

17 Mitchell remembers Schapiro and Chicago steering visiting feminist luminaries, including Gloria Steinem, Linda Nochlin, and Anaïs Nin, away from her room toward installations with more legibly articulated feminist points of views — in other words figurative representations or appropriations of objects from the real with figurative and representational elements built in. And people would ask me what *Red Moon Room*, my piece in *Womanhouse*, had to do with the theme of women's liberation, of which the house was thought to be an embodiment, even though my painting was figurative, including a self-portrait within a landscape with two red moons. The fact that the (barely) metaphorical aspects of my subject matter (red moon=menstruation) could not be read as relating to women's liberation confirmed my growing sense that there was a problem for painting within a political project in relation to artworks that incorporated the real — in this case the menstruation-related paraphernalia and "bloody" tampons in Judy Chicago's *Womanhouse* installation, *Menstruation Bathroom*. Even representational paintings were less clear than works that involved the appropriated (in sculpture) or incorporated (in performance) real, because the potential for slippage into metaphor and private symbolism in painting would prevent a painting from translating into a clear feminist statement.

18 Pollock, "Killing Men and Dying Women," 283.

19 Alice Neel, qtd. in Hills, *Alice Neel*, 80.

20 Ibid., 90. In speaking of "New Realism," Neel seems to be alluding to the objective approach espoused by contemporaneous realist artists such as Philip Pearlstein.

21 *The Spanish Family* is reproduced in Carr, *Alice Neel*, 25, plate 4.

22 Pollock, "Killing Men and Dying Women," 262.

23 Neel, qtd. in Hills, *Alice Neel*, 30.

24 Neel, qtd. in *Alice Neel*, dir. Andrew Neel, a feature documentary (SeeThink Productions, LLC, 2006). Here Neel is most likely referring to the valorization of the personal, and thus the autobiographical, by feminist artists in the 1970s.

25 Neel, in Hills, *Alice Neel*, 62.

26 The importance of Chaïm Soutine's work to artists such as Willem de Kooning is discussed in Stevens and Swan, *de Kooning: An American Master*, 312–13. Soutine's work was featured in a retrospective at the Museum of Modern Art in 1950. The abstract-expressionist painter Jack Tworkov's review of that exhibition, "The Wandering Soutine," published in *ARTnews* in November 1950, has been a touchstone for the history of Soutine's influence. Tworkov, "The Wandering Soutine," in *The Extreme of the Middle*, 157–61. *Thanksgiving*, Neel's deceptively simple, memorably brutal still-life painting from 1967 of a raw turkey in a sink was included in "The New Landscape / The New Still Life: Soutine and Modern Art" at the Cheim and Read Gallery, New York, June 22 to September 8, 2006. See Tuchman and Dunow, *The New Landscape / The New Still Life*.

27 The connection to Barnett Newman is also made by Jeremy Lewison in his description of another Neel portrait from this period, *Black Spanish Family* from 1950, where the background is a richly painted Indian red: "Behind them the red wall, an interesting echo of Barnett Newman's *Onement I* (1948) and *Onement III* (1949), creates a somber if not mournful backdrop to life in Spanish Harlem." Lewison, "Alice Neel," n.p.

28 Neel, in Hills, *Alice Neel*, 112; my emphasis. The painting is reproduced in Hills, *Alice Neel*, 114.

29 The portrait of Andy Warhol is reproduced in Hills, *Alice Neel*, 138.

30 Allara, *Pictures of People*, 164.

31 Here I am quoting from Barnett Newman's description of Schapiro's views as he expressed them in Emile de Antonio's film documentary on the New York School, *Painters Painting* (Turin Film Corp., 1972).

32 Neel, voice over in *Alice Neel*, dir. Andrew Neel.

33 Elke Solomon, qtd. in Carr, *Alice Neel*, 18 n. 10.

34 Neel, qtd. in Carr, *Alice Neel*, 4.

Like a Veneer

1 Schor, "Patrilineage," in *Wet*, 100.

2 Siegel, "Blonde Ambition," 157; my emphasis.

3 Yuskavage, qtd. in Solomon, "Art Girls Just Wanna Have Fun," 38.

4 Yuskavage, qtd. in Charles Gandee, "I Am Curious (Yellow)," *Talk*, April 2000, 60.

5 Julie Joyce, "Lisa Yuskavage at Christopher Grimes, 6 January–17 February," *Art Issues*, March–April 1996, 37.

6 I was unable to obtain permission from the David Zwirner Gallery to reproduce Lisa Yuskavage's painting *Northview* (2000). However, this painting, along with other Yuskavage works relevant to this essay, appears on the gallery's official website: http://www.davidzwirner.com, accessed July 21, 2009.

7 Nancy Bowen, personal correspondence, May 2001.

8 Baudelaire, "The Painter of Modern Life," 36.

9 Ibid., 30.

10 Solomon, "Art Girls Just Wanna Have Fun," 38; Peter Plagens, "Lady Painters? Smile When You Say That: Surrealism's the Name, Postfeminism Is the Game," *Newsweek*, September 30, 1996, 82–83; Deborah Solomon, "A Roll Call of Fresh Names and Faces," *New York Times*, April 16, 2000, sec. 2, 35.

11 In "A Painter Who Loads the Gun and Lets the Viewer Fire It" (*New York Times*, January 12, 2001, E53), Roberta Smith claims some degree of professional life for Yuskavage's models, although not the one I am suggesting. "With their elaborate country house interiors, these paintings suggest a more real, more sophisticated world. Their occupants seem almost normal, possibly career women, and are in charge of their lives and their pleasures. Some exude a post-orgasmic glow, others just seem grateful to be sitting down after a long day." The reproduction positioned inches from this statement is a large detail of Yuskavage's *Northview*, which represents two women: one is sitting in an Empire-style nightgown from which her very large breasts spill out toward the edge of the canvas, while another young lady in a negligee stands around behind her. A hard day's orgasmic work indeed.

12 Jones, "Uta Barth at Domestic Setting," 41.

13 Barth, qtd. in Smith, *Uta Barth*, 6. In an interview with Sheryl Conkelton, Barth repeats this story slightly differently, underlining the initial unintentionality of her link with Vermeer: "At a certain point of that project [the *Ground* series], I realized that one of the images I had made [*Ground #30*] had the exact same proportions, layout of the room and quality of light as that of a Vermeer painting (*The Milk Maid*, 1658–60) that I had spent much of my life looking at. This was unintentional on my part when I made this photograph, but it seemed that Vermeer was the perfect subtext for this body of work, and as a reference I made an additional image in the series [*Ground #42*] which included, in the background, the two small Vermeer reproductions I had grown up with in my home." Conkelton, "Ground and Field, Before and After," in Conkelton, Ferguson, and Martin, *Uta Barth*, 20.

14 Rob Storr identifies the origin of dark background of *Betty*: "The opaque background of the picture is one of the large gray monochromes Richter painted shortly before the photograph from which *Betty* was derived was taken, sometime in 1977." Storr, *Gerhard Richter: October 18, 1977*, 134.

15 Richter's work has also been discussed elsewhere in relation to Vermeer. As is his usual mode, he articulates the patrilineal reference via the negative: "I don't paint as well as Vermeer—we have lost this beautiful culture, all the utopias are shattered, everything goes down the drain, the wonderful time of painting is over. It is an inclination of mine to see it that way. I don't know anybody else who is so attached to the history of art and loves the old masters as much or wants as much to paint like them. . . . It is a reality that is unreachable. It is a dream. It's over. But I am old-fashioned enough or stupid enough to hang on. I still want to paint something like Vermeer. But it is the wrong time and I cannot do it. I am too dumb. Well, I am not able to." Storr, "Interview with Gerhard Richter," in *Gerhard Richter: Forty Years of Paintings*, 297. Earlier in the interview, Richter discusses light, again taking a negative stance toward something he is said to be working on: "I have a problem with the term *light*. I never in my life knew what to do with that. I know that people have mentioned on some occasions that, 'Richter is all about light,' and that, 'the paintings have a special light'; and I never knew what they were talking about. I was never interested in light. Light is there and you turn it on or you turn it off, with sun or without sun. I don't know what the 'problematic of light' is. I take it as a metaphor for a different quality, which is similarly difficult to describe. Good" (291–92). On Richter, Vermeer, and the political valence of beauty, see Perling Hudson, "Beauty and the Status of Contemporary Criticism," 119–20.

16 Robert Irwin, "Part I: Times 18 Cubed," April through December 1998, and "Part II: Homage to the Square Cubed," January through June 1999, DIA Center for the Arts, New York.

17 Jean Baudrillard, "The Precession of Simulacra," 254. See also Baudrillard, *Simulations*.

18 Jean Baudrillard, "The Precession of Simulacra," 256.

19 Ibid., 257.

20 Schjeldahl, "The Elegant Scavenger," 174.

Modest Painting

A shorter version of this essay appeared in *Art Issues*, January–February 2001.

1 Tanizaki, *In Praise of Shadows*, 3.

2 Even Tanizaki knew that one couldn't go back: as Thomas Harper notes in his afterword to *In Praise of Shadows*: "But for Tanizaki a museum piece is no cause for rejoicing. An art must live as a part of our daily lives or we had better give it up. We can admire it for what it once was, and try to understand what made it so—as Tanizaki does in *In Praise of Shadows*—but to pretend that we can still participate in it is mere posturing. Mrs. Tanizaki tells a story of when her late husband decided, as he frequently did, to build a new house. The architect arrived and announced with pride, 'I've read your *In Praise of Shadows*, Mr. Tanizaki, and

know exactly what you want.' To which Tanizaki replied, 'But no, I could never *live* in a house like that'" (48).

3 Ibid., 9.

4 When Tanizaki writes about painting, it is to place it in (and subsume it under) the architectural context of the alcove set in shadowy rooms without any other ornamentation, in a strange parallel to Mondrian's wish for painting to eventually disappear into architecture: "We have all had the experience, on a visit to one of the great temples of Kyoto or Nara, of being shown a scroll, one of the temple's treasures, hanging in a large, deeply recessed alcove. So dark are these alcoves, even in bright daylight, that we can hardly discern the outlines of the work; all we can do is listen to the explanation of the guide, follow as best we can the all-but-invisible brush strokes, and tell ourselves how magnificent a painting it must be. Yet the combination of that blurred old painting and the dark alcove is one of absolute harmony. The lack of clarity, far from disturbing us, seems rather to suit the painting perfectly. For the painting here is nothing more than another delicate surface upon which the faint, frail light can play; it performs precisely the same function as the sand-textured wall." Tanizaki, *In Praise of Shadows*, 19–20.

5 Bryson, "Rhopography," in *Looking at the Overlooked*, 61.

6 Ibid.

7 Christoph Büchel's aborted exhibition at Mass MOCA in 2007 is perhaps a cautionary but indicative case in point: among other factors, the enormity of the institution's square footage available for installations and the seeming eagerness of the curators to accept the artist's ambitious proposal to fill it with the work "Training Ground for Democracy," which included such large scale real-life spaces and objects as a movie theater, tanker trucks, and houses, came to grief as the artist's plans escalated in cost and in size. His request for the museum to acquire and install the burned out fuselage of a large jetliner proved to be one of the deal breakers for the institution. Its efforts to show an unfinished version of the work was the subject of a lawsuit adjudicated in federal court in Massachusetts.

8 Two responses to the then new Tate Modern, both published in the summer 2000 issue of *Modern Painters*, articulate some of the attraction and the problems of this trend toward gigantism in exhibition spaces. Trevor Winkfield took a primarily critical point of view: "Perhaps I should declare at the outset that I've always preferred cottages of art to temples of art, so my initial dismay when I first set foot on the gargantuan ramp of Bankside's Turbine Hall (which masquerades as an entrance hall) surprised me not at all, though the depression it triggered did not lift until I staggered outside again. Having visited Germany and Italy, I'm quite familiar with totalitarian architecture. I'm presuming that totalitarian architecture has now become one of the many unacceptable faces of capitalism. . . . This feeling of being dwarfed pursues the visitor (or should that be the consumer?) throughout the entire complex." Winkfield notes the effect on artworks of having to function in such huge spaces: "Only by adopting the banal

equation, Size + Importance, can art-works hope to compete with the inhuman scale of the building." Winkfield, "Bankside Blues," 62–63. Tom Lubbock seems to enjoy the theatricality and the spectacle of the place. But he also points to the same effect on artworks noted by Winkfield: "It's a spectacle, all right—and one where the most spectacular work, the biggest, brightest, buzziest, which is basically to say the most recent, makes the going. . . . In this setting, it is very hard for a small painting not to appear as an especially boring kind of video." Lubbock, "Bankside Ride," 59–60. Winkfield's and Lubbock's comments are similar to my response to the Museum of Modern Art's new building in New York: I disliked the large, noisy, poorly organized lobby with little art on view and no sense of aesthetic moment or direction except to direct one right out the back of the space into the next street; the atrium whose principal purpose or effect seems to create an as yet unused opportunity for an artist to commit suicide by throwing himself from the top floor, and which caused Matisse's *Dance I* (1909) to be placed in a staircase during the inaugural installation (so that it can be seen through a window from across the atrium but not comfortably viewed up close); the rooms with extra-large doorways presumably designed to improve traffic flow and to allow the viewer to make visual connections with strategically placed works in other rooms (the initial installation created an optical line-up of a Motherwell and a Frankenthaler!) but that also overload one's peripheral vision, shifting focus from the art to the crowd and interfering with the intimate yet shocking experience one could once have with an individual work. Lost is the experience available to the museum visitor in the 1960s and 1970s in MoMA's old building of going through a normal-size portal from one moderately sized room to another, to round a corner and find oneself looking head-on at Picasso's *Les Demoiselles d'Avignon* (1907) with few other works competing for one's attention. The special exhibition space on the top floor has been a disaster for every show installed there, because the overly high ceilings create an uncomfortable scale for almost any wall arrangement or installation, even of large works, with only the largest works made for (and in the era of) just this kind of spectacular exhibition space, being able to surmount the circumstance. One example is Douglas Gordon's four-channel video installation *Play Dead: Reel Time* (2003), which shows an *elephant* lumbering around and playing dead within a white-cube art gallery of proportions gigantic enough to house such a behemoth, a space just like the one in which the large video screens are installed at MoMA.

9 This is the expression often used by Clement Greenberg. Since *picture* references the representational, the photographic, or even the cinematic, all of which were anathema to his aesthetic, it is an amusing linguistic quirk that he preferred *picture* to *painting*. Perhaps it reflects a kind of tough-guy pose of not speaking too reverentially about the medium he sought to police the most tightly.

10 "The Art Colony's First Century, Part Two, 1933–1966," curated by Bob Bailey and Brenda Horowitz, July 7–24, 2000; and "Hofmann Students from the Collection,"

curated by Robert Henry, Brenda Horowitz, and Tony Vevers, July 28–August 14, 2000 (in conjunction with "Hans Hofmann Paintings," curated by Lillian Orlowsky, July 28–October 1, 2000), all held at the Provincetown Art Association and Museum, Provincetown, Mass. That these two exhibitions appeared in Provincetown was fortuitous, but not a coincidence, since Provincetown was a significant site in the history of mid-twentieth-century American art and, as it happens, one of the primary sites of my artistic inculturation.

11 Jim Forsberg (1919–1991) was a painter who, for many years, also owned the Studio Shop, a small but excellent art supply store in Provincetown, Mass.

12 This painting puts me in mind of *Dunes, Provincetown* (1957), a painting by Rudy Burckhardt, which hangs in my bedroom in Provincetown. I enjoy the little painting's quiet distillation of the atmosphere of Cape Cod. On a small wooden panel, framed by thin wooden strips that have darkened with time, it depicts, through a series of horizontal zones of color, a grey-blue wavy ocean against a grey sky, foregrounded by dunes with banks of dune grass and blossoming rose hips bushes. The surface has been produced mainly through small palette knife marks. But, whereas the palette knife is often an assertive tool, used for creating more concrete physicality than the brush, here it is used like the finest sable brush. The painting is simple, verging on the naive, yet marked by the hand of someone who knows the language of painting but is completely open to the grey haze of the place in which he stands.

13 I use the term "unofficial art" because by the mid-1950s, abstract expressionism was not only the dominant art movement in New York City and the United States, it was also promoted by the U.S. government as emblematic of American freedom of expression during the Cold War, making it a kind of de facto official American art. See Guilbault, *How New York Stole the Idea of Modern Art*.

14 Downes, "What the Sixties Meant to Me (1973)," 17.

15 This anecdote was at the service of a "modest" painting, yet it betrays some of the homicidal competition for attention at work in many artists' identity and career formations, evidenced earlier in Alex Katz's fury at having been eclipsed by another artist in a group show.

16 Jack Tworkov, journal entry, December 30, 1954, reprinted in "By Jack Tworkov," in Armstrong, *Jack Tworkov*, 130. See also Tworkov, "Journals and Diaries 1949–1963," in *The Extreme of the Middle*, sec. 3.65, 75.

17 Schwartz, *Myron Stout: The Unfinished Paintings*, n.p.

18 This painting is reproduced in the exhibition catalogue *Jack Tworkov: Paintings and Drawings* (New York: Mitchell-Innes and Nash, 1999), n.p., reproduction no. 41.

19 I am grateful to Amelia Jones for pointing this out to me in her careful reading of a draft of "Modest Painting" in the spring of 2001. She wrote: "Modesty in painting is linked to modesty as a personal trait—really? This [raises] the old dilemma of how to theorize the *person* in relation to the *work*; was Pollock an egomaniac?

Seems like Greenberg was more of one . . . , etc." (email to the author, April 13, 2001). I appreciated her critique but nevertheless answered, "I do think people's work is somehow of a piece with at least some of who they are as a person, even though you are right that there are so many examples of artists with ghastly personal traits and wonderful works, but among my friends as among so many artists of the past there is a sense of a consistent utterance, for better or worse. It is a complex issue for sure. . . . Maybe Greenberg and Pollock were just two sides of the same incubus" (Schor, email to Jones, April 13, 2001).

20 One such minute yet influential exhibition space is the Wrong Gallery, run by Maurizio Cattelan, Ali Subotnick, and Massimiliano Gioni, originally located in an interstitial urban space at 516½ West Twentieth Street in Chelsea in New York City. It is now housed at the Tate Modern until December 21, 2009, an amusing instance of the huge incorporating the tiny. Other influential examples include galleries emerging from conceptual artists' curatorial experiments, such as Reena Spaulings Fine Art or Orchard Gallery in New York City.

21 See Alex Kwartler's show at John Connelly Presents, New York, November 19–December 17, 2005.

22 Avgikos, "Luc Tuymans, David Zwirner Gallery," 84–85.

23 Quotation from a press release for "Painters without Paintings and Paintings without Painters," curated by Gareth James, Orchard Gallery, New York, December 10, 2005, to January 15, 2006.

24 Having heard Dan Colen give an artist's talk at the Rhode Island School of Design in May 2008, I think he would embrace the term *idiot* as a compliment.

25 Calvin Tomkins, "The Pour," *New Yorker*, March 13, 2006, 32, 34.

26 Jack Tworkov, undated note, qtd. in Mira Schor's introduction to *The Extreme of the Middle*, xxi.

27 Tanizaki, *In Praise of Shadows*, 22, 23, 30.

Blurring Richter

1 Richter, "Conversation with Jan Thorn Prikker concerning the cycle '18 October 1977,' 1989," in *The Daily Practice of Painting*, 189. Richter's use of the photograph as a mediating device has been central to Benjamin Buchloh's interpretation of the significance of Richter's work as a commentary on the end of painting. As noted in my introduction, this essay was set into motion in part by a line in Buchloh's essay "Divided Memory and Post-Traditional Identity: Gerhard Richter's Work of Mourning" from 1996, which caught my attention like a garment of fine mohair is caught on a thorn: "A full-size portrait of the artist's uncle in the uniform of the German *Wehrmacht*, the painting retains the naive central composition typical of a family photograph (which was its source), thereby generating *a first conflict within the reading of the painting*" (62–64; my emphasis). My first conflict "within the reading of the painting" is that it represents a Nazi.

2   Richter, "Interview with Peter Sager," in *The Daily Practice of Painting*, 70.

3   Richter, "From a Letter to Edy de Wilde, 23 February 1975," in *The Daily Practice of Painting*, 82–83. Richter returns to the use of grey in his *October 18, 1977* paintings because "it's partly a way of establishing distance." Richter, qtd. in Storr, *Gerhard Richter: October 18, 1977*, 112. In "18. Oktober 1977: Gerhard Richter's Work of Mourning and Its New Audience," Rainer Usselmann notes that, "the contrast between evasive Grisaille, and suggested historical facticity creates a sense of unease, which invites speculation on a dark episode but fails to spells it out" (6). Usselmann suggests that Richter's "use of photographic signifiers" in combination with painterly "facticity," creates "an extraordinary aura [that] shields these paintings from a penetrating, critical gaze" (6). Quoting Walter Benjamin's emphasis, in "The Work of Art in the Age of Mechanical Reproduction," on "the phenomenon of distance as a pre-requisite for aura," Usselmann summons up an amusingly heretical view of the auratic nature of Richter's work, vis à vis Buchloh's complex balance between his support of Richter's work and his general critique of painting. Usselmann received the College Art Association's *Art Journal* Award for this essay in 2002. For further discussion of the use of grey, see "Work Document: *Grey*" in this volume.

4   Richter, "Notes, 1964–1965," in *The Daily Practice of Painting*, 37.

5   "Speaking to an interviewer in 1990, Richter explained his earlier evasions and mixed messages this way: 'My own statements about my lack of style and lack of opinion were largely polemical gestures against contemporary trends that I disliked—or else they were self-protective statements designed to create a climate in which I could paint what I wanted,' later adding, 'If I ever did admit to irony, I did so for the sake of a quiet life.'" Storr, *Gerhard Richter: October 18, 1977*, 132–33. And, in a 2001 interview with Robert Storr for the exhibition catalogue *Gerhard Richter: Forty Years of Paintings*, in discussing misreadings of his work as "cynical," Richter says, "The second reason [for people to have such reactions] could be that I made a few remarks that have circulated, things like: 'I don't believe in anything'; and 'the motifs in my paintings have no meaning whatsoever, I might have just as well painted cabbage.' These remarks gave people a certain impression of me. That's how they saw me. People still claim that only painting has an important story, never the subject." Storr then asks, "Why did you say those things? What was the context?" Richter continues, "I made those statements in order to provoke and in order not to have to say what I might have been thinking at that point, not to pour my heart out. That would have been embarrassing, I didn't know why I painted *Uncle Rudi* or *Aunt Marianne*. I refused to admit any kind of meaning that these paintings would have had for me. Therefore, it was easier to say what I said" (288).

6   Buchloh, "Divided Memory and Post-Traditional Identity," 68, 78–81; Buchloh, "Gerhard Richter's *Atlas*," 141.

7   I had two Uncle Moishes. Moses Ajnsztajn (my grandfather's family adopted

a Polonized spelling of Einstein) was my mother's youngest brother. Beyond a few photographs, the only other trace of his existence was the intensity of my mother's love for the baby brother whose birth she had attended. I have always felt that much of what I know about devotion, and much of the love I was given, was result of my mother's surplus of love for Moishe, who was in some sense her "first" child. It is the burning quality of that love that has always made it difficult for me to accept the validity of Richter's key strategy for remembering and mourning the past through contemporary art: lack of affect articulated through the use of photography, with the use of grey and the use of blurring as concomitant visual strategies. Moses Schorr was my father's oldest full-brother (an older half-brother, Abraham, had immigrated to America before my father was born). The very fact that my parents had photographs from before the war is part of my family's foundational "fairy tale," which I was told throughout my childhood— the true story of how my parents survived the war. It seemed like a fairy tale, primarily because of my parents' own sense of the miraculous about their escape and also because of the surrealism of the tale when heard in the safety of our apartment on the Upper West Side of Manhattan (a security always tempered by the substance of their story). My parents left Paris in late May 1940, just before the Germans entered the city. They had been sitting in a café with friends, wondering what to do. When my mother saw French peasants (gentiles) from the Eastern provinces pushing wheelbarrows with their belongings and their sick and elderly relatives through the city, she understood that she and her friends, all young Polish Jews, had to leave at once, which they did with just a change of underwear, a gas mask, and a few lumps of sugar in a small rucksack. Of the ten or so friends who left with them that day, only my parents survived the war. After a series of the kind of adventures one now associates with Humphrey Bogart movies or recitations of the last days of Walter Benjamin, they made it first to Marseilles, where they stayed for a year, and then to America, in December 1941, arriving in New York City a few days before Pearl Harbor. One of their closest friends from art school in Warsaw, Fiszel (Fishel) Zylberberg, known as Zber, had left Paris with them, but he returned to Paris because he had recently fallen in love with a woman whose husband had been killed. She appealed to him to stay with her and so, in my mother's wording, "he perished," but not before he was able to send some of my parents' belongings to them in Marseilles, including the family pictures.

8 Art Spiegelman, *Maus II*, 113.

9 Ibid., 114–16.

10 Ibid., 134.

11 For information about the anti-Nazi activities of Serge Klarsfeld and his wife, Beate Klarsfeld, including their long campaign to bring Klaus Barbie to justice in France, see the Beate Klarsfeld Foundation website, http://www.klarsfeld foundation.org.

12 Klarsfeld, quoted in Ralph Blumenthal, "The Holocaust Children Who Did Not Grow Up," *New York Times*, December 5, 1996, C15, C18.

13 Klarsfeld, *French Children of the Holocaust*, xv.

14 Ibid., 624.

15 Ibid., 450.

16 Ibid., 436.

17 See Schaffner and Winzen, eds., *Deep Storage*.

18 Numerous texts on Holocaust-related art have focused not only on Adorno's statement that "to write poetry after Auschwitz is barbaric" (see Adorno, *Prisms*) but also on his own later commentary on this much debated declaration. Marianne Hirsch explores Adorno's various statements in *Family Frames* (274 n. 10). Gertrude Koch pursues the implications of Adorno's statements on poetry after Auschwitz in "The Aesthetic Transformation of the Image of the Unimaginable," in which she proposes that Claude Lanzmann's *Shoah* is not only a documentary but also a work of art that achieves "a radical aesthetic transformation of this problematic" (20). According to Koch, Lanzmann attains this through witness narratives, unorthodox interview practices including strategic locations that act as spurs or expressive counterpoints to the content of the elicited narrative, and through his refusal to use archival footage of the camps: "in the elision, it offers an image of the unimaginable" (21). Klarsfeld can be said to use a similar strategy in juxtaposing pre-Shoah photographs of the children with a synopsis of the archival documentary information available on each child's fate in the Shoah. The reader creates the image of the unimaginable, or the juxtaposition creates the full horror of the unimaginable in the gap between image and text. Further thoughts on the use of the blur in depiction of horror and tragedy, as well as on the role of text in such narratives, emerged in panel discussions at "Picturing Atrocities: Photography in Crisis," a conference held at the Graduate Center, City University of New York, December 9, 2005. On the panel "Photography in the World: A Conversation," moderated by Nancy K. Miller, Ellen Tolmie of UNICEF discussed how children are photographed in order to generate (manipulate) sympathy and thus financial and political support for children in perilous or exploitative situations around the world without exploiting the children further. Representing the child's face is seen to enact such further exploitation, so the photographers seek situations and create compositions where the child's face is obscured or blurred: for example, in a series of photographs of child soldiers in Africa, a photo will include a child holding a gun — the gun is in focus, the child soldier's face is blurred. In these humanitarian projects the blur is a protective device. Fred Ritchin, formerly a photo editor at the *New York Times Magazine*, spoke of the importance of giving the subject of photographs a voice, and he emphasized the necessity of text, placing the importance on the explicit or enriched narrative of the written story or explanatory caption, rather than on the implicit narrative of the visual image.

19 Young, *At Memory's Edge*, 140.

20 Klarsfeld, *French Children of the Holocaust*, 508.

21 Ibid., 443.

22 Young, *At Memory's Edge*, 1.

23 Ibid. Chronologically I belong to the generation Young describes as "post-Holocaust," which can only experience "the Holocaust as a vicarious past." I did not experience the Holocaust directly. Further, in the hierarchy of Holocaust survivors, my parents were not survivors of concentration camps, so one might say that for them too the Holocaust was a vicarious experience, if not a past one. Their direct experience was of forced and dangerous flight, wartime deprivation and fear, loss of their entire families and most of their childhood and school friends, and finally, life in a country they would not have chosen to live in under normal circumstances. So my own relationship to the Holocaust bears some of the degrees of separation that Young suggests can only be dealt with in art via distancing devices referencing the simulacrum. When I was in my twenties, a non-Jewish friend, who had been raised in an affluent (and primarily Jewish) Long Island suburb whose mores were later to become the subject of his painting, casually dismissed my mention of the role of the Holocaust in the formation of my life and my character as inauthentic. He didn't "buy it." And, perhaps precisely because of my family's destabilized identity and insecure status in American society, I was actually willing to consider his point of view—that is, as I recall, I didn't argue the point. Only years later, in the years of commodified recovered memory, post-traumatic stress syndrome, and other confessional returns to pasts real and imagined on national television, did another response occur to me: "If I told you that my entire extended family had been the victims of a mass murder—an *American*-style mass-murder, a serial killer, like *In Cold Blood*, or a shoot-out in a McDonald's—you would believe that such a trauma would have profoundly permeated my affective being and world view, instead of dismissing my claim to this background as inauthentic." It would be saleable; he would "buy it."

    Even in my family the impact of the Holocaust and yet its distance from our actual lived lives was the subject of a recurring joke: if I acted in a certain manner, for example expressing anxiety about not getting enough food at the family dinner table because, in a somewhat counterintuitive practice, as the youngest I was served last, my sister would say, "*you* weren't at Auschwitz." But I should more accurately say "joke," because in a family where that can be said with some direct relationship to the truth, traumatic discontinuity is a real factor. My experience of the loss of family and the fear of death for unreasonable cause ensured that my experience of the Holocaust was not entirely vicarious and most certainly constitutive. During my childhood it was loosely assumed that my Uncle Moishe on my mother's side had perished at Auschwitz. However, my mother thought or perhaps had heard that Moishe had found refuge working with his teacher, the famed Polish doctor, educator, and author Janusz Korczak (1879–1942). In the Warsaw ghetto in the summer of 1942, Korczak, although offered his own life, chose to accompany the orphans in his charge to their deaths at Treblinka: they were marched out of Warsaw on August 6, 1942. In this case, Moishe may have perished at Treblinka. The degree of separation from the Holocaust that my cohort of first-generation Americans experience is smaller than that experienced by American Jews of my age with no ties to Europe and much smaller than that of younger Americans with no living ties to World War II. Thus I find that Young's thesis does not take the full measure of the intermediary generation of which I am a member. Significantly Norman Kleeblatt looked to the "second or third generation after the Holocaust" for his choice of artists to be included in "Mirroring Evil: Nazi Imagery / Recent Art" at the Jewish Museum in 2002. In an interview with Sarah Boxer, Kleeblatt, himself the child of German refugees and the grandson of Holocaust victims, said that "this new generation 'learned the lessons of the Holocaust,' . . . not in school and not from their parents but from cartoons and films." Sarah Boxer, "Man behind a Museum Tempest: A Curator Defends His Show Exploring Nazi Imagery," *New York Times*, February 6, 2002, E1.

24 Young, *At Memory's Edge*, 44–46, 4.

25 See Kleeblatt, *Mirroring Evil*. On cue, in the months leading up to the March 2002 opening of "Mirroring Evil," organizations of Holocaust survivors protested the exhibition based on early reports of some of the works, including Alan Schechner's *It's the Real Thing—Self Portrait at Buchenwald* (1993), in which the artist has digitally inserted an image of himself in a concentration-camp striped uniform holding a can of Diet Coke into a photograph of emaciated prisoners at Buchenwald. See my discussion of this work in "Recipe Art," this volume. The museum promised to set up warnings, disclaimers, and alternate exits from the exhibition space so that viewers could avoid possibly offensive works if they wished (Barbara Stewart, "Jewish Museum to Add Warning Label on Its Show," *New York Times*, March 2, 2002, B1). Elderly Holocaust survivors picketed the museum when the show opened: " 'It's painfully trivializing,' said Isaac Leo Kram, 81, who was held at three concentration camps, including Buchenwald. He stood outside the museum yesterday wearing a placard saying: 'I was there. I testify: Genocide is not art!' " (Sarah Kershaw, "Exhibition with Nazi Imagery Begins Run at Jewish Museum," *New York Times*, March 18, 2002, B2). These demonstrators had not seen the works they were protesting. Further, subtly discrediting their demonstrations, the uproar was compared in the news to similar protests, engineered primarily by Mayor Rudolph Giuliani, of the "Sensation" exhibition at the Brooklyn Museum in 1999.

26 Levinthal, qtd. in Young, *At Memory's Edge*, 51.

27 Young, *At Memory's Edge*, 53–54.

28 Quotation from Richter, *The Daily Practice of Painting*, 37.

29 Ibid., 35, 37.

30 See Storr, *Gerhard Richter: October 18, 1977*, 100.

31 The blur has been used to connote the appearance of the spectral or the super-natural almost since the beginning of photography; indeed, the ability to ma-nipulate effects in the photo-development process and via double exposure gave new energy to the age-old human desire to believe in the presence of spirits of the dead. There has been in recent years a resurgence in interest in this late-nineteenth-century usage of photography to enable exploration of the spiritual, and, by extension, in the blur's usefulness to connotations of the spectral or the supernatural. See "The Perfect Medium: Photography and the Occult," an exhi-bition at the Metropolitan Museum of Art, New York, September 27, 2005, to December 31, 2005; Chéroux et al., *The Perfect Medium*; and Ferris, *The Disembod-ied Spirit*. In his catalogue essay, "Haunted History: Uncanny Modernity," Tom Gunning writes, "Recognition of spirits as identifiable persons now deceased usually depended on either a very blurry photograph and a willing imagination, or the fact that, to contact the spirit of a specific deceased, the medium often requested an existing photograph." Ferris, *The Disembodied Spirit*, 11.

32 Sheryl Conkelton and Uta Barth, "Ground and Field, Before and After," in Conkle-ton, Ferguson, and Martin, *Uta Barth: In Between Places*, 12.

33 Elizabeth A. T. Smith, "At the Edge of the Decipherable: Recent Photographs by Uta Barth," in *Uta Barth: At the Edge of the Decipherable*, 4.

34 Quotation from Wolf, "First Exposure," n.p.

35 Ibid.

36 Bill Jacobson, artist's statement addressed "To the Museum of Modern Art," 4 February 1994, Museum of Modern Art Library Photo Bio File for Bill Jacob-son.

37 Simon Watney, "Reviews," 101. For reproductions of Jacobson's work, see Eugenia Parry, *Bill Jacobson: Photographs* (Ostfildern-Ruit, Germany: Hatje Cantz, 2005); and Bill Jacobson, *Bill Jacobson, 1989–1997* (San Francisco: Twin Palms, 1998).

38 Cousseau, "L'usage du flou," n.p.

39 According to Young, "Levinthal accomplished this ambiguity by shooting these tableaux at Polaroid's New York City studio with a 20×24 Land camera, its aper-ture set wide open, to create an extremely shallow focal plane—hence the blurry fore- and backgrounds." Young, *At Memory's Edge*, 51.

40 Ibid., 51–52.

41 Barthes, *Camera Lucida*, 47. Barthes defines the *studium* as the general informa-tional field that countless photographs offer and the *punctum* as the element that breaks that field.

42 Ibid., 43.

43 The phrase "the banality of evil" entered the contemporary idiom through Hannah Arendt's perception of the character of Adolf Eichmann as described

in her report of his 1961 trial, *Eichmann in Jerusalem: A Report on the Banality of Evil*. At the time her work provided a startling analysis of the character of a man involved in state-organized mass murder, but her phrase "banality of evil" has become a sound bite. (The book itself is quite shocking in some of its legal conclusions, namely that, along the legal grounds chosen by the prosecution and to some extent followed by the court, Eichmann—although he, as they say in Texas, "needed killing"—was not guilty of the actual crimes for which evidence was brought against him. He was, however, guilty of the new, unprecedented category developed by the Nuremberg trials, of "crimes against humanity.") What is pertinent to a critique of indifference and lack of affect is the tone of Arendt's book: for though it is often bitingly ironic, mordantly comic—in a darkly sharp manner of a Billy Wilder script—it is not empty or morally ambivalent; it is full and complex in its moral arguments. Richter discusses Arendt's famous phase in his interview with Robert Storr in 2001. Storr suggests that Richter's "range of subjects goes from things that are totally banal, like *Toilet Paper*, to images that are not so banal, like *Mr. Heyde*." (*Mr. Heyde* being an early Richter painting of a Nazi war criminal.) Richter first defends the painting of toilet paper from the term *banal*: "In relation to the history of art, where nobody had ever painted toilet paper, it was time to paint toilet paper, which is not really banal. . . . It's important; it cannot be banal. Then there's the 'banality of evil.' It's a beautiful term—what Hannah Arendt said about [Adolf] Eichmann. And the same for Mr. Heyde. This is important." Further, "*Banality* means a little bit more than *unimportant*. . . . I mentioned 'the banality of evil' in order to show that banality has at some point been described as something horrific. It can be a concern to describe the banal as something terrifying." Richter, quoted in Storr, "Interview with Gerhard Richter," *Gerhard Richter: Forty Years of Paintings*, 293–94.

294 | 295

44 Levi, "Chemical Examination," in *Survival at Auschwitz*, 105–6. I have experienced for myself the impact of such a look mediated through the intervention of a photo-based medium, television. In April 1961, my parents borrowed a television set so that they could watch the Eichmann trial. The television was placed in our living room but in an odd location, away from the couch and easy chair, blocking an archway passage to the kitchen and the front door. My father sat in a hard chair in front of the TV as if it was there only for him. This configuration seemed to enact the drama of an individual confrontation with the unthinkable: the death of every beloved member of his family and of the civilization he had been born into was now brought to the vivid reality of his mind's eye by trial testimony. And as we know, throughout, Eichmann had a rather prissy expression on his face, like there was a bad smell in the room. In the face of not only a confrontation with the horrors of their own past but also with this affectless figure, men who came to court to testify against him fainted away and had to be carried out. My father died in June 1961: the physiological cause of death was complica-

tions from a succession of small heart attacks he suffered in the weeks after the trial began. Many years later I discovered that my sister and I independently of each other had come away with the belief that he had "died of Eichmann."

45 Buchloh, "Gerhard Richter's *Atlas*," 142.

46 Quotation from ibid.

47 Heschel, "A World of Palimpsests," in *The Earth Is the Lord's*, 56.

48 Buchloh has noted, with regards to *Uncle Rudi*, that "frontality and centrality in painting traditionally indicate the prominence of the sitter, transcoding in spatial terms the figure's legitimacy as an object of historical representation. In Richter's portrait of his Nazi uncle, however, these conventions clash with a heretofore unrepresentable *subject* of history" (Buchloh, "Divided Memory and Post-Traditional Identity," 64). Richter has been placed within a dual legacy that determined his distrust of ideology: the politics and the aesthetics of both the Nazi era and the Soviet era. As Buchloh and Storr emphasize, at least Richter did try to represent the "unrepresentable subject" at a time when German culture generally preferred a collective amnesiac silence although, as Paul Jaskot has suggested, in "Gerhard Richter and Adolf Eichmann," in the period in which *Uncle Rudi* was painted, just following the Eichmann trial in Israel in 1961 and synchronous with the Frankfurt trial of Auschwitz guards, "the evasion of the Nazi past was neither as complete nor as monodimensional as is usually assumed" (Jaskot, "Gerhard Richter and Adolf Eichmann," 459; Jaskot's essay was originally delivered as a paper at the same CAA panel on Richter where I delivered the talk "Blurring Richter," which forms the foundation of this essay: Gerhard Richter panel, moderated by Robert Storr, CAA annual conference, New York, February 22, 2003). Buchloh, Storr, and Richter himself confront the particular problematics adhering to the notion of the father for post-War Germans. Richter says of his own father's return home at the end of the war, "He shared most fathers' fate at the time. . . . Nobody wanted them" (Richter, interview with Robert Storr, April 21–23, 2001, trans. Catharina Manchanda, in Storr, *Gerhard Richter: Forty Years of Painting*, 19). Buchloh notes that Richter is involved in a critique of paternal influence and inheritance, emerging from his dual heritage: the necessity of escape and recovery from the paternalism of the Führer and of Stalin (Buchloh, "Divided Memory and Post-Traditional Identity," 75). But he quickly places Richter into a safer patrilineage, one that includes Marcel Duchamp and Jasper Johns, and perhaps Richter himself sought these ironic, yet neutral in terms of German heritage, masters. Oedipal wrangling in the aesthetic arena is safe, for the artist and the author, compared to the more personal problematics of having an *Uncle Rudi*. Buchloh notes that Richter and Palermo "also seem to recognize the loss of the commemorative function as an element of a larger process of destruction — the destruction of subjectivity" (68). He praises Richter precisely for attempting such an *amnesis*, a remembering and a mourning of the past. In the light of my own patrilineal narrative, I cannot but wonder, what is

Richter mourning? Or, What is *Richter* mourning? Is it the loss of the German Father/land? Loss of identification with a national character, a German nature? I have to confess this is a dilemma I have never found it in myself to be completely sympathetic with. And how does he accomplish this amnesis of destruction of subjectivity? Through visual strategies that (re)enact "lack of affect."

Off the Grid

This essay first appeared in *Provincetown Arts*, summer 2002.

Trite Tropes, Clichés, or the Persistence of Styles

1 Müller, "Portrait of the Museum as a Chair," 72.
2 In 2006 a jury review yielded a surfeit of birds, often appropriated from the same general library of nineteenth-century illustrations and Audubon guides. After I called my fellow jurors' attention to their frequency, my colleagues started poking me in the ribs every time birds appeared. We speculated on why they were there: was it to telegraph the artist's interest in Nature or in Freedom? My guesses were based in personal experience. Very recently a friend sent me a picture of me taken in 1973 in my studio at the California Institute of the Arts when I was a graduate student: on the wall behind me are numerous gouache and pencil works on paper representing the very same birds from the very same sources, with poetic or political words scrawled next to them (therefore replicating some of the persistent styles I discuss in this essay). I doubt if I had much of a reason then for using these images. I was influenced by other artists who used them, from various surrealist artists I admired to Pat Steir, who used such images in her work around 1970, at a time when I often visited her studio.
3 Actually my notes from that day clearly say "tripe and trippy," which would indicate that the work included ornamental loops suggestive of an intestinal origin; however, I have changed it here to "trite and trippy" for purposes of immediate clarity.
4 I discuss the mechanism of these more recent tropes in "Recipe Art" in this volume. See also Roland Barthes's distinctions between language, style, and writing: "A language is therefore a horizon, and style a vertical dimension, which together map out for the writer a nature, since he does not choose either. . . . Now every Form is also a Value, which is why there is room, between a language and a style, for another formal reality, writing"(*Writing Degree Zero*, 34). "A language and a style are blind forces; a mode of writing is an act of historical solidarity. A language and a style are objects; a mode of writing is a function: it is the relationship between creation and society, the literary language transformed by its social finality, form considered as a human intention, and thus linked to the great crises of History" (35). For a comprehensive examination of the meaning and usages

of the word *style*, see Meyer Schapiro, "Style" (1962), included in his *Theory and Philosophy of Art*, 51–101. See also Jas Elsner, "Style."

5 See http://afonline.artistsspace.org.

6 Under "Media," you have a choice of "architecture, books, collage, computer, drawings, film-video, mixed media, mural painting, performance, prints, sculpture, wall-relief, installation, digital, works on paper." Under "Materials": "canvas, charcoal, clay, fiber, found/used, glass, light, metal, oil paint, paper, pastel, pen and ink, graphite, photographs, plaster, plastics, sound, stone, watercolor, wax, Xerox, natural elements, latex, computer, text, projection, vcr/monitor, mass produced, clothing/fabric, electricity, motors, chemicals, casting."

7 Email to author from Artists File Coordinator, Artists Space, July 10, 2007.

8 Barthes, *Writing Degree Zero*, 36–37.

9 Noel Robbins, *New American Paintings*, 173. At the same time, this artist engages in another very common career strategy that I have previously identified as the mechanism of "patrilineage," placing his name in the general vicinity of artists such as Jackson Pollock and Hans Hofmann.

10 Close, quoted in Newman, "Part I: Late 1950s–Early 1960s, The Experimental Education of Artists," *Challenging Art*, 37.

11 Buchloh, "Figures of Authority, Ciphers of Regression," 53.

12 I was a visiting faculty member in the department of art at the University of California, Berkeley, in 1987. The faculty and students exhibited strong loyalty to noted Bay Area artists of the 1950s and 1960s. Compared to the way my New York students (mainly the men) approached influence, with an Oedipally homicidal competitiveness, here even the youngest students admired and emulated in their work the style of local masters, including David Park, Emerson Woelffer, and Richard Diebenkorn. I told one student that I thought Diebenkorn was one of the most overrated artists; he reacted as if I had stabbed him. I ran into the chair of the art department later that day and said, "I just earned my salary for the semester."

13 Barnett Newman, "Art of the South Seas," in *Barnett Newman*, 101–2.

14 I should note for the record that as a young painter struggling to insert personal content into painting in the context of late Greenbergian formalist structures that opposed my doing so, I was drawn to early Renaissance art, Flemish painting, Indian Miniatures, and surrealist painting, for many of the same reasons they remain popular today. I understood them to be oppositional to the formalist norm of the day, and as such they were imbued for me with a gendered political content, as they had been for predecessors that I only learned about just a bit after my aesthetic development had begun, notably Florine Stettheimer and Frida Kahlo.

15 Marshall, *New Image Painting*.

16 These works are presented by Thomas Lawson in his essay "Last Exit" from 1981.

17 Newman, "The Ideographic Picture" (catalogue essay for the exhibition of the same name, Betty Parsons Gallery, New York, January 20 to February 8, 1947), in *Barnett Newman*, 102. See also Harrison and Wood, eds., *Art in Theory*, 573–74; and Adolph Gottlieb, "My Painting," originally published in *Art and Architecture*, September 1951, and reproduced in David and Cecile Shapiro, eds., *Abstract Expressionism*, 261–63. Gottlieb writes, "My work has been called abstract, surrealist, totemistic and primitive. To me these labels are not very accurate. Therefore, I chose my own label and called my paintings pictographs." Further, he provides a metaphor for the compartmentalized, grid-based composition of the pictograph-filled paintings, which remains an accurate description of many paintings done in the genre: "I am like a man with a large family and must have many rooms. The children of my imagination occupy the various compartments of my painting, each independent and occupying its own space. At the same time they have the proper atmosphere in which to function together, in harmony and as a unified group. One can say that my paintings are like of [*sic*] house, in which each occupant has a room of his own" (262–63).

Recipe Art

1 Ken Johnson, "A. B. Normal," Art in Review, *New York Times*, July 29, 2005, B31; my emphasis.

2 Michael Kimmelman, "A Global Village Whose Bricks Are Art," *New York Times*, June 16, 2005, E1; my emphasis.

3 Jeffrey Kastner, "On Form in Emptiness: A Zen Way," *New York Times*, December 17, 2000, Arts and Leisure, 43; my emphasis.

4 Randy Kennedy, "Master of the Dark Ages: The Artist behind the Whitney's Foray into Arson, Suicide, and Black Metal," *New York Times*, May 15, 2005, sec. 2: 1, 30; my emphasis.

5 Tom Sachs, qtd. in "Questions for Tom Sachs: Designer Death Camp," The Way We Live Now, *New York Times Magazine*, March 10, 2002, sec. 6: 19.

6 This note describes Michael St. John's "Let Us Go Then, You and I," as seen at Caren Golden Fine Art, September 9–October 21, 1995.

7 Lawrence Weiner, "Untitled Statement" (1970), in Stiles and Selz, eds., *Theories and Documents of Contemporary Art*, 839.

8 Advertisement for the exhibition "Dave Cole: The Knitting Machine," at Mass MoCA from June to December 2005, *New York Times*, June 30, 2005, B6; my emphasis.

9 Kozloff, "The Kudzu Effect," 41.

10 See, for example, Holland Cotter, "Fanciful to Figurative to Wryly Inscrutable," *New York Times*, July 8, 2005, Boston edition, B31. In an article about thematic summer group shows, Cotter includes a review of "Idols of Perversity" at Bellwether Gallery: "Surrealism is the prevailing mode; academic painting, the pre-

ferred style; the contemporary art star John Currin, the patron saint." See also Maura Egan, "The Remix; School of Ghoul: Today's Art Stars Find Their Muse in the Devil Inside," *New York Times*, September 18, 2005, Men's Fashion Magazine, 6: 76: "While his technique is steeped in the Renaissance, Roger Andersson's subject matter is culled from the slacker-stoner genre." See also Jerry Saltz, "The Pursuit of Happiness: Damien Hirst Goes for Baroque," *Village Voice*, October 17, 2000, 69: "Hirst has broken his realism into surrealism." Saltz's ability to describe Hirst's work as "Goth Minimalism: Donald Judd filled with creepy stuff," is a perfect example of the tandem dance between the recipe artist and the critic, and of the kind of formulaic predictability of the stylistic mutants that characterize the low of trite tropes and clichés, and the market high of recipe art. It also accurately predicts and describes one of the breakout hit works of the 2004 Whitney Biennial, David Altmejd's *Delicate Men in Positions of Power* (2003).

11 Cotter, "Multitude," Art in Review, *New York Times*, October 11, 2002, E38.

12 Ellegood and Burton, *The Uncertainty of Objects and Ideas*. Work of this style and by some of the same artists was featured in "Unmonumental," the first series of shows at the New Museum's new building, December 1, 2007–April 9, 2008.

13 Margo Jefferson, "Critic's Notebook: The Avant-Garde, Rarely Love at First Sight," *New York Times*, July 8, 2005, E1. Jefferson instructs the prospective audience of an avant-garde artwork, specifically a theatrical work, on what to expect, including: "Don't look for a straightforward storyline. Or at least, don't expect the story to be told in a straightforward way. It may emerge in pieces." Jefferson instructs her readers further, "Remember, the avant-garde is not a designated tribe of rebel outsiders anymore. It is a set of tools and practices; certain styles and attitudes." She continues, "Is a urinal art? Is elephant dung a fit substance for creating art? . . . Are fractured words and stories truer to the shape of our experience than traditional narratives? . . . At one time all these things were controversial. Now they are familiar." But Jefferson's own instructions belie this positive assertion: clearly these things are *not* familiar, or she wouldn't need to explain them to the presumably educated readers of the *Times*.

14 "The Brand Called You: Self-Promotion for Artists and Designers," sponsored by Parsons Alumni Relations and Career Services, November 1, 2004, New School University, Parsons School of Design. This symposium was possibly suggested by or in reference to Peter Montoya's *The Brand Called You: The Ultimate Step-by-Step Guide to Branding and Business Development* (Santa Ana, Calif.: Personal Branding Press, 2002). "Internet Famous" is a course run by Jamie Wilkerson through Parsons. See the course website, http://internetfamo.us/class; and S. James Snyder, "Googling for Your Grade," *Time*, December 20, 2007, http://www.time.com.

15 See the PainterNYC blog, http://painternyc.blogspot.com.

16 Chuck Close, qtd. in Newman, *Challenging Art*, 37.

17 Tomkins, "Dept. of Precocity," 31.

18 Mia Fineman, "Portrait of the Artist as a Paint-Splattered Googler," *New York

Times, January 15, 2006, Sec. 2, 16. Paumgarten's *New Yorker* article begins with Koenig and his best friend drinking themselves into a stupor before his first gallery's premiere opening only to come to and "[discover] that the gallery was full—some seven hundred guests," and it ends with him finishing off the evening of his current Chelsea gallery's first show "in Williamsburg, at May's, watching five women dance on top of a bar" (144, 155). In between, one meets such characters as the young woman artist who has only painted six canvases, ever (of the David Salle school of female representation)—with a three-hair brush. (This detail is important because in the current art world, Labor=Value just as Sex Sells. One could see this as a kind of reaction formation against the elimination of human manual labor by technological advances, and in ironic contradistinction to the fact that for most of the world, labor=no value. Consider the unwillingness of the most recent Bush administration to raise minimum wages while the top 1 percent of the population has seen its wealth greatly increased.) According to Paumgarten, Koenig is sure he can sell this artist's paintings for up to fifty thousand or more.

19 It must have been a slow news day: the front-page headlines that day were, from left to right, "Bird Flu Virus May Be Spread by Smuggling," "For Leading Exxon to Its Riches, $144,573 a Day," "For Immigrants and Business, Rift on Protests," "Rumsfeld Gets Robust Defense from President." The lead picture was a dramatic shot of Christians carrying a large wooden cross into the Church of the Holy Sepulcher in Jerusalem, in a Good Friday ritual ("Retracing Jesus' Steps"). The worshippers are barely visible, except for the top of their hands grasping the cross, which gleams in the light. "Warhols of Tomorrow" was on page 1 accompanied by a picture of a Columbia student in her studio with a painting of long red fingernails, shades of Marilyn Minter, in the background. ("'I don't want to be discovered and then canned in five years,' said Emily Mae Smith, a graduate art student at Columbia University.") Granted, this article was below the fold, but the Tilton show was old news: the *Times* was picking up a month-old *New Yorker* item and repeating some of the reportage almost verbatim, down to the brand of beer drunk at the opening. So, why?

20 Jori Finkel, "Tales From the Crit: For Art Students, May Is the Cruelest Month," *New York Times*, April 30, 2006, sec. 2: 34. The cutthroat, make-the-girls-cry, boot-camp crit is a standard feature of art school, as are tales of such early ignominious treatment of artists who later show up their teachers by scoring big in the art world. Thus the article is principally noteworthy in that it *is* focusing on such an *old* story, in order to serve the current art market's speculative interest in getting them as young as possible.

21 Mia Fineman, "Looks Brilliant on Paper: But Who, Exactly, Is Going to Make It?," *New York Times*, May 7, 2006, 1, 18.

22 Dorothy Spears, "The First Gallerists' Club," *New York Times*, June 18, 2006, 33.

23 Tomkins, "Dept. of Precocity," 31.

24 Tomkins, "The Creative Life," 32, 34.

25 Eric Wilson, "Little Prada in the Desert," Front Row, *New York Times*, September 29, 2005, G9. Sometime later the "vandals took the handles," giving this project further press attention; see Barbara Novovitch, "Vandal Hated the Art, but, Oh, Those Shoes," *New York Times*, October 8, 2005, A11.

Work and Play

This essay first appeared in the *Brooklyn Rail*, February 2006.

1 See http://www.peacecandy.com and http://angrycandy.wordpress.com.

2 See the BateMania website, http://www.batemania.com/bateman365.

3 "Citizen Twain" took toostupidtobepresident.com down on January 20, 2009. However, in May 2009 the artist indicated plans to create an archive of this material accessible at this URL.

4 See these videos at Camp Chaos Entertainment, http://www.campchaos.com.

5 See the Dubya movie at http://www.dubyamovie.com.

6 For "Fake State of the Union Address," see the Peace Candy website, http://www.peacecandy.com.

7 See Ze Frank's website, http://www.zefrank.com.

8 See the Yes Men website, http://yesmen.org.

9 For an example of Ferrell's parodies, see the short video of Bush shooting a "down-on-the-ranch" political ad while fearfully trying to avoid the harmless attentions of a friendly horse (Peace Candy website, http://www.peacecandy.com). Andy Dick's video is available at his website, http://andydick.com.

10 See Kaprow, "The Education of the Un-Artist I," in *Essays on the Blurring of Art and Life*, 97–109.

New Tales of Scheherazade

1 The video for Will.i.am's "Yes We Can" (2008) can be viewed at YouTube, http://www.youtube.com.

2 See Julia Meltzer and David Thorne, http://www.meltzerthorne.com/nota.

3 In this passage, unbracketed ellipses indicate pauses and bracketed ellipses indicate editorial omissions. This segment can be seen as a video sample at the *New York Times* website: Neil MacFarquhar, "Video-Sampling Syria: Global Politics from a Ground's-Eye View," *New York Times*, March 6, 2008, http://www.nytimes.com, accessed in May 2008.

4 *Laocoön and His Sons* is attributed to Athanadoros, Hagesandros, and Polydoros of Rhodes. The date is unknown but thought to be ca. 175–20 B.C.E. This work is in the collections of the Vatican Museums.

5 Over thirty video clips related to *Winter Soldier* are available on YouTube, http://

www.youtube.com; see also the Iraq Veterans against the War website, http://ivaw.org/media.

6 Smit's work was included in "Melodrama," a screening of short videos organized by Laura Parnes at the Sarah Meltzer Gallery, New York, June 4, 2008.

Appendix

1 See notes 2 and 3 to "Blurring Richter" in the present work.

2 Storr, *Gerhard Richter: October 18, 1977*, 112–13.

3 Levi, *The Drowned and the Saved*, 43, 49.

4 I am indebted here to conversation with the noted neuroscientist Joseph LeDoux, although I'm sure that the act of drawing his brief explanations out of my memory has radically mauled a much more complex understanding. See LeDoux, *The Emotional Brain*; and "Parallel Memories: Putting Emotions Back Into The Brain; A Talk With Joseph LeDoux," with an introduction by John Brockman, *Edge* website, February 17, 1997, http://www.edge.org.

5 Levi, "A Conversation with Primo Levi," an interview conducted by Philip Roth, in *Survival at Auschwitz*, 182.

6 Storr, *Gerhard Richter: October 18, 1977*, 112.

7 Spielberg did not choose to film *Saving Private Ryan* in black and white, perhaps because the subject is more familiar and easier to absorb; the hero is one of us and his heroism is part of his job, whereas Schindler's heroism is less easily comprehensible, and the action took place in a more foreign domain. Also, *Saving Private Ryan* involves military action, and whereas grey would imply reflectiveness and passivity, Spielberg wanted to depict battle as it really was, gory—but was the Shoa any less bloody, and did green grass not grow beyond the barbed wire?

8 Godard, qtd. in Sterritt, ed., *Jean-Luc Godard*, 181–82.

9 Keneally, *Schindler's List*, 108.

10 Godard, qtd. in Sterritt, ed., *Jean-Luc Godard*, 182.

11 "Shattered," *Star Trek: Voyager*, season 7, episode 11, first broadcast January 17, 2001, CBS Paramount Television, directed by Terry Windell; teleplay by Michael Taylor; story by Michael Sussman and Michael Taylor.

12 "An unfinished repetition of the celebrated Grand Odalisque of 1814 in the Louvre, is cited in a list compiled by Ingres of works he had painted between 1824 and 1834." "Jean-Auguste-Dominique Ingres and Workshop: *Odalisque in Grisaille* (38.65)," in *Heilbrunn Timeline of Art History* (New York: Metropolitan Museum of Art, 2000–), available at http://www.metmuseum.org/toah, accessed in December 2008.

Adorno, Theodor. *Minima Moralia: Reflections from Damaged Life*. New York: Verso, 1978.

———. *Prisms: Cultural Criticism and Society*. Translated by Samuel Weber and Shierry Weber. c.1967. Cambridge: MIT Press, 1981.

Allara, Pamela. *Pictures of People: Alice Neel's American Portrait Gallery*. Hanover, N.H.: University Press of New England for Brandeis University Press, 1998.

Arendt, Hannah. *Eichmann in Jerusalem: A Report on the Banality of Evil*. 1963. New York: Penguin, 1994.

Armstrong, Richard. *Jack Tworkov: Paintings, 1928–1982*. Philadelphia: Pennsylvania Academy of the Fine Arts, 1987.

Avgikos, Jan. "Luc Tuymans, David Zwirner Gallery," Reviews. *Artforum*, January 1997, 84–85.

Barrett, Liz, Catherine Hollander, and Andrea Richards. "Schism-ism: Thoughts on Intergenerational Feminisms." *Documents*, no. 16 (fall 1999): 38–47.

Barthes, Roland. *Camera Lucida: Reflections on Photography*. Translated by Richard Howard. New York: Farrar, Straus, and Giroux, 1981.

———. Part 1 of *Writing Degree Zero*. In *A Barthes Reader*, edited by Susan Sontag, 31–61. New York: Hill and Wang, 1982.

Baudelaire, Charles. "The Painter of Modern Life." In *The Painter of Modern Life and Other Essays*, translated and edited by Jonathan Mayne, 1–40. New York: Da Capo, 1986.

Baudrillard, Jean. *The Conspiracy of Art: Manifestos, Interviews, Essays*. Edited by Sylvère Lotringer, translated by Ames Hodges. New York: Semiotext(e), 2005.

———. "The Precession of Simulacra." In *Art After Modernism: Rethinking Representation*, edited by Brian Wallis, 253–81. New York: New Museum of Contemporary Art; Boston: David R. Godine, 1984.

———. *Simulations*. Translated by Paul Foss, Paul Patton, and Philip Beitchman. New York: Semiotext(e), 1983.

Benjamin, Walter. *The Arcades Project*. Translated by Howard Eiland and Kevin McLaughlin. Cambridge: Belknap, 1999.

Boogs, Jean Sutherland. *Degas*. New York: Metropolitan Museum of Art, 1988.

Brennan, Marcia. *Modernism's Masculine Subjects: Matisse, the New York School, and Post-Painterly Abstraction*. Cambridge: MIT Press, 2004.

Broude, Norma, and Mary D. Garrard, eds. *The Power of Feminist Art*. New York: Harry N. Abrams, 1994.

———. *Reclaiming Female Agency: Feminist Art History after Postmodernism*. Berkeley: University of California Press, 2005.

Bryson, Norman. *Looking at the Overlooked: Four Essays on Still Life Painting*. Cambridge: Harvard University Press, 1990.

Buchloh, Benjamin H. D. "Divided Memory and Post-Traditional Identity: Gerhard Richter's Work of Mourning." *October* 75 (winter 1996): 61–82.

———. "Figures of Authority, Ciphers of Regression." *October* 16 (spring 1981): 38–68.

———. "Gerhard Richter's *Atlas*: The Anomic Archive." *October* 88 (spring 1999): 117–45.

———. "A Note on Gerhard Richter's *October 18, 1977*." *October* 48 (spring 1989): 86–109.

Buck-Morss, Susan. *The Dialectics of Seeing: Walter Benjamin and the Arcades Project*. Cambridge: MIT Press, 1989.

———. *Thinking Past Terror: Islamism and Critical Theory on the Left*. London: Verso, 2003.

Butler, Cornelia, and Lisa Gabrielle Mark, eds. *WACK! Art and the Feminist Revolution*. Los Angeles: Museum of Contemporary Art; Cambridge: MIT Press, 2007.

"Capitol Hill: Shoe Show," Periscope. *Newsweek*, October 26, 1998, 8.

Carr, Carolyn. *Alice Neel: Women*. New York: Rizzoli, 2002.

Center for Constitutional Rights. *Articles of Impeachment against George Bush*. Hoboken, N.J.: Melville House Publishing, 2006.

Chave, Anna C. "Minimalism and Biography." In Broude and Garrard, eds., *Reclaiming Female Agency*, 385–407.

———. "Minimalism and the Rhetoric of Power." *Arts Magazine*, January 1990, 44–63.

———. "'Normal Ills': On Embodiment, Victimization, and the Origins of Feminist Art." In *Trauma and Visuality in Modernity*, edited by Lisa Saltzman and Eric Rosenberg, 133–57. Hanover, N.H.: University Press of New England, 2006.

Chéroux, Clément, Andreas Fischer, Pierre Apraxine, Denis Canguilhem, and Sophie Schmidt. *The Perfect Medium: Photography and the Occult*. New Haven: Yale University Press, 2005.

Chicago, Judy. *Through the Flower: My Struggle as a Woman Artist*. New York: Penguin, 1975.

Conkleton, Sheryl, Russell Ferguson, and Timothy Martin. *Uta Barth: In Between Places*. Seattle: Henry Art Gallery Association, 2000.

Connor, Maureen. "(Con)testing Resources." In *Making Art History: A Changing Discipline and Its Institutions*, edited by Elizabeth C. Mansfield, 245–63. New York: Routledge, 2007.

Cousseau, Henry-Claude. "L'usage du flou." In *Jack Pierson*, exhibition catalogue, n.p. Bordeaux: CAPC Musée D'Art Contemporain de Bordeaux, 1997.

Debord, Guy. *Comments on the Society of the Spectacle*. Translated by Malcolm Imrie. London: Verso, 1998.

————. *The Society of the Spectacle*. Translated by Donald Nicholson Smith. New York: Zone, 1995.

Downes, Rackstraw. "What the Sixties Meant to Me (1973)." In *In Relation to the Whole: Three Essays from Three Decades*, 11–31. New York: Edgewise, 2000.

Duncan, Michael. "Buggy-Making in Tulip Time." In Rubinstein, ed., *Critical Mess*, 109–14.

Eagleton, Terry. *After Theory*. New York: Basic, 2004.

Eklund, Douglas. *The Pictures Generation, 1974–1984*. New York: Metropolitan Museum of Art, 2009.

Ellegood, Anne, and Burton, Johanna. *The Uncertainty of Objects and Ideas: Recent Sculpture*. Washington: Hirshhorn Museum and Sculpture Garden, Smithsonian Institution, 2006.

Elliott, Jane. "The Currency of Feminist Theory." *PMLA* 121, no. 5 (2006): 1697–1703.

Elsner, Jas. "Style." In *Critical Terms for Art History*, 2nd edition, edited by Robert S. Nelson and Richard Schiff, 98–109. Chicago: University of Chicago Press, 2003.

Feminist Art Program, California Institute of the Arts. *Anonymous Was a Woman: A Documentation of the Women's Art Festival; A Collection of Letters to Young Women Artists*. Valencia: Feminist Art Program, California Institute of the Arts, 1974.

Fernandez, Maria, Faith Wilding, and Michelle M. Wright, eds. *Domain Errors! Cyberfeminist Practices*. New York: Autonomedia, 2002.

Ferris, Alison. *The Disembodied Spirit*. Exhibition catalogue. Brunswick, Maine: Bowdoin College Museum of Art, 2003.

Finkel, Jori. "Saying the F-Word." *ARTnews*, February 2007, 118–19.

Foster, Hal. *Design and Crime (and Other Diatribes)*. London: Verso, 2002.

————. "The Expressive Fallacy." In *Recodings: Art, Spectacle, Cultural Politics*, 59–78. New York: New Press, 1999.

Godard, Jean-Luc. *Godard on Godard; Critical Writings*. Edited by Tom Milne and Jean Narboni. New York: Viking, 1972.

Griffin, Tim. "Show and Tell: Tim Griffin Talks with Curator Robert Storr about the 52nd Venice Biennale." *Artforum*, May 2007, 181–84.

Gubar, Susan. "Feminism Inside Out." *PMLA* 121, no. 5 (2006): 1711–1716.

Guilbault, Serge. *How New York Stole the Idea of Modern Art: Abstract Expressionism, Freedom, and the Cold War*. Translated by Arthur Goldhammer. Chicago: University of Chicago Press, 1983.

Harrison, Charles, and Paul Wood, eds. *Art in Theory, 1900–2000: An Anthology of Changing Ideas*. Oxford: Blackwell, 2003.

Hertz, Richard. *Jack Goldstein and the CalArts Mafia*. Ojai, Calif.: Mineola, 2003.

Heschel, Abraham Joshua. *The Earth Is the Lord's: The Inner World of the Jew in Eastern Europe*. Illustrated with wood engravings by Ilya Schor. 1949. New York: Farrar, Strauss, and Giroux, 1984.

Hess, Elizabeth, and Mel Bochner. *In the Lineage of Eva Hesse*. Exhibition catalogue. Ridgefield, Conn.: Aldrich Museum of Contemporary Art, 1994.

Hills, Patricia. *Alice Neel*. New York: Harry N. Abrams, 1983.

Hirsch, Marianne. *Family Frames: Photography, Narrative, and Postmemory*. Cambridge: Harvard University Press, 1997.

Huxley, Aldous. *Brave New World*. New York: Doubleday, Doran, 1932.

Irigaray, Luce. *Speculum of the Other Woman*. Translated by Gillian C. Gill. Ithaca, N.Y.: Cornell University Press, 1985.

Jaskot, Paul. "Gerhard Richter and Adolf Eichmann." *Oxford Art Journal* 28, no. 3 (2005): 459–78.

Jones, Amelia. "Faith Wilding and the Enfleshing of Painting." *n.paradoxa*, June 1999. http://web.ukonline.co.uk/n.paradoxa/.

———. "Lari Pittman's Queer Feminism." *Art+Text*, no. 50 (1995): 36–42.

———, ed. *Sexual Politics: Judy Chicago's Dinner Party in Feminist Art History*. Los Angeles: UCLA at the Armand Hammer Museum of Art and Cultural Center in association with University of California Press, Berkeley, 1996.

———. "Uta Barth at Domestic Setting." *Art Issues*, November–December 1994, 39–41.

Jones, Leslie C. *Abject Art: Repulsion and Desire in American Art*. New York: Whitney Museum of American Art, 1993.

Kaprow, Allan. *Essays on the Blurring of Art and Life*. Berkeley: University of California Press, 1993.

Kelly, Mary. *Post-Partum Document*. London: Routledge and Kegan, 1983.

Keneally, Thomas. *Schindler's List*. New York: Simon and Schuster, 1982.

Klarsfeld, Serge. *French Children of the Holocaust: A Memorial*. Edited by Susan Cohen, Howard M. Epstein, and Serge Klarsfeld. Translated by Glorianne Depondt and Howard M. Epstein. New York: New York University Press, 1996.

———. *Le Mémorial des Enfants Juifs Déportés de France*. Paris: Les Fils et les Filles des Déportés Juifs de France and the Beate Klarsfeld Foundation, 1995.

Kleeblatt, Norman L., ed. *Mirroring Evil: Nazi Imagery / Recent Art*. New York: Jewish Museum; New Brunswick, N.J.: Rutgers University Press, 2001.

Koch, Gertrude. "The Aesthetic Transformation of the Image of the Unimaginable: Notes on Claude Lanzmann's *Shoah*." *October* 48 (spring 1989): 15–24.

Kozloff, Joyce. "The Kudzu Effect, or The Rise of a New Academy." *Public Art Review*, fall–winter 1996, 41.

Lawson, Thomas. "Last Exit: Painting." *Artforum*, October 1981, 40–47.

Ledoux, Joseph. *The Emotional Brain: The Mysterious Underpinnings of Emotional Life*. New York: Simon and Schuster, 1996.

Levi, Primo. *The Drowned and the Saved*. Translated by Raymond Rosenthal. New York: Vintage, 1989.

———. *The Periodic Table*. Translated by Raymond Rosenthal. New York: Schocken, 1984.

———. *The Reawakening*. Translated by Stuart Woolf. New York: Simon and Schuster, 1995.

———. *Survival at Auschwitz*. Translated by Stuart Woolf. New York: Simon and Schuster, 1986.

Levin, Gail. *Becoming Judy Chicago: A Biography of the Artist*. New York: Harmony, 2007.

Levinthal, David. *David Levinthal: Work from 1975–1996*. Essays and interview by Charles Stainback and Richard B. Woodward. New York: International Center of Photography in association with D.A.P., 1997.

Lewison, Jeremy. "Alice Neel: A Chronicler of Her Times." In *Alice Neel: A Chronicle of New York, 1950–1976*, n.p. Exhibition catalogue. New York: Victoria Miro Gallery, 2004.

Lippard, Lucy. "Biting the Hand: Artists and Museums in New York since 1969." In *Alternative Art New York, 1965–1985*, edited by Julie Ault, 79–120. Minneapolis: University of Minnesota Press, 2002.

———. *From the Center: Feminist Essays on Women's Art*. New York: E. P. Dutton, 1976.

Lord, Catherine. *CalArts Skeptical Beliefs*. Chicago: Renaissance Society at the University of Chicago, 1988.

Lovelace, Carey. "Weighing in on Feminism." *ARTnews*, May 1997, 140–45.

Lubbock, Tom. "Bankside Ride: The Tate Modern Experience." *Modern Painters*, summer 2000, 59–60.

Marshall, Richard. *New Image Painting*, New York: Whitney Museum of American Art, 1978.

Meyer, Laura, ed. *A Studio of Their Own: The Legacy of the Fresno Feminist Experiment*. With essays by Laura Meyer and Faith Wilding. Fresno: Press at the California State University, Fresno, 2009.

Morris, Catherine, and Ingrid Schaffner. *Gloria: Another Look at Feminist Art of the 1970s*. Exhibition catalogue. New York: White Columns, 2002.

Moyers, Carrie. "Feminist Art: Viva." *Modern Painters*, March 2007, 70–77.

Müller, Christian Philipp. "'Portrait of the Museum as a Chair,' Artist Questionnaire: 21 Responses." *October* 100 (spring 2002): 72.

Newman, Amy. *Challenging Art: Artforum, 1962–1974*. New York: Soho Press, 2000.

Newman, Barnett. *Barnett Newman: Selected Writings and Interviews*. New York: Alfred A. Knopf, 1990.

———. Interview, *Painters Painting*. Dir. and prod. Emile de Antonio, Turin Film Corp., 1972.

Nochlin, Linda. "Why Have There Been No Great Women Artists?" *ARTnews*, January 1971, 22, 39, 67, 71.

Paumgarten, Nick. "Salesman: Days and Nights in Leo Koenig's Gallery." *New Yorker*, October 17, 2005, 144–55.

Payne, Michael, and John Schad, eds. *Life.after.Theory*. London: Continuum, 2003.

Perling Hudson, Suzanne. "Beauty and the Status of Contemporary Criticism." *October* 104 (spring 2003): 115–30.

Phelan, Peggy, and Helena Reckitt, eds. *Art and Feminism*. New York: Phaidon, 2001.

Pollock, Griselda. "Killing Men and Dying Women: A Woman's Touch in the Cold Zone of American Painting in the 1950s." In *Avant-Gardes and Partisans Reviewed*, edited by Fred Orton and Griselda Pollock, 221–94. Manchester: Manchester University Press, 1996.

Princenthal, Nancy. "Feminism Unbound." *Art in America*, June–July, 2007, 142–52, 221.

———. "Issues and Commentary: Art Criticism, Bound to Fail." *Art in America*, January 2006, 43–47.

Reilly, Maura, and Linda Nochlin, eds. *Global Feminisms: New Directions in Contemporary Art*. New York: Merrell, 2007.

Reyla, Lane. "Lisa Yuskavage / Christopher Grimes Gallery." *ArtForum*, November 1994, 92.

Richter, Gerhard. *The Daily Practice of Painting: Writings and Interviews, 1962–1993*. Edited by Hans-Ulrich Obrist. Translated by David Britt. London: Anthony d'Offay Gallery; Cambridge: MIT Press, 1995.

Robbins, Noel. *New American Paintings* 5, no. 5 (2000): 170–73.

Rothfuss, Joan. *New American Paintings* 5, no. 4 (2000): 3.

Rowe-Finkbeiner, Kristin. *The F-Word, Feminism in Jeopardy: Women, Politics, and the Future*. Emeryville, Calif.: Seal, 2004.

Rubinstein, Raphael, ed. "Art Schools: A Group Crit." *Art in America*, May 2007, 99–113.

———. *Critical Mess: Art Critics on the State of Their Practice*. Lenox, Mass.: Hard Press Editions, 2006.

Saltz, Jerry. "The Pursuit of Happiness: Damien Hirst Goes for Baroque." *Village Voice*, October 17, 2000, 69.

Saltzman, Lisa. "Reconsidering the Stain: On Gender and the Body in Helen Frankenthaler's Painting." In *Reclaiming Female Agency*, edited by Broude and Garrard, 373–83.

Schaffner, Ingrid, and Matthias Winzen, eds. *Deep Storage: Collecting, Storing, and Archiving in Art*. Munich: Prestel, 1998.

Schapiro, Meyer. *Theory and Philosophy of Art: Style, Artist, and Society*. Vol. 4, *Selected Papers*. New York: George Braziller, 1998.

Schell, Jonathan. "Letter from Ground Zero: The Fall of the One-Party Empire." *Nation*, December 12, 2005, 9.

Schjeldahl, Peter. "The Elegant Scavenger: John Currin's Low Comedy of High Style." *New Yorker*, February 22, 1999, 174–75.

———. "Girls, Girls, Girls: Lisa Yuskavage Raises Trashiness to High Art." *New Yorker*, January 15, 2001, 100–101.

Schneir, Miriam. *Feminism: The Essential Historical Writings*. New York: Vintage, 1972.

Schor, Mira. "Backlash and Appropriation." In *The Power of Feminist Art*, edited by Broude and Garrard, 248–63.

———. "Cassandra in the City." *Art Journal*, summer 2006, 133–35.

———. "Contemporary Feminism: Art Practice, Theory, and Activism—An Intergenerational Perspective." *Art Journal* 58, no. 4 (1999): 8–29.

———. "Waiting for the Big Show." *Ms. Magazine*, March–April 1996, 72–75.

———. *Wet: On Painting, Feminism, and Art Culture*. Durham, N.C.: Duke University Press, 1997.

Schor, Naomi. *Reading in Detail: Aesthetics and the Feminine*. 1987. New York: Routledge, 2007.

Schwartz, Sanford. *Myron Stout: The Unfinished Paintings*. Exhibition catalogue. New York: Washburn Gallery, 1997.

Schwendener, Martha. "Lisa Yuskavage at Marianne Boesky." *Flash Art*, March–April 1999, 111.

Seager, Joni. *The Penguin Atlas of Women in the World*. New York: Penguin, 2003.

Shapiro, David, and Cecile Shapiro, eds. *Abstract Expressionism: A Critical Record*. Cambridge: Cambridge University Press, 1990.

Siegel, Katy. "Blonde Ambition." *ArtForum*, May 2000, 156–59.

———, ed. *High Times, Hard Times: New York Painting, 1967–1975*. New York: Independent Curators International and D.A.P., 2006.

Simpson, David. *9/11: The Culture of Commemoration*. Chicago: University of Chicago Press, 2006.

Smith, Elizabeth A. T. *Uta Barth: At the Edge of the Decipherable; Recent Photographs*. Exhibition catalogue. Los Angeles: Museum of Contemporary Art, 1995.

Solomon, Deborah. "Art Girls Just Wanna Have Fun." *New York Times Magazine*, January 30, 2000, 36–39.

Spiegelman, Art. *Maus II*. New York: Pantheon, 1986.

Sterritt, David, ed. *Jean-Luc Godard: Interviews*. Jackson: University Press of Mississippi, 1998.

Stevens, Mark, and Annalyn Swan. *De Kooning: An American Master*. New York: Alfred A. Knopf, 2005.

Stiles, Kristine, and Peter Selz, eds. *Theories and Documents of Contemporary Art: A Sourcebook of Artists' Writings*. Berkeley: University of California Press, 1996.

Stoops, Susan L. "From Eccentric to Sensuous Abstraction: An Interview with Lucy Lippard." In *More than Minimal: Feminism and Abstraction in the '70s*, edited by Stoops, 26–31. Exhibition catalogue. Waltham, Mass.: Rose Art Museum, Brandeis University, 1996.

Storr, Robert. "All in the Family: Is the New Art History a One-Party State?" *Frieze*, November–December 2005, 25.

———. *Gerhard Richter: Forty Years of Painting*. New York: Museum of Modern Art, 2002.

———. *Gerhard Richter: October 18, 1977*. New York: Museum of Modern Art, 2000.

Tanizaki, Jun'ichiro. *In Praise of Shadows*. Translated by Thomas J. Harper and Edward G. Seidensticker. New Haven, Conn.: Leete's Island, 1977.

Taylor, William R., ed. *Inventing Times Square: Commerce and Culture at the Crossroads of the World*. Baltimore: Johns Hopkins University Press, 1996.

Temkin, Ann. *Alice Neel*. Philadelphia: Philadelphia Museum of Art, 2000.

Tomkins, Calvin. "The Creative Life: The Pour," Talk of the Town. *New Yorker*, March 13, 2006, 32, 34.

———. "Dept. of Precocity: Artists in their Youth," Talk of the Town. *New Yorker*, February 27, 2006, 31.

Toobin, Jeffrey. "The Bench: Girls Behaving Badly." *New Yorker*, May 30, 2005, 34–35.

Tuchman, Maurice, and Esti Dunow. *The New Landscape / The New Still Life: Soutine and Modern Art*. New York: Cheim and Read, 2006.

Tucker, Marcia. *Bad Girls*. Exhibition catalogue. New York: New Museum of Contemporary Art; Cambridge: MIT Press, 1994.

Tworkov, Jack. *The Extreme of the Middle: The Writings of Jack Tworkov*. Edited by Mira Schor. New Haven: Yale University Press, 2009.

Usselmann, Rainer. "18. Oktober 1977: Gerhard Richter's Work of Mourning and Its New Audience." *Art Journal* 61, no. 1 (2002): 4–25.

Watney, Simon. "Reviews." *Artforum*, April 1995, 101.

Weinberger, Eliot. *What Happened Here: Bush Chronicles*. New York: New Direction, 2005.

Wilding, Faith. "Don't Tell Anyone We Did It!" *Documents*, no. 15 (spring–summer 1999): 16–27.

Winkfield, Trevor. "Bankside Blues: A Museum Wanting the Human Touch." *Modern Painters*, summer 2000, 62–63.

Wolf, Sylvia. "First Exposure: Sharon Harper, Photographs from the Floating World." Exhibition brochure. New York: Whitney Museum, 2001.

Woolf, Virginia. *A Room of One's Own*. 1929. New York: Harcourt, Brace, and World, 1957.

Yee, Lydia. *Division of Labor: "Women's Work" in Contemporary Art, 1970–1995*. Exhibition catalogue. New York: Bronx Museum of Contemporary Art, 1995.

Young, James E. *At Memory's Edge: After-Images of the Holocaust in Contemporary Art and Architecture*. New Haven: Yale University Press, 2000.

Zelevanky, Lynn. *Sense and Sensibility: Women Artists and Minimalism in the Nineties*. Exhibition catalogue. New York: Museum of Modern Art; distributed by Harry N. Abrams, 1994.

Page numbers in *italics* refer to illustrations.

Mira Schor is a painter and writer living in New York. She is on
the fine arts faculty at Parsons the New School for Design. She
is the author of *Wet: On Painting, Feminism, and Art Culture*; the
co-editor (with Susan Bee) of *M/E/A/N/I/N/G: An Anthology
of Artists' Writings, Theory, and Criticism*; and the editor of
The Extreme of the Middle: Writings of Jack Tworkov. Schor is a
recipient of the College Art Association's Frank Jewett Mather
Award in Art Criticism.

Library of Congress Cataloging-in-Publication Data
Schor, Mira.
A decade of negative thinking : essays on art, politics, and daily
life / Mira Schor.
p. cm.
Includes bibliographical references and index.
ISBN 978-0-8223-4584-8 (cloth)
ISBN 978-0-8223-4602-9 (pbk.)
1. Feminism and art—United States. 2. Art, American—21st
century. 3. United States—Politics and government—21st
century. 4. United States—Social conditions—21st century.
I. Title.
N72.F45S35 2009
701'.03—dc22   2009032834